STRONG SOCIETIES
AND WEAK STATES

JOEL S. MIGDAL

Strong Societies and Weak States

State-Society Relations and
State Capabilities in the Third World

PRINCETON UNIVERSITY PRESS

Princeton, New Jersey

Copyright © 1988 by Princeton University Press
Published by Princeton University Press
41 William Street, Princeton, New Jersey 08540
In the United Kingdom:
Princeton University Press, Chichester, West Sussex

This book has been composed in Linotron Baskerville

Princeton University Press books are printed on acid-free paper
and meet the guidelines for permanence and durability of the
Committee on Production Guidelines for Book Longevity of the
Council on Library Resources

Printed in the United States of America

Library of Congress Cataloging-in-Publication Data

Migdal, Joel S.
Strong societies and weak states : state-society relations and
state capabilities in the Third World / Joel S. Migdal.
p.   cm.
Includes index.
ISBN 0-691-05669-2 (alk. paper) ISBN 0-691-01073-0 (pbk.)
1. Developing countries—Politics and government. 2. Developing
countries—Social conditions. 3. Social control. I. Title.
JF60.M54 1988
306′.2′091724—dc19   88-17614

        14   16   18   20   19   17   15   13

ISBN-13: 978-0-691-01073-1

ISBN-10: 0-691-01073-0

To Marcy, my inspiration

CONTENTS

THIS BOOK has been a long time in gestation. The original idea for such a book came in a graduate seminar I taught at Tel-Aviv University in 1974–1975. At that time, the notion of writing such an ambitious work seemed overwhelming, and I ended up instead spending the next few years writing *Palestinian Society and Politics* (Princeton University Press, 1980), which worked out some of the same ideas within a more limited framework. I returned to *Strong Societies and Weak States* at Harvard University, where I had the benefit of the supportive atmosphere of the Center for International Affairs, headed by Samuel P. Huntington.

In 1980, I moved to the University of Washington, where the lion's share of my time was spent building and heading the new and now highly successful International Studies Program in the Henry M. Jackson School of International Studies. A wonderful year at the Hebrew University of Jerusalem in 1985–1986 finally gave me the time to complete the manuscript. My debt of gratitude is especially large to the Harry S. Truman Institute for Peace Research at the Hebrew University, to its staff and faculty, and to its director, Harold (Zvi) Schiffrin.

I have presented faculty seminars on parts of the manuscript in numerous universities from Haifa, Israel, to Stanford, California, to Mexico City. The book, quite simply, is much better because of the help I received from the colleagues, far too many to name, who participated in these seminars. Over the last decade, some colleagues were so provoked that they wrote lengthy comments for me to assimilate; although my ego was somewhat battered, I am deeply indebted to these fellow scholars, including Michael Barnett, Myron Glazer, Penina Glazer, Merilee Grindle, Fen Hampson, Reşat Kasaba, Baruch Kimmerling, David Laitin, Peter Lange, the late Arthur Liebman, John Montgomery, Eric Nordlinger, Daniel Pearson, Dov Ronen, Howard Spodok, Mark Tessler, and my wonderful friend Ted Stein, who died in 1985. Myron Aronoff not only read the manuscript himself, but he also asked the members of his graduate seminar to write papers on it.

Three colleagues read the entire penultimate version and sent me long sheafs of comments; to Aaron Klieman, Alan Zuckerman, and

John Waterbury, I owe special thanks. Kerry Berger, Samuel Carradine, Jill Crystal, Mary Dunn, Donna Eberwine, Mary Fiksel, Michael Furtado, Ann Goldstein, Mary Hilderbrand, and Todd Larson all assisted in parts of the research. Nancy Acheson has been a superb typist (and editor!). Parts of earlier versions of the manuscript went into two articles I wrote: "A Model of State-Society Relations," in Howard J. Wiarda, ed., *New Directions in Comparative Politics* (Boulder: Westview Press, 1985); and "Strong States, Weak States: Power and Accommodation," in Myron Weiner and Samuel P. Huntington, eds., *Understanding Political Development* (Boston: Little, Brown, 1987).

When I first began to articulate a new way of thinking about social and political change in the Third World, two of my children, Tamar and Amram, were not even born, and one, Ariela, was still in diapers. My wife Marcy did much more than put up with me. She has been the life partner who has been able to renew me continually with new energy, curiosity, and understanding. It is to her that I have dedicated this book.

IN ONE section of France, the evening prayers of peasants long included the line, "Deliver us from all evil and from justice."[1] Certainly, French peasants have not been alone in their equivocal or antagonistic relationship with "justice" and the state that represents the rules of justice. In the following pages, I will explore some central relations between people and the states that seek to make the rules of justice to govern their lives.

Do states actually make a difference in the lives of the people they seek to govern? Undoubtedly yes. Even in the most remote corners of those societies with the newest states, the personnel, agencies, and resources of the state have reshaped political and social landscapes. Have these contours of society been redrawn more or less as state leaders envisioned? Here I must equivocate: only in a handful of cases and in realms involving some issues more than others. This book offers a set of tools—a model and a theory—for approaching the difficult question of why some states succeed more and some less in realizing the visions of their leaders.

The main issues will be state capabilities or their lack: the ability of state leaders to use the agencies of the state to get people in the society to do what they want them to do.[2] Focusing merely on the direct im-

---

[1] Quoted in Eugen Weber, *Peasants into Frenchmen: The Modernization of Rural France* (Stanford: Stanford University Press, 1976), p. 50.

[2] Our view of the state, then, corresponds to Max Weber's notion of the state as institutional—an organization—enforcing regulations, at least in part through a monopoly of violence. States vary in the degree to which they actually approach such an ideal type. I will expand more on the meaning of the state in Chapter 1. Here, it is worth quoting from Bertrand Badie and Pierre Birnbaum to give a glimpse of how the concept of the state and its relationship to capabilities will be developed in this study.

> The progress of state building can be measured by the degree of development of certain instrumentalities whose purpose is to make the action of the state effective: bureaucracy, courts, and the military, for example. Clearly, the more complex and highly developed these instrumentalities are, the greater the capacity of the state to act on its environment and to autonomously impose collective goals distinct from the private goals generated within the social system itself. In this situation, the state's autonomy corresponds to a tangible reality.

Badie and Birnbaum, *The Sociology of the State* (Chicago: University of Chicago Press, 1983), p. 35.

pact of states on societies, however, would give us only a partial view of the relations between peoples and states and would miss important aspects of why some states are more capable than others. Societies also affect states. We will look at how the structure of society affects state capabilities. We will also explore how societies influence the character and style of states encountering great difficulties in getting people to follow their leaders. In addition, a full view of relations between a people and its state requires looking beyond domestic society. The calculus of state-society relations has changed dramatically, as we shall see, because of forces outside the society altogether.

All states have had limited capabilities at some time, or with some groups, or on some issues. Note a recent description of a small fringe group, the Posse Comitatus, and its disregard for laws in the United States: "If you are Posse, you do not bother with a driving licence; you get rid of your birth certificate and marriage licence; you do not have a bank account and you keep your children away from school. . . . You arm yourself with a gun and several thousand rounds of ammunition, and train at weekends."[3] Nevertheless, the limitations of state capabilities, including tax collection and regulation of personal behavior, have been especially acute for state leaders in Asia, Africa, and Latin America. Only a mere handful of these states—China, Cuba, Israel, Japan, North Korea, South Korea, Taiwan, and Vietnam—have ended up on the "strong states" end of a scale of state capabilities. I will primarily focus on states and societies on these continents. Why have so many of these states failed so often to get their populations to do as state leaders legislate and decree, and why have a few others been so much stronger?

This book stems from two paradoxes I troubled over as I reviewed some of the vast literature on political life, particularly regarding various Third World countries.[4] The first concerns the incredible change in the political landscape of even the most remote villages in Asia, Africa, and Latin America in the last generation. In all sizes and shapes,

---

[3] *The Economist*, November 2, 1985, p. 22.

[4] I tried to synthesize and review critically some of this literature in Joel S. Migdal, "Studying the Politics of Development and Change: The State of the Art," in Ada W. Finifter, ed., *Political Science: The State of the Discipline* (Washington, D.C.: American Political Science Association, 1983). "Third World" here is used as a loose, inclusive term, encompassing Africa, Asia (except the USSR and Japan), the Americas from Mexico southward, and the oceanic islands (excluding Australia and New Zealand). As we shall see in Chapter 2 and thereafter, Third World societies were deeply and universally affected by the spread and intensification of the world economy in the half-century or so leading up to World War I. The changes in these societies, I will argue, had a lasting and profound impact on state-society relations until the present.

state institutions from health clinics to marketing boards have established a permanent presence among the populations of these countries, resulting in income transfers, a changing quality of life, new social hierarchies, and more. But a close look at the performance of
these agencies reveals that often they operate on principles radically
different from those conceived by their founders and creators in the
capital city. The second paradox seems even more bizarre. Another
close look at accounts of the political behavior of top state leaders revealed, strange as it may seem, that many have persistently and consciously undermined their own state agencies—the very tools by which
they could increase their capabilities and effect their policy agendas.
Primarily I sought to discover some solution to or explanation of these
paradoxes.

I found the literature I studied both indispensable and frustrating.
It was indispensable in helping me construct for myself broad outlines
of difficult and complex processes. Numerous articles and books,
many of which I do not even mention in the chapters that follow, contained important, keen insights into states and societies. I am indebted
to them for countless sources of inspiration. But that literature was
also full of unresolved contradictions, and I took issue with much of
it, particularly the self-consciously theoretical materials. I have re-
strained myself (quite admirably, I think) from lengthy critiques of
this literature and past approaches to the subject of political and social
change in the Third World. My purpose has been to discuss, as directly as possible, the components and logic of a different approach
and explanation for understanding social and political organization
and the relationship between them. The reader familiar with the literature on social and political change in the Third World will note
how my approach differs from those dominating the subject in recent
decades.

I reject, for instance, the teleological, unilinear assumptions of modernization theory, which have been at pains to explain the various
types of emergent political and social organization. I argue implicitly
against modernization theory's preoccupation with the effect of center
on periphery and its lack of interest in the impact of periphery on the
center. Also, I emphasize fragmented social organizations and their
impact on politics, bringing into sharp relief the limitations of the concept of social class, as used by Marxist theorists and others, to explain
many dynamics of Third World societies. Although I have relied on
some conceptions developed in world system theory, my approach re-
jects the tendency of both that theory and dependency theory to see
the dynamics of Third World social organization and politics almost

exclusively in terms of processes in the metropolitan or core countries. World economic and political forces have presented opportunities and constraints, as Chapters 2 through 4 make clear, but the dynamics of state-society relations have a life that considerably exceeds the effects of core-periphery interactions. I have tried to show, in opposition to much scholarship on the impact of capitalism, that the social dislocations associated with the spread of the world economy did not automatically answer how society would be restructured.

My approach, too, takes issue with empiricists, those area specialists and historians who claim to lack any preconceived notions or approaches and simply present what they see. Of course, all observers are aided and limited by their mental constructs, whether explicit or implicit. So often the works of the empiricists, especially the more common literature focusing on capital city or palace politics and even those on the hinterlands, have missed intense state-society struggles in remote parts of the country as well as the pressure of forces from outside the society.

In general, the literature on the Third World falls into two categories. The first looks at societies at the ground level, focusing on peasant communities, patron-client ties, urban neighborhoods, and the like; these studies, while occasionally referring to state policies and resources, often remain enmeshed in the intricacies of social life at the local level. The second category focuses on life among the most influential elements—powerful elites, large capital, foreign investment, and so on. Studies here much too facilely assume that those at the pinnacle of politics can effectively repress or transform or reform the rest of society.

My chief complaint about the literature I reviewed was that so many prevailing approaches—modernization theories, Marxist theories, dependency and world system theories, empiricist descriptions—were both too uncritical about the power at the top and too state-centered. For the Third World, at least, a state-centered approach is a bit like looking at a mousetrap without at all understanding the mouse. Somehow the focus of attention on centerstage in so many books and articles seemed to take as given what I found so open to question: the issue of the autonomy and strength of the state. Also, I do not think the rediscovery of the state in recent years by those writing on Europe has been terribly helpful in this regard. These authors have either dismissed the state entirely outside Europe and North America, talking at times of stateless or nonstate societies, or else they have developed notions of state autonomy extended fairly indiscriminately to Third World cases.

State-centered approaches do have a certain intuitive attractiveness about them. The state's home base in the capital city, after all, is the place where the action seems to occur—the appearance of swanky limousines, the machinations of the high politics of society, the workings of the security nerve centers for army and police, the concentration of foreign and domestic capital. In this book, I hope to convince the reader that even capital city politics can best be understood, counterintuitively perhaps, by expanding one's field of vision. There is a need constantly to look back and forth between the top reaches of the state and local society. One must see how the organization of society, even in remote areas, may dictate the character and capabilities of politics at the center, as well as how the state (often in unintended ways) changes society. I have been very gratified in my final examination of the literature to find a number of very recent works, some still unpublished, that reflect aspects of the new approach developed here.[5] These studies look at both local society and the state; many stress how state policies are deflected and how state resources are redirected as they filter down to society, and the studies analyze, as well, the unexpected effects state and society have on one another.

Convincing readers to change their way of looking at political and social change and inertia is an ambitious undertaking indeed. To do that, I have written this book as an integrated general essay, one that is more suggestive than definitive. Its very scope has forced me to leave important questions open or incompletely addressed.[6] In this

[5] See, for example, Frances Hagopian, "The Politics of Oligarchy: The Persistence of Traditional Elites in Contemporary Brazil" (Ph.D. diss., M.I.T., 1986); Akhil Gupta, "Technology, Power and the State in a Complex Agricultural Society: The Green Revolution in a North Indian Village" (Ph.D. diss., Stanford University, 1987); Richard H. Adams, Jr., *Development and Social Change in Rural Egypt* (Syracuse: Syracuse University Press, 1986); Sevket Pamuk, "Government Policies and Peasant Resistance in Turkey during World War II" (Paper presented at the annual meeting of the Middle East Studies Association, Boston, November 1986); Vivienne Shue, *The Reach of the State: Sketches of the Chinese Body Politic* (Stanford: Stanford University Press, 1988); Donald Rothchild and Naomi Chazan, eds., *The Precarious Balance: State and Society in Africa* (Boulder, Colo.: Westview Press, 1987); and Victor Azarya and Naomi Chazan, "Disengagement from the State in Africa: Reflections on the Experience of Ghana and Guinea," *Comparative Studies in Society and History* 29 (January 1987): 106–31.

[6] Any theory of this sort should be viewed as prolegomena to more systematic inquiry. Among the issues raised (or ignored) in the book that I felt could be full studies of their own are: (1) the role of state leadership in state-society relations; (2) the influence of war and the threat of war on state and society; (3) the influence of the post–World War II, multinational-corporation-dominated world economy on state-society relations; (4) the impact of old social structure on the emergence of new social structure after exogenous, "catastrophic" forces have precipitated major social changes; (5) the difference of pat-

manner I could develop an approach inclusive enough to digest varieties of political experiences, especially in the post–World War II era, and make some sense of them.

My model and theory should present, if successful, an approach to understanding the capabilities of all modern states, but in the essay, I have turned repeatedly to the experiences of five states: Egypt, India, Israel, Mexico, and Sierra Leone. These countries are by no means a representative sample but a selection;[7] their examples help to give a suppleness, subtlety, and complexity to the material that would be impossible to achieve simply by presenting an abstract theory. I have not compared these countries systematically, nor have I seen each of them through all facets of the theory. My purpose is not to tell and explain each country's story. The story here is the theory, which explains the varying capabilities of states and the character of weak states. The five countries are only illustrations, highlighting portions of the argument.

Why were these five countries selected above all others? I would be less than candid if I did not admit these are states and societies about which I knew a bit more than others or, at least, about which I wanted to learn a lot more. My selection also sought a range of cases along a spectrum of state capabilities. As a result, the five illustrative cases run the gamut of possibilities from one with a very weak state, Sierra Leone, to one with a relatively strong state, Israel.

Egypt, India, and Mexico have each displayed remarkable instances of both high and low state capabilities in different realms. Mexico, for example, has been singled out many times as a strong state with corporatist or bureaucratic-authoritarian tendencies. Similarly, researchers have pointed to the historically high penetrative capabilities of the

terns of social and political change in colonial and noncolonial societies, as well as societies that experienced different sorts of colonialism; (6) a classification of state capabilities according to different sorts of policies; (7) the effect of different types of government (e.g., democracy) on state-society relations, and the opposite: the effects of different types of state-society relations on the type of government. Other questions I have sometimes approached obliquely because of my dissatisfaction with the terminology that has been commonly used to deal with important relationships. I have avoided using the words "political corruption" and "nationalism," for example, except in a few isolated instances, although readers will immediately note for themselves their relationship to the ideas in this book. On nationalism, I agree with Arthur Waldron, who wrote, "Enough is unexplained about nationalism itself as to cast real doubt upon its usefulness in explanation." Waldron, "Theories of Nationalism and Historical Explanation," *World Politics* 37 (April 1985): 416.

[7] See Gabriel A. Almond, Scott C. Flanagan, and Robert J. Mundt, *Crisis, Choice, and Change: Historical Studies of Political Development* (Boston: Little, Brown, 1973), p. 23. Also, see Adam Przeworski and Henry Teune, *The Logic of Comparative Social Inquiry* (New York: Wiley-Interscience, 1970).

Egyptian state or the extraordinary capabilities of the Indian civil service. All three states have developed a myriad of new governmental
institutions that have irrevocably changed daily lives in towns and villages throughout their countries. Nevertheless, all three have shown
astonishing weaknesses, as well, as they have attempted to mobilize
and appropriate resources to change daily habits in intended ways.
Mexico, for example, has been very low in its extractive capabilities,
with the state share of GNP at just over 10 percent.[8] All three have
found rich peasants in rural areas redirecting state resources to effect
results not at all intended in state legislation and policy. Thus, these
three states are at a middle level of capabilities between the states in
Israel and Sierra Leone. Together, the five cases provide the kinds of
differences in state capabilities that could enrich the theory.

I also picked these particular countries because they vary in a number of other important ways. As in a "most different systems" research
design, I sought cases different enough in certain key regards so that
I could eliminate these differences as possible explanations of state
capabilities because these differences did not correlate with variations
in these capabilities. The cases thus range from ones displaying extreme ethnic heterogeneity in society, such as in India, to unusual homogeneity, as in Egypt; from small populations, as in Sierra Leone
and Israel, to extremely large, as in India. I also wanted cases from a
variety of culture areas. All these differences suggest, although I have
far from proved the case, the general applicability of the approach
developed here.

The selection of these five countries was also influenced by the importance of colonialism in affecting later state-society relations. I decided to concentrate on the impact of one colonial power, Great Britain. Four of the five countries were greatly affected historically by
Great Britain, which played a leading role in the expansion of the European world system in the late nineteenth and early twentieth centuries. This expansion and the various direct and indirect forms it
took, as I posit in Chapters 2, 3, and 4, were very important for understanding current state capabilities. Although there may indeed be
important differences for societies that came under other Western influences, the sheer scope of British influence made it worth a special
focus of concern. By the early twentieth century, the British ruled
about two-thirds of all colonized peoples. On the eve of World War II,

[8] On the debate of the discretionary power of Mexico's state leaders to make policy
unencumbered by societal constraints, see Fen Osler Hampson, *Forming Economic Policy:
The Case of Energy in Canada and Mexico* (New York: St. Martin's Press, 1986), p. 26.

the British Empire embraced roughly one-quarter of the world's population and land surface. The one case of our five that Britain did not rule directly or indirectly is Mexico. Nonetheless, I thought it important to draw illustrations from a major Latin American country as well. Also, it is worth noting that the British did dominate external economic relations with Mexico well into the nineteenth century.[9]

This book presents both a model and a theory for understanding state-society relations in Third World countries. Part I offers the model: an approach for analyzing the diverse and complex societies that make up the Third World. It emphasizes the distribution of social control among the many organizations in society that vie to make the rules about how people should behave. In Parts II and III, a theory is developed to answer the central question of the book: Why have many Third World states had such difficulty in becoming *the* organization in society that effectively establishes those rules of behavior? Part II delves into a critical period of history to demonstrate the circumstances that led to social control in societies being distributed as it is. The focus will be on a tandem of international forces, those paving the way for the expansion of the world economy and those involving European rule of non-Western societies, which worked somewhat independently and combined with indigenous forces to produce some very long-lasting results. Part II asks how things became what they are at the societal level. The analysis in Part III centers on why the social patterns that developed, which have impeded the growth of state capabilities, have not been overturned in the last generation. Why, even after the crumbling of Western empires, have many states continued to encounter insurmountable forces in their society and what results have such forces had on states and political life generally in these countries?

In grappling with the question of state capabilities, I have sought to treat Third World societies—but not necessarily Third World states—sympathetically, if unsentimentally. This is a book on how to understand state capabilities; it does not offer prescriptions on how to enhance them. My own bias does not run toward uncritical support for increased state strength. All too often that process has been accompanied by attacks on the identities and lives of the most vulnerable elements in society, minorities and the poor. The struggles for social control in the Third World, at the heart of the following analysis, have

---

[9] Until the last quarter of the nineteenth century Mexico traded predominantly with Britain. In 1860, 48 percent of all Mexico's trade was with Britain, almost three times as much as with the United States or France.

been over the control of these peoples. For vulnerable individuals, that struggle for control of their lives has frequently been little more than a conflict between the evils of exploitative local powers and the "justice" of an aggrandizing state intent on transforming them and ridding them of some of their most cherished values.

PART ONE

States and Societies

FROM 1947 to 1965, the world witnessed a massive change, indeed a revolution, in its political map. The unraveling of empire in Asia and Africa during these years took on numerous different guises. In Egypt, Jordan, and Iraq, for example, there was an almost imperceptible transfer of authority over several decades from British officials to indigenous leaders. Other cases had sharper demarcations, but even these differed substantially. The British transferred power to Sierra Leone blacks in 1961 in as fraternal a fashion as one could imagine, but in India and Palestine their departure came only after bitter struggles and opened the way to new, even more bloody battles.

Several countries' decolonization and independence experiences stood out in particular, and these rippled throughout what came to be known as the Third World. The dogged success of civil disobedience in India, the disorders in the Gold Coast in 1948, the ignoble defeat of the French at Dien Bien Phu in Vietnam, Gamal Abdul Nasser's surprising nationalization of the Suez Canal, and the battle of the revolutionary National Liberation Front (FLN) in Algeria against France's last ditch stand for empire all had wide reverberations. From his vantage point in North Africa, Franz Fanon, echoing a refrain of Lenin, reflected the powerful influence of an experience such as Dien Bien Phu on others: "The great victory of the Vietnamese people at Dien Bien Phu is no longer, strictly speaking, a Vietnamese victory. Since July 1954, the question which the colonized peoples have asked themselves has been, 'What must be done to bring about another Dien Bien Phu? How can we manage it?' "[1]

To both contemporary and aspiring state leaders, these landmark cases were speeding an end to European empire and suggesting the potential political strength in poor, subjugated countries. Daring leadership, such as that of Mohandas Gandhi, Kwame Nkrumah, and Gamal Abdul Nasser, together with imaginative political organization, as that found in India's Congress, the FLN, and the Vietnamese Communist party, could topple the rich and powerful. An imperial state could be reduced to a Gulliver among the Lilliputians. Even to Third

[1] Franz Fanon, *The Wretched of the Earth* (New York: Grove Press, 1963), p. 70.

World leaders who eluded explosive anticolonial struggles, events in distant India or Algeria lent confidence about the important role that centralized, mobilizing politics could play in their countries after independence.

Western imperial powers were not only the *bêtes noires* in the transition from colony to statehood, but they were also models to be emulated. The founding fathers of new states shaped their goals on the basis of those of already established states and the dominant European nationalist ideologies of the nineteenth century.[2] As in both the West and the Socialist bloc, the new political leaders of Asia and Africa came to believe in their states' potential to mold their societies through virtuous planning and meticulously laid out policies. Even in Latin America, where many state organizations had been exceedingly weak and corrupt during the first half of the century, a new "can-do" spirit gripped many who aspired to state leadership. The state organization became the focal point for hopes of achieving broad goals of human dignity, prosperity, and equity; it was to be the chisel in the hands of the new sculptors. This new state, it was believed, could create a very different social order, a unified channel for people's passions that until now had run in countless different streams.

This book is about the capabilities of states to achieve the kinds of changes in society that their leaders have sought through state planning, policies, and actions. Capabilities include the capacities to *penetrate* society, *regulate* social relationships, *extract* resources, and *appropriate* or use resources in determined ways.[3] Strong states are those

---

[2] See, for example, two articles by Benjamin Neuberger: "The Western Nation-State in African Perceptions of Nation-Building," *Asian and African Studies* 11 (1976): 241–61; and "State and Nation in African Thought," *Journal of African Studies* 4 (Summer 1976): 198–205.

[3] By using the term "capabilities of states" as the dependent variable here, I have two goals in mind for this book. First, I aim to probe the variation of states in social control—getting people to behave differently from what they would otherwise do—which highlights the *regulation* and *extraction* components of "capabilities." Second, I argue that variations in social control, in turn, affect the other aspects of "capabilities"—the capacity to *appropriate* or use resources in determined ways and the nature of the state's *penetration*. Many political scientists have written about political capabilities, using a variety of definitions and criteria. The most notable work is Gabriel A. Almond and G. Bingham Powell, Jr., *Comparative Politics: A Developmental Approach* (Boston: Little, Brown, 1966). By capabilities, they refer to the overall performance of a political system in its environment. They list five clusters of activities: extractive, regulative, distributive, symbolic, and responsive. Their work and others' have been criticized by Harry Eckstein, "The Evaluation of Political Performance: Problems and Dimensions," Sage Professional Paper, Comparative Politics Series, Vol. 2 (Beverly Hills: Sage, 1971). Unfortunately, Eckstein's alternative understanding of political performance is much too comprehensive and unwieldy

with high capabilities to complete these tasks, while weak states are on the low end of a spectrum of capabilities.

Have states in the Third World lived up to their billings in the generation since decolonization? Have they become strong states? Certainly, in terms of penetration, many states have demonstrated impressive capabilities, changing the very nature of institutional life even in distant villages and towns. However, the answer to the question for most states is negative when one looks at some other aspects of state capabilities, especially the abilities to regulate social relations and use resources in determined ways. The bright hopes of those heady years surrounding decolonization have faded considerably.

In all fairness, the standards set were unrealistic. As the depth of the problems to be solved became apparent, it became more and more difficult to sustain an image of these states and societies performing, as Albert Hirschman once put it, like wind-up toys lumbering single-mindedly through the various stages of development.[4] Even by more modest standards, however, a good many states have faltered badly in building the capabilities to change their societies in particular ways. The central question in the rest of this volume is why so many states have sputtered in amassing such capabilities, although a handful of others have increased their capabilities dramatically. Beyond that question, I argue that the failure of states to have people in even the most remote villages behave as state leaders want ultimately affects the very coherence and character of the states themselves.

What kinds of capabilities have Third World states developed to achieve planned social change and what kinds of limitations have they manifested? Unfortunately, it is hard to answer that question straightforwardly. We still do not have even a generally acceptable characterization of how Third World states have fared, let alone pictures to convey the major varieties of experiences or theories to explain why things are as they are. An odd duality, or even contradiction, has marked the social science literature. One version gleaned from scholarly works shares many assumptions held by those with such high hopes about the possibilities for progressive change. It has set politics, especially state politics, center stage, kneading society into new forms

---

for evaluating what states can do. His concept of decisional efficacy comes closest. The best basis for evaluating states is to measure what states actually do in the four activity clusters I have set out against their declared intentions as established in legislation, policy statements, and so on. See Appendix A.

[4] Albert O. Hirschman, *Essays in Trespassing: Economics to Politics and Beyond* (Cambridge: Cambridge University Press, 1981), p. 24.

and shapes and adapting it to the exigencies created by industrialization or other stimuli. This is the image of the strong state.

Scholars have described how states, for better or worse, have become the constant and formidable presence even in the most remote villages, especially in regions such as Latin America and East Asia. They have stressed how states reshaped societies by promoting some groups and classes while repressing others and simultaneously maintaining autonomy from any single group or class.[5] Theories of corporatism and bureaucratic authoritarianism have emphasized the activism and strength of the state in regulating, even shaping, the eruptive conflicts that develop from industrialization and the mobilization of new social groups.[6] The state, wrote James M. Malloy, "is characterized by strong and relatively autonomous governmental structures that seek to impose on the society a system of interest representation based on enforced limited pluralism."[7]

A second perspective, in contrast, has portrayed the state as almost totally impotent in the swirl of dizzying social changes that have overtaken these societies, changes largely independent of any impetus from the state itself. Some scholars have viewed the dynamics of these changes within the country's borders, while others have seen these uncontrollable forces coming from large powers and the world economy. In both instances, the state's image is weak.

This portrait has come from journalists and social scientists alike, who have described the activist state as more often illusion than reality. They have remarked on the inept, bumbling nature of states as well as on the instability and ineffectiveness governing bodies have demonstrated in trying to carry out their grand designs. C. L. Sulzberger, for example, reported in the *New York Times*: "One remarkable feature of the two-generation period covered by my working years was the creation of new states, most of them backward and weak. There

---

[5] Autonomy in the domestic context means that state officials can act upon their own preferences. In this way the state can reshape, ignore, or circumvent the preferences of even the strongest social actors. See Eric A. Nordlinger, "Taking the State Seriously," in Myron Weiner and Samuel P. Huntington, eds., *Understanding Political Development* (Boston: Little, Brown, 1987), pp. 353–90.

[6] See, for example, the articles by Graham and by Bennett and Sharpe in Sylvia Ann Hewlett and Richard S. Weinert, eds., *Brazil and Mexico: Patterns in Late Development* (Philadelphia: Institute for the Study of Human Issues, 1982); and Guillermo O'Donnell and others in David Collier, ed., *The New Authoritarianism in Latin America* (Princeton, N.J.: Princeton University Press, 1979).

[7] James M. Malloy, "Authoritarianism and Corporatism in Latin America: The Modal Pattern," in Malloy, ed., *Authoritarianism and Corporatism in Latin America* (Pittsburgh: University of Pittsburgh Press, 1977), p. 4.

are, of course, exceptions to this rule. . . . But the majority are help-less."[8] Or, as Stephen Krasner summarized the situation, "Most developing countries have very weak domestic political institutions."[9]

Planning new social orders has taken on a surrealistic quality in societies where, as Huntington put it, "governments simply do not govern."[10] Governments have been unable to achieve that which had been so widely assumed inevitable. As Wildavsky noted, "Planners begin by attempting to transform their environment and end by being absorbed into it. This pattern of failure is most evident in the poor countries of the world where glittering promise has been replaced by discouraging performance."[11]

Those portraying the weak states have dwelt not only on states in sub-Saharan Africa, where even some proponents of the strong state image admit the rule of state leaders has extended beyond the capital city or the main port only in the most tenuous and intermittent ways. But their image of weak states has also extended to the so-called "bureaucratic-authoritarian" states of Latin America. One serious doubter about how strong and active Latin American states have been is Linn A. Hammergren; "It is true that constitutions and legislation often accord enormous powers of control to central governments, but the question remains as to whether this control is actually exercised or exists only on paper. The limited success of Latin American governments in enforcing their own legislation suggests that the extent of this control is not great."[12] Similar statements have come out of Asia, especially some fine recent work on India. "Three decades of democratically planned development have failed to alleviate India's rural pov-

[8] *New York Times*, December 24, 1977, p. 19.

[9] Stephen D. Krasner, *Structural Conflict: The Third World Against Global Liberalism* (Berkeley: University of California Press, 1985), p. 28. See also, Joseph La Palombara, "Political Science and the Engineering of National Development," in Monte Palmer and Larry Stern, eds., *Political Development in Changing Societies* (Lexington, Mass.: Heath Lexington, 1971), p. 53.

[10] Samuel P. Huntington, *Political Order in Changing Societies* (New Haven: Yale University Press, 1968), p. 2.

[11] Aaron Wildavsky, "If Planning is Everything, Maybe It's Nothing," *Policy Sciences* 4 (June 1973): 128.

[12] Linn A. Hammergren, "Corporatism in Latin American Politics: A Reexamination of the 'Unique' Tradition," *Comparative Politics* 9 (July 1977): 449. A couple of older works on Latin America voiced this refrain, as well. See Charles W. Anderson, *Politics and Economic Change in Latin America: The Governing of Restless Nations* (New York: Van Nostrand, 1967), pp. 105–6; and Merle Kling, "Toward a Theory of Power and Political Instability in Latin America," in James Petras and Maurice Zeitlin, eds., *Latin America: Reform or Revolution* (New York: Fawcett, 1968), p. 93.

erty," writes Atul Kohli.[13] With some variation from region to region within India, he notes, the state's policy performance can be characterized overall as a "failure to pursue the regime's own professed goals."[14]

If we can make any sense at all from these diametrically opposed images of strong and weak states, perhaps opposing scholars are looking for strength in different realms. The major focus of proponents of the strong state image has been on capabilities involving state penetration of society and extraction of resources. Many of these researchers have written about macrolevel state policies, such as regulation and taxation of foreign corporations or certain types of income transfer. In these areas, some states have been more accomplished. These somewhat more potent states have been found most commonly in several places: in parts of Latin America, they have evolved as a presence in their societies because independence was achieved more than a hundred years ago; in parts of South and East Asia, some complex political organizations were built in the framework of anti-imperial struggles; and in parts of the Middle East, imperial forces opposing the emergence of strong state organizations were often the weakest.

Those favoring the weak state image, meanwhile, have examined capabilities involving regulation of social relationships and appropriation of resources in determined ways. They have often studied social policy implementation, especially the difficulties state leaders have had in ensuring intended widespread changes in people's social behavior and planned overall transformations in social relations. Many states have tended to encounter particular difficulties in achieving their leaders' aims at the local level. A number of scholars have concentrated on sub-Saharan Africa, where leaders have had grave difficulties implementing social policies that call upon individuals down to the lowest status groups and out to the most remote areas to change their behavior and beliefs.[15]

This dual nature of states is at the heart of any possible understand-

[13] Atul Kohli, *The State and Poverty in India: The Politics of Reform* (Cambridge: Cambridge University Press, 1987), p. 224.

[14] Ibid., p. 8. Also, see Akhil Gupta, "Technology, Power, and the State in a Complex Agricultural Society: The Green Revolution in a North Indian Village" (Ph.D. diss. Stanford University, 1987); and Francine R. Frankel, *India's Political Economy, 1947–1977: The Gradual Revolution* (Princeton, N.J.: Princeton University Press, 1978).

[15] See, for example, Victor Azarya and Naomi Chazan, "Disengagement from the State in Africa: Reflections on the Experience of Ghana and Guinea," *Comparative Studies in Society and History* 29 (January 1987): 106–31.

ing of the Third World today. States have become a formidable presence in their societies, but many have experienced faltering efforts to get their populations to do what state policy makers want them to do. States are like big rocks thrown into small ponds: they make waves from end to end, but they rarely catch any fish. The duality of states—their unmistakable strengths in penetrating societies and their surprising weaknesses in effecting goal-oriented social changes—is my central concern in the following chapters.

Of course, significant differences exist from state to state and from region to region in the Third World in the capabilities of states—that is, in their ability to determine how social life should be ordered. All societies have changed enormously in the Third World over the last generation but not necessarily accòrding to the designs of state leaders. States have had unprecedented revenues at their disposal; they have built huge armies, police forces, and civil agencies. But with such resources, why have so many Third World states been so ineffective in accomplishing what their leaders and others had so eagerly expected of them, while a few others have done so much better in developing capabilities in social planning, policy, and action? That is the central question of this book.

The answers to that question, one might assert, lie in the particular events and history of each state. On one level, that is certainly true. On another level, however, propositions can be fashioned that not only help illuminate the relevant events and history in each case but also demonstrate why the question of unfulfilled expectations arises at this juncture in history for so many states. Answering the question on this level, the one used in this book, demands an understanding of the sources of resistance to the designs of state leaders and of the factors that make state leaders unable or unwilling to overcome such resistance. The next chapter offers a model of state-society relations which highlights the struggles that states face in attempting to fashion social relations. The remaining chapters of the book suggest a theory—an answer to the question of why so many formidable looking Third World states have not been able to change their societies in the ways political leaders have intended and why a few such states have succeeded. The explanation I develop in the following chapters will take note of why certain societies in the Third World came to be organized so that some social elements could resist the initiatives of their states. My aim is to explain how, despite the many advantages the state has had, these elements have managed to continue to oppose state leaders successfully, sometimes to reach unexpected accommodations with state officials, and even at times to capture parts of the state.

CHAPTER ONE

A Model of State-Society Relations

GENERATING HIGH EXPECTATIONS FOR STATES

Anticipation of the capabilities states could develop and what they could achieve with those newfound capabilities ran high as Third World societies threw off the shackles of colonialism. These hopes were fueled by a cultural artifact of their former masters, the social sciences of the 1950s and 1960s. Although the term "state" was rarely used then, many social scientists came to think of politics—or better yet, policy and planning—as a subject of almost boundless possibilities.[1] The limits of states became unclear as scholars lost a sense of what states could and could not effectively do. Complex and only vaguely understood social processes in Western societies, resulting in such disparate phenomena as neglect of the aged, regional poverty, overpopulation, and migration, came to be seen as utterly malleable in the face of policy interventions. Social scientists were thought able to unlock the secrets of social engineering. United States social science, especially, burned with an excitement about what was "do-able" through policy interventions.[2] But social science learned little about government's limitations during the 1950s and 1960s because very few studies investigated what actually happened after policy was enunciated.

In the years immediately after World War II, political science continued to treat comparative politics as a host of institutional histories or analyses of formal constitutional principles of regimes. The emphasis was much more on the structure of institutions than on an examination of whether the institutions were doing what they purported to be doing. Only in the years following, the 1950s, were new methodologies and concepts brought to the study of comparative politics.[3] The

---

[1] A number of works have mistakenly assumed that because the term "state" was not used, earlier authors did not use the concept. See, for example, Peter B. Evans, Dietrich Rueschemeyer, and Theda Skocpol, eds., *Bringing the State Back In* (Cambridge: Cambridge University Press, 1985).

[2] Robert A. Packenham, *Liberal America and the Third World: Political Development Ideas in Foreign Aid and Social Science* (Princeton, N.J.: Princeton University Press, 1973).

[3] Two landmark books pioneering a comparative approach were Daniel Lerner, *The Passing of Traditional Society* (New York: Free Press, 1958); and Gabriel A. Almond and

new techniques led to both more truly comparative studies and increased concern with the interaction of populations of countries with their governments. However, even after the new methodologies took hold only one direction of this interaction was widely examined—the effects of the attitudes and participation of the population on leadership and policies.[4] The new tools, such as survey research, were geared toward studying this "input" side of the equation, and in large part they shaped substantive concerns. Social scientists focused on representation rather than delivery; preoccupied with details of recipes, they neglected to taste the finished dishes. One finds only rare questioning of regime infallibility: most often they simply assumed the impact of policies upon the population would be identical to what policy makers projected. It was taken for granted that actions at the institutional level of the regime would be reflected faithfully at the level of the individual citizen.

Social scientists from all the disciplines were not content merely to observe and analyze; they became avid advocates of state activism, tending to obscure failures and limitations even more. Social scientists had a stake in development. Prescriptions became as common as descriptions, and state failures became imperceptibly intertwined with the professional failures of social scientists.

In recent years, there has been widespread disillusionment among many social scientists with the capacity of even Western states to plan and to transform their societies.[5] Misconceived or not, the notions of Western thinkers helped create a great sense of expectation about the potential capabilities of states not only in the West but also in the Third World. There was a stark confidence in the 1950s and 1960s that the chaos of the moment would pass as new and renewed states would pull themselves together and create "modern" national societies. It was eagerly anticipated that the new states could lay the way for directing the economic and social changes already engulfing their societies.

James S. Coleman, eds., *The Politics of the Developing Areas* (Princeton, N.J.: Princeton University Press, 1960).

[4] See Thomas B. Smith, "The Policy Implementation Process," *Policy Studies* 4 (June 1973): 198. Note, in its emphasis on the regime level and the input side of politics, a book such as Jean Blondel's *Comparing Political Systems* (London: Weidenfeld and Nicolson, 1972).

[5] See, for example, Aaron Wildavsky, "If Planning is Everything, Maybe It's Nothing," *Policy Sciences* 4 (June 1973): 127–53; Horst W. J. Rittel and Melvin M. Webber, "Dilemmas in a General Theory of Planning," *Policy Sciences* 4 (June 1973): 155–69; and Theodore J. Lowi, *The End of Liberalism*, 2d ed. (New York: W. W. Norton, 1979), especially Part II, "Why Liberal Governments Cannot Plan."

Strikingly similar to thinkers of the Enlightenment, such as M. de Condorcet, or to those philosophers in the late nineteenth century, social scientists saw the world beyond Europe and North America as open to intelligently planned, progressive change. They imagined the futures of the "emerging" continents to be reflected in what they took to be the presents and pasts of the Western states. Benedetto Croce's comment about the nineteenth-century philosophers applies to many of these social scientists as well: "There was a living and general consciousness of progress, not only as a concept of historical interpretation, but as a certainty that the royal road had been entered upon at last, that the human race now had acquired the mastership over things and, what was more important, over itself, and that it would not again abandon or lose this road but would follow it forever."[6]

Implicitly and explicitly, the twentieth-century social scientists utilized what they perceived to be the European and American experiences of change to build theories about subjects ranging from economic growth of entire societies to psychic changes in identity of individuals. Imagery of lags and sleeping giants connoted that there could and would be evolution across a threshold from "backwardness" and "underdevelopment" to "modernity" and "development" along Western lines.[7] The role of the state as the principal tool in transforming the society along these progressive lines was often taken to be self-evident.

Probably even more important than Western social science in generating expectations about the capabilities of Third World states to shape their societies has been a web of international norms and institutions. In the years since the major anticolonial struggles ended, many broad aims of how states should change their societies have been carefully specified. Numerous goals for the transformation of societies have become the canon of international organizations, especially the United Nations. Plans for social changes and the role of the state in effecting those changes are no longer simply general hopes and beliefs widely shared around the world; they are also the written norms of legitimate world bodies. The charter of the United Nations opens with

[6] Benedetto Croce, *History of Europe in the Nineteenth Century* (London: Allen and Unwin, 1934), pp. 243–44. Also, see Robert A. Nisbet, *History of the Idea of Progress* (New York: Basic Books, 1980).

[7] On the concept of crossing such an historical threshold, see Leonard Binder, "Crises of Political Development," in Binder, James S. Coleman, Joseph La Palombara, Lucian W. Pye, Sidney Verba, and Myron Weiner, *Crises and Sequences in Political Development* (Princeton, N.J.: Princeton University Press, 1971), pp. 3–17. Also, see Lerner, *Passing of Traditional Society.*

the basic postulates of such transformation—"to promote social progress and better standards of life in larger freedom"—and from these
a much more elaborate set of goals has been developed in the agencies
and conferences of the world body.

The United Nations Universal Declaration of Human Rights approved by the General Assembly in 1948, especially the social and economic rights espoused, was of particular importance in initiating a debate on the guidelines for state goals. The independence documents
of Third World states began to reflect the new emphasis of the charter
and the Universal Declaration of Human Rights. Where earlier independence documents, such as that of the Mexican state, emphasized
the formal constitution of authority and relationships to their former
colonial rulers, those of newer states, such as India and Israel, also
stressed social and economic justice and "development."[8]

Even after the Declaration of Human Rights, the great new labyrinth of the postwar era, the so-called United Nations system, generated an endless stream of actions that continued the specification of
international norms for states. Both the 1960s and 1970s, for example, were designated as UN Development Decades with particular importance placed on the role of states in accelerating national economic
growth. Using organs such as the United Nations Development Program (UNDP) and the Food and Agriculture Organization (FAO), the
world body specified its aim of ensuring a higher standard of living
through numerous state programs.

The United Nations, it can be said, canonized a paradoxical view of
change in the contemporary world. On the one hand, it hallowed the
status quo by making the large territorial state, a political form of a
limited period of all human history, inviolable. States were to be the
building blocks of the United Nations, while the United Nations, in
turn, would attempt to safeguard them from aggression. At the same
time, the United Nations was elaborating comprehensive plans for undermining the status quo through economic and social programs promoted by states. Little concern was exhibited for the near impossibility
of undermining the status quo in one realm without also disturbing it
in the other and the very real possibility of social and economic change
bringing domestic and international political instability. Broad acceptance of UN plans and goals by populations throughout the world was

---

[8] See the Treaty of Peace between the Armies of Spain and Mexico, signed at Cordova,
August 24, 1821; the Constitution of India, January 26, 1950; and the Declaration of the
Establishment of the State of Israel, May 14, 1948. These documents and many others
have been collected in Albert P. Blaustein, Jay Sigler, and Benjamin R. Beede, *Independence Documents of the World* (Dobbs Ferry, N.Y.: Oceana, 1977).

simply assumed. In fact, resistance to state designs by unassimilating minorities or vulnerable peasants and workers clinging for security to tried and true folkways has often been quite significant. Some groups have viewed an expansion of state capabilities with grave suspicion, as a process presaging dire threats to their income, their autonomy, even their lives. The Kurds in Iraq, Iran, and Turkey, for example, have stood as witnesses during the last generation to the determination of some groups to stop the state from doing what many others assume to be the state's unquestionable duty.

Specification of norms and goals for leaders of state organizations through the United Nations has been part of a much longer process of normative change in the international environment about what sorts of capabilities states should have. Since the beginnings of the contemporary state system in the fifteenth to seventeenth centuries, change has moved toward accepting an axiom that the state organization *should* provide the predominant (if not exclusive) set of "rules of the game" in each society. These game rules involve much more than broad constitutional principles; they include the written and unwritten laws, regulations, decrees, and the like, which state officials indicate they are willing to enforce through the coercive means at their disposal. Rules encompass everything from living up to contractual commitments to driving on the right side of the road to paying alimony on time. They involve the entire array of property rights and countless definitions of the boundaries of acceptable behavior for people.

There is little doubt that contemporary state leaders have rhetorically accepted the axiom that states should provide such rules. In fact, as Poggi contends, "one can visualize the whole state as a *legally* arranged set of organs for the framing, application, and enforcement of *laws*."[9] For many state leaders, the set of rules they have aspired to has been characterized by the vague term "modernity." By 1965, C. E. Black classified 91 out of 115 Third World countries as having begun the "consolidation of modernizing leadership," the first criterion of which "is the assertion on the part of political leaders of the determination to modernize."[10] For example, Black dates the consolidation of such leadership for Mexico, 1867–1910; for India, 1919–1947; for Israel, 1920–1948; for Egypt, 1922–1952; and for Sierra Leone, from

[9] Gianfranco Poggi, *The Development of the Modern State: A Sociological Introduction* (Stanford, Calif.: Stanford University Press, 1978), p. 102.

[10] C. E. Black, *The Dynamics of Modernization* (New York: Harper and Row, 1966), pp. 90–94, 71. I arrived at the total of 115 Third World countries by taking all Black's listings for Latin America, Asia, and Africa other than Japan, Hong Kong, South Africa, and Rhodesia.

1961 on. Even in the few cases where "modernity" has been rejected as the fount for the new rules, as in postrevolutionary Iran, the goal of the state's providing some set of rules has been embraced avidly; in the case of Iran, of course, the set of rules derives largely from an interpretation of Islam.

The periodic conferences of leaders of Third World states have reiterated time and again their goals of effecting deep social change in their societies. The final communiqué of the 1955 Asian-African Conference in Bandung made only brief mention of "the urgency of promoting economic development," but by the time of the Cairo Declaration of Developing Countries in 1962 detailed statements were made about needs for mobilizing resources (including human resources), drawing up and implementing "national development plans," accelerating economic growth, dealing with population problems, instituting agricultural reforms, training skilled manpower, mobilizing capital through community development techniques, and more. Despite an increasing emphasis on trying to change the terms of trade and other aspects of the international economic regime, state leaders have continued to make pledges geared toward the domestic front; for example, the Third Conference of Heads of State or Government of Non-Aligned Countries in Lusaka (1970) pledged "to promote social justice and efficiency of production, to raise the level of employment and to expand and improve facilities for education, health, nutrition, housing and social welfare; to ensure that external components of the Developmental process further national objectives and conform to national needs." These are no mean ends to achieve. They assume a state with overpowering dimensions and capabilities.

THE DRIVE TOWARD STATE PREDOMINANCE

Today, for those of us in the West, the state has been part of our natural landscape. Its presence, its authority, its place behind so many rules that fashion the minutiae of our lives, have all been so pervasive that it is difficult for us to imagine the situation being otherwise. We accept the rightness of a state's having high capabilities to extract, penetrate, regulate, and appropriate—in short, a strong state. Galbraith has remarked on the omnipresence (some would say omnipotence) of the strong contemporary state. "There is, first of all, the large and pervasive apparatus of the modern state. In the nonsocialist countries it can be a little larger or a trifle smaller as conservatives or liberals,

Social Democrats or democratic socialists will it; but as all practical people must agree, it will continue to be very large."[11]

Even when the state is in the process of shedding whole bureaus and rule-making functions—"in deregulating society"—no one can doubt that when markets now take over these functions the state still authorizes the new arrangement. And, if there are those who do not play by the market's rules, the state will use its authority to enforce contracts made in the marketplace. Perhaps, the neglect of the concept of the state in so much of the earlier social science literature, commented on by scholars such as Nettl and Skocpol,[12] stemmed from the fact that the state has been too much with us and, as a result, has been wholly unremarkable.

What may seem as much a part of the natural order as the rivers and mountains around us is, in fact, an artifact of a small segment of human history. To be sure, the goal of uniform rules—a common law and broadly accepted norms—is not totally a novelty of the modern era; one need only think of the monism of certain city-states in European history or tribal states in African history among many other examples. The difference in the modern period has been how state officials have acted to impose one set of rules over so large a territory and how this goal has spanned the globe. What marked off this age from previous periods was the creation of a number of states, a state system. The state organizations in that system have ruled across large territories and populations, which have become highly homogeneous in their sense of identity and moral order. Nation-states have grown out of powerful state organizations and their increasingly homogeneous societies. Charles Tilly has given a sense of how far some states have come in imposing themselves on everyday life by reference to some interesting French statistics. He calculated the amount of time a hypothetical average Frenchman spent working to generate revenue for the state (through tax payments); in 1600, he estimated 50 hours of work per year; in 1966, 650 hours—a thirteenfold increase.[13]

Others, outside Europe, have latched onto these accomplishments in Europe as their ideal. Although there have been few universals in processes of social and political change, one can generalize broadly on

---

[11] John Kenneth Galbraith, *The Voice of the Poor: Essays in Economic and Political Persuasion* (Cambridge, Mass.: Harvard University Press, 1983), p. 66.

[12] J. P. Nettl, "The State as a Conceptual Variable," *World Politics* 20 (1968): 559; Theda Skocpol, "Bringing the State Back In: Strategies of Analysis in Current Research," in Evans, Rueschemeyer, and Skocpol, eds., *Bringing the State Back In*, pp. 3–37.

[13] Charles Tilly, *As Sociology Meets History* (New York: Academic Press, 1981), pp. 203–4.

this issue: by the mid-twentieth century, in practically every society on earth, political leaders had adopted the end of creating a state organization in a given territory, through which they could make a set of common rules that govern the details of people's lives and could authorize, if they choose, other organizations to make some of these rules. Planners and policy makers have so internalized these goals that sometimes they seem a bit startled when others may not accept the same ends. John P. Lewis, a planner par excellence, wrote of India, "One element of the strategy—the proposition that it is the business of government to be the principal planner, energizer, promoter, and director of the accelerated development effort—is so fundamental and so little disputed in India that one probably would not bother even to mention it to an Indian audience."[14] At least to an audience of Indian planners, I might add.

Goals set by the United Nations or by the heads of state of nonaligned countries have aimed to influence the choice of rules by states but not to question the state's making and implementing the rules. If anything, the international environment demands more of states, especially those facing impoverished populations, than ever before. It has been taken as a sine qua non by planners, such as Lewis, that nonindustrialized societies engaged in what Gerschenkron used to call "late development," and what others have now dubbed "late, late development," require the active guidance and participation of the state.[15] Ambitious aims by leaders to use the state to precipitate industrialization, to raise the level of nutrition, to regulate all loans are only parts of a much larger ambition.

The danger in taking the state for granted is that we begin to assume states in all times and places have had a similar potential or ability to achieve their leaders' intentions; the varying roles states have played in different societies may be lost. Just when the state's role was changing most dramatically in Europe, during the seventeenth century, philosophers such as Thomas Hobbes and John Locke focused on this new leviathan; they made clear distinctions between the state and other components of society. The need is no less pressing today; although the goal of creating a state organization that makes all the rules or at least authorizes others to make some of them has been uni-

[14] John P. Lewis, *Quiet Crisis in India: Economic Development and American Policy* (Garden City, N.Y.: Doubleday, 1964), p. 26.

[15] Alexander Gerschenkron, *Economic Backwardness in Historical Perspective: A Book of Essays* (Cambridge, Mass.: Harvard University Press, 1962); and Albert O. Hirschman, "The Political Economy of Import-Substituting Industrialization in Latin America," *The Quarterly Journal of Economics* 82 (1968): 2–32.

versal among state leaders, the ability to achieve such a goal has been another matter entirely. Political leaders have faced tremendous obstacles in their drive, and by no means have all overcome the formidable barriers.

The ability to neutralize opposition against a state's drive toward predominance—toward supplying and authorizing the innumerable written and unwritten rules that dictate daily behavior in a society—has varied markedly. Some states have gained much more mastery than others in governing who may heal the sick and who may not; the duration, content, and quality of children's education; numerous specifications of a house one may build for oneself; with whom one may or may not have sexual relations; and countless other details of human actions and relationships. It is not simply that some states have leaders who purposely have the state do less. Although there are important differences in declared intentions by state leaders of what their states should do, there are no states whose intentions would demand much less than a quarter of the society's total GDP, if they were to be implemented properly (see Appendix A). Gunnar Myrdal wrote that "soft states" are ones in which "governments require extraordinarily little of their citizens" and "obligations that do exist are enforced inadequately if at all."[16] Even if that were true two decades ago when Myrdal wrote (and I do not think it was), today all states demand much of their citizens, but the enforcement in many cases remains inadequate.

Understanding differences in states' capabilities in various periods and places needs more than a simple definition of the state as a political organization that is the basis for government in a given territory and then leaves it at that. Differences among states have related to variations in certain attributes of "stateness" for which political leaders have striven.[17] First, leaders aim to hold a monopoly over the principal means of coercion in their societies[18] by maintaining firm control over standing armies and police forces while eliminating nonstate controlled armies, militias, and gangs. Second, through state autonomy from domestic and outside forces state officials have sought to act

[16] Gunnar Myrdal, *Asian Drama: An Inquiry Into the Poverty of Nations*, vol. 2 (New York: Twentieth Century Fund, 1968), p. 896.

[17] Nettl, "The State as a Conceptual Variable," introduced the idea of variability or "the degree of stateness." I believe he went too far in rejecting the concept as at all applicable to certain entities, such as those in the United States and Britain. Alfred Stepan introduced the question of the degree to which states structure relations within civil society in his fine book, *The State and Society: Peru in Comparative Perspective* (Princeton, N.J.: Princeton University Press, 1978), pp. xii–xiii.

[18] Weber emphasized "the monopoly of the legitimate use of violence." See H. H. Gerth and C. Wright Mills, *From Max Weber* (New York: Oxford University Press, 1958), pp. 78, 334.

upon their own preferences, making decisions that reshape, ignore, or circumvent the preferences of even the strongest social actors. Third, state leaders have aimed for significant differentiation of its components; thus, numerous agencies can take on the specialized, complex tasks of governing the details of people's lives. And, fourth, state builders have sought these components to be explicitly coordinated, allowing a coherence of the parts of the state and shared purposes by those working in the various agencies. The distortion arising from taking the state for granted is an implicit assumption that all governing authorities are more or less equal in these four attributes.[19] They are not.

In short, following Max Weber, I use an ideal-type definition of the state: it is an organization, composed of numerous agencies led and coordinated by the state's leadership (executive authority) that has the ability or authority to make and implement the binding rules for all the people as well as the parameters of rule making for other social organizations in a given territory, using force if necessary to have its way.[20] Real states, it is important to remember, vary considerably in how closely they fit the ideal-type. From the first monarchical states in Europe, as Otto Hintze showed, there existed severe limits in states' rule-making powers.[21]

[19] On this point and on the performance of functions by "amorphous *ad hoc* communities," see Weber's discussion of the state. Max Rheinstein, ed., *Max Weber on Law and Economy and Society* (Cambridge, Mass.: Harvard University Press, 1954), p. 342. Some of the best Marxist literature has been less sensitive than one might have hoped about the variability of state capabilities. Alavi, for example, simply assumed that postcolonial states, without differentiating among them, would have mediating capabilities and relative autonomy. Part of his problem lay in wrongly assuming a unity or consciousness of bureaucratic-military oligarchies. These oligarchies have strength, he wrote, because of an absence of other classes that could control the state and because of the activist role of the state in economics. Hamza Alavi, "The State in Post-Colonial Societies: Pakistan and Bangladesh," *New Left Review* (July–August 1972): 59–81, esp. pp. 62, 64, 72. Robert Brenner, an astute and penetrating Marxist, seemed to fall into a similar trap. He argued against viewing states quantitatively—according to their strength or weakness—and, instead for looking at the state in relationship to class structure. The problem with such a "qualitative" perspective is its assumption that each state is capable of enforcing policies that strengthen the mode of production indicated by the society's particular class structure. It does not leave open the possibility that the state is *not* simply an expression of the dominant class in the society or that, conversely, questions of overall class relations *may* be beyond the influence of the state. Robert Brenner, "The Origins of Capitalist Development: A Critique of Neo-Smithonian Marxism," *New Left Review* (August 1977): 63–66.

[20] See Max Weber, *The Theory of Social and Economic Organization*, ed. Talcott Parsons (New York: Free Press, 1964) p. 156.

[21] Otto Hintze, "The Preconditions of Representative Government in the Context of

In speaking of the state as an organization, we refer to it here in the singular, much as we would in talking about a corporation such as General Motors. Although there is important utility in placing the state as an *entity* in its social environment (as we do later in this chapter), there is also a danger in making it seem anthropomorphic, as if it were motivated solely by the will of a single individual leader. Where state coherence is low, reference to the state leadership or executive authority as if it *were* the state or, worse yet, reference to *the* state without regard to differences within it could be downright misleading in certain circumstances. After introducing the state in this chapter in the singular for heuristic purposes, I will elaborate a more complex view of real states, especially in Part III, demonstrating some important internal tensions and divisions within them and how those affect state-society relations.

Why has it been so important for state organizations since the sixteenth century to seek predominance, to make or authorize *all* the rules, and to move up the scale of state attributes? After all, central political organizations have not taken such an aggressive and ambitious stance in all times and places. It must be fairly evident to state leaders that constant assaults on existing ways of making the rules are very risky indeed. They can threaten to sap the state's strength and eventually topple it or, at least, its leaders. Belatedly, Mohammad Reza Pahlavi, the deposed Shah of Iran, noted this point:

> Bazaars are a major social and commercial institution throughout the Mideast. But it remains my conviction that their time is past. . . . The bazaaris are a fanatic lot, highly resistant to change because their locations afford a lucrative monopoly. I could not stop building supermarkets. I wanted a modern country. Moving against the bazaars was typical of the political and social risks I had to take in my drive for modernization.[22]

His lofty ambitions, the Shah suggests, led to his tumultuous downfall. But why this compulsion to build supermarkets in the first place? What is the historical source for state leaders' voracious appetites for widespread and pervasive rule changes—whether those rule changes were called "modernization" or any other term?

The answer lies in the wider setting within which states exist. Threats to the survival of states and their leaders do not come only

---

World History," in Felix Gilbert, ed., *The Historical Essays of Otto Hintze* (New York: Oxford University Press, 1975).

[22] Mohammad Reza Pahlavi, *Answer to History* (New York: Stein and Day, 1980), p. 156.

from groups in their own societies. The backdrop for state aggressiveness has been the special character of the world system during the last half millenium. The role and effectiveness of the state domestically is highly interdependent with its place in the world of states.

When the new state entered into the tumble of history's events, it did not do so in splendid isolation.[23] It appeared with a handful of other similar political entities that together constituted a new state system. They formed a system because, as one would move up the scale of the attributes of "stateness," it would precipitate changes in the others, stemming from the fear leaders had of the growing strength of their neighbors. From the time that states began to appear in northwestern Europe four hundred to five hundred years ago and form a state system, they gravely threatened not only one another but also all other existing political forms, both local political entities and those outside the boundaries claimed by the new states. The state's fantastic advantage over other political entities in mobilizing and organizing resources for war, as well as for other purposes, brought the survival of the other political forms into question. A prime motivation for state leaders to attempt to stretch the state's rule-making domain within its formal boundaries, even with all the risks that has entailed, has been to build sufficient clout to survive the dangers posed by those outside its boundaries, from the world of states.[24]

How does an increasing capacity to dictate society's rules improve the state's prospects in the international arena? A state's ability to survive has rested on a number of factors, including the organizational capabilities of its leaders, population size, potential material and human resources available, and larger international configurations at the moment. Probably none has been more important in marshaling strength for the state, though, than the ability to mobilize the society's population.[25] Mobilization involves channeling people into specialized

---

[23] This seemingly obvious point has often been lost in analysis, as noted by Otto Hintze, "The Formation of States and Constitutional Development: A Study in History and Politics," in *The Historical Essays of Otto Hintze*, pp. 159 ff.

[24] For major books that develop variations of this theme, see Perry Anderson, *Lineages of the Absolutist State* (London: NLB, 1974); and Theda Skocpol, *States and Social Revolutions* (Cambridge: Cambridge University Press, 1979).

[25] Krasner has made the point quite well. A state's strength in external relations rests on its strength in relation to its own society. Stephen D. Krasner, "Domestic Constraints on International Economic Leverage," in Klaus Knorr and Frank N. Trager, eds., *Economic Issues and National Security* (Lawrence, Kan.: Regents Press of Kansas, 1977). To be sure, the state is dealing in two different domains and internal social control is not totally and immediately fungible to power in the world of states. Nonetheless, such social control is a necessary, if not sufficient, condition to exercise power internationally. Also see Bar-

organizational frameworks that enable state leaders to build stronger armies, collect more taxes (especially important in maintaining those armies), and complete any other number of complicated tasks.[26] "The foundation of power in the global system," wrote Kugler and Domke, "is the relationship between state and society. Governments acquire the tools of political influence through the mobilization of human and material resources for state action."[27]

It is not surprising that the growth of the very first modern states in Europe included building a triad of essential state tentacles—a standing army, a vastly improved tax-collecting mechanism, and an expanded set of judicial courts. The implantation of state law in place of fragmented customary or feudal law through the extension of the court system was essential in inducing people to behave as state leaders wanted them to behave and not according to dictates of local lords or others; in other words, the courts, along with the police and others who fed into the workings of the courts, were essential for shifting social control to the state. Improved tax collecting allowed expanded agencies of the states, including the courts and a standing army. The army, of course, provided the force necessary to back up the demands and decisions of the tax collectors and judicial authorities.

State social control involves the successful subordination of people's own inclinations of social behavior or behavior sought by other social organizations in favor of the behavior prescribed by state rules. Social control is power or, more precisely, what Michael Mann has called infrastructural power.[28] Increased capabilities of states include and rest

---

bara Haskel, "Access to Society: A Neglected Dimension of State Power," *International Organization* 34 (Winter 1980): 89–120. Haskel links the state's control to the ability of outsiders to gain access to society and to circumvent the state and state policies.

[26] Nettl notes that political mobilization "is the collective and *structured* expression of commitment and support within society. Such expression may take the form of political parties or quasi-parties—interest groups, movements, etc., anything that has a well-articulated structure" (emphasis added). J. P. Nettl, *Political Mobilization: A Sociological Analysis of Methods and Concepts* (New York: Basic Books, 1967), p. 123.

[27] Jacek Kugler and William Domke, "Comparing the Strength of Nations," *Comparative Political Studies* 19 (April 1986): 40.

[28] Michael Mann, "The Autonomous Power of the State: Its Origins, Mechanisms and Results," *Archives Européenes de Sociologie* 25 (1984): 189. I avoid the term power for the most part because I take social control to mean infrastructural power only. I do not want to confuse that concept with what Mann called despotic power, "the range of actions which the elite is empowered to undertake without routine, institutionalised negotiation with civil society groups" (p. 188). In Mann's example, the Red Queens may have the despotic power to shout "off with his head" and have their wish granted, if they have the infrastructural power to find the offender. Social control (or infrastructural power) "denotes the power of the state to penetrate and centrally co-ordinate the activities of civil

upon increased state social control. Mobilization of the population to serve in and financially support a standing army or other tasks could only grow out of the state's increasing social control made possible by the expanded domain of the courts. In brief, the drive towards predominance in their own societies among the earliest states grew out of their interaction with one another in a new state system. Getting the population to obey the rules of the state rather than the rules of the local manor, clan, or any other organizations arose much less from lofty visions of universal justice and what society should be than from the need for political leaders to ensure their own survival. There was a driving compulsion to establish state social control within society, for that was the key that could unlock the doors to increased capabilities in the international arena. Mobilization of the population into disciplined standing armies or into other state institutions could grow out of social control, the new ability to have people follow the state's rules. Such mobilization could provide the human and material machinery to fight for survival among political entities that were sharpening their claws on their neighbors.[29] It could lead to political entities of unimagined strength. The new state was to political-social organization what nuclear weapons much later came to be to warfare.

Even in periods of intense state competition in Europe, some weaker states managed to take advantage of the balance of power, which created "some nook or cranny in which a militarily impotent minor state could nestle." As Toynbee put it so vividly, "Rival Great Powers around them had bestowed an independence that these pigmies would have been incapable of either winning or keeping by force of their own arms."[30] The bipolar configuration of world politics in the aftermath of World War II has made it more possible than in many previous periods of history for states that have failed miserably in gaining predominance in their societies to survive by nestling in such nooks and crannies.[31] Yet, it could not have gone unnoticed that when

society through its own infrastructure" (p. 190). The term "social control" itself was used in classical sociology by Durkheim and others in reference to organization and regulation on a societal level—a question related to the bases of social order. In this tradition my use of the term stands, not in that of more recent social psychology, which is ahistorical and apolitical and emphasizes socialization. See Stanley Cohen and Andrew Scull, "Introduction: Social Control in History and Sociology," in Cohen and Scull, eds., *Social Control and the State* (New York: St. Martin's Press, 1983), pp. 5–6.

[29] V. G. Kiernan, "State and Nations in Western Europe," *Past and Present* 31 (July 1965): 20–38.

[30] Arnold J. Toynbee, *A Study of History*, vol. 9 (London: Oxford University Press, 1954), p. 240.

[31] For a somewhat different explanation, see Robert H. Jackson and Carl G. Rosberg,

the *ancien régime* collapsed in both Ethiopia and Iran during the 1970s neighboring Somalia and Iraq used the breakdown of state social control as an opportunity to press old territorial claims through war. Internal weakness has continued to invite international aggression. The territory of one of the states with the least social control of all, Lebanon, served as a playground for three non-Lebanese armies in the 1970s and 1980s in addition to a gaggle of nonstate militias, gangs, and international and multinational forces. The compulsion to extend state social control—to build supermarkets, as it were—derives from the most Hobbesian qualities of the world system; it has been reinforced in the last generation, as noted earlier, by its set of widely shared norms—especially those put forth by the UN system and others that have assumed the state's domestic hegemony.

MODELING STATE-SOCIETY RELATIONS

State leaders have adopted the ambitious goal of making their organizations overpowering in their own societies. They have built massive state organizations with a myriad of tentacles reaching out toward society. At the same time, journalists, social scientists, and planners, as we have seen, have been divided about the ability of many Third World states to achieve predominance. At the local level, many states have faced tremendous difficulty in effecting intended changes. Some have even been characterized as inept. How are we to understand this gap between aspirations and achievements?

The disparity demands, in the first place, an approach that focuses attention on the sources of resistance to the state's efforts at achieving predominance. Many earlier models falter in precisely this regard: they fail to account for powerful forces of resistance. Social scientists such as Daniel Lerner, Walt Rostow, and Edward Shils (in their respective traditional-modern, stages of growth, and center-periphery models) imputed a deus ex machina quality to the changes overtaking Third World societies.[32] The direction of "historical development or evolution," as Shils put it, is away from the primordial (biological cri-

---

"Why Africa's Weak States Persist: The Empirical and the Juridical in Statehood," *World Politics* 35 (October 1982): 1–24.

[32] Lerner, *The Passing of Traditional Society*; W. W. Rostow, *The Stages of Economic Growth: A Non-Communist Manifesto* (Cambridge: Cambridge University Press, 1960); Edward Shils, *Center and Periphery* (Chicago: University of Chicago Press, 1975). Others have made similar critical points about these dichotomies. See, for example, Dean C. Tipps, "Modernization Theory and the Comparative Study of Societies," *Comparative Studies in Society and History* 15 (1973): 199–240.

teria of affinity) and toward attachment to the larger territory. The assumed inevitability of this powerful dynamic leading societies from lower stages to higher ones, or from traditional patterns to modern ones, obviated the need for scholars to analyze closely those forces of resistance that would, in any case, fall by the wayside. Such resistance, they implied, was crumbling.

What sort of model, then, would center attention on the frequently tenacious elements blocking state aspirations, those forces that do not so easily fall by the wayside, as well as on those abetting the state in its designs? Such an approach must start with the actual way the rules of the game have been made and maintained in societies, with a focus on *all* the social organizations that have exercised social control.[33] Informal and formal organizations are the settings within which people have had structured, regularized interactions with others. These organizations have ranged from small families and neighborhood groups to mammoth foreign-owned companies. These organizations—all the clans, clubs, and communities—have used a variety of sanctions, rewards, and symbols to induce people to behave in their interactions according to certain rules or norms, whether those were interactions between father and son, employer and employee, landlord and tenant, priest and parishioner, and so on. These rules may include what age to marry, what crop to grow, what language to speak, and much more.

The people of any country, especially peasants, workers, and those in other vulnerable social groupings, have been sensitive to what the social organizations around them have prescribed. These organizations have most often been dominated, after all, by people with the means to deny others a livelihood—that is, those making the key decisions about production and distribution of goods—and those who could offer organized physical defense. A careful weighing of the incentives social organizations use to gain conformance has been necessary to gain personal mobility, even at times just to assure personal survival. Friedrich Heer spoke of such weighing of incentives by European peasants in the fourteenth and fifteenth centuries. He noted the conflicting forces, the pull and counterpull, between which the peasants were caught. The "good old law" of the state (in fact, very

[33] Baldwin has written of "power" and the ability to make others conform to one's set of rules. He refers to "situations in which A gets B to do something he would not otherwise do." David A. Baldwin, "Power Analysis and World Politics: New Trends versus Old Tendencies," *World Politics* 31 (January 1979): 162–63. Baldwin notes that it is important to denote both the scope and domain of such concepts. The issue of domain, who is influencing whom, is at the heart of the rest of the discussion.

recent law) promised the peasants a new status in society, but the nagging fear of abject poverty, of impotence before the law, of landlessness, all made the peasants hesitate before abandoning those forces that opposed the imposition of state law.[34]

The incentives peasants and workers weigh include rewards, such as a way to make a living, protection from marauders, and security in old age; they also incorporate sanctions, such as physical violence, withdrawal of status, and ostracism. These incentives to behave according to a set of prescribed norms and rules, however, involve more than only rewards, threats, and punishments. Various rewards and sanctions are not simply discrete, individual incentives but are ordered and packaged by those seeking social control to be as attractive and compelling to people as possible. Such packaging rests, of course, on the bedrock of material needs, but it also lends meaning to people's behavior as they meet those needs. A consciousness about social behavior aims to tie actions together in some meaningful or purposeful way, to transcend through action the specific act itself. These systems of meaning or symbolic configurations, whether ideology or beliefs or anything else, make manageable a universe, which could otherwise seem overwhelmingly threatening and impenetrable. They address cravings and needs, such as salvation, affection, and respect. William H. McNeill spoke of these symbolic configurations as myths:

> Myth lies at the basis of human society. That is because myths are general statements about the world and its parts, and in particular about nations and other human in-groups, that are believed to be true and then acted on whenever circumstances suggest or require common response. This is mankind's substitute for instinct. It is the unique and characteristic human way of acting together. A people without a full quiver of relevant agreed-upon statements, accepted in advance through education or less formalized acculturation, soon finds itself in deep trouble, for, in the absence of believable myths, coherent public action becomes very difficult to improvise or sustain.[35]

Symbolic configurations are thus intimately tied to rewards and sanctions. They integrate a transcendental purpose into otherwise mundane behavior needed for survival. Attempting to distinguish whether peasants act according to a "moral economy," emphasizing

[34] Friedrich Heer, *The Medieval World: Europe 1100–1350* (New York: New American Library, 1962), p. 51.

[35] William H. McNeill, "The Care and Repair of Public Myth," *Foreign Affairs* 61 (Fall 1982): 1.

the symbolic configurations, or are "rational actors" driven only by material needs is a futile exercise; it loses sight of the integration of the material and the moral. Together with the symbolic configurations, the various arrays of rewards and sanctions have determined the characteristic forms of social control in a society; through time, they have constituted the specific institutional arrangements that have distinguished one people's history of control from that of others; they have marked off one culture from another.

All people combine available symbols with opportunities to solve mundane needs for food, housing, and the like to create their *strategies of survival*—blueprints for action and belief in a world that hovers on the brink of a Hobbesian state of nature. Such strategies provide not only a basis for personal survival but also a link for the individual from the realm of personal identity and self-serving action (a personal political economy) to the sphere of group identity and collective action (a communal moral economy).

In stitching together strategies of survival, people use myths or symbols to help explain their place and prospects in an otherwise bewildering world. Their strategies rest upon concrete foundations; they provide material needs and aspirations, such as jobs, housing, and protection. These strategies of survival, sewn from the symbols, rewards, and sanctions, are the roadmaps used to guide one through the maze of daily life, ensuring one's existence and, in rare instances, pointing the way toward upward mobility.

The choice of components for one's strategy of survival is severely constrained by available resources, ideas, and organizational means. Even though each person constructs his or her own strategy, the existing resource base and the control over access to resources limit the range of strategies in an area. Social control rests on the organizational ability to deliver key components for individuals' strategies of survival. Most such strategies have coincided with existing, accepted modes of behavior and belief, reinforcing the characteristic forms of social control. However, sometimes components for strategies have been offered that lock horns with prevalent norms and modes of social control, proposing new forms of social life.

Through most of human history, legions of strategies have been at work in areas today claimed by single states. Territories have hosted a diversity of rules of the game—one set for this tribe and another for a neighboring tribe, one for this region and another for that. Social control has not been of a piece, but it has frequently been highly fragmented through a territory. The central political and social drama of recent history has been the battle pitting the state and organizations allied with it (often from a particular social class) against other social organizations dotting society's landscape. Although state leaders have aimed for ultimate uniform social control inside its boundaries, diverse heads of these other organizations have striven fiercely to maintain their prerogatives.

In parts of Asia and Africa, this drama began during the period of the colonial state. In India, for example, the battle for social control was reflected in the new approach the British took towards local police systems. "The other great empires—Maurya, Gupta, and Moghul— were content to establish contact with the autonomous villages but not to reorder policing within them. The details of structure as well as the names of agents within the imperial organization changed from empire to empire, but the traditional police system persisted mutely."[36] British policy, in contrast, openly challenged the autonomy of the village and its right and ability to maintain its own rules of policing. From passage of the Police Act of 1861 into the period following independence, the state sought to appropriate for itself the spelling out of police structures and functions.

Even more intense struggles have occurred in many societies during the postcolonial period and over numerous issues besides policing. The overall encounter concerns which strategies are to be adopted, who will make the rules, and who will determine the property rights that define the use of assets and resources in the society. This struggle for social control must be brought into stark relief even before we can begin asking why some states have succeeded in their drive towards predominance and others have not.

The model suggested here depicts society as a mélange of social organizations, rather than the dichotomous structure that practically all past models of macrolevel change have used (e.g., center-periphery, modern-traditional, great tradition–little tradition). The image of a mélange conveys two facets of the model. First, the groups exercising social control in a society may be heterogeneous both in their form (for example, a small family and a sprawling tribal organization) and in the rules they apply (for example, based on personal loyalty and founded on profit maximization). Second, the distribution of social control in society may be among numerous, fairly autonomous groups rather than concentrated largely in the state. In other words, the overall sum of authority may be high in the society, but the exercising of that authority may be fragmented. In this mélange, the state has been

---

[36] David H. Bayley, *The Police and Political Development in India* (Princeton, N.J.: Princeton University Press, 1969), p. 38.

one organization among many. These organizations—states, ethnic groups, the institutions of particular social classes, villages, and any others enforcing rules of the game—singly or in tandem with one another, have offered individuals the components for survival strategies. The actual strategies individuals have pieced together have been based on the material incentives and coercion organizations can bring to bear on them and on the organizations' manipulation of symbols about how social life should be ordered.

To be sure, there have been cases of the state's overcoming the dogged resistance of other social organizations and achieving predominance. In such instances, the state may make and enforce nearly all rules in the society as in a totalitarian state, or it may choose to delegate some of that authority to other mechanisms, such as the church or market, as in the case of a liberal democratic state. Its rules and norms as well as those of organizations it has dominated have offered the cues to individuals on how to act to maintain or advance their status. There are other societies, however, where social organizations have been in conflict with one another in proposing different rules of the game. They have split on such fundamental questions as what is proper human behavior and how should the society be constituted. Here, the mélange of social organizations has been marked by an environment of conflict, denoting an active struggle for social control of the population among organizations.[37] Here, individuals must choose among competing components in making their strategies of survival; these are difficult choices when people also face the possibility of competing sanctions.

The state, too, has been part of such an environment of conflict. In Senegal, for example, Minister of the Interior Cisse Dia depicted the confrontation between the state and an organization with different rules of the game: "The clan is a Senegalese evil, which has been with us for long generations, constantly denounced by the party, but always increasing in strength."[38] Never mind that these clans are not what they were in the past, no longer based on kinship, a common ancestor, or a shared taboo; more important, the effective political competition in Senegal has come, as the minister put it, in "passionate confrontation, occasionally armed struggle, between clans" that are not sanc-

[37] On "conflict groups" and "conflict organizations," see Eric A. Nordlinger, *Conflict Regulation in Divided Societies*, Occasional Paper No. 29 (Cambridge, Mass.: Center for International Affairs, Harvard University, January 1972), p. 7.

[38] Quoted in Donald B. Cruise O'Brien, *Saints and Politicians: Essays in the Organization of a Senegalese Peasant Society* (Cambridge: Cambridge University Press, 1975), p. 149.

tioned by the state and operate under rules different from those propounded by the state.[39]

In these sorts of cases, political leaders have not achieved predominance for their states through the ability to fashion rules and to have
those rules broadly accepted, but these state leaders have accepted the
goal that they *should* be predominant. The state's battles may be with
families over the rules of education and socialization, with ethnic
groups over territoriality, or with religious organizations over who
sanctifies sexual unions. For example, Mustafa Kemal of Turkey
locked horns with religious organizations over whether men should
wear hats with brims or without. As with so many other skirmishes,
the issue was not so inconsequential as it may first appear; over 70
people were hanged for wearing the wrong hats. In reality, the conflict
was over who had the right and ability to make rules in that society.
The model of society as a mélange lends importance to such issues by
placing them in the context of an existing environment of conflict.

Perhaps, because the state's role in making and authorizing rules
about public affairs and the intimacies of private life is so much taken
for granted in the West, many social scientists have lost sight of the
major struggle in societies with relatively new states. In fact, in my
reading of the social science literature, only the legal anthropologists,
as a group, have brought attention to the multiple sets of rules of the
game in society. Leopold Pospíšil, for example, remarked critically
that

> in our Western civilization we are accustomed to regard the law of
> the state as the primary, almost omnipotent standard to which the
> individual looks for protection and with which he tries to conform
> in his behavior. Only within the framework of this basic conformity,
> we tend to think, may there exist additional controls of the family,
> clique, association, and so on. In other words, in the West it is as-
> sumed that the center of power controlling most of the behavior of
> the citizens of a modern nation lies on the level of the society as a
> whole.[40]

Even the legal anthropologists, however, have paid scant attention to
the conflict among organizations offering the different rules.

In many societies, state officials have simply not gained the right

---

[39] Ibid.

[40] Leopold Pospíšil, *Anthropology of Law* (New Haven: Human Relations Area Files
Press, 1974), p. 115. Also, see Sally Falk Moore, *Law as Process* (London: Routledge and
Kegan Paul, 1978), who writes about "reglementation," the variety of orders and types of
control in a society.

and ability to make many rules they would like. Families and clans may seek to marry off children at ages quite different from the minimum age of marriage set by state law. Landlords and shopkeepers may seek interest rates for loans at variance with those legislated by the state. The major struggles in many societies, especially those with fairly new states, are over who has the right and ability to make the countless rules that guide people's social behavior.

Noncompliance here is not simply personal deviance or criminality or corruption; rather, it is an indication of a more fundamental conflict over which organizations in society, the state or others, should make these rules. These struggles are not over precisely which laws the state should enact or how the state's laws or constitution should be interpreted; these, after all, are decided within *state* organs, legislatures and courts. Instead, these struggles are much more fundamental, reaching beyond marginal deviance and beyond the formal roles of any existing political institutions in the society. These struggles are over whether the state will be able to displace or harness other organizations—families, clans, multinational corporations, domestic enterprises, tribes, patron-client dyads—which make rules against the wishes and goals of state leaders.

Many existing approaches to understanding social and political change in the Third World have either downplayed conflict altogether (for example, much of "modernization" theory) or missed these particular sorts of conflicts, which only on occasion are class-based (for example, much of the Marxist literature), or skipped the important dynamics within domestic society altogether (for example, dependency and world system theories). Focusing on these struggles within society, between states and other social organizations such as clans, tribes, language groups, and the like, will give new insights into the processes of social and political change. The very purposes for which leaders employ the state in seeking predominance through binding rules automatically thrust it into conflict with other organizations over who has the right and ability to make those rules.

It is far from inevitable that state leaders achieve predominance for the state. In cases where it has been unattainable, the state has neither simply disappeared nor has it always continually incurred the high costs of battling those who have effectively made the rules in this realm or that, in one locality or another. The most subtle and fascinating patterns of political change *and* political inertia have resulted from the accommodation between states and other powerful organizations in society; such accommodations could not be predicted using existing models and theories of macrolevel social and political change.

The struggles over the state's desire for predominance, the accommodations between states and others, and the maneuvers to gain the best deal possible in any impending accommodation have been the *real* politics of many Third World societies; moreover, these politics have often taken place far from the capital city. These processes can help give a clearer portrait of the state and its real capabilities. We will look more carefully at these accommodations in the final chapter of this book. But for the moment, it is important to note that the state leaders' drive for predominance—their quest for uncontested social control—has stalled in many countries because of tenacious and resilient organizations scattered throughout their societies.

Social control is the currency over which organizations in an environment of conflict battle one another. With high levels of social control, states can mobilize their populations, skimming surpluses effectively from society and gaining tremendous strength in facing external foes. Internally, state personnel can gain autonomy from other social groups in determining their own preferences for what the rules of the society should be; they can build complex, coordinated bureaus to carry out those preferences; and they can monopolize coercive means in the society to ensure that other groups do not stand in the way of enforcing state rules. Increasing levels of social control are reflected in a scale of three indicators.

Compliance.   At the most elementary level, the strength of the state rests on gaining conformance to its demands by the population. Compliance often first comes with the use of the most basic of sanctions, force. Who controls the local police is often one of the most important questions one can ask about the distribution of social control. The ability to control the dispersal of a broad scope of other resources and services also determines the degree to which the state can demand compliance.

Participation.   Leaders of the state organization seek more than compliance; they want to gain strength by organizing the population for specialized tasks in the institutional components of the state organization. In practical terms, the leaders may want peasants to sell produce to the state cooperative or to employ state-licensed clinics instead of unauthorized healers. Participation denotes repeated voluntary use of and action in state-run or state-authorized institutions.

Legitimation.   The most potent factor accounting for the strength of the state, legitimation, is more inclusive than either compliance or participation. It is an acceptance, even approbation, of the state's rules of the game, its social control, as true and right. As Poggi has written, state leaders want "citizens to comply with its authority not from the inertia of unreasoning routine or the utilitarian calculation of personal advantage, but from the conviction that compliance is right."[41] Whereas compliance and participation may result from calculations by individuals of the array of rewards and sanctions at hand, legitimacy includes the acceptance of the state's symbolic configuration within which the rewards and sanctions are packaged. It indicates people's approval of the state's desired social order through their acceptance of the state's myths.

The strength of the state organization in an environment of conflict has depended, in large part, on the social control it has exercised. The more currency—that is, compliance, participation, and legitimation— available to state leaders, the higher the level of social control to achieve state goals. Leaders of many other social organizations in an environment of conflict have not shared the belief that the state should be predominant in the entire society, and they, too, have desperately sought social control. They have used the same currency of compliance, participation, and legitimation to protect and strengthen their enclaves, in which they have also tried to determine how social life should be ordered and what the rules of the game should be. In Appendix A, I discuss various ways that have been used and can be used to assess and measure social control.

STATES AND WEBLIKE SOCIETIES

In parts of the Third World, the inability of state leaders to achieve predominance in large areas of their countries has been striking. A central argument I elaborate in this book is that the capacity of states (or incapacity, as the case may be), especially the ability to implement social policies and to mobilize the public, relates to the structure of society. The ineffectiveness of state leaders who have faced impenetrable barriers to state predominance has stemmed from the nature of the societies they have confronted—from the resistance posed by chiefs, landlords, bosses, rich peasants, clan leaders, za'im, effendis, aghas, caciques, kulaks (for convenience, "strongmen") through their various social organizations.

There can be no understanding of state capabilities in the Third World without first comprehending the social structure of which states

[41] Poggi, *The Development of the Modern State*, p. 101.

are only one part. In those countries where states have faced the greatest obstacles in their leaders' quest for predominance, a social environment continues in which many structures conflict with one another over how social life should be ordered. In fact, this is the environment of conflict. Grindle quoted one Mexican state official's description of such an environment: " 'Going out and meeting with peasants can be a dangerous business in Mexico. It threatens a lot of people.' In some remote areas, the *caciques* were considered to be an unassailable force, even by the party."[42]

Even in these cases, the state's impact should not be underestimated. The image of the strong state is certainly well grounded. In many countries the state still is the most prominent organization in this environment, but its leaders have not established it as predominant, able to govern the details of most people's lives in the society. The leaders have been unable to transform many aspects of the society according to their liking. In Egypt, as we shall see in Chapter 5, the state undertook a major onslaught in the 1950s and 1960s against wealthy landlords and their rules of the game. State policies did radically alter rural social structure, but President Nasser witnessed the emergence of new patterns, not at all to his liking and not at all what he had expected. The old landed class was gone, but Nasser's regime was being forced "to rely on the well-to-do peasants as a 'mediator' between the government and the mass of the peasantry. In this the Nasserites resembled every previous administration of rural Egypt, despite the former's very different ideology and social base. Government regulations certainly did little to weaken the strength of the rural middle class."[43] As we shall see in later chapters, state actions frequently have brought social changes even when the state has not been predominant and in ways quite different from those set out in official policy.

Many Third World countries have differed from those of both the West and the Socialist bloc, not so much in the amount of social control in the society but in its distribution and its centralization. Both these types of societies, the highly centralized and the more diffused, can be considered "strong" because the overall level of social control is high. They differ because in one the pyramidal structure of society concentrates social control at the apex of the pyramid, in the state, while in the other social control is spread through various fairly auton-

[42] Merilee Serrill Grindle, *Bureaucrats, Politicians, and Peasants in Mexico: A Case Study in Public Policy* (Berkeley: University of California Press, 1977), p. 160.

[43] Alan Richards, *Egypt's Agricultural Development, 1800–1980: Technical and Social Change* (Boulder, Colo.: Westview Press, 1982), p. 179.

omous social organizations.[44] Both these sorts differ from "weak" societies in which the overall level of social control is low; the latter have
often appeared in the wake of cataclysmic events. Natural disaster,
war, and other extraordinary circumstances can greatly decrease the
overall level of social control in societies by taking rewards and sanctions out of the hands of leaders of social organizations or by making
the strategies of survival they offer irrelevant to the new exigencies
people face. Table 1.1 presents a matrix differentiating types of societies by the distribution and overall amount of social control exercised.

Strong Third World societies, then, are not mere putty to be molded
by states with sufficient technical resources, managerial abilities, and
committed personnel. Although the set of organizations ranging from
small kinship groups to large tribes and ethnic groups has been
thought as anachronistic as the hand plow, it has often not simply disintegrated under the impact of state policies or even in the wake of
increased urbanization and industrialization.[45] The tenacity of these
groups and their strongmen leaders can enrage determined state officials.

Prime Minister Indira Gandhi of India experienced such frustration
when, as Francine Frankel put it, "the government appeared powerless to carry out its own program of institutional reform," even after
her party in 1971 and 1972 had achieved its largest popular mandate

TABLE 1.1. *Social Control of States and Societies*

		state	
		strong	weak
society	strong	————	diffused (Sierra Leone)
	weak	pyramidal (France, Israel)	anarchical (China, 1939–1945; Mexico, 1910–1920)

[44] Michael Mann has spoken of the "essentially *federal* nature of extensive preindustrial societies." *A History of Power from the Beginning to A.D. 1760*, vol. 1 in *The Sources of Social Power* (Cambridge: Cambridge University Press, 1986), p. 10.

[45] Suzanne Berger and Michael J. Piore, *Dualism and Discontinuity in Industrial Societies* (Cambridge: Cambridge University Press, 1980).

in twenty years of electoral politics.[46] Her inability to get people to adopt the state's codes and norms led her to new responses—authoritarianism, harsh methods, including widespread reports of forced sterilization—that still ran headlong into the same brick wall. "Heredity caste groups, each placed in a position of ritual superiority or inferiority to the others, and all governed in their mutual relationships by customary norms of reciprocal, nonsymmetrical rights and obligations, continued to provide the building blocks of social organization in the hundreds of thousands of India's villages."[47]

These castes, and other groups with their own rules in other countries, have continued to exhibit a hard-nosed persistence to survive in many areas and to resist the replacement of their social control by that of a state. It has been far too common in the literature on the Third World to dismiss with a wave of the hand the importance of the local, small organizations with rules different from those of the state. They have seemed so inconsequential, especially to someone who has rarely left the capital city. A book on Sierra Leone demonstrates how easy it is to denigrate local struggles.

> Such struggles tend to be largely personal or factional, not based on any broader social divisions. Since the participants tend to be largely in the "residual" sector, their actions will have little if any impact upon the national arena. And even if their actions do affect the national arena, local leaders have to operate within both legal and financial frameworks set by the national leaders, and are open to fairly drastic coercion if they overtly oppose the national leadership.[48]

In fact, events and struggles at the local level can have a momentous impact on both the state and the goal of state predominance. The reasons for the continued vitality of such groups in many societies (but not, interestingly, in some others) and the impact that these organizations have on the state are the subject of the remaining chapters of this book. For the moment, though, it is worth looking more closely at the nature of social structures in order to understand their relationship to the state.

For each Third World society as a whole, some important commonly shared values and memories provide the bases for the symbolic configuration underpinning social control. Many of these evolved during

---

[46] Francine R. Frankel, *India's Political Economy, 1947–1977: The Gradual Revolution* (Princeton, N.J.: Princeton University Press, 1978), p. 4.

[47] Ibid., p. 5.

[48] John R. Cartwright, *Political Leadership in Sierra Leone* (Toronto: University of Toronto Press, 1978), p. 116.

colonial administration. Yet these shared experiences have often paled next to the radically different sets of beliefs and recollections dispersed throughout the society. In fact, the very boundaries of these societies may be vague and uncertain.[49] The strength of shared memories and beliefs within various subunits—the clans, tribes, linguistic groups, ethnic groups, and so on—suggests an image for many societies of the Third World quite different from the centralized, pyramidal structure found, say, in many European countries. Numerous Third World societies have been as resilient as an intricate spider's web; one could snip a corner of the web away and the rest of the web would swing majestically between the branches, just as one could snip center strands and have the web continue to exist. Although there certainly have been connections between the parts and some parts have been obviously more important than others, often no single part has been totally integral to the existence of the whole.

The difficulties state leaders have had in many Third World countries in achieving social control relate to the state's place in these web-like societies. True, every society, including those of the West, has comingled multiple sets of beliefs and memories. However, the diversity in many Third World societies taken as a whole compared to other societies can be striking. Weblike societies host a mélange of fairly autonomous social organizations. Although Table 1.2 by no means covers all types of subunits that have maintained social control in various societies, it does reflect at least the differences in ethnic and linguistic fractionalization between the Third World and elsewhere.

Well over half the Third World countries are either "very high" or "high" in ethnic and linguistic fractionalization, while less than a third of other countries fall into these categories (see Table 1.2). Such statistics have severe limitations; for instance, they camouflage the tremendous differences among Third World societies themselves. Moreover, Table 1.2 does not show how such fragmentation relates to actual social control. Nevertheless, it does convey a warning that Third World societies and states may not fit well into molds shaped on the basis of European or North American experiences. In Table 1.3 I demonstrate the range of such fractionalization among our five selected countries, from India's highly fragmented society to Egypt's unusually homogeneous one.

Our analytic lenses have conditioned us to view *all* modern societies

---

[49] See Anthony Giddens, *The Nation-State and Violence*, vol. 2 of *A Contemporary Critique of Historical Materialism* (Cambridge: Polity Press, 1985), ch. 1. Giddens argues that boundaries are so fuzzy in such cases that one better speaks of frontiers.

TABLE 1.2. *Ethnic and Linguistic Fractionalization*

Level of Fractionalization	First World Countries		Second World Countries		Third World Countries	
	No.	%	No.	%	No.	%
Very high	2	7.7	1	11.1	31	30.7
High	6	23.1	2	22.2	26	25.7
Low	7	27.0	2	22.2	25	24.8
Very low	11	42.3	4	44.4	19	18.8
Totals	26	100.0	9	100.0	101	100.0

Source: Adapted from Charles Lewis Taylor and Michael C. Hudson, *World Handbook of Political and Social Indicators*, 2d ed. (New Haven: Yale University Press, 1972), pp. 271–74. They rank 136 countries on the basis of three scales using 1960–1965 data. The scales are those of Janet Roberts, Siegfried H. Muller, and *Atlas Nardov Mira* (Moscow).

Note: Very high represents the first quartile of the most fractionized thirty four countries; *High* represents the second quartile, and *low* the third quartile; *Very low* represents the fourth quartile of the least fractionized thirty four countries.

TABLE 1.3. *Ethnic and Linguistic Fractionalization in Selected Countries*

Country	Rank among 136 Countries in Fractionalization Level
India	4.5
Sierra Leone	15.0
Mexico	72.5
Israel	84.5
Egypt	121.5

Source: Adapted from Charles Lewis Taylor and Michael C. Hudson, *World Handbook of Political and Social Indicators*, 2d ed. (New Haven: Yale University Press, 1972), pp. 271–74. They rank 136 countries on the basis of three scales using 1960–1965 data. The scales are those of Janet Roberts, Siegfried J. Muller, and *Atlas Nardov Mira* (Moscow).

in ways attuned to their centralization of power, rather than in ways suited to weblike structures. We look for cleavages between "social classes," or we look at "national entities." Social change is analyzed in terms of centers conquering peripheries or modern sectors clashing with traditional ones or, perhaps, class conflicting with class. We examine politics in the capital city to see who precisely holds the reins of power; which social class dominates, or who authoritatively allocates values. We have a penchant for seeking out where the ballgame is being played, but our lenses and predilections may have misled us. There may be no one ballgame, no single manager of power. Overarching concepts, such as cohesive social classes or nationalism, may belie the reality of how social control has been exercised and how that has been changing. In many Third World countries, many ballgames may be played simultaneously. In weblike societies, although social control is fragmented and heterogeneous, this does not mean that people are not being governed; they most certainly are. The allocation of values, however, is not centralized. Numerous systems of justice operate simultaneously. The new lenses can give us very different insights into political inertia and political change.

STATES AND STRONGMEN STRUGGLE FOR SOCIAL CONTROL

The political shape of the world changed as dramatically in the quarter of a century following World War II as in any previous period of history. Vast empires crumbled, and the number of independent states just about tripled. With the revolution in the global map hopes and aspirations were reborn. New states, as in most of Africa, and renewed versions of old states, as in China, the most populous nation on earth, came to hold the promise for a better life. Those states, it was thought, would reshape their venerable societies, eliminating the old parochial fissures and replacing them with a unified nation. Statesmen and scholars expected the states in Asia, Africa, and Latin America to steer the way to unprecedented levels of prosperity and new heights of human dignity through a host of both macrolevel and microlevel social and economic policies.

Unfortunately, the achievements were beyond the grasp of most societies. Some important accomplishments by state leaders have followed those energizing years of decolonization. Many states have become formidable presences even in the far reaches of their societies, especially in North Africa, South America, and Asia. They have greatly affected the course of social and economic change, maintained territorial unity, represented their societies with single voices in world forums, and provided a major source for new employment. At the same time, state leaders in many societies have found it exceedingly difficult to bring about intended social changes.

Formerly optimistic planners have turned to despair. A new cynicism has crept into scholarship on the Third World. Hammergren has noted for Latin America, "The tradition of local caudillos, caciques, or *gamonales*, especially in more isolated areas of the country, the presence of regional elites even in more developed areas, the maintenance of economic ties between internal and external groups with minimal participation by the state, all point to a very limited penetration of society by the national center."[50]

The difficulties many states have had in displacing the caudillos and other strongmen operating with different rules of the game—not *individual* strongmen so much as the pattern of fragmented social control—have been hard for state leaders to accept. Third World states have been initiated into a political world that has been, above all else, a system of states. The goal of state predominance has been evident at every turn in that system. Every international organization that has bestowed legitimacy on the state organization from outside (for example, the UN agencies and the Non-Aligned Movement) has reinforced the assumption that states succeed, and succeed fairly rapidly, in their drives toward increasing levels of social control. That same state system has been organized historically, making any diffidence toward driving for predominance in society a very risky posture for state leaders to maintain. Increased social control is needed minimally for the mobilization of people and material resources against potentially avaricious neighbors.

Understanding the differing abilities of states to achieve social control, and in particular the difficulties many Third World states have had in their own societies, demands an appreciation of the nature of the resistance states have encountered. There has been nothing inexorable about the move toward state predominance. The state, as this chapter's model portrays it, has been only one organization in a mélange within the boundaries in which it seeks to rule. Where an environment of conflict persists, states have been at loggerheads with kinship and ethnic groups and others. Each has struggled to establish the currency of social control in what its leaders consider its domain; each has offered the wherewithal for people's strategies of survival. The results of such struggles are by no means self-evident. In many cases, weblike societies have survived with social control dispersed among various social organizations having their own rules rather than centralized in the state or organizations authorized by the state.

This chapter has been heuristic. In it I have presented a model for or approach to looking at Third World societies to begin to understand the difficulties so many states have had in increasing capabilities and securing uncontested social control. The question we face now is

---

[50] Linn A. Hammergren, "Corporatism in Latin American Politics: A Reexamination of the 'Unique' Tradition," *Comparative Politics* 9 (1977): 449.

why many Third World states—given the resources and recognition they garner internationally, their mass of bureaus and agencies, their armies and police—have stumbled so in their attempts to increase their capabilities. Why has the goal of achieving a universal set of rules within their boundaries (a common law) and a single political status (citizen) for all inhabitants been so elusive? And why has a handful of Third World states achieved the coveted predominance through vastly increased capabilities?

PART TWO

Crisis and Reconsolidation:
The Impact of
Capitalism and Colonialism

THE TWO DECADES following World War II brought a feverish pitch of optimistic excitement to political leaders in Africa and Asia. Sierra Leone, for example, bustled with "a great outburst of political party activities"[1] in the years and months leading up to independence. To the surprise of almost everyone, the British and Sierra Leoneans alike, the political jockeying finally resulted in a united group of politicians negotiating earnestly with Great Britain over the conditions of independence. "In these rather unexpected circumstances," wrote one party activist engaged in those negotiations, "the Sierra Leone Constitutional Independence Conference turned out to be an exercise in mutual admiration with the British congratulating the Sierra Leoneans and the Sierra Leoneans congratulating the British."[2]

A far less demure sort of excitement gripped India and Israel upon their independence in 1947 and 1948. Eventual statehood in both cases had been much less assured than it had been in the last years of colonial rule in Sierra Leone. Also, mutual admiration was much less the order of the day between the British and their former subjects. Both Israelis and Indians felt they had realized their dreams despite the British, not because of them, and the long bitter struggles were not easily put aside. Abba Eban's description is representative of how the Jews of Palestine perceived the end of British rule.

In Palestine, the last High Commissioner prepared for the end of the Mandate. He was adamant in refusal to permit the orderly handing over of authority. British policy was to avoid doing anything which might be construed as cooperating with the UN resolution [which partitioned Palestine and authorized the creation of a Jewish state]. There was to be non-cooperation to the last moment in the setting up of the Jewish State. Railways ceased to run. The post ceased to function. Official files were burnt. The assets of the State were transferred to England, offered for auction, or turned over to the Arabs. Though there had been a substantial surplus, not

[1] Gershon Collier, *Sierra Leone: Experiment in Democracy in an African Nation* (New York: New York University Press, 1970), p. 24.
[2] Ibid., p. 29.

a penny was left in the Treasury for the use of a successor government.[3]

As the mandate drew to a close, "one of the most abject failures in
British Imperial history," as the *New York Times* put it,[4] was immediately followed for the Jews by a rush of contrasting events and emotions. Feelings of wariness about renewed hostilities could not be put
aside for long. War with the Arabs of Palestine had actually begun five
months before the May 14, 1948, declaration of independence, and
the final withdrawal of the British now brought full-scale invasions
from the Arab states. The declaration establishing the new state was
read in a ceremony whose details were kept secret until the last possible moment. Yet, as word traveled through Tel Aviv, throngs immediately surrounded the hall and cheered the new state ministers. The
feeling that an independent state could somehow achieve for the Jews
all the good things that statelessness had denied them simply could not
be dampened. That night people poured into streets and cafes to continue celebrating. At home, David Ben-Gurion, the formidable leader
of the Jews and the reader of the declaration, said to his wife, "I feel
like the bereaved among the rejoicers." Twelve hours after the declaration, Egyptian bombs struck the city. The revelry quickly ended.

India's moment of independence also brought soaring hopes mixed
with a strong dose of realism. As the chimes of the clock struck mid-
night on August 14, 1947, the Indian nationalist leaders stood silently
in the Grand Hall in New Delhi. At the last ringing, one participant
blew a conch shell, similar to those used in Hindu temples summoning
the gods to witness a great event. A tremendous cheer then arose from
the crowd in the assembly hall. Only Gandhi was conspicuously absent,
mourning the partition of the subcontinent into two separate domin-
ions, the states of India and Pakistan. In the street, wild crowds celebrated and later in joy seized the new prime minister, Jawaharlal
Nehru. In Calcutta, countless numbers of Hindus and Muslims alike
danced in the streets. Bombay witnessed a massive parade of four
hundred thousand people. Colorful decorations splashed across
smaller towns and villages. Optimism over all the good an independent state would bring mixed uneasily, however, with the gravity of the
problems facing the new state. One year prior to the sounding of the
conch shell, "the people of Calcutta hacked, battered, burned, stabbed

---

[3] Abba Eban, *My People: The Story of the Jews* (New York: Behrman House and Random
House, 1968), p. 452.
[4] *New York Times*, May 14, 1948, p. 1.

or shot 6,000 of each other to death, and raped and maimed another 20,000."[5]

For the state leaders of India and Israel, the challenges to state predominance by various social groups came almost immediately, indicating to still heady state leaders how Herculean a task getting the state to dictate the rules of the game throughout its territory would be. Societal resistance to the order state leaders sought to impose gave instant evidence of the difficulties new states would face. Communal violence simply engulfed India. Even on the day of independence itself, reports filtered back from the Punjab of hundreds killed in Muslim-Hindu fighting and vultures openly preying on the dead bodies. Prior to independence, sixteen million Muslims and twelve million Hindus and Sikhs lived in the Punjab. Similarly Bengal had had a small Muslim majority. But each was now divided between the new states of India and Pakistan. In Calcutta, the sheer force of Gandhi's presence calmed the near hysterical emotions of those bent on fratricide. However, in the Punjab and elsewhere pleas from the new independent states' leaders went unheeded. Leonard Mosley wrote:

> In the nine months between August 1947 and the spring of the following year, between fourteen and sixteen million Hindus, Sikhs and Muslims were forced to leave their homes and flee to safety from blood-crazed mobs. In that same period over 600,000 of them were killed. But no, not just killed. If they were children, they were picked up by the feet and their heads smashed against the wall. If they were female children, they were raped. If they were girls, they were raped and then their breasts were chopped off. And if they were pregnant, they were disembowelled.[6]

At the moment of independence, as one observer put it, "there was a naive assumption that the British having withdrawn, the problems would vanish. Politicians spoke eloquently of great plans and world leadership."[7] Only a day or two after independence, however, new state leaders began to realize how difficult it would be for the state to establish a single set of effective rules. Reflecting on that moment a decade later, one of the great Indian nationalists, Abul Kalam Azad,

[5] Leonard Mosley, *The Last Days of the British Raj* (London: Weidenfeld and Nicolson, 1961), p. 11.

[6] Ibid., p. 243.

[7] Donald F. Ebright, *Free India: The First Five Years, An Account of the 1947 Riots, Refugees, Relief and Rehabilitation* (Nashville, Tenn.: Parthenon Press, 1954), p. 26. Ebright lived in India from 1936 to 1952. The final three years he served as the director of Refugees and Famine Relief of the National Christian Council of India.

still seemed a touch incredulous about how wide the gulf between state leaders and Indian society had been. The two major political groups, the Moslem League and the Congress party, had had considerable support, after all, and one would have expected that their acceptance of the partition plan "would normally have meant that the whole country had accepted partition. The real position was, however, completely different. . . . The people of India had not accepted partition."[8]

On August 17, Nehru stood in Lahore with the new prime minister of Pakistan and observed in his own words how "anti-social elements were abroad, defying all authority and destroying the very structure of society."[9] Nehru later toured the Punjab hoping to restore order, but the situation only worsened. The state could not achieve even its leaders' minimal goal of domestic tranquility, let alone the great plans that sat on the shelves of its bureaus.

Likewise, the Israeli state encountered an early challenge to its claimed prerogatives that, in some ways, was even more worrisome than the attack launched by the Arab states. Before the end of the British mandate, Ben-Gurion had failed in one of his major goals. He had sought, even before independence, a unified army under the control of the national administration (what was to become the new cabinet after independence). As it stood, several Jewish fighting forces had existed surreptitiously during the mandate, largely controlled by particular political parties. The Haganah and the crack Palmach troops had been directed by the left-wing parties, and the Irgun had been under Menachem Begin's right-wing Revisionists. Begin announced on Independence Day that the Irgun was now to be at the disposal of the new government. In June, he ordered his troops to join the national army, although until they were integrated they were to have their own commanders. Israel now put an army of 30,000 armed people in the field. On May 26, the new government issued an ordinance creating the Israel Defense Force and forbidding the existence of any other armed forces.

Coordination of the Irgun with the new army, however, did not proceed smoothly. As part of its absorption into the state army, the Irgun had relinquished the right to make independent arms purchases. But the residue of mistrust lingered. Irgun leaders did not forget that Ben-Gurion's political cronies and members of the Haganah had undertaken a campaign against the Irgun in the last year of World War

[8] Maulana Abul Kalam Azad, *India Wins Freedom: An Autobiographical Narrative* (New York: Longmans, Green, 1960), p. 241.
[9] Quoted in Ebright, *Free India*, p. 31.

II and in some of the period following the war. At one point, Irgun members and leaders had even been kidnapped and handed over to British authorities.

During a ceasefire just over a month after Independence Day, an Irgun ship, the *Altalena*, approached the Israeli shore laden with arms and ammunition. The government refused to let the ship unload unless the material was put at the disposal of the army. Irgun leaders negotiated with the government, in the end demanding a fifth of the arms and ammunition for its units in Jerusalem, still operating semi-autonomously. Ben-Gurion met with the cabinet, emphasizing the challenge to the status of the new state that Begin had precipitated. "This affair is of the highest importance," he exhorted the reluctant ministers. "There are not going to be two states and there are not going to be two armies. Begin will not be allowed to do as he likes." The ship was fired upon and sunk. Irgun cadres throughout the country were arrested, and its units disbanded; its members then joined the national army as individuals.

In the same month, Ben-Gurion challenged the still autonomous character of the Haganah and Palmach, units allied with Ben-Gurion's political organizations but resistant to the discipline and chain of command imposed by a state structure. A week after the sinking of the *Altalena*, he elicited oaths of allegiance from the commanders of the units and then immediately announced a reorganization of the new army. The High Command resigned, trading charges with Ben-Gurion. He upbraided them for what he termed an attempt at revolt by the army, and the commanders accused Ben-Gurion of imposing a dictatorship on the army. Once again Ben-Gurion triumphed, repelling the first challenges to state predominance.

India and Israel are examples of states that faced immediate, dramatic challenges to their claims of predominance, even in the midst of the jubilation of independence. Other political leaders discovered the limitations of their state organizations only in the incremental frustration that came with trying to get things done. State social control remained a mirage-like goal on some far horizon. For example, prior to decolonization, "the glories and prosperity of an independent Sierra Leone were often painted in attractive colors to cheering audiences who had been led to believe that there was an inherent magic in the word 'independence.' "[10] Once independence was achieved, however, the tribal chiefs, whom the British had courted, proved difficult to move, and affairs of state inched along in the form of tribal politics.

[10] Collier, *Sierra Leone*, p. 97.

Early governments lacked the temerity to seek much more than the preservation of their own privileges. Even with the imposition of authoritarian rule in later years, the existing configuration of social control still kept state advances in check.

Other state leaders found the same sort of slowly growing frustration even when decolonization was not a major breakpoint. Gamal Abdul-Nasser, president of Egypt, reflected on the state's inefficacy after a dozen years of his highly popular rule. "We need to struggle," he exhorted the people, "against ourselves and to realize our responsibilities. Fighting against ourselves is naturally much more difficult than fighting against an outside enemy. The question is not simple."[11] Perhaps the opposition to state designs in Egypt was not as blatant as in an earlier period of Mexico's history, where agents of landlords and the church in the 1930s killed the new representatives of the expanding state, the school teachers. Nonetheless, in Egypt, noncompliance with state policies and laws continually muted the impact of reforms. Nasser labored in an environment of conflict in Egypt from which he could find no escape, even as he gained increasing stature and respect in the world arena.

Why have these and other states in the Third World encountered such difficulties in achieving predominance in their own societies? What enabled these societies to resist efforts at state predominance? Why was Ben-Gurion able to overcome the challenges to the new Israeli state's authority and establish effective rules and social control, but Nehru could only stand helplessly by as Indians massacred one another and Sierra Leonean political leaders could not budge the entrenched chiefs?

The answers to these questions begin at a point long before the feverish excitement that erupted in the period of decolonization. The consolidation of strong social organizations, such as those led by Sierra Leone's chiefs, able to oppose the state and create an environment of conflict happened even before the creation of the independent state. Contrary to common opinion, however, these organizations were not simply "traditional" forces whose beginnings lay in the dim recesses of history. If one were to examine closely social structure and social control of societies in Asia, Africa, and Latin America in 1950 and compare them to those found in, say, 1850, one would discover that a profound transformation had already occurred. In fact, it is terribly

---

[11] Quoted in Raymond William Baker, *Egypt's Uncertain Revolution under Nasser and Sadat* (Cambridge, Mass.: Harvard University Press, 1978), p. 114.

misleading to speak of these twentieth-century forces as "traditional" at all.

When and how, then, did the social organizations that now stand in the way of state predominance establish their social control? How were their leaders able to offer effective components for the strategies of survival for large portions of the population? These answers are fascinating, and they will fill the next three chapters. At the core are two sets of related forces that had revolutionary effects on many Third World societies in the mid-to-late nineteenth century; they were revolutionary in the sense of creating sudden, disruptive types of political and social change and transforming substantially the character of social control in these societies. One set involves the expansion of the world economy out of Europe and its penetration to all levels of societies in Asia, Africa, and Latin America. This process was as much political as economic, as we shall see momentarily, for it involved deliberate government policies that undermined existing strategies of survival and social control in societies. The expanding world market gave the Humpty Dumpty of existing social organizations the mighty shove off the wall.

The other set was connected with the establishment and maintenance, mostly through colonialism, of political hegemony, the force most responsible for the manner in which Humpty Dumpty was put together again. How political hegemony managed that will be the topic of Chapters 3 and 4. For the moment, let us turn to the forces that paved the way for a major restructuring of many societies in Asia, Africa, and Latin America—a transformation that in many cases resulted in social organization capable of resisting the expansion of state social control.

CHAPTER TWO

The Weakening of
Patterns of Social Control

TIES TO THE WORLD ECONOMY

The types of social structures found in the Third World and the ways in which social control is distributed in different societies affect the capabilities and character of contemporary states. In many respects, these social structures derive from the unique cultures, environments, and histories of each society. But key common factors have also deeply influenced Third World societies. These forces date back centuries to the expansion of the trade routes that ultimately tied together the remote corners of the globe. Diverse cultures have witnessed the shrinking of the globe through the development of a single world market, introducing an economy that eventually encompassed nearly every person on earth.

Since the late fifteenth century, such trade increasingly linked European states and entrepreneurs to others around the world.[1] Sturdier ships and daring seamen took Europeans farther and farther from their home ports. For some areas, contact with the Europeans was not very different from attacks through history by other fierce and plundering conquerors. The experience was as sudden and intense as being drawn into a vacuum, and the results for the non-Europeans were frequently disastrous. While the *encomienda* system of forced labor took hold as a typical form of enterprise in New Spain (Mexico), for example, the country's population fell from about 11 million at the beginning of the sixteenth century to as low as 1.5 million by the middle of the seventeenth century. The disruption of the existing society and its strategies for survival was practically total as the Indians rarely survived their mobilization to extract silver from the land and perform other back-breaking and spirit-breaking services. Similarly, the slave trade in Africa and forced labor there and elsewhere exacted a terrible toll in human suffering.

The global impact of European expansion, however, was quite un-

[1] The effect of the European economy beyond Europe from 1400 until the Industrial Revolution is the subject of Parts 1 and 2 of Eric R. Wolf's wonderful book, *Europe and the People Without History* (Berkeley: University of California Press, 1982).

even. For many areas in Asia and Africa, the results in the sixteenth century did not totally disrupt old forms of social organization and social control; in fact, penetration was quite limited in scope in many regions until well into the nineteenth century when a true worldwide economy developed through a qualitative leap in European manufacturing and demand for raw materials. After all, even in the Mediterranean region itself in the sixteenth century, "the market economy covered only a fraction of economic life. More primitive forms—barter and autarky—rivalled it everywhere."[2] There, the market included only about one-third of all goods produced. In regions far from Europe, the embryonic world economy of the sixteenth century encompassed a proportion far less than that.

European economic relations in Asia, Africa, and Latin America during much of the sixteenth through eighteenth centuries and even in the first half of the nineteenth century were usually limited to coastal enclaves. Important exceptions stand out, to be sure. The switch to the cash crop of cotton under Muhammad Ali in the first half of the nineteenth century, for example, brought new forms of economic relations all along the Nile River. For most non-Europeans, however, those in coastal trading areas faced the most direct and profound effects of European expansion. Beyond these coastal enclaves, the rippling effects of the European economy varied considerably. In the hinterlands of some regions, life changed drastically, although most people never even set eyes on a European face.[3] In other areas, mediated and sporadic ties to the world economy left existing social organizations and strategies of survival relatively unscathed.

European companies often established themselves in the ports and then relied on indigenous middlemen or a particular foreign group for any trade with the interior. Sometimes, fierce battles, even wars, raged over who the intermediaries would be. The peasants, laborers, and gatherers had to deal with new lords or chiefs as a result of the fighting, and strategies of survival changed drastically as well. In other cases, the inland areas were affected only intermittently and selectively by the new forces emanating from Europe. In eighteenth-century Palestine, for example, only those peasants whose ruling *shaykhs* had linked up with French merchants on the Lebanese coast found it necessary to grow the cash crop of cotton; even then, they could still maintain a largely subsistence-oriented production.

[2] Fernand Braudel, *The Mediterranean and the Mediterranean World in the Age of Philip II*, vol. 1 (New York: Harper and Row, 1972), p. 438.

[3] See Wolf, *Europe and the People Without History*, Part 2.

In the course of the sixteenth century, Latin America, as much as any region, became an artifact of the expanding European market. Oddly, the role of the European economy there subsequently diminished and began to play the same intermittent role as in some inland regions of Asia and Africa. After the silver boom, the seventeenth century brought economic contraction and decline. One can speak of a partial disengagement of those in much of Latin America from the European economy at that time, allowing new systems of social control to enter. The new social control was exercised with only irregular contact with the European market. New "indigenous" societies emerged made up of Indians, Iberian settlers and their descendants (*criollos*), and descendants of mixed unions (*mestizos*).

Those societies revolved around the largely self-sufficient estates, *haciendas*. As the owners and managers of the haciendas and as officials, the new settlers and later the criollos were at the top of the status hierarchy in the colonies; meanwhile, the Indians gave their land and labor and fell to the bottom of the hierarchy. Indian peasantry, re-established in the seventeenth century on the haciendas or in small corporate villages on marginal lands, was subject to types of social control only tenuously related to the European economy. Even with the reinvigoration of trade in the eighteenth century, the peasants of New Spain, like many elsewhere, found the effects of the European economy intermittent and selective. Although existing forms of social organization, especially those on the haciendas and in the corporate villages of the Indians, may have had to adapt to market pressures, they endured.

In short, many non-Europeans were able to insulate themselves somewhat from the European economy through the mid-nineteenth century—able to keep the market at arm's length, as Redfield once wrote.[4] Existing patterns of social control and strategies of survival adapted in varying degrees to the new circumstances of European expansion, but it is striking how much existing social structure endured.

All that changed around the globe in a relatively short period. Both those who had shielded themselves through venerable social organizations and those in societies whose social patterns had already changed drastically in the previous centuries as a result of European influence experienced socially explosive changes in the span of only a few critical decades beginning about a hundred years ago. Wolf wrote, "During the latter part of the nineteenth century, production under capi-

[4] Robert Redfield, *Peasant Society and Culture* (Chicago: University of Chicago Press, 1960), p. 29.

talism took a great leap forward, escalating the demand for raw materials and foodstuffs and creating a vastly expanded market of worldwide scope. Whole regions became specialized in the production of some raw material, food crop, or stimulant . . . [which] had consequences at the level of household, kin group, community, region, and class."[5] New industrialists and reinvigorated traders permanently transformed any intermittent, tenuous, and selective connections producers had had to the European economy. Peasant economic crises and the crumbling or radical alteration of existing social organizations and social control ensued. The catastrophic change in conditions between the mid-nineteenth century and the beginning of World War I—in Asia, Africa, and Latin America alike—is central for our story here. The rapid and deep transformations of a century ago, I will argue, have had an enduring impact on state-society relations today. To understand why so many Third World states today have grave difficulties in establishing effective social control, we must first understand the disruptive changes that began in the middle of the last century.

The societies of Asia, Africa, and Latin America turned from being strong societies with viable strategies of survival into weak societies in which crises pushed the population into desperate search for new strategies. The irrelevance of old rewards, sanctions, and symbols came universally and nearly simultaneously to the producers of each society; barely a society on earth remained untouched. The European economy now became the world economy for peoples from East Asia to South America. Reasons for the suddenness and depth of the world market's penetration to all segments of society relate to a number of technological and administrative breakthroughs and new needs that developed during Europe's Industrial Revolution.[6] By the beginning of this century few people in the world were not consuming European manufactured products and producing raw materials for Europeans or, at least, servicing those who did produce. These changes have been dealt with extensively by historians and others.

However, less frequently examined is the means by which European traders, industrialists, and investors achieved two primary goals (1) guaranteeing access to distant markets and suppliers who could pro-

---

[5] Wolf, *Europe and the People Without History*, p. 310.

[6] "There had occurred already before 1850 significant technological advances in textiles, and to a lesser extent in coal, iron, and transport." Philip S. Bagwell and G. E. Mingay, *Britain and America 1850–1939* (London: Routledge and Kegan Paul, 1970), p. 7. In the cotton industry, for example, the period from 1820 to 1850 saw powerweaving and steam power come to dominate the industry, and the productivity of workers rose rapidly; the increase was sometimes as great as 300 percent in hourly output per worker.

vide raw materials vital for European food needs and industry; and
(2) assuring that the commodities most needed in Europe (rather than
commodities simply for local consumption) would be produced and in
sufficient quantity. Despite the nineteenth-century liberal credo of
free trade and the belief in the invisible hand, the hand that helped
achieve these goals was actually quite visible. European states, through
specific policies, played an integral role in achieving these two aims so
critical to the success of the contemporary economic order. While important questions of production, allocation, wealth, and opportunities
remained in the private sector, out of the hands of state officials, public policies did play active and critical roles in gaining access to peasant
producers in Asia, Africa, and Latin America and in assuring that
those peasants produced for the needs of the international market.
The European economy did not become the first worldwide market
through some inexorable process. Various peoples threw a panoply of
barriers and diversions at it. No, its success took political might and
directed political policies to pave the way for its worldwide expansion—doctrines of "free trade" notwithstanding. These policies went
beyond colonial rule. Even in long-standing colonies, such as Indonesia, new policies assaulted the means people had used to hold the market at arm's length.

Hegemonic Western states, epitomized by Britain, adopted a series
of policies in areas they ruled that facilitated rapid, nearly universal
penetration of the European-dominated market. These policies left
practically no peasant or gatherer, even in the most remote corners of
the globe, untouched.

Indigenously ruled regimes, such as those in Mexico, often ended
up employing much the same set of policies as the Western powers did
in colonial territories. As we shall see, their leaders hoped that by em-
ulating the West they could unlock the European secret of concentrating vast wealth and power and could thereby ward off the threats
Western powers posed internationally. Or, in bleaker circumstances,
they employed such policies as a means of complying with the wishes
of the overpowering Western states.

Three types of state policies underlay the rapid and widespread
weakening of old social and politcial arrangements: (1) effecting important changes in *land tenure* patterns; (2) adopting new forms and
procedures of *taxation*; and (3) instituting new modes of *transportation*.
By first understanding the colossal impact these policies had on social
structure in Asia, Africa, and Latin America, we can later analyze how
and why the resultant social structure has had such important effects
on contemporary Third World politics.

Land Tenure Laws

In disparate parts of the world ruled by different states and empires, small freeholding peasants almost simultaneously faced catastrophic changes in the rules of landholding and land use. It is striking that these land tenure changes came in a number of countries almost at the same moment in history. As if in a flash, government after government came to see the hidden potential of changing landholding rights.

In 1856, Mexico passed its *Ley de desamortización*, also known as *Ley Lerdo*; in 1858, the Ottoman Empire enacted the *Tapu* law; in 1858, the British rulers issued the Proclamation of 1858 for the province of Oudh in North India; and, also in 1858, Said Pasha issued a law strengthening private landowning rights in Egypt. And that is not all. Legislation and administrative decrees changing proprietary and social relationships to the land could be found from South America to East Asia in the single generation following the late 1850s. Bolivia's *Ley de Exvinculación de Tierras* in 1874, for example, capped an eight-year process of abolishing communal holdings. In Guatemala, the legal onslaught against communal Indian lands began around 1870; and, in Venezuela, a series of policies culminated in 1882.[7] The Dutch enacted the Agrarian Land Law in Indonesia in 1870. Only sub-Saharan Africa largely escaped the effects induced by transformations in land tenure. In other parts of the non-European world, land changes in the latter 1800s had momentous results.

In striking at existing land tenure patterns, the new policies hit at what was inevitably the critical set of rules of the game in agrarian societies. Property rights consist of the rules for employing productive factors in a society. What better way to assure the unviability of the old ways of producing than to attack the most important property rights of all in such societies, those involving land? In so doing, successful policies would greatly affect existing social control. So many rewards, sanctions, and symbols that underlay social control, after all, stemmed directly from questions of access to and use of land. In societies with more than 90 percent of the population in agriculture, changes in land tenure were bound to upset people's strategies of survival. Social structure was in for some momentous changes.

Often, there were multiple purposes for these changes in land tenure, whether effected by indigenous states or outside rulers. In many areas, for example, one goal was to establish and maintain as secure a hegemonic rule as possible. Wherever enacted, however, these laws

---

[7] International Labour Office, *Indigenous Peoples*, Studies and Reports, New Series, No. 35 (Geneva: International Labour Office, 1953), pp. 296–99.

primarily aimed to facilitate changes in agricultural production that would increase yields and lead to planting crops suitable for export. The bevy of landholding changes in such a short period was not mere coincidence. Simultaneous shifts in land tenure in seemingly unrelated parts of the globe came in large part because of vastly increased demand in Europe and the United States for cotton, sugar, coffee, jute, indigo, and a number of other select crops. The world economy was bursting at its seams, overflowing into places far beyond the North Atlantic and the Mediterranean. The textile industry, Britain's biggest exporter, for example, increased its imports of raw cotton by more than 100 percent between the early 1850s and the early 1880s.[8]

The unquenchable thirst for raw materials in Europe motivated actors in Asian, African, and Latin American countries. State leaders, whether indigenous rulers or the European governors of colonies, were prodded by opportunistic European traders to change land tenure laws. Increasingly powerful rural or urban entrepreneurs, also keenly interested in such laws, aimed to exploit the new commercial opportunities by gaining control of vast tracts of cultivable land and arranging for production of lucrative export crops. New production techniques developed at this time for certain crops also led to increased pressure for new laws; thus, land could be consolidated to gain greater economies of scale.

Surprisingly, state leaders drafting new land laws frequently discovered their policies did not have the intended impact. Instead of affecting more secure central control over a territory, they found that they had fostered the growth in power of landlords hostile to state centralization. Whatever the result, it turns out, land tenure rules are such sensitive instruments that even when goals were not achieved they could have monumental unintended effects on peasant societies—on strategies of survival and the patterns of social control.

Rationalization for the new laws came cloaked in the rhetoric of nineteenth-century liberal ideology. This was the period, after all, of the Emancipation Proclamation and the emancipation of Russian serfs. For example, the Ottoman Empire's land law came on the heels

[8] See Sir John Clapham, *An Economic History of Modern Britain* (Cambridge: Cambridge University Press, 1952), p. 225; Hugh Bodey, *Twenty Centuries of British Industry* (London: David & Charles, 1975), p. 156; and Abbott Payson Usher, *An Introduction to the Industrial History of England* (Boston: Houghton Mifflin, 1920), p. 305. A. E. Musson, *The Growth of British Industry* (New York: Holmes and Meier, 1978), p. 80, wrote, "The main incentive to mechanization in the industry seems to have been the growth of demand." During the same period, the import of wool increased 400 percent; flax, almost 25 percent; hemp, 40 percent; and jute, about 1200 percent (see Clapham, p. 225).

of the Crimean War and the consequent need by the Ottoman sultan to curry favor with the liberal European powers that had saved the teetering empire from the brink of disaster. As one of a cluster of reforms, including a new charter of rights dealing with the Sublime· Porte's Christian subjects, the land law was intended to demonstrate the Turks' seriousness about reform and their commitment to liberal tenets. The empire's leaders aimed to undermine tribal shaykhs and create, instead, a free peasantry. The shaykhs exercised significant social control nearly free of restraints imposed by the Ottomans. Now officials in Constantinople aggressively sought to topple the shaykhs and establish their own social control among the new free peasants. As it turned out, the shaykhs indeed fell from power, but the Sublime Porte was not the organization to step in and develop social control instead.

Mexican leaders, likewise, tied the *Ley de desamortización* to the liberal credo; it ended the differentiations based on race as well as the special status of the church's holdings. In Mexico, as in almost every other area where land tenure changes were introduced, state rulers offered the new regulations as a step against the mortmain, that anachronism of feudalism which preserved the inalienable right of communal organizations to hold land in perpetuity. Modeled after the antifeudal and antiecclesiastic Statutes of Mortmain in Europe, the new laws provided for individual ownership and registration of plots and attempted to eliminate various types of communal rights to land by church, village, or clan found characteristically in Mexico, India, Palestine, and elsewhere. The lofty vision was of peasants *cum* capitalists, of countless freeholders acting in economically rational ways and thus increasing yields of cash crops. And, as in the Ottoman Empire, the goal was to undercut the existing bases for social control from communal landholding and substitute the control of a reinvigorated Mexican state.

Despite the precise purposes and rationalizations for the changes in land tenure from one place to another, they precipitated eruptive, universal dislocations wherever enacted. Peasants' stable world suddenly became topsy-turvy. The new laws signaled changes in agricultural production and rural relations that entered so deeply into the fabric of societies that their effects are often still readily discernible today. The Ottoman *Tapu* law in Palestine, for example, must be considered a failure from the perspective of the Ottoman authorities who devised and implemented it, but it still had cataclysmic effects on the relationship of the poor *fellahin* (peasants) to the land and the classes above them.

The Ottomans aimed to precipitate a permanent division of village lands that previously had been periodically redistributed to the various clans (*musha'a*) and of state lands that had also been continually redivided (*miri*). Also, the laws required the proper registration of all land parcels; until then formal registration of property had been the exception, not the rule. Ottoman authorities hoped that in Palestine, Iraq, and elsewhere firm rights for proprietors would sever the dependency of the rural population on the powerful shaykhs. The undermining of the shaykhs, they believed, would initiate political centralization. In fact, events did not turn out that way at all. Even after the Ottoman Empire had slipped almost silently into extinction, musha'a lands continued to constitute a significant part of all Arab landholdings in Palestine, and land registers there were nearly useless.

Even though the new laws were inadequate to prop up the empire sufficiently to prevent its demise, the *Tapu* law did transform the nature of rural relations. Ottoman authorities, seeking quick, easy ways to gain state revenues, claimed unregistered tracts in the most fertile parts of Palestine and then sold them off for a pittance to wealthy urban entrepreneurs (*a'yan*). The most noted case involved land in the Jezreel Valley, including twenty villages with 4,000 inhabitants, sold in a single transaction.[9] In other instances fellahin, fearful of shedding their precious anonymity, registered their plots under the name of a single village elder or urban notable. The results were the same: these ploys dispossessed numerous fellahin. Many became tenants, especially on the land most suitable to increased economies of scale in the burgeoning central and western portions of the country. Others were left with small, unviable plots.

Alongside the peasants' small fragmented plots in Palestine, there came to be huge holdings owned by city dwelling lords and populated by poor tenants. "Only rarely," wrote Granott, "did the estate owners live on their property. Their land was cultivated for the most part by tenants who rented the lands on various terms, and with the help of overseers and supervisors."[10] At the end of the Ottoman rule of Palestine, in a country still largely underpopulated, about one-half the landowning families had insufficient land for subsistence, and about

---

[9] Z. Abramovitz and Y. Gelfat, *The Arab Holding in Palestine and in the Countries of the Middle East* (Palestine: Hakibutz Hameuchad, 1944) (text in Hebrew; title translated), p. 16; A. N. Polak, *The History of Land Relations in Egypt, Syria and Palestine at the End of the Middle Ages and in Modern Times* (Jerusalem: Avar, 1940) (text in Hebrew; title translated), p. 86; and A. Granott, *The Land System in Palestine* (London: Eyre and Spottiswoode, 1952), p. 80.

[10] Granott, *The Land System in Palestine*, p. 40.

one-third of all cultivated lands were rented to tenants.[11] On their own plots, peasants were drawn into the wider markets slowly; for example, in Palestine the British estimated early in their rule that the fellahin marketed about 15 percent of their yield. But larger landowners, even while avoiding full-scale plantation-like agriculture, exported increasing amounts of citrus fruits and bananas.

The supposed intermediaries between Constantinople and the local population, the a'yan, entrenched themselves locally through a niche in the world market economy and at the expense of the Ottoman authorities, who saw only a meager share of the profits, and the country's fellahin. The question here probably should not have been "who will guard the guardians" as much as "who will keep an eye on the a'yan"? Social control had indeed been wrested from the clutch of the shaykhs, but the land tenure policies and the new production for export had done little to give social control to the central authorities.

In Iraq, a profound change in rural relations occurred too, although again it was not at all what the Ottomans expected. Note Batatu's description:

> The decline of the political and military power of the shaikhs, aghas, and begs was unmistakable. The military confederations and principalities were destroyed. . . . On the other hand, the groundwork was laid for the economic growth of the shaikhs and aghas by the granting or leasing to them or the registering in their name, through fraud or bribery, of vast estates supporting many tribes or whole villages, tribal and nontribal, in utter disregard of the prescriptive right of rank and file tribesmen or nontribal cultivators.[12]

New land tenure laws brought changes for Mexican *campesinos* similar to those for fellahin in Palestine and Iraq—only much more extreme. The 1856 *Ley de desamortización* states that all landed property held by civil or religious corporations would be divided in ownership among those who actually worked the plots. A clause exempted land,

[11] The situation in nearby Lebanon differed from that in Palestine and other countries of the Fertile Crescent. Already in the eighteenth century, Lebanon was divided into twenty-four districts, each having a ruling family with extensive taxing, judicial, land, and other rights. Although formally many peasants owned their land, the social control of these families was very high. During the latter third of the nineteenth century this situation reversed and a more equitable distribution of land rights ensued especially following the bloody clashes and revolt ending in 1861. See Gabriel Baer, *Introduction to the History of Agrarian Relations in the Middle East 1800–1970* (Israel: Hakibutz Hameuchad, 1971) (text in Hebrew; title translated), ch. 4.

[12] Hanna Batatu, *The Old Social Classes and the Revolutionary Movements of Iraq* (Princeton, N.J.: Princeton University Press, 1978), pp. 77–78.

such as the *ejidos*, held in common for the use of the people actually working it. If anything, the edict seemed to secure a stronger foothold for the precariously perched campesinos, while attacking church holdings and community corporations.

The results, however, were anything but encouraging for poor farmers. The new constitution of 1857 dropped the exemption for ejidos. The Indians now became individual proprietors of the plots they had farmed and of the former common land in their villages and towns; but these gains were illusory. The new legislation did not achieve the aims of state leaders, particularly President Benito Pablo Juarez, of ensuring the existence of a landed peasantry with firm title to individual holdings. Instead the law had catastrophic consequences for the campesinos.[13] Speculators, corrupt officials, *hacendados*, and others exploited the new right of the campesinos to dispose of their land freely by freely disposing them of their land.

In a country already characterized by the big hacienda, the result was a rapid consolidation of former communal lands into super-haciendas and other big farms and ranches. As in Palestine and Iraq, the primary effects of the legislation came in the last quarter of the nineteenth century. Additional legislation reinvigorated the process alienating campesinos from their land during this period. The Act of 1876 and then the so-called Law of Colonization in 1894 followed several presidential decrees. All these made it easier to seize properties that lacked properly registered titles. They reiterated the need to parcel out any remaining communal land and grant individual title through the *Gran Registro de la Propriedad*. Hacendados, in particular, took advantage of the provision of the law allowing them to denounce imperfect titles—through neglect, fear, or ignorance many Indian titles were imperfect—and acquire the plots attached to such titles.[14] Haciendas now absorbed the former members of inward-oriented, corporate villages as peons, or else such people lived precariously as landless laborers. The life of two centuries crumbled, leaving campesinos in a world almost beyond recognition. Old strategies of survival were nearly useless in the transformed landscape of the late nineteenth century.

Laws or decrees, such as the *Ley de desamortización*, produced a new social topography. They helped induce very different rural relations from what the peasants had known—relations more suited for export-

[13] See George McCutchen McBride, *The Land Systems of Mexico* (1923; reprint New York: Octagon Books, 1971), pp. 133, 69–70; and Diego G. López Rosada, *Agricultura y ganaderia. La propriedad de la tierra*, vol. 1 of *Historia y pensamiento económico de México* (Mexico City: Universidad Nacional Autónoma de México, 1968), pp. 191–93.

[14] McBride, *Land Systems of Mexico*, pp. 74–81.

oriented production.[15] As in Palestine during the last quarter of the century, production of Mexican campesinos on their own plots did not change immediately and totally from its subsistence orientation, but the proportion of campesinos able to maintain their own holdings was low indeed (estimates range from 80 to 95 percent landless).[16]

The law resulted, as in Palestine and Iraq, in a land-grab of stupendous proportions. The figures are truly dramatic. At the start of the Revolution in 1910, 300 haciendas contained at least 25,000 acres each, and 11 haciendas had more than 250,000 acres apiece. Estate owners had acquired more than 2.25 million acres of communal property. "By 1910," wrote Robert A. White, "less than 1 per cent of the families of Mexico controlled 85 per cent of the land, and 90 per cent of the villages and towns on the central plateau had almost no communal land."[17] Although Palestine is a much smaller country, the land law there produced comparable results. By the beginning of the twentieth century in Palestine, about 140 wealthy families owned large estates averaging 5,500 acres in size. In Iraq, two major families controlled more than 250,000 acres apiece, while more than forty others each owned 25,000 acres or more.

Where communal land was not an immediate barrier to land consolidation in the second half of the nineteenth century, no single law had as overwhelming an effect as in the Ottoman Empire or Mexico. In countries such as Egypt (only nominally in the Ottoman domain) and India, authorities paved the road for rapid land consolidation much earlier than the mid-nineteenth century. Both Egypt and India had enacted a series of acts, laws, and proclamations that allowed for the same market-oriented production and growing peasant landlessness as elsewhere. In Egypt, Muhammad Ali as early as 1812–1815 had achieved a state monopoly over landownership, and a number of other land tenure changes had followed until mid-century. Said's

[15] Daniel Cosío Villegas, *Vida Económica*, vol. 7 of *Historia moderna de México* (Mexico City: Editorial Hermes, 1965), p. 2, states, "*La obra de la Reforma desata un cambio extenso y profundo en el régimen de la propiedad de la tierra al favorecer la propiedad privada y crear un verdadero proletariado agrícola.*"

[16] See *Indigenous Peoples*, p. 298; Manning Nash, "The Impact of Mid-Nineteenth Century Economic Change Upon the Indians of Middle America," in Magnus Morner, ed., *Race and Class in Latin America* (New York: Columbia University Press, 1970), p. 174; López Rosado, *Historia y pensamiento económico de México*, p. 103; and McBride, *Land Systems of Mexico*, ch. 3.

[17] Robert A. White., S.J., "Mexico: The Zapata Movement and the Revolution," in Henry A. Landsberger, ed., *Latin American Peasant Movements* (Ithaca: Cornell University Press, 1969), p. 115. Another estimate is that 1 percent of the population owned 70 percent of the land. *Indigenous Peoples*, p. 298.

Land Law of 1858, intending to increase market-oriented production, served to strengthen large private holdings by facilitating land transfers.[18] By that time, obstacles to alienating the peasants from the limited land rights they had retained were much less formidable than in Mexico or the Ottoman Empire.

Abrogation of peasant land rights had already occurred prior to the mid-nineteenth century in parts of India as well. British land policies in India had affected different parts of the country at various times. By the mid-nineteenth century a map of Indian land rights would have looked like a patchwork quilt. The most notable change in land tenure, the Permanent Settlement of Bengal in 1793, had established *zamindars*, mostly Calcutta businessmen, as the proprietors of land—a sharp departure from previous Indian history. The results of that and ensuing land changes were far-reaching. Holt MacKenzie, the secretary of the Supreme Government in the Territorial Department, reported as early as 1819 that there had occurred "in the landed property of the country a very extensive and melancholy revolution." The result was "to disjoint the whole frame of the village societies, to deprive multitudes of property which their families had held for ages; and to reduce a high-spirited class of men from the pride of independence to the situation of labourers on their paternal fields."[19]

[18] See Gabriel Baer, *A History of Landownership in Modern Egypt 1800–1950* (London: Oxford University Press, 1960); and Baer, *Introduction to the History of Agrarian Relations.*

[19] Quoted in Eric Stokes, "Northern and Central India," in Dharma Kumar, ed., *c. 1757–c. 1970*, vol. 2 of *The Cambridge Economic History of India* (Cambridge: Cambridge University Press, 1983), p. 43. On land tenure changes and their results see the articles by Stokes and B. Chaudhuri in the Cambridge volume. Also see B. M. Bhatia, "Agriculture and Co-operation," in V. B. Singh, ed., *Economic History of India 1858–1956* (Bombay: Allied, 1965); George Campbell, "The Tenure of Land in India," in J. W. Probyn, ed., *Systems of Land Tenure* (1881; reprint London: Cassell, Petter, Galpin, n.d.); Dvijadas Datta, *Landlordism in India* (Bombay: D. B. Taraporevala Sons, 1931); and Peshotan Nasserwanji Driver, *Problems of Zamindari and Land Tenure Reconstruction in India* (Bombay: New Book Company, 1949). In addition to the *Zamindari* system, the British adopted another type of land tenure, the *Ryotwari* system. This latter system was geared to create small landholders but largely failed, as we shall see momentarily, because of other aspects of the penetration of capitalism. It should be noted that the fantastic heterogeneity of India and the waves of changing land tenure resulted in diverse patterns from area to area. Different authors have come up with radically divergent characterizations based on their samples. Stokes, for example, basically accepted the characterization of a "melancholy revolution." In the same volume, H. Fukazawa wrote, "To conclude, there is little support for the view that from the middle of the nineteenth century there was a marked transfer of land to moneylenders or a sustained proletarianization of rural labour. The pace of change was much slower, and much more mixed than these overdramatic pictures suggest" (p. 206). In South India, Kumar reports in the same volume, events varied

In many parts of India, the consolidation of land progressively squeezed out the middle-sized owners, leaving the large owner, the cultivating owner or tenant, and increasing numbers of landless laborers, many of whom did retain microplots of their own. In 1858, the British reconfirmed this method of land consolidation for a part of India by issuing a proclamation that enabled the *taluqdars* of Oudh to gain large tracts of land following the outbreak of a peasant revolt there.[20] By the late nineteenth century, loss of land and indebtedness by rural cultivators were becoming worrisome problems, even to the British rulers. Policy changed in the course of time from ones disregarding small cultivators, especially tenants, to ones offering legal protection to them.[21] By the time such policies took hold, however, tremendous changes had occurred in rural landholding patterns and social organization.

Even in cases, such as those of Egypt and India, where authorities enacted a series of land tenure changes over a number of decades rather than in a single major law, some of the most decisive effects of these changes came in the few decades following mid-century. The land tenure policies transformed social structure. Social control changed irrevocably as big landowners consolidated holdings and integrated themselves (and, along with them, their workers and tenants) much more fully into the world market economy. Landowners in region after region increased the resources at their disposal, which could be used to build new strategies of survival through their direct ties to the world market. Additionally, these ties often made them somewhat impervious to any attempts by ambitious political authorities to bring them under control. The stage was set for the recreation of weblike societies that would characterize so much of the Third World in the late twentieth century.

Meanwhile, the rural poor throughout Asia, North Africa, and Latin America found that the land tenure changes, whether effected starting in the mid-nineteenth century or in an even earlier series of decrees, prevented them from producing as they had in the past. The new conditions, which pressed inexorably upon them, tied the tenants, laborers, and small landholders to the tastes, needs, and demands of people in far-flung places on the globe. Their old strategies of survival

so from area to area that sometimes Stokes's description is apt and at other times Fukazawa's description seems to fit.

[20] Jagdish Raj, *The Mutiny and British Land Policy in North India 1856–1868* (Bombay: Asia Publishing House, 1965).

[21] Dietmar Rothermund, *Government, Landlord, and Peasant in India: Agrarian Relations under British Rule 1865–1935* (Wiesbaden: Franz Steiner Verlag, 1978), ch. 6.

were in disarray, and their old safeguards against demonic outside forces proved useless. Changes in land tenure placed those who seemed the most remote from the cyclone of world capitalism into a path that swirled inextricably toward its vortex.

TAXES

Land tenure laws prepared the way for the rapid growth in scope of the nineteenth-century world economy. The spate of land grabs, the mushrooming of export-oriented plantations, and the vast increases in numbers of tenants and landless laborers meant new rural relations and whole new sets of needs for the producers—the peasants and workers. Rather suddenly and almost universally, the new land policies rocked existing forms of social control to the foundation. Two additional factors reinforced the world trend toward land consolidation; both involved what peasants already took to be the bane of their existence, taxes. First, ruling states increased revenues collected from the peasants and others, and second, the states switched from taxes collected in kind to those collected in cash. These two factors also had a major impact, even when land consolidation was not achieved, on those fortunate enough to hold onto a cherished plot of land.

Increases in Revenues

High taxes were certainly not new experiences for many peasants. Even prior to the nineteenth century, Indian, Egyptian, Palestinian, and other cultivators went so far as to abandon their land in certain periods on account of high exactions by officials and tax-farmers. But the increases in taxes during the late nineteenth century differed from those of the past. Now the state, rather than local tax-farmers or other intermediaries, relentlessly administered the new revenue policies down to the level of the individual. Like Cain after the slaying of Abel, cultivators found it impossible to flee or hide, particularly in the face of new administrative revenue-collection techniques copied or imported from Europe. Not only did states raise rates and collect taxes more efficiently, but they also often fixed the tax rates instead of varying them according to the peasants' ability to pay in a given year. "Nothing about the colonial order," James C. Scott concluded about Southeast Asia, "seemed to infuriate the peasantry more than its taxes."[22] The heavy increases in tax burdens often worked together

[22] James C. Scott, *The Moral Economy of the Peasant* (New Haven: Yale University Press, 1976), p. 91.

with land tenure laws like a vise, putting tremendous pressure on existing rural relations and patterns of social control.

The effects of tax increases in Egypt during the late nineteenth century, for example, differed from the pattern of land abandonment characteristic of Egypt in many previous instances of higher exactions from fellahin. Now the state oversaw the tax increases directly. State leaders packaged them with important changes in land tenure laws and applied the new taxes only to certain classes of land. Said, in the 1850s, increased the tax for *kharajiya*, those lands inhabited mostly by poor peasants with something less than full ownership rights to the land; but his regime did not raise tax rates for *ushuriya*, those lands usually held by large owners with full ownership rights.[23] Said's land tenure changes during this period both strengthened full ownership rights on land and opened the way for foreign ownership of Egyptian land. Later, in 1876, the state established Mixed Courts to handle problems arising from transactions with foreigners.

The upshot of all these changes was that peasants experienced severe problems of indebtedness by the 1860s due to the higher taxes on kharajiya. Peasants, consequently, abandoned plots, but now new land tenure policies allowed numerous sequestrations of either the abandoned land or the land with unpaid taxes, a practice previously unknown in Egypt and now promoted through the new Mixed Courts. In addition, the representative of the state in each village, the *umda*, now not only assessed many of the taxes, but he also received part of the profit on the sale of sequestered land. There was a pot of gold at the end of his rainbow: he had only to assess high taxes and step in at the moment of default.

As a result of the inability to keep up with the new rates, fellahin found their kharajiya, increasingly falling into the hands of officials and other wealthy people, transformed into ushuriya. The state's need for increased revenues to undertake major public works, especially building the Suez Canal, put new burdens onto the shoulders of the peasantry. Peasants, of course, benefited little from the canal or many other public works of the time. With Egypt's deteriorating balance of payments, the state sought greater exactions from the fellahin and a change to estates that could produce foreign capital through production of export crops.

Higher taxes and the resulting rural indebtedness had a similarly

[23] "In 1877 total tax receipts from *kharājīya* amounted to £E3,143,000, or 9.4 times the £E333,000 from *ushūrīya*, although the area of the former was only 2.6 times larger." Baer, *A History of Landownership in Modern Egypt*, p. 31.

devastating impact on small landholders in India. Here, too, peasants paid for the grand technological schemes of Europe. Even though British capital primarily, as we shall see momentarily, financed the Indian railroads, the British raj could provide a quick return on investments to the numerous British investors by increasing taxes on the Indian peasant. The swelling peasant indebtedness that resulted in India from the new taxes had an unprecedented effect, for the new British codes transformed land into a commodity able to be held as security against loans by the moneylender. "Once an agriculturist fell into his clutches," wrote Bhatia, "he (the agriculturist) rarely got out before his land was sold in satisfaction of his creditor's debt."[24] Even where the British did not institute the *zamindari* system of large owners and opted instead for the *ryotwari* system of smaller holders, the new rigidity of land revenue collection still led to many peasants' losing their land through debt collection. Also, the new civil courts introduced by the colonialists made it much more likely that creditors could actually expropriate the land from the cultivator.

British perplexity about the causes of the new severe rural debt in India, as evidenced by their numerous inquiries into the subject, came as their collected land revenue grew by 50 percent and their gross revenues by 200 percent in the second half of the nineteenth century. Blame was more apt to be placed on the poor peasant than on the pressures generated by high taxes, as seen in the following statement by P. J. Thomas: "If the ignorant pariah does not mind selling his labour for life for having the pleasure of seeing his kith and kin get drunk on his wedding eve—a common occurrence among the labourers in several parts—many a brahmin will encumber his whole property and exhaust even his personal credit for celebrating marriages and paying dowries."[25]

Land revenue per acre in relation to the value of net output remained high in India into the twentieth century. Even wealthier peasants complained that the high taxes made it impossible to fund the traditional village ceremonies. These festive ceremonies were part of local strategies of survival, giving strongmen the opportunity to reward poorer village members in order to shore up their social control. Although the new high taxes did not generally lead to the creation of large surplus-producing estates or plantations in India, they did have reverberating effects nonetheless. They displaced the peasantry as landowners

[24] Bhatia, "Agriculture and Co-operation," p. 147.

[25] P. J. Thomas, *The Problem of Rural Indebtedness* (Madras: Diocesan Press, 1934), p. 2.

and led to a deteriorating or stagnating standard of living for the majority of India's population through the end of the nineteenth century and into the twentieth.[26]

The Ottoman Empire also did not succeed in creating estates with much greater economies of scale. Likewise, it coupled the pressures generated by new land tenure arrangements with increased taxes. The Sublime Porte raised the tithe in Palestine from the customary 10 percent of yield to 11.5 percent in 1886 and then to 12.5 percent in 1897.[27]

Although large parts of sub-Saharan Africa escaped the "liberal" land tenure laws of the 1850s through 1880s, colonial states there, too, subjected the population to the ravages of increased revenue collection. Involvement with the European economy dated to the fifteenth century for parts of Africa, and the New World slave trade that developed in the next century testified to the momentous impact of the European market. Swift and universal penetration of the world market to the level of practically all individuals' daily lives, however, came somewhat later than for other parts of the world. In fact, not until the eve of the twentieth century for most areas of sub-Saharan Africa did new policies, such as major changes in revenue collection, upset old social arrangements.[28] The colonialists harbored complex motivations at this moment in Africa, including heightened European demand for raw materials, growth of exportable capital in Europe, imperial competition, and technological innovations allowing for easier and less

[26] There had been some controversy over whether there really was an absolute decline in the standard of living in the second half of the nineteenth century. For a summary of this debate, see Daniel Thomer, "Long-term Trends in Output in India," in Simon Kuznets, Wilbert E. Moore, and Joseph J. Spengler, eds., *Economic Growth* (Durham, N.C.: Duke University Press, 1955), pp. 103–19. It is especially unclear, given the falling value of the rupee and the lack of disaggregated statistics, exactly how much the standard of living varied for those directly or indirectly involved with farming through cultivation or services to cultivators. See M. Mukerje, "National Income," in Singh, ed., *Economic History of India*, esp. pp. 689–90. For the falling wages of industrial workers, see K. Mukerji, "Levels of Living of Industrial Workers," in Singh, ed., *Economic History of India*, pp. 656–60.

[27] Chaim Halperin, *The Agricultural Legislation in Palestine* (Tel-Aviv: Sifriat HaSadeh, 1944), p. 119 (text in Hebrew; title translated).

[28] It may be argued that by the end of the nineteenth century, the great attractiveness of land tenure laws in order to promote new forms of production and to generate higher state revenues had disappeared for state officials. The side effects of such laws, particularly the promotion of a difficult to control, wealthy landowning class, may have directly led to the search for a new panacea, new types of taxation, to benefit in the world market economy and generate new state revenues.

costly physical penetration of the interior. Michael Crowder, writing on West Africa, summarized the essence of the changes in production:

> Before the establishment of colonial rule, European firms were for the most part content to trade on the coast and rely on African middlemen for the penetration of the interior. . . . Whereas before colonial occupation groundnuts and palm-oil had been produced by the African in a situation where he could balance the comparative advantage of concentration on subsistence crops against growing export crops to exchange for imported goods, the colonial system, primarily through taxation, forced him to concentrate on export crops to the detriment of his subsistence crops.[29]

Through the new taxes they imposed in the late nineteenth and early twentieth centuries, the colonial powers specifically intended to change the nature of production down to the lowest level. Sir Frederick Lugard, the renowned British governor general of Nigeria, wrote mellifluously in 1906, for example, that "direct taxation is a moral benefit to the people by stimulating industry and production."[30] Similarly, Gabriel Angoulvant, who became French governor of the Ivory Coast in 1908, believed that the potential wealth of the country could be achieved only by proper French policy toward the inhabitants: "that being the payment of taxation which would stimulate them to produce for export."[31]

The British and French, particularly the latter, used forced labor (*corvée*) in Africa both as a direct form of taxation and as an outgrowth of other types of taxation. One French report to the International Colonial Congress in 1900 stated, "The idea that seems the best for achieving the employment of native labour, would be to impose on the blacks relatively high taxes . . . and in default of payment they would incur a sentence of forced labour."[32] The French went so far as to demand compulsory planting of certain crops and to recruit labor for commercial enterprises. Through the various forms of taxation, Europeans mobilized Africans for building railways and other public works, as well as for seasonal migrations to commercial plantations.

The migration, forced labor, and production for export that resulted from the new tax policies took a high toll on existing social organizations and the social control they had exercised. Felix Chau-

[29] Michael Crowder, *West Africa under Colonial Rule* (Evanston, Ill.: Northwestern University Press, 1968), pp. 286, 274.

[30] Quoted in ibid., p. 206.

[31] Ibid., p. 110.

[32] Quoted in ibid., p. 186.

temps, former minister of colonies in France, recognized in 1913 this dislocation and the native's loathing of the colonial rulers that accompanied it: "We came, officials and traders alike, to live at his expense; we levy a tithe on his goods under the pretext of humanity. We upset his institutions and in the guise of justice we contravene his customs—the native does not like us; he is afraid of us."[33]

Some of Britain's most difficult moments in imposing its new state revenue plans in Africa came immediately after it proclaimed a British protectorate over Sierra Leone in 1896; this was in addition to its already existing Colony of Sierra Leone in the small coastal peninsula of Freetown. The hut (or house) taxes imposed in 1898, principally to finance the adminsitration of the protectorate, resulted in the Hut Tax War, a widespread rebellion directed against British rule. Although the period of violence lasted nearly a year in some areas, the British maintained the tax. The colonial governors' main adaptation seems to have been the change to an administration of tax through the local chiefs (see Chapter 3).

From Kind to Cash

Indebtedness for cultivators was further assured, in many countries, through laws and administrative decrees demanding that taxes be paid in cash rather than simply as a percentage of one's yield. The British considered one of their main achievements in India to have been "the systematic commutation of the share of produce into a money tax."[34] In Lebanon and Palestine, Ottoman increases in the rate of the tithe during the last quarter of the nineteenth century accompanied sputtering attempts to change payment to cash. The shift put severe pressure on farmers. Previously, imperial officials set tax rates on the basis of the average yield for the five preceding years, but the faltering attempts to collect cash meant that yearly fluctuations in crop prices could have disastrous effects.[35] Egyptian officials made more headway, as usual, in changing to money taxes; a decree in 1880 recognizing only cash payments capped a series of administrative changes under Said and his predecessor Abbas I.

The change to cash taxes during the late nineteenth century forced farmers more and more into market relations and stimulated them toward production for export: peasants, it was assumed, would produce the higher paying export crops in order to gain sorely needed

[33] Quoted in ibid., p. 187.

[34] C. K. Meek, *Land Law and Custom in the Colonies*, 2d ed. (London: Oxford University Press, 1949), p. xvii.

[35] Granott, *The Land System in Palestine*, p. 60.

cash for tax payment. Almost universally, however, the new rigid tax systems and the vagaries of production and of the money economy simply overwhelmed small peasants living on the margin of survival. Money-lending elements, who frequently used the change to money taxes as yet another basis for land consolidation, grew in size and power. In India, Egypt, Palestine, Sierra Leone, and elsewhere, the land itself became the security upon which lenders advanced their credit. Baer described the Egyptian fellahin's plight that followed from the shift to cash crops, particularly cotton for British manufacturers, to satisfy the tax collector:

> Many of the fellahs now needed to buy the foodstuffs they had replaced by cash crops. Whereas they would formerly have had to abandon their plots or starve, in the event of drought or some other calamity, they could now borrow from a money-lender. Often, however, they were unable to redeem these debts. . . . Now that the fellahs owned their land, they could be granted credit on its security, with the result that, after an enormous growth in money-lenders' credit, much fellah land was foreclosed, some of it remaining with the money-lenders.[36]

Lenders came from different elements of the population in various countries. At times they were people of the village, usually either shopkeepers or larger landowners; in other instances, urban entrepreneurs or big landowners from outside the village added moneylending to their repertoire. Also, in numerous countries, members of ethnic or religious minorities assumed the moneylending role. Frequently, where cash was still scarce but evermore essential, colonial rulers influenced who would and could be in a position to lend money.

The broad and deep penetration of the world economy came on the coattails of the change to cash taxes. Cash allowed for a much freer exchange and movement of goods. Almost all cultivators—some quicker, some slower—came to gear larger shares of their production according to market dictates. Just as important, the change promoted the mobility of labor critical to the operation of a capitalist market economy. With the galloping increases in rural debt and subsequent sequestration of peasant lands, peasants first sold their land, then their labor. Landlessness "freed" former small landowners and those who retained only microplots to fill the ranks of the new urban and rural workforce. Alienation from the land further aided the establishment of the world market in many areas by precipitating land consolidation

---

[36] Baer, *A History of Landownership in Modern Egypt*, p. 34.

where conditions were suitable for the highly demanded crops amenable to new technologies and greater economies of scale.

Tax policies and land tenure laws constituted a double-barrel shot that blasted rural life from its moorings. The timing of the deep penetration of the world market in each case, however, depended on one final factor that guaranteed the freer exchange of peoples and especially goods. That factor, the symbol of the new technological age—the railroad—allowed the world economy to permeate non-Western parts of the globe.

New Modes of Transportation ✗

Western societies drew closer to societies in Asia, Africa, and Latin America as the nineteenth century progressed. Steamships, for example, displaced sailing vessels for standard cargo runs on the high seas between the 1870s and 1890s. In addition, large increases in investments abroad by Western private entrepreneurs and states transformed the relationship between the imperial powers, particularly Great Britain, and others. At the same time that British total domestic investment increased only 13 percent (from 1841–1850 to 1851–1860), net investment abroad grew by more than 200 percent.[37] Besides the mushrooming of exportable capital, increased European demand for raw materials, both crops and mineral resources, and technological changes associated with the grand development of railroads precipitated a revolution in transport in Asia, Africa, and Latin America.

The laying of railway track from the mid-nineteenth century on was the great trailblazer of the expanding world economy. One might even venture to say that railways became the locomotive of change.

[37] *Cambridge Economic History of Europe*, vol. 7, part 2, pp. 91, 69. E.A.J. Johnson, *An Economic History of Modern England* (New York: Thomas Nelson 1939), p. 111, wrote that British foreign investments "made possible not only the construction of railways but the digging of mines, the building of factories, the erection of public utilities, and the establishment of plantations." Also, see Matthew Simon, "The Pattern of New British Portfolio Foreign Investment, 1865–1914," in A. R. Hall, ed., *The Export of Capital from Britain 1870–1914* (London: Methuen, 1968). Large increases continued later. From 1874 until the outbreak of World War I, British gross foreign investments outstanding grew more than 300 percent; France's and Germany's increased even faster. See Simon Kuznets, *Modern Economic Growth* (New Haven: Yale University Press, 1966), p. 322; and A. K. Cairncross, *Home and Foreign Investment 1870–1913* (Cambridge: Cambridge University Press, 1953), p. 203. Feinstein's estimates show an increase of over 1500 percent in accumulated net investment abroad from 1845 to 1913. C. H. Feinstein, *National Income, Expenditure and Output of the United Kingdom 1855–1965* (Cambridge: Cambridge University Press, 1972), p. 205.

Trains broke down isolation and inaccessibility. The speed with which they could carry people and freight was itself dazzling, let alone the amount they could convey. The new market economy became an everyday reality as the giant freight cars forged through forests and over mountains and deserts to move manufactured goods, people, and perhaps most striking, the raw commodities produced outside Europe. Expansion of the railroads continued through the nineteenth century and into the twentieth century, but a tremendous surge of growth that opened up the most populated and rich areas came for many countries in a relatively short period. From 1850 to 1880, rail lines worldwide increased almost tenfold, and between 1880 and World War I another threefold. By the onset of the Great War, about two-thirds of a million miles of track were in use. Other qualitative and quantitative changes in conveyance teamed with rail growth, the grandest and most visible of all, to create a veritable revolution in transport. Road improvements began worldwide. And, with the addition of steamships to merchant marines, the tonnage of shipping rose from 280,000 gross tons in 1850 to over 37 million by World War I.

In India in 1853, Governor-General Lord Dalhousie expressed the frustration and motivation that were to cause the 1860s to begin explosive social and economic changes in India:

> Great tracts are teeming with produce they cannot dispose of; others are scantily bearing what they would carry in abundance if only it could be conveyed whither it is needed. England is calling aloud for the cotton which India does already produce in some degrees and would produce sufficient in quality and plentiful in quantity if only there were provided the fitting means of conveyance for it from distant places to the several ports adapted for its shipment. Ships from every part of the world crowd over ports in search of produce which we have, or could obtain in the interior, but which at present we cannot profitably fetch to them. . . . It needs but little reflection on such facts to lead us to the conclusion that the establishment of a system of railways in India judiciously selected and formed, would surely and rapidly give rise within this empire to the same encouragement of enterprise, the same multiplication of produce, the same discovery of latent resources, to the same increase of national wealth, and the same similar progress in social improvement, that have marked the introduction of improved and extended communication in various kingdoms of the Western world.[38]

[38] Quoted in Tarasankar Banerjee, *Internal Market of India (1834–1900)* (Calcutta: Academic, 1966), pp. 83–84.

Dalhousie's naive hope was the kind soon in short supply among the jaded colonialists of the late nineteenth and twentieth centuries.

With the new methods of machine textile production in Europe, the search for raw cotton grew tremendously. Along with the increased demand was the need to build means to transport that cotton. And build they did! Dalhousie's policies transformed transport in India from the enormously costly means of buffalo, camels, and pack bullocks to the faster, far less costly trains. After four days of transport, an oxen consumes more grain than it carries. Such impediments alone prevented deep penetration of international markets.[39] More than three-quarters of a century earlier, Adam Smith had made clear in *The Wealth of Nations* how the means of conveyance determine the practical reach of the market. In fact, since the patenting of the locomotive was still several years away when Smith published his book, he was much more sanguine about markets' linking world ports than their ability to encompass inland areas.[40]

Trains pried the inland areas open. In 1858, about 430 miles of track were open, only about 1 percent of India's eventual railway lines. The increases thereafter were phenomenal; five years later, the British already achieved a 400 percent increase with considerably more than 2,000 miles open for transport. Growth in cotton exports reflected the greatly expanded rail system. With the disruption caused by the American Civil War, Indian cotton exports rose more than 500 percent from 1859–1860 to 1864–1865. In the five years from 1863 to 1868, the British companies managed another approximately 100 percent growth in rail lines, and then about *another* 100 percent increase over the next fifteen years. By 1882, the trains transported about *five thousand times* more freight tonnage than they had in 1858, much of that the raw cotton so important to British manufacture.[41]

Although the railroads were the most striking part of the opening of village India to the full force of the European world economy, new roads also played an important role in procuring raw materials from peasants easily and at low costs. Before the Select Committee on In-

[39] Michelle Burge McAlpin, "Railroads, Prices, and Peasant Rationality: India 1860–1900," *The Journal of Economic History* 34 (September 1974): 682.

[40] Adam Smith, *The Wealth of Nations*, vol. 1 (New York: E. P. Dutton, 1957), book I, ch. 3.

[41] See Banerjee, *Internal Market of India*, pp. 334–35; Nolinaksha Sanyal, *Development of Indian Railways* (Calcutta: University of Calcutta, 1930), esp. diagram 1 and p. 35; Vinod Dubey, "Railways," in Singh, ed., *Economic History of India*, p. 336; and Romesh Dutt, *The Economic History of India in the Victorian Age*, vol. 2 (1904; reprint New York: Augustus M. Kelley, 1969), p. 548.

dian Territories, 1852–1853, A. S. Finlay stated "I consider that at present there are no roads in India suitable for commercial purposes of any extent."[42] Dalhousie remedied this situation, as well, by creating public works departments that vastly expanded the road network during and following the 1850s.

British capital and administrative skills played important roles in the rapid construction of India's railway system and road network. Before the completion of the conquest of India in 1857, there had been a net outflow of capital from India to Britain. After that, however, the situation reversed itself, and British export capital to India played a major role in several sectors of the economy.[43] Initially, a guaranteed 5 percent return attracted British capital to railroad enterprises. Many investors were middle class; by 1868, there were almost fifty thousand share and debenture holders. Eager to gain as much profit as possible, they pressured the British government to accelerate railway construction in India, forcing a parliamentary inquiry and a new regime in India "which promised to be more directly responsive to the wants and interests of the people of the British Isles."[44] Within a short period, however, state rather than private capital became most important. Until late 1891, for example, the British state accounted for almost 60 percent of all expenditures on railroads.[45] A quite visible hand directed the forward march of the world market economy.

Where states were less well endowed and less capable than India, railroad construction proceeded much less smoothly. For example, in Egypt Muhammad Ali had several railroad schemes founder in the 1830s and 1840s because he lacked Western support and was unable to proceed alone. Only during the reign of Said in the 1850s did railway transport get underway, and during the era of Ismail in the 1860s and 1870s it boomed. The Cairo-Alexandria line, opened in 1856, was

[42] Quoted in Banerjee, *Internal Market of India*, p. 63. According to Sanyal, *Development of Indian Railways*, p. 3, the beginning of road construction preceded that of railway construction by more than a decade, with 30,000 miles of road laid in the 1840s. It is doubtful, however, how many of these roads were useful for commercial purposes.

[43] Arun Bose, "Foreign Capital," in Singh, ed., *Economic History of India*. He writes, "It was not until after 1857, however, that we find British capital flowing into India to any appreciable extent. And when it did, non-railway investment clearly went chiefly into raw material production for export, tea plantations becoming the most important, and later jute manufactures" (p. 506). About £150 million in British capital were invested in India between 1854 and 1969 and approximately £5 million per year during the 1870s. Leland Hamilton Jenks, *The Migration of British Capital to 1875* (New York: Alfred A. Knopf, 1927), p. 225.

[44] Jenks, *The Migration of British Capital*, p. 215.

[45] Dutt, *The Economic History of India*, p. 549.

the first in either the Middle East or Africa. Of course, Egypt did not have the same problems of penetrating the hinterlands that many other countries did. The natural communications and transport medium of the Nile River solved that problem, and building the Suez Canal lessened the reliance on rail transport.

The rest of the Ottoman Empire was even slower in entering into the "age of the locomotive."

> But in the vast area east of the Canal, as far as the borders of India, the picture was very different. For centuries this had been the great "cross-roads" of the civilised world, where East met West and the great caravans from Cathay and Samarkand came down through Tehran to Baghdad, Damascus and the Mediterranean. So it comes as something of a shock to realise that even as late as 1886, by which time railways had penetrated to all sorts of strange and exotic parts of the world, there was not a single mile of railway track anywhere in this particular area. The countries now known as Israel, Jordan, Lebanon, Syria and Iraq were then part of the Ottoman Empire, and there was not even a carriage road in the region until 1863 when a French company completed one from Beirut to Damascus. Moreover in neighbouring Persia (now Iran) communications were scarcely any better.[46]

The absence of important raw materials in Palestine and Lebanon detracted from any sense of urgency about railway construction there. Only in the 1890s with competition between French influence in what was to become Lebanon and British influence in what was to become Palestine did the Western powers stimulate railway building.

As in Egypt, problems beset initial efforts in Mexico at constructing a railway system. The emergence of a reinvigorated Mexican state during the last quarter of the nineteenth century finally brought significant construction. During that period, the system expanded very rapidly, largely with the aid of adventurous foreign investors, spurred on by government subsidies. In 1876, the Mexicans had laid only about 640 kilometers of track, but by 1884 the line had increased 800 percent, in large part because of the construction of the Mexico City–Paso del Norte line to the border with the United States. Investors designed the Mexican railway to reach the most productive areas of the country, unlike some others in Latin America, which were used to

[46] Hugh Hughes, *Middle East Railways* (Middlesex, England: Continental Railway Circle, 1981), p. 7.

stimulate settlement.[47] (In still other parts of the world, military and security motives determined where new lines were built.) Railroad construction increased another 100 percent in Mexico by the end of the century, and, by the eve of the revolution in 1910, the complex railroad grid laced the entire country.

The railroad induced spectacular economic and social changes. Freight savings and indirect benefits, Coatsworth estimated, accounted for more than half the increase in the productivity of the Mexican economy prior to the revolution. Production of minerals and fibers for export rose dramatically, in great part due to the new railways. In other areas, too, the effects of railroads rippled through the society, abetting the trend toward land concentration and influencing any number of other areas.

In the mountainous plateaus of Indo-Latin America particularly, railroads radically altered supply and demand schedules for agricultural products. By reducing transport costs dramatically and by connecting distant (domestic and international) markets with previously isolated rural areas, railroads made landowning more profitable than ever before. . . . Transport innovation was the cause of important shifts in crop structure, estate management, labor arrangements, land tenure patterns and rural welfare. Rural populations shared few of the benefits of this modernization and frequently suffered as a result.[48]

Penetration to the interior of Sierra Leone, as for most of sub-Saharan Africa, came latest of all. Builders did not even begin the Sierra Leone railway until 1896.[49] Yet it and the road system that followed had an enormous impact. Crowder wrote,

If colonial powers can be said in any way to have brought about an economic revolution in West Africa, it was through the construction of railways. Built over uncharted country, through thick forest, over

---

[47] McBride, *The Land Systems of Mexico*; and Don M. Coerver, "The Perils of Progress: The Mexican Department of Fomento during the Boom Years 1880–1884," *Inter-American Economic Affairs* 31 (Autumn 1977): 41–62.

[48] John Coatsworth, "Railroads, Landholding, and Agrarian Protest in the Early *Porfiriato*," *Hispanic American Historical Review* 54 (February 1974): 48–49; also his article, "Indispensable Railroads in the Mexican Economy," *The Journal of Economic History* 39 (December 1979): 939–60; also, see Cosío Villegas, *Historia moderna de México*, vol. 7, part 4. In 1867, the date that C. E. Black marks as the beginning of Mexico's consolidating leadership, there were only 272.7 kilometers. See López Rosado, *Historia y pensamiento económico de México*, vol. 3, p. 54.

[49] Lionel Wiener, *Les chemins de fer coloniaux de l'Afrique* (Brussels: Goemaere, 1930), pp. 299–303.

massive hill ranges, and often marked by the gravestones of workers, they were an immense stimulus to the production of the cash crops which they were designed to evacuate.[50]

Although less than 500 miles total in length, Sierra Leone's rail system facilitated the world market's penetration to areas that had not yet been commercialized. The Liverpool and Manchester Chambers of Commerce pressured Britain's Colonial Office to build the Sierra Leone line. They sought to gain access to the areas rich in palm products, in high demand for use in glycerin and margarine.[51]

All through Asia, Africa, and Latin America, the new paths to the interior forged by the railroad, accelerated social change and weakened the old forms of social control. S. R. Sharma opened his article on cottage industries by calling India prior to the advent of the Europeans "the industrial workshop of the world."[52] He closed the same piece by writing, "The construction of railways helped the replacement of home-made by foreign goods and facilitated the export of raw material. The Indian handicrafts were doomed and the labour displaced from them served to increase the pressure upon agriculture."[53] And the railroad profoundly affected agriculture itself. The greater economies of scale associated with those crops that the railroads most commonly transported, such as sugar or cotton, made small peasants' production and the social institutions catering to that production noncompetitive and unsuitable. With the extension of rail lines in Mexico in the 1880s, for example, "planters began importing heavy machinery and setting up big sugar mills to supply the large new markets now opened."[54] For many small farmers, these innovations made life an evermore desperate struggle; their ability to hold onto small plots of land slipped all the more.

In many countries, the opening of the railways changed the nature of rural labor in another way too; it greatly expanded the mineral extraction industries. Indian coal production, for example, was negligible until the mid-nineteenth century. The expansion of the rail system "gave a fresh impetus to the industry . . . not only as a carrier but

[50] Crowder, *West Africa under Colonial Rule*, p. 276.

[51] Margarine had only been invented in 1869; this in part explains the growing European demand for palm kernels toward the end of the century.

[52] S. R. Sharma, "Cottage Industries: 1857–1947," in Singh, ed., *Economic History of India*, p. 281.

[53] Ibid., p. 296.

[54] John Womack, Jr., *Zapata and the Mexican Revolution* (New York: Alfred A. Knopf, 1969), p. 15.

as a large consumer of coal."[55] Even if roads and canals would have better served the penetration of the world market (as has been argued for India, for example), the railroads had an additional value—their symbolic power. The *Economist* in 1857 spoke of the "civilizing influence" of the railroad, promoting "principles of secular government which, without any touch of intentional proselytism, have struck so effectually at the rapidly decomposing structure of native superstition."[56]

SOCIAL CHANGE AND SOCIAL CONTROL

Effective social control depends first on regulation of resources and services. Beyond that it entails an effective use of symbols to give meaning to social relationships. The package of rewards, sanctions, and symbols offers people the components to construct strategies of survival relevant to their particular life situation—a way to meet their mundane needs as well as their material and spiritual aspirations. Changes in land tenure laws, tax procedures, and transportation laid the way for a fundamental, rapid, and nearly universal transformation in these life situations. The basic life conditions—their homes, their work, their agriculture—that had related to particular forms of social control were no longer. They disappeared in an eruptive change that deeply affected all parts of society in one way or another within the brief span of only a couple of decades (often in even less time).

The commercialization of everyday lives that accompanied the spread of the European-based economy hastened a vast process of what others have called proletarianization. In order to survive, peasants and workers now increasingly sold their labor power as a means to survive, whether in agricultural enterprises or in other, mostly new, service and manufacturing jobs. In Europe, Tilly noted, this process resulted from the substitution of wages for other forms of compensation and, even more important, the expropriation of the means of production from the producers themselves.[57] In Asia and Latin America, expropriation was also critical through the land tenure changes. In Africa, commercialization through tax changes and improved transportation led the way in creating proletarianization.

---

[55] Bishnupada Guha, "The Coal Mining Industry," in Singh, ed., *Economic History of India*, p. 310. For the relationship of railroads to the growth of mineral industries in sub-Saharan Africa, see Robert H. Bates, *Rural Responses to Industrialization* (New Haven: Yale University Press, 1976), pp. 18–19.

[56] Quoted in Jenks, *Migration of British Capital*, p. 216.

[57] Charles Tilly, *As Sociology Meets History* (New York: Academic Press, 1981), p. 195.

The nature and impact of change differed from place to place. Microregional disparities could be tremendous. Ecological variations, as Elizabeth Perry has demonstrated for North China, or previous agricultural organization for export, as discussed by Jeffrey Paige, could make huge differences as the world economy relentlessly pushed forward outside Europe.[58] These differences deserve much closer attention by scholars in the future, but here I want to note the larger contours of change and the more general impact of the new economy. In many parts of Asia, Africa, and Latin America, gaps in international stratification widened beyond all previous imagination and then froze in place. Before the Industrial Revolution, the gap between the poorest and richest societies, Bairoch reports, was in the range of only 1.0 to 1.5. In the mid-eighteenth century, Europe's standard of living was probably a bit below that of the rest of the world. However, after the Industrial Revolution, as Europe's standard rose dramatically and as other areas' standards of living fell, the gap widened to the range of 1.0 to 3.4 in 1913 and to 7.7 in 1977.[59] The West rose to the top and then seemed immovable.

The same widening of the stratification gap occurred within non-Western societies. Land tenure laws, new tax policies, and transportation initiatives reinforced each other's effects. Those with resources to take advantage of new economic opportunities, which the new state policies propitiated, leapfrogged ahead of all others in their wealth and control of productive factors in society. Change beyond the widening differences in income between the haves and have-nots reached the very foundations of social and political life—where people lived, the jobs in which they worked, the nature of agricultural organization. Relative changes in wealth proved only a small part of the story; the new conditions actually undermined people's strategies of survival.

Large numbers of people changed their place of residence. Mining towns often mushroomed almost overnight. Bustling cities grew out of sleepy villages and towns, beginning a process of urbanization in the Third World that has still not abated. Some city populations today are

[58] Elizabeth J. Perry, *Rebels and Revolutionaries in North China, 1845–1945* (Stanford, Calif.: Stanford University Press, 1980); and Jeffrey M. Paige, *Agrarian Revolution: Social Movements and Export Agriculture in the Underdeveloped World* (New York: Free Press, 1975).

[59] Paul Bairoch, "The Main Trends in National Economic Disparities since the Industrial Revolution," in Bairoch and Maurice Levy-Leboyer, eds., *Disparities in Economic Development since the Industrial Revolution* (New York: St. Martin's Press, 1981); and Paul Bairoch, "Historical Roots of Economic Underdevelopment: Myths and Realities," in Wolfgang J. Mommsen and Jürgen Osterhammel, eds., *Imperialism and After: Continuities and Discontinuities* (London: Allen and Unwin, 1986).

growing as much as 3 percent annually due to net migration alone and
another 3 percent due to natural increase. Rapid urbanization began
during those critical decades of the late nineteenth century (and early
twentieth century for most of Africa). Beirut, for example, was a quiet
port of 6,000 people toward the end of the eighteenth century; by
1885, it already had 100,000 inhabitants, and that growth even preceded its rebuilding as a modern port in 1890. The city then stood at
the mere beginning of an upward slope that would eventually show an
increase of another fifteenfold, ultimately incorporating more than
half of all Lebanon's inhabitants.

Cairo grew in size by about 50 percent from 1850 to 1880.[60] In Palestine, the whole center of gravity of the country's population began
to shift in the last quarter of the nineteenth century. Fellahin in the
rocky hills of the eastern portion of the country and even Arabs from
neighboring countries moved into the more commercialized central
plain and western coastal region, where Western activity and Zionist
settlement sparked new opportunities. In these regions, towns and cities far exceeded the country's general increase of population. In port
cities, such as Jaffa, the numbers grew 100 percent in a decade. Indian
cities and towns, too, grew rapidly, already increasing by about 1 percent a year in the 1880s.[61]

The new cities spawned whole new classes of jobs, especially in the
service sector. Even for those who did not shift their place of residence
permanently, however, many experienced important new changes in
life conditions. Coal mines, sugar mills, and any number of other types
of enterprises geared to provide goods for the world market transformed countless villagers into daily commuters or seasonal migrants.
And for every person landing a job in production, a number of others
worked in new service jobs in rural areas, too. Land consolidation and
new manufactured products made the old forms of survival through
subsistence agriculture and handicraft production untenable.

The lack of fit between the numbers displaced from old types of
employment and the available positions in new kinds of enterprise
often complicated the search for new means of survival. As Clark
Reynolds wrote of Mexico in the period immediately prior to the revolution of 1910, "The growth of machine manufacturing . . . tended
to displace artisans at a greater rate than workers were absorbed into

---

[60] Adna Ferrin Weber, *The Growth of Cities in the Nineteenth Century* (1899; reprint Ithaca:
Cornell University Press, 1963), p. 137; and Tertius Chandler and Gerald Fox, *3000 Years
of Urban Growth* (New York: Academic Press, 1974), pp. 196–97.

[61] Weber, *The Growth of Cities*, p. 126.

the new plants and mills."[62] In many countries of Asia and Africa, the momentous increase in the population growth rate that followed the colonial powers' pacification efforts and the introduction of the West's new public health measures also contributed to a worsening employment situation in many areas.

Even those fortunate enough to find jobs frequently faced severe economic crises. "Increased income associated with rapid growth of the economy, attributable particularly to extractive industries, cash crops, and manufacturing," wrote Reynolds on Mexico, "did not transmit itself to the labor force in terms of proportional increases in wages and salaries. Instead, income growth in the leading sectors was being captured by the owners of capital, land, and subsoil resources."[63] Many of these owners, as in Egypt and India, were foreigners; many were the same people who profited so handsomely from landgrabs in the countryside.

Life situations and the types of social control relevant to them changed rapidly and irreparably during those critical decades even for those, the clear majority, who altered neither their place of residence nor their occupation. The social changes associated with the spread of the world economy were largely rural, not terribly different from those in the initial phases of European social transformation before 1800. Agriculture remained the way most people made a living. Even after Mexico's two-decade spurt of social and economic changes beginning about 1870, for example, agriculture still supported more than 80 percent of the population. The proportion remained similarly overwhelming in Egypt, Sierra Leone, India, and Palestine.

What changed during those years, as we have seen, was people's agricultural production, their relationship to the land, and their position with respect to those in other social classes. Production shifted clearly toward cash crops and especially those in high demand for export. Although growing for export was most pronounced on estates and plantations, small landowners and peasants, even in the most noncommercialized parts of Mexico or Palestine, moved away from farming exclusively for subsistence needs. Peasants often tried to continue as much subsistence growing as possible while simultaneously expanding, to the degree they could, into commercial agriculture. Only the fortunate few, however, retained title to their land. Life situations changed most drastically as strongmen consolidated land into hacien-

[62] Clark W. Reynolds, *The Mexican Economy* (New Haven: Yale University Press, 1970), p. 25.
[63] Ibid., p. 24.

das, *fazendas*, estates, and the like. In areas where new economies of scale entered agricultural production, peasants often became day laborers in large commercial enterprises, while in other areas they became tenants or joined the growing world ranks of wandering landless laborers.

The position of peasants compared to those in other social classes changed in varying ways. In Egypt, for example, the landowning class became overwhelmingly absentee landlords with a high percentage of foreign owners; Palestine's Arab landowners were also absentee but less likely to be foreign, and, by the turn of the century, Jews began to enter the land market.

At times the landlord and moneylender were one and the same, but in other instances moneylenders made up a distinct, often an ethnically distinct, group. Almost everywhere, however, peasants found growing social gaps between them and those who controlled resources crucial for their survival. Peasants' relationships to landowners did vary from place to place, of course, especially according to the degree an area became commercialized and the type of commercialization that occurred.[64] In general, however, widening income gaps, different places of residence, varying styles of dress and speech, all increasingly separated peasants from those in the classes above them. Many found supervisors and overseers now mediating between them and their landlords or creditors. The personal relationships peasants had maintained with culturally similar large landowners had protected them, in some measure, from capriciousness. These now gave way to more business-like ties.

With all these changes in life situations—in occupation, place of residence, production, relationship to the land, and ties to other classes—people's needs changed drastically, too. The overall weakening of societies resulted as old means of social control throughout the society crumbled simultaneously. Old sanctions, such as community ostracism or gossip, became less powerful as many commuted from the village, finding new reference groups, or moved from the village altogether. Old rewards, such as the benefits of mutual work teams to harvest specific crops, became meaningless in environments where many became landless or production shifted to new cash crops. Old means, such as settling disputes through the mediation of the village headman, be-

---

[64] For an excellent contrast of peasants in Egypt, where commercialization occurred simultaneously in nearly all parts of the country, and in Turkey, where commercialization was much less homogeneous, see Dani Rodrik, "Rural Transformation and Peasant Political Orientations in Egypt and Turkey," *Comparative Politics* 14 (1982): 417–42. Also, see Paige, *Agrarian Revolution*.

came more and more irrelevant as interactions grew with those who neither knew nor respected the headman.

In all the countries I have studied, the environment of the peasant or laborer changed drastically in only a short period beginning sometime in the latter nineteenth century. Land tenure changes, higher taxes, demands for taxes in cash, and railroad construction paved the way for changes in the environment that made old strategies and solutions irrelevant to the new problems. True, important variations existed in the rate of change and the degree to which changes debilitated old forms of social control. Such differences from community to community were especially evident in countries with varying topographical and climatic regions. Areas differed significantly in the degree to which world market forces found them both readily accessible and attractive to penetration.

In Mexico for example, those Indians on the coast experienced the most severe change as social control by local community organizations disintegrated rapidly in the face of expanding plantations and estates, but those Indians in the more remote highlands at times maintained some semblance of what Nash called "defensive corporate communities."[65] In the poor and isolated state of Oaxaca, the market system stretching from Mexico City and beyond did not overwhelm the limited peasant markets altogether until well into the twentieth century. Large concentrations of land did not appear there as in districts to the north.[66]

A similar pattern of internal variation occurred in Palestine. By the turn of the century, up to 80 percent of the peasants in the more accessible and fertile Galilee and central plains had no land, compared to 50 percent in the rocky, remote hills in the eastern regions (what

[65] Nash, "The Impact of Mid-Nineteenth Century Economic Change," p. 183.

[66] Ralph L. Beals, *The Peasant Marketing System of Oaxaca, Mexico* (Berkeley: University of California Press, 1975), pp. 11–12. Also, see Ronald Waterbury, "Non-revolutionary Peasants: Oaxaca Compared to Morelos in the Mexican Revolution," *Comparative Studies in Society and History* 17 (October 1975); and Charles R. Berry, "The Fiction and Fact of the Reform: The Case of the Central District of Oaxaca, 1856–1867," *Americas* 26 (January 1970): 286. Katz gives a vivid picture of the variations from region to region in Mexico. He notes that differences were great even within haciendas. In southern Mexico, for example, "laborers on haciendas clearly did not constitute a mass of peons living under identical conditions but a very complex hierarchy of social groups. There were differences in access to land, differences in access to resources, differences in access to the hacienda's paternalism, and differences in ethnic and social origin." Friedrich Katz, "Labor Conditions on Haciendas in Porfirian Mexico: Some Trends and Tendencies," *The Hispanic American Historical Review* 54 (February 1974): 21.

today is called the West Bank).[67] Only in a country such as Egypt with
its single link, the Nile, for the great majority of villages and with similar topography and climate, did internal variations have much less
importance.

It must be stressed, nevertheless, that in all but the most remote
areas of Asia, Africa, and Latin America, the steady onslaught of the
world market weakened old forms of social organization and social
control substantially. The new land laws, tax procedures, and railway
construction made existing strategies of survival anachronistic. In
some cases, the old forms of social organization and control had survived for centuries, and in others they had been the products of other
recent changes, such as peasants' settling on frontier land or earlier
impacts of Western economic activity. Whatever the case, the expansion of the world economy had a sudden and momentous effect on
people's social relations. Whether thrust into a growing urban prole-
tariat or able to maintain a foothold in a still viable village community,
people universally found themselves parts of enterprises linked directly or indirectly to the expanding market economy. In each country, the environment changed drastically for individuals as the society
as a whole transformed its place and role in that world economy. Although a revisionist school has attempted to argue, especially in the
case of India, that market forces caused much less disruption than I
(and others) have inferred from accounts of that period, even its authors' own evidence intimates that market forces must have battered
old strategies considerably (see Appendix B). These forces pushed
Humpty Dumpty off his wall.

The shockwaves of a rapidly changing environment stemming from
the society's new role in the world market first affected India and
Egypt, among the cases to which I have made reference. Their social
and economic transformations accelerated rapidly starting in the early
1860s. Due to the disruptions in Atlantic trade resulting from the U.S.
Civil War, the demand for cotton elsewhere rose rapidly, spurring tremendous new production. The total value of exports from India grew
a whopping 140 percent in the twenty-year period after 1860 and another 140 percent in the next twenty-seven years.[68] In fact, India's absolute growth in trade trailed only that of the United States in the last

[67] Abromovitz and Gelfat, *The Arab Holding*, p. 154.

[68] Figures adapted from Bhatia, "Agriculture and Co-operation," p. 124. Exports had
begun to grow even prior to 1857, but the total value exported in 1857 amounted only
to £27 million. More important exports went from "drugs, dyes, and luxuries" to foodgrains and other raw materials. See R. L. Varshney, "Foreign Trade," in Singh, ed., *Economic History of India*, p. 445.

quarter of the nineteenth century. Furthermore, the opening of the Suez Canal in 1869, reducing the sea voyage from Europe to India by thousands of miles, impelled major changes in India's economic environment.

Overall growth in trade, including flourishing exports, however, did not assure those displaced from their old occupations or those who remained in agriculture a share of the new wealth. True, Europeans demanded the products of rural India. Even though cotton exports declined somewhat after the U.S. Civil War, the level of demand for foodgrains, oil seeds, jute, tea, opium, indigo, and animal hides and skins rose to unprecedented levels. At the same time, the changing economic environment brought tremendous pressure on Indian cultivators. Wages fell, and by the year of India's independence "at least one-fifth of the total area under cultivation even in Ryotwari tracts could be said to have passed under open tenancy while an unknown, though substantial proportion of area was worked under forms of crop-sharing, in essence no different from tenancy."[69] India's countryside now hosted a permanent army of landless rural workers.

Although India's rush into the world market hinged mostly on demand for cotton, it did include a number of other highly valued crops. The average annual British imports of jute, for example, which came almost solely from India, grew approximately 1200 percent from the early 1850s until the early 1880s. Egypt's new role in the world economy, on the other hand, was built almost solely around cotton. The effect of that precious fiber, wrote E.R.J. Owen, was felt "throughout every other part of the economy. From the early 1860s onwards it provided never less than 70 per cent of the country's export earnings. In those years it was the major source of income for almost every proprietor in the Delta."[70]

Egypt had already developed a much more integral place in the world economy under Muhammad Ali in the first half of the century, but it found that old role dwarfed by its participation in the world market beginning in the 1860s. Under Muhammad Ali cotton exports had risen threefold, but by the 1890s the Egyptians exported more than twenty times as much cotton as at the end of Muhammad Ali's reign.[71] The value of Egypt's exports increased almost 300 percent be-

---

[69] A. M. Khurso, "Land Reforms Since Independence," in Singh, ed., *Economic History of India*, p. 183.

[70] E.R.J. Owen, *Cotton and the Egyptian Economy* (Oxford: Clarendon Press, 1969), pp. xxiv, vii.

[71] Baer, *A History of Landownership in Modern Egypt*, pp. 22–23.

tween the late 1850s and the late 1870s.[72] And these changes precipitated others in class relations. "From the 1880s onwards," wrote Baer, "a new class, the urban rich, rapidly became the chief class of landowners."[73] By the turn of the century, 43 percent of the total area of landholdings consisted of large estates, and 23 percent of those estates were foreign-owned. These large holdings formed the backbone of the greatly expanded cotton trade with the West.

A second wave of eruptive changes began to occur in other parts of Asia and in Latin America a decade or so later than in India or Egypt. For most of Asia and Latin America, the tremendous confluence of changes began around 1870 and permeated throughout each society by the early 1890s. In Palestine, for example, where commercialization was far less extensive than in India or Egypt, the massive changes in the economic environment began during the 1870s, about a decade before Zionist settlement activity accelerated the pace of commercialization even more.

So, too, in Mexico: the 1870s witnessed the beginning of a galloping rate of social and economic change. There, the renewed relationship with the world economy had a devastating effect on peasant land ownership (by the revolution in 1910, there were over 8,000 haciendas) as well as a great impact on raw materials production, whether in the form of goods for import-substituting industries or for export. Production increased an average of only 0.65 percent annually from 1877 to 1907 in the troubled agricultural sector, but in that sector raw materials for export grew during the same period by a hefty average of 7.45 percent annually.[74] Among the major select export crops of Mexico, growth was even more dramatic. From 1877 to 1880, for example, the value of coffee exports increased 55 percent; henequen, 80 percent; and vanilla, 58 percent. For the years 1881–1882 to 1891–1892, the increases were 128 percent for coffee, 138 percent for henequen, and 398 percent for tobacco.[75] All this occurred while the buying power of agricultural laborers fell an estimated 20 to 30 percent and per capita crop production grew at a rate of −0.8 percent annually (1877–1910).[76] The overall result of changes in agriculture was that most Mexicans were eating less while some were exporting more.

[72] Derived from Owen, *Cotton and the Egyptian Economy*, p. 168.

[73] Baer, *A History of Landownership in Modern Egypt*, p. 70.

[74] Cosío Villegas, *Historia moderna de México*, vol. 7, pp. 3, 107.

[75] Figures adapted from López Rosado, *Historia y pensamiento económica de México*, vol. 1, pp. 66–71, 95–100.

[76] See Friedrich Katz, "Labor Conditions on Haciendas in Porfirian Mexico," 1; and Reynolds, *The Mexican Economy*, p. 96.

In all these countries of Latin America, Asia, and the Middle East, the spread of the world economy came in fits and starts. The world market's unpredictability demonstrated poor people's vulnerability and dramatized the failures of old strategies of survival. The years immediately following the opening of the Suez Canal were among the most uneven and disruptive. New shipping possibilities on top of the railroad building boom brought a surge in trade for India and other countries, leading to an increasing pace of change in production patterns to satisfy strong European demand. The Great Depression of 1873, however, brought a jolting reduction in demand, testing existing social organization and strategies of survival. As Wolf noted, "Capitalism encroached ever more intensively on the social arrangements predicated upon tributary or kin-ordered modes of production."[77]

The latest wave of eruptive changes in the environment due to the penetration of the world economy came in sub-Saharan Africa. Most societies there did not face the far-reaching, revolutionary changes associated with the triumph of the world economy until the two-decade period following the mid-1890s and leading up to World War I. For Sierra Leone, the value of exported palm kernels, the main cash crop, more than doubled in only three years once railway line had been laid in 1904 to the palm-rich Upper Mende country. Total export revenues in Sierra Leone grew almost 250 percent between 1896 and 1912.[78] West Africa as a whole saw the total value of its exports increase more than 350 percent during that period.[79] Even without the potent land tenure laws, the new niche West Africa took in the world economy had a debilitating effect on existing forms of social organization and social control. As Nash wrote, "In any 'foreign factor economy,' the economically weakest go to the wall and find themselves at the bottom of the stratification order and in the least skilled and remunerative niches in the ethnic and occupational division of labor."[80]

CRISIS AND INSTITUTIONAL CHANGE

The shortness of the time period in which world forces changed societies, rocking them to their foundations in less than a generation, is

---

[77] Wolf, *Europe and the People Without History*, p. 311.

[78] Figures adapted from J. Barry Riddell, *The Spatial Dynamics of Modernization in Sierra Leone* (Evanston, Ill.: Northwestern University Press, 1970), pp. 21–23.

[79] From 1895 to 1912. Figures adapted from Crowder, *West Africa under Colonial Rule*, p. 288. Crowder shows that this boom did not continue from 1913 until the Great Depression.

[80] Nash, "The Impact of Mid-Nineteenth Century Economic Change," p. 171.

not incidental to understanding the momentous nature of social transformation in this period. Sudden disruptions in life patterns give people precious little time to adapt their life strategies. Fine tuning is not
enough. For peasants and workers these years were ones of crisis. This
period was a turning point in their lives, marked by difficulty, insecurity, and movement from one set of survival strategies while searching
for new ones. It also included a sudden, radical change in the institutions with which they interacted; those institutions are simply the established systems of rules and roles within which people deal with one
another.

The notion of crisis in nineteenth-century non-Western societies
suggests an understanding of institutional change that departs from a
common view in the social sciences. A standard outlook on institutional change has been expressed best by the neoclassical economists.[81]
An institution changes, according to the neoclassical formulation, at
the margins. That is, when certain parameters or environmental conditions change—for example, the appearance of people with different
abilities or of a shifting capital stock due to varying population numbers and human knowledge—a corresponding adjustment results in
the rules.

Thus, institutions change incrementally; each new benefit or cost
accorded by varying conditions modifies rules for human behavior
and interaction. People are willing to change the rules when expected
benefits of the new institutional arrangements outweigh expected
costs. A system of rules, or an institution, includes innumerable, individual prescripts; thus, the system as a whole, bound by written laws
as moral codes, will change slowly and at the margins.

The experience of eruptive change and crisis in the nineteenth century indicates that another perspective may tell us more than the con-
ventional neoclassical approach about major institutional changes. A
convergence of powerful forces can precipitate rapid institutional disintegration; this occurred with the tremendous dynamism of late nineteenth-century capitalism, spurred by new policies in land tenure, taxation, and transportation. Historical crises or turning points involve
wholesale changes in institutions touching many aspects of people's
lives. Institutions weaken as their rules become irrelevant to matters at
hand. Crisis means that a great proportion of these rules simultaneously becomes irrelevant to broad segments of the population. The

[81] See Lance E. David and Douglass C. North, *Institutional Change and American Economic Growth* (Cambridge: Cambridge University Press, 1971); and Douglass C. North, *Structure and Change in Economic History* (New York: W. W. Norton, 1981).

model of institutional change here is not one of a continuous curve representing incremental alterations at the margins; rather, it is an image of history as discontinuous, as bursting at rare moments with catastrophic suddenness.[82] In between those bursts, incremental change can tell us much about societies, but the disintegration and recreation of institutions at particular moments—the fall of Humpty Dumpty and the act of putting him together again—instructs us on the landmark changes that hit societies.

A Look Aside at Theory and Back in History

During the nineteenth century Latin American, African, and Asian societies were by no means the first to undergo such wholesale institutional disintegration. The societies that existed in northwest Europe toward the end of the feudal period faced similar changes and discontinuities. This is not the place for a full elaboration of the structure of late feudal societies, especially those in which feudal elements were most rapidly disappearing, such as England and the Netherlands (and less so France and Scandinavia), but several points reveal how crisis was critical in allowing the restructuring of those societies.

The Black Death had occurred about a century prior to some of the major institutional innovations in politics and economics that began in Europe after about 1450. By killing one-third to one-half of Europe's population, it wreaked havoc on the control and capabilities of almost all leaders and their organizations. The problems of these leaders intensified through the rest of the fourteenth century with at least four plague recurrences. The Black Death undermined the organizational bases of the local power of lords (when they survived). Also, depopulation made the lowly serfs' labor much more in demand than before. Rents diminished, the amount of land cultivated declined, and wages rose. In some areas, the changes ruined entire landowning classes. A distinct weakening of local and regional social organization ensued.

---

[82] A number of other social scientists have written about discontinuous institutional change. See, for example, Suzanne Berger, *Peasants Against Politics: Rural Organization in Brittany 1911–1967* (Cambridge, Mass.: Harvard University Press, 1972); Stephen D. Krasner has written of "punctuated equilibrium" in "Approaches to the State: Alternative Conceptions and Historical Dynamics," *Comparative Politics* 16 (January 1984): 223–46; also see his "Regimes and the Limits of Realism: Regimes as Autonomous Variables," *International Organization* 36 (Spring 1982): 497–510; and Alfred Stepan, *The State and Society: Peru in Comparative Perspective* (Princeton: Princeton University Press, 1978), p. 47; Fen Osler Hampson, *Forming Economic Policy: The Case of Energy in Canada and Mexico* (New York: St. Martin's Press, 1986), ch. 2; Michael Mann, *The Sources of Social Power*, vol. 1, "A History of Power from the Beginning to A.D. 1760" (Cambridge: Cambridge University Press, 1986), p. 3, notes "the discontinuous nature of power development."

Although by no means as universal or as devastating as the Black
Death, the Hundred Years War, fought intermittently from 1337 to
1453, extended the havoc in some areas. The squandering of crucial
resources and the general destruction of the War placed great strains
on many elements of the society in the century before one of the most
institutionally innovative periods in human history, the years from
1450 to 1600.

As early as the mid-fourteenth century, then, the major social organizations of parts of Europe began to be weakened when, as E. J.
Hobsbawm wrote, "something clearly began to go seriously wrong
with European feudal society."[83] After the sixteenth century's innovations, including a state with significantly more social control than previous political units and a much more inclusive and far-ranging European economy dominated by maritime powers, conditions in the
seventeenth century compounded the earlier weakening of the local
social organizations. In the seventeenth century, economic decline, faltering population growth (with the worst epidemics in more than two
hundred years), the Thirty Years War (1618–1648), splits in the
church, and a series of revolts and civil wars (led by the Puritan Revolution in England) all helped strike the final death knell in many
areas for the dominant local and regional social organizations of medieval Europe.

Existing institutional orders do not give up easily. Only severe crisis,
as in fourteenth- and seventeenth-century Europe or nineteenth-century non-Western societies, could induce people to abandon in droves
tried and tested strategies for survival, even when those strategies demanded unspeakable hardships. The weakening of society through
the crumbling of social control has occurred broadly only at rare moments of human history. In the nineteenth century, the dislocating
force was the spreading world market; in previous periods other
forces shattered existing patterns of social control. The important
point is not that capitalism was the immediate cause but that its effects
were institutionally devastating. Once old institutional arrangements
disintegrate, no ineluctable force necessarily leads society to a "higher
level" of civilization. The problem of disintegration of institutions does
not necessarily dictate its own solution—the blueprint for the new institutional arrangements. In Europe, a few new strong, centralizing
states followed disintegration. It is worth noting that many other
forms of political organization appeared in Europe, from reformed

---

[83] E. J. Hobsbawm, "The Crisis of the Seventeenth Century," in Trevor Aston, ed.,
Crisis in Europe 1560–1660 (London: Routledge and Kegan Paul, 1965), p. 5.

principalities to reconstituted empires to renewed arrangements of serfdom. All the forms other than the state, however, largely failed to last into the second quarter of the twentieth century.

The catastrophic changes that engulfed Latin America, Africa, and Asia, did not necessarily lead to strong, centralizing states—even after independence. Sudden, eruptive changes in the late nineteenth and early twentieth centuries, nonetheless, had momentous and long-term effects on social organization and social control. Such catastrophic changes prime a society for a major institutional transformation. "This fluid and indeterminate state," wrote Pitirim Sorokin, "affords a *favorable ground for the swift transformation of social institutions—for the emergence of radically different social forms.* Society is now in a plastic state, like half-melted wax out of which anything can be molded."[84]

The Deterioration of Old Social Control

The liberalism that had made headway in Europe for half a century worked its way into the heartlands of other parts of the globe by the late nineteenth century. Once there, however, it took some odd twists and turns. The land consolidation, disenfranchisement of peasants from the land, growing gaps in social status, and *corvée* labor did not seem very liberal at all. The survival of a liberal international order, nonetheless, came to depend on the ability of the world market to insinuate itself down to the lowest levels of far flung societies. European state leaders knew from the experiences of their own societies in the seventeenth and eighteenth centuries that prosperity came from commercialization. In those centuries, Tilly pointed out, "promoting the national market became something of a state religion, and resisting it, a civil sin."[85] Now their goals of commercialization remained, but their aims went beyond the narrow countrywide market. Their vehicles to accomplish that task and ensure the enforcement of rules to create the necessary conditions for a worldwide division of labor were the land, revenue, and transportation policies adopted by both the colonialists and the indigenous regimes seeking a toehold in the new world order.

With the rapid and deep penetration of the world economy, leaders of existing social organizations in each society frequently found what they offered irrelevant to the needs and problems of their constituencies. As people lost their land or moved far from ancestral villages

[84] Pitirim A. Sorokin, *Man and Society in Calamity: The Effects of War, Revolution, Famine, Pestilence upon Human Mind, Behavior, Social Organization and Cultural Life* (New York: E. P. Dutton, 1943), p. 120.

[85] Tilly, *As Sociology Meets History*, p. 206.

or changed the sort of work they did, their old survival strategies became inadequate or inappropriate. They experienced a sudden weakening of their societies throughout Asia, Africa, and Latin America, where levels of social control declined substantially. The ability to enforce old sets of rules on how people should behave withered under the new conditions. Existing sanctions and rewards were geared to another age.

Social organizations and social control, of course, differed considerably from one society to another, but in every society one comes across familiar laments. The prevalent organizations suffered during this period of increased world market penetration. In India, T. N. Madan complained of the decline of the Hindu joint family.[86] Wolf wrote of the demise of Mexico's self-governing landholding *pueblos*.[87] The powerful shaykhs of Palestine's countryside were victims of the changes in the last part of the nineteenth century, as well. The world economy's almost total shift away from slavery by the middle of the nineteenth century left local leaders of Sierra Leone without one of their main bases of social control.

To be sure, the deterioration of these old forms of social control did not signal an end to a romantic and harmonious precapitalist era.[88] The old configurations of social control could be demeaning, exploitative, and personally debilitating. Also, the deterioration of these forms did not preclude their ultimate rehabilitation based on people's new strategies of survival. The shaykhs of Palestine did fade almost totally from the stage of history, but in Iraq they staged a remarkable comeback in the 1900s after almost a half century of decline. In some tribal groups in Sierra Leone, local leaders also enjoyed a revival as British-appointed chiefs. India's Hindu joint family remained, not unscathed, an important factor in people's lives.

Which leaders and organizations resurrected themselves was not simply a matter of serendipity. We shall see in Chapters 3 and 4 how this recreation of social control and social organization occurred in colonial societies. In countries that did not experience rule by Westerners, those who already had the contacts and capital to take advantage of opportunities presented by the encroaching market often built up their roles as powerbrokers. They enhanced their position and refashioned their old organizations to provide components for new, rel-

---

[86] T. N. Madan, "Social Organization," in Singh, ed., *Economic History of India.*

[87] Eric R. Wolf, *Peasant Wars of the Twentieth Century* (New York: Harper and Row, 1969), p. 17.

[88] Samuel L. Popkin, *The Rational Peasant* (Berkeley: University of California Press, 1979), calls this the "myth of the village."

evant strategies of survival. Some of these societies had had a fair degree of upward and downward mobility. Now, through their ties to foreign entrepreneurs, the strongmen could freeze the social structure with themselves at the top. The new resources available to them could be used to solidify their positions as powerbrokers to the population and to limit the ambitions and autonomy of the indigenous state.

Whether in colonial or independent societies, the recreation of social control through the construction of new institutional arrangements was necessitated by general crisis. The crisis of the peasantry, of the new urban working class, and of rural landless laborers consisted of the demise of their strategies of survival. Old rules were simply not working; the old forms of social control were gone.

They were moribund not because capitalism ineluctably washed over these societies, much as the tide would suck the coastal sands into the sea; markets did not stretch to encompass additional chunks of the world automatically. Instead, they were propelled by those able to control political policies. Where no colonial administration was in place, powerful figures manipulated governing organizations to pass such legislation or exploited legislation passed for other purposes. Independent states or empires sought to protect themselves from powerful insiders and outsiders with policies that would unlock the secrets of the West.

In colonial states, Westerners used the policies to ensure access to producers and to guarantee that those producers would supply the products demanded in the West. In both colonial and noncolonial cases, these policies refashioned land rights; they drove people into the world of cash; and they laid open for penetration even remote hinterlands. Other political policies in colonial regimes—the subject of the next two chapters—injected crucial new resources into societies at this moment helping to determine who could and would take advantage of the weakening of old forms of social control in order to introduce new ones.

I have now taken the first step in my attempt to answer why many contemporary Third World states have stumbled in their attempts at increasing their capabilities and their social control while a few others have had much greater success. The policies that facilitated the incorporation of African, Asian, and Latin American societies into the European-dominated world economy had a radically transforming effect on those societies. When world forces made the old forms of social control suddenly less suited to the daily exigencies of most people's lives, old institutional arrangements unraveled. The old rewards, sanctions, and strategies no longer provided the same solutions to people's most pressing needs and problems or the same compelling dictates to behave and believe one way rather than another.

I now turn to the restructuring of those societies. Social control had to be reestablished; Humpty Dumpty had to be put together again. In the next two chapters, I seek answers to the question of how to explain the manner in which people subject to Western colonialism recreated the fabric of society. In other words, how did they construct new institutional arrangements? Who rose to the top of indigenous societies subjected to Western rule? How did outside forces condition the ways in which the new social control would be exercised? After my analysis of certain types of emerging social organization in Chapters 3 and 4, I can demonstrate in Part III the impact of the new patterns of social control on the capabilities and nature of Third World states in the post–World War II era.

CHAPTER THREE

Laying the Basis for a Weak State: British Colonialism and the Fragmentation of Social Control in Sierra Leone

WHO BENEFITED?

Social Control in Independent Regimes

As parts of a larger world social system, Third World societies have adapted to the tugs and pressures originating outside their borders. Forces associated with the spread of world markets and those tied to the far-reaching power of Western states have had a profound impact on the overall structures of these societies and on the daily lives of individuals. A century ago, representatives of huge joint-stock companies and other enterprising entrepreneurs trailblazed evermore direct access for Westerners to producers in exotic, remote corners of the world and often displaced indigenous traders or small overseas or minority middlemen. As discussed in the preceding chapter, hegemonic Western states, such as France and Great Britain, introduced important policies involving land tenure, taxation, and the improved physical access to the hinterland. Even in areas they did not rule directly, the Western traders and state officials prepared the way for the introduction of the same sorts of policies by local political leaders.

In both Western-ruled and indigenously ruled societies, these policies facilitated deep, rapid, and almost universal penetration of world markets emanating from Western Europe and precipitated the emergence of new forms of production. Even when the policies did not achieve the specific aims of those who conceived and implemented them, they still opened the way for elements of change so powerful they rocked many existing social organizations, toppling some and precipitating wild adjustments in others. Some disappeared altogether; others endured but barely recognizable in the functions they performed; and still others drew succor from the new conditions.

The taxation, land, and transportation policies greased the wheels for European market penetration, making old strategies of survival unviable. With old means of social control crumbling—old rewards, sanctions, and symbols deprived of relevance and meaning in the new circumstances—people still needed strategies of survival, ways to improve their life chances. It is not surprising, then, that new patterns in the distribution of social control began to emerge immediately in Asia, Africa, and Latin America. In fact, the seeds of new strategies appeared as quickly as the old routines died. But the disruption of the old through the deepening of the world market in the late nineteenth century did not bring with it a necessary blueprint for new strategies. From an analytic perspective, it is worth separating the debilitation of old strategies and the creation of new ones. An important reason for the varying capabilities among contemporary Third World states is the differences among them in which groups and individuals created new strategies in the atmosphere of rapid change. Who could offer components for strategies suitable to new proletarians and farmers caught in the throes of commercial agriculture? Who was able to take advantage of the new circumstances and reestablish social control? This question guides Chapters 3 and 4. By offering a partial answer to it, I can present some understanding of the roots of the social structures that emerged in these societies. Then I can proceed with the central question of what impact these structures have had on the capabilities and characters of contemporary states.

The rejoinders to the question of who could capitalize on the weakening of old forms of social control are, on one level at least, as numerous and diverse as the societies in the Third World. Scholars have barely scratched the surface in their efforts to comprehend the input of old patterns on emerging new ones. Certainly, any full-blown theory of the effect of previous social structure on the rate, direction, or content of change during a period of catastrophic transformation is beyond the scope of the present work. We shall see, however, that previously existing social differences within the native societies influenced who could provide capital, use contacts, and marshall other resources to exploit the new opportunities created by the rapidly spreading market.

There is little doubt that the individual character of each society helped determine the ultimate impact of the world economy in that country. A well-oiled market neither simply pulverizes the old, irrespective of the structure of traditional society as so many theories of change imply, nor does it necessarily afford equal or nearly equal opportunities for garnering resources to a mass of undifferentiated economic "actors." On the contrary, factors as basic as social class, race, religion, ethnicity, sex, existing distributions of capital stock, and pure luck impinged mightily in each case; they influenced the operation of the market and, ultimately, determined who could make binding rules, create effective social control, and organize new strategies of survival.

In addition to looking at the influence of old patterns on new ones, other sorts of approaches may also help identify who benefited from the spreading world market by suggesting more general answers that exceed country-specific conditions. Important commonalities exist, for example, among societies run by indigenous regimes able to escape Western colonial rule. Often unwittingly and ironically leaders of such states or empires aided in creating new forms of social control inimical to their own aims. Their actions stemmed from the vulnerability of their regimes in a world increasingly marked by gaps in capabilities among political units; some states possessed an overwhelming share of destructive and economic power while others lagged far behind. In the last quarter of the nineteenth century, Ottoman and Mexican political leaders, among others, attempted to influence shifts in patterns of social control within their societies as a major means to increase the resources available for international use. They desperately sought the formula that would allow them to increase their power, just as European states had. The new orientation these regimes displayed toward their own populations in policies involving taxation, land tenure, and railroad construction largely stemmed from the rulers' desire to attenuate their obvious vulnerability during the fifty or so years around mid-century. They had good reason to feel vulnerable: they had witnessed such events as the conquests of Muhammad Ali, the Crimean War, the Mexican-American War, and the reign of Maximilian.

Their very weakness in the international arena, however, also worked against them domestically. As they implemented their new policies, they sought to release the genie that would bring them vast new revenues and power from the bottle. These leaders found, to their dismay, that there were no quick fixes or secret formulas for accumulating surplus capital, industrializing their societies, and developing impressive military power.

At the same time, certain domestic groups had already enhanced their own positions through direct ties to foreign capital and foreign traders. The growing strength of these people in places such as Mexico or various districts of the Ottoman Empire resulted in their ability to twist liberal public policies to their advantage. One might have expected certain reforms, such as giving farmers deeds to the land they cultivated, could have led to new state strength or helped ward off threatening outsiders while creating a more liberal social order at home. Instead, these reforms resulted in the concentration of wealth in the hands of a small minority; poor rural people came under the control of this small group of powerful landlords. An independent peasantry, beholden to the state and able to give state leaders the wherewithal needed to act against other social groups and threatening outsiders, simply did not appear in most such societies. These conditions of fragmented social control among the landowners, who both controlled the peasantry and maintained independent ties to foreign traders, made it highly unlikely that an independent state leadership could emerge.

Political leaders in independent Mexico or the Ottoman Empire, then, faced severe constraints. Without social control, they could neither mobilize the human and material resources necessary to develop significant autonomy nor regulate social relationships and appropriate resources at the local level. Resources for agricultural production and the even more important ability to disburse those resources, the bedrock of any new possible strategies of survival, accumulated in the hands of a relatively small group of landowners, not in those of autonomous state leaders. Despite the tremendous cultural differences between Mexican and Ottoman societies (or among other indigenously ruled Latin American, Asian, and African societies, for that matter), there were astonishing commonalities in the new forms of social organization and social control. From Mexico to Turkey, from El Salvador to Iran, from Colombia to Egypt, a rather small class of landowners—sometimes even designated by only a few families, 12 or 200 or some other number—benefited from the new conditions through the accumulation of huge tracts of cultivable land.

Social Control in Colonial Regimes

My primary interest in this chapter, however, is not the indigenously led regimes but the question of who reestablished social control in Western-ruled Asian and African societies in the late nineteenth and early twentieth centuries. Which indigenous elements benefited from the new conditions and formulated the new rules of social relations? Again, although still far from definitive answers, I can suggest some common factors that influenced the character of the new social structure.

Beyond the impact on social control of the Western-dominated market and the state policies that facilitated the deepening of that market, the colonial powers in Asia and Africa influenced social life in other important respects as well. In this chapter and the next, I argue that the reconstitution of social control and distribution of that control depended, to an important degree, on other actions of Western states beyond policies of land tenure, taxation, and transportation. While the Westerners staffing the colonial state often shared viewpoints with entrepreneurs investing in and trading with non-Western societies, those state officials were not driven exclusively by an interest in extending the market. These men deviated in important respects from businessmen in their perspectives.

Differences in viewpoint also split the Western state officials themselves, based on what they perceived the state interests to be. Where they sat in the state organization and how they perceived their own career chances affected officials' understanding of the state's interests. Foreign ministry officials, for example, frequently advocated policies based on grand strategic views, but those in colonial offices looked for administrative efficiency and social accommodations in a local territory. At the same time, those stationed in the territories often fought to reduce risks in their domains that might create unwanted, damaging publicity about any existing difficulties. In short, a mix of political and personal motives by colonial rulers had important effects on native social structure, the reconstitution of social control in indigenous African and Asian societies.

Cross-pressures and diverse perspectives of colonial officials produced policy in the governed territories. The concerns of all these sorts of officials sitting in different chairs of the colonizing state went beyond ensuring the flow of local products to national and international markets, the creation of new forms of production to generate commodities demanded in Europe, and the development of new consumers for European manufactured products. For independent reasons, they wanted to choose who among the natives would take advantage of the opportunities generated by the spreading world market and thus who would be able to establish social control. In other words, the colonial leaders wanted to manipulate the rules and makers of the new social control.

The independent political and personal considerations of colonial officers have remained shadowy subjects. British officials obfuscated their differences with British entrepreneurs and the degree to which they independently effected social relations. Sir Harry Johnston remarked to the Foreign Office in 1895, "All that needs now to be done is for the Administration [in Sierra Leone] to act as friends of both sides, and introduce the native labourer to the European capitalist."[1]

[1] Quoted in A. P. Kup, *Sierra Leone: A Concise History* (New York: St. Martin's Press, 1975), p. 192.

The role of colonial officials and administrators, however, far sur-
passed serving as beaming matchmakers. By analyzing the independent role of state actors in light of the effects of spreading capitalism,
we begin to uncover the changes that occurred in nineteenth-century
colonial societies. These changes greatly affected for decades to
come—until this very day, in fact—the meaning and salience of terms
such as "class," "tribe," and "ethnicity" in particular countries and the
relations of state and society in them.

POLITICAL HEGEMONY AND THE NEW DISTRIBUTION OF SOCIAL CONTROL

Social scientists have often disregarded the long-term intended and
unintended effects of outside *political* forces—particularly the assertion of autonomous state interests—on colonized societies, especially
compared to the attention given the impact of the expanding world
market.[2] By no means did all forms of outside rule and influence have
the same results. Variations in directness or intensity of the rule and
influence of outside states, as well as differences in the mix of outside
forces with indigenous social structure, led to differing abilities of particular indigenous social organizations ultimately to gain social control.
Colonialism, as in Britain's rule in India or in the Crown Colony of
Sierra Leone, was the most intense form of Western political hegemony, involving formal appropriation of the key decision-making posts
in the society. No colonial regime ruled without significant participation and assistance by indigenous people, who in turn benefited
greatly from the authority gleaned from the colonial state. Outside
powers were in the best position to thwart or abet the development of
indigenous centralized leadership and a competent administrative
staff, together forming the basis for an eventual, centralized state organization. The colonizers could allocate the right to disburse resources, opportunities, and sanctions to various indigenous groups;
these in turn could fashion new strategies of survival for peasants and
workers. Officials, meanwhile, withheld resources from others. Allocation could either favor a single, central group in a position to consolidate social control or tilt toward a legion of other social organizations to fragment social control and engender an environment of
conflict.

[2] Ralph Braibanti talks of the literature's "neglect of the experience of the former colonial powers especially Britain, France, the Netherlands, and the United States in the construction of political systems within the context of imperial rule." "Political Development:
Contextual Nonlinear Perspectives," *Politikon* 3 (October 1976): 8.

In this chapter and the next I argue that the colonizers' actions greatly affected which indigenous figures were able to reconstitute social control in the wake of the catastrophic changes wrought by the spreading world market. Whether the colonized countries would end up with weblike or pyramidal societies, then, was not only a result of previous social structure. The new distribution of social control stemmed, too, from actions and alliances by the Western powers. These powers were in the best position to shape events where they established colonial states. Other forms of rule, such as Britain's League of Nations Mandate in Palestine or the British Protectorate in Sierra Leone, came close to colonialism in directness and intensity. In Chapters 3 and 4 I detail the impact of British decisions on society in two cases of the most intense sort of hegemonic rule, Sierra Leone and Palestine.

It is important to note, however, that other sorts of political hegemony by Western powers could greatly influence social structure as well, although not as decisively as in cases of colonialism. A second type of political hegemony involved the direct influence of an outside state on questions of power—who rules, how wealth is spent, what institutions may exist, and the like—but this type did not involve the actual appropriation of most key decision-making posts. A nominally independent indigenous regime, as in Egypt in parts of the late nineteenth and twentieth centuries, still existed. Here, outside powers were somewhat more constrained in determining the actual distribution of social control in the society, especially between the indigenous political leadership and other social organizations, but outside influence was still considerable. This type of hegemony characterized the United States's position in the Caribbean in the first decades of this century or Britain's role in Transjordan in the years leading up to World War II.

Finally, in a third and least intense type of political hegemony, the outside power set important structural parameters but was not involved with the details of ruling. A classic set of cases was United States influence in the Caribbean from the 1930s through the early 1960s. British influence over the Porte in the Ottoman Empire for parts of the nineteenth century and in the hinterland of Sierra Leone prior to the Protectorate or United States concern with Mexico through the early decades of this century also fall into this category. In each of these cases, the state interests of the outside power affected relations between the indigenous governing organization or organizations and society. But the impact was far less than in the instances of more direct and intense Western colonialism or even protectorates, such as in Great Britain's post-1882 role in Egypt.

Even within each of these three types of political hegemony, there was tremendous variation from country to country. For example, British colonialism differed from that of the French, and both varied substantially from Belgian and Portuguese colonialism. Moreover, the policies of each colonial power varied from place to place (for example, compare French rule in Senegal and Morocco), especially because local colonial governors often had such great leeway in determining policy in the field. Also, the manifold differences in the societies and cultures upon which outside powers acted affected the nature of colonial rule, as well as the outcomes in the newly established patterns of social control.

Some attempts have been made to sort out a number of these differences. For African colonialism, for example, scholars have long differentiated among the policies associated with "direct rule" of the French in which Frenchmen filled even fairly low-level administrative offices, "indirect rule" of the British in which the indigenous population played these roles, and the hybrid case of "quasi-indirect rule" used by the Belgians.[3] In another classification, again from Africa, David Apter differentiated societies according to social structure and belief systems; he looked at precolonial societies having consummatory or instrumental value systems and hierarchical, pyramidal, or segmental authority systems with important consequent variations in societies' reactions to the impact of the West.[4]

Important differences exist, then, in the long-term influence of Western states on the type of indigenous social control encouraged, permitted, or even unintentionally spawned in Asia, Africa, and Latin America. The type of social control Western states fostered was particularly important in the wake of the disruptive impact of the expanding world market and the crumbling forms of previous social control. Economic crises and dislocation forced peasants and workers into new relationships with those who could address their new needs and problems. Lowering the overall level of social control precipitated a scramble by those with some resources at hand to adapt old social organizations or create new ones with which they could gain social control under these new circumstances.

[3] See James S. Coleman, "Tradition and Nationalism in Tropical Africa," in Martin Kilson, ed., *New States in the Modern World* (Cambridge, Mass.: Harvard University Press, 1975), p. 17; also, Thomas Hodgkin, *Nationalism in Colonial Africa* (London: Frederick Muller, 1956), Part 1. For a critique, see Immanuel Wallerstein, *Africa, The Politics of Independence* (New York: Vintage Books, 1961), ch. 4.

[4] David E. Apter, *The Politics of Modernization* (Chicago: University of Chicago Press, 1965), ch. 3.

Success or failure in this scramble depended not only on the existing social structure (that is, who was in a position to take advantage of new resources or to survive the current crisis), or on individual skill, but also on the specific policies undertaken by the colonizing state. Much of the means by which indigenous strongmen could reconstitute social control during this critical period flowed intentionally and unintentionally from the hands of the colonizing states' rulers. Through specific policy decisions, colonizing rulers made crucial economic and political resources available to some but not to others in the local societies.

In brief, these colonial policies permitted or encouraged creating a firm base of social control for particular indigenous leaders and their social organizations. Of all the distinctions in the local population these policies fostered, one stands out in its long-term effect on state-society relations. Colonizing rulers could either give preferential access to resources to many local indigenous leaders, each of whom could establish social control in only a circumscribed part of the society, or the foreigners could support those in a position to create central, countrywide institutions capable of forming an eventual, centralized state.

For the indigenous society, these differences in privileged access to resources proferred by the colonial power had prolonged effects. They determined who could offer components as people sought to reconstitute viable strategies of survival—organizations broad and strong enough to be incipient states or scattered local organizations that could never hope to achieve countrywide control. Adroit use of the resources made available by the colonizing state's policies enabled some social organizations, and not others, to reestablish social control. If, in fact, organizations broad enough eventually to rule the entire territory could devise such strategies, the chances of a strong state emerging with significant capabilities rose dramatically.

Once certain local strongmen implemented successful strategies of survival, however, it became exceedingly difficult to change, in great measure, the overall distribution of social control in the society. Although successful challengers to social control arise here and there in a society, attempts at universal transformation of existing strategies and control have encountered great obstacles, for reasons that will become clearer in Chapters 5 and 6. Only rare circumstances, as in the penetration of the cash market, create deep and universal disruptions in a society making a large share of the population's strategies unviable simultaneously. By extending considerable latitude and resources to some types of indigenous organizations to take on new tasks while clamping down harshly on the activities, or even the very existence, of others, colonizing states made deep imprints on indigenous social structure.

These Western states, then, played a great role in influencing the pattern of social control, a pattern that often remained intact even after their own rule and influence had dwindled or long ended. They influenced who would have the resources and authority to offer effective components for strategies of survival to the population—local strongmen or those who could create the basis for an eventual centralized, indigenously ruled state. For a strong incipient state organization to develop, its creators first had to assume the disposition of material resources, such as land, credit, and jobs, critical for people's survival and social mobility. On the symbolic level, they had to fashion a worldview that accepted, even legitimated, the particular disposition of resources and the social hierarchies related to the form of production and distribution in the society. Most often, they offered variants of nationalist ideologies.

For the colonizing power itself, the question of who benefited from its rule was also vitally important. Its own ability to maintain secure rule depended on what forms of native social control existed in the governed society. Because even in the most direct forms of colonial rule, the colonial power depended greatly on indigenous social organizations for implementing policy and maintaining domestic order, rulers had to choose carefully their alliances with indigenous strongmen. The new form of social control, in short, stemmed from a convergence of disparate interests of colonizers and some of the colonized.

Two cases—those of colonial Sierra Leone and the Jewish community in mandatory Palestine—demonstrate how different goals for the territories on the part of the outside rulers led to varying conceptions of their own state interests and their policies on how local societies should be controlled. The case of Sierra Leone constitutes the remainder of this chapter, while that of Palestine forms the basis for Chapter 4. The British encouraged very different distributions of social control among the local populations of these two societies; consequently, the decisions taken by British colonial officials have had lasting but different effects on social structure and political rule in the two, extending well into the period of independence. Their influence stretched beyond the distribution of social control to the very meaning of the most central social terms, such as tribe, party, and chief, extant in the societies.

RECREATING SOCIAL CONTROL: BRITS AND CHIEFS

The West African territory that came to be known as Sierra Leone fell under British rule in fits and starts. Individual Britons settled in coastal parts of Sierra Leone under the protection of African rulers during the eighteenth century, and toward the end of that century British businessmen already held sway in some coastal areas. The British project to resettle freed slaves in Freetown, together with the related incorporation of the Sierra Leone Company in 1791, led to increasing British domination. Finally, in 1808, the coastal area became a Crown Colony, and, in 1896, the inland areas became a British Protectorate. Only in 1951 did a new constitution finally treat the colony and protectorate as a single unit.

For the people of Sierra Leone contacts with Europeans date back half a millennium. By the beginning of the sixteenth century, trade with Portuguese and other Europeans already had a recognized set of rules. The slave trade was the linchpin of this contact legally through the eighteenth century and illegally midway into the nineteenth, but exports of ivory, palm kernels and oil, groundnuts, and other products also brought Europeans and Africans together. Many local strongmen reinforced their social control through a barter system that included everything from highly prized salt to silks and human beings, and other new indigenous rulers rose through similar trade networks.

Even as the end of the slave trade in the latter half of the nineteenth century deprived chiefs and other strongmen of important resources in maintaining social control, the growth in palm oil trade enabled "those who controlled the river-heads beyond which the rivers were no longer navigable, where traders congregated to buy produce brought from the interior [to grow] rich from rents and duties."[5] At times, contests for these crucial locations bubbled over into bitter local wars and feuds, as chiefs from the interior sought control of the profitable river heads and access to the Europeans' coastal enclaves.

Maintaining order in the hinterland, for most of the nineteenth century, rested upon those indigenous leaders who were able to use their highly prized resources as a basis for social control in the interior. By the last quarter of the century, increasingly frequent British military expeditions influenced the outcomes of the local conflicts and wars, usually waged over control of trade routes. The colony governors were not reticent to interfere in inland disputes, even to the point of

[5] Christopher Fyfe, *Sierra Leone Inheritance* (London: Oxford University Press, 1964), p. 226.

installing leaders of their liking. Even so, large parts of the interior remained beyond effective British influence until the very end of the nineteenth century.

Only with the creation of the protectorate in 1896 did the British assume the ongoing responsibility for administering more directly all of Sierra Leone. In those heady years of the colonial scramble in Africa during the late nineteenth century (and even after), the British and other colonial powers did not contemplate the end of their rule on that continent. For all the rhetoric of their civilizing role, the colonialists were trying, at the time, to establish permanent rule or at least direct control through the foreseeable future. The concern of British Governor Frederic Cardew, then, went beyond ensuring stability needed for the increased extraction of palm oil so important for the manufacture of both glycerine used in explosives and margarine. Even with precious few British officials to assist in establishing and maintaining empire in Sierra Leone, he pursued the ambitious goal of laying the foundation for indefinite British rule. One piece of that administration was a corps of police, reputed to have used force quite liberally.

Social control and social order, however, depended on much more than a police force spread thinly over the countryside. Although Cardew and others bandied about many words about new judicial, administrative, and fiscal institutions, much of the protectorate's actual administration came through a set of indigenous leaders. Sierra Leone was no different from all other European colonies in this regard. The essence of imperialism, as Ronald Robinson indicated so well, was the technique of collaborating elites.[6] Even after the uprising of many chiefs and their followers against the British in the Hut Tax War near the end of the century, those determining British policy maintained their belief that economical rule demanded relying heavily on the chiefs, now more shored up by British personnel.

The major alternative to the chiefs as allies to the British was the growing corps of Western educated elites. In fact, the twentieth-century history of Sierra Leone and many other African and Asian countries, both before and after independence, has centered around the overt and covert struggles between strongmen and more urbane elites, who were products of Western education and culture. The outcomes of these struggles in the postindependence era, have varied from case

[6] Ronald Robinson, "The Excentric Idea of Imperialism, with or without Empire," in Wolfgang J. Mommsen and Jürgen Osterhammel, eds., *Imperialism and After: Continuities and Discontinuities* (Boston: Allen and Unwin, 1986), pp. 267–89.

to case, in some part due to the preferences of the colonizers prior to independence. In French colonies, notes Christopher Clapham, the "highly sophisticated indigenous elite . . . were indeed, in many respects, almost indistinguishable from Frenchmen, . . . whose priviliged position was recognised both legally and politically." For the British, in contrast, "the highly Europeanised Asian or African . . . was the subject of suspicion and stereotyped contempt."[7] British officials reacted with open disdain to the new elites as a possible alternative to the chiefs. Albertini wrote of the feelings "of the governors, residents, and district commissioners, who because of birth and upbringing got on much better with the emirs, chiefs, and notables than with the members of the new elite. The claims of the latter to be spokesmen for the African population were rejected with unconcealed scorn."[8]

As in colonies throughout Africa and Asia, social control in Sierra Leone did not become a monopoly of the foreigners. Quite the contrary, indigenous forces shared this control in important ways. Those who shared control with the British, however, were carefully selected: chiefs, yes; the new educated elites, no. The preference for chiefs by no means eliminated the more educated elites as contenders to social control forever after. It did, nonetheless, affect the long-term balance of power in Sierra Leone and elsewhere.

The British conception of "ruling through traditional chiefs" has a deceptive ring to it. For the Limba chiefs of northern Sierra Leone, for example, the traditional institution of chiefship had very little traditional about it.[9] Until the protectorate period, in fact, the Limba had no defined chiefships at all, contrary to British assumptions; only with the dangling of British resources did the informally defined rulers of the earlier period become the chiefs of the protectorate. Sierra Leone is not an exception in this regard. In other territories, too, the British created traditional roles and offices. The position of Grand Mufti of Jerusalem, for example, was a creation of the British after World War I and became an important stepping stone for the man handpicked by the British rulers to become the most important Muslim leader in Palestine, Haj Amin al-Husayni.

Dramatic changes in the bases of indigenous leaders' social control among the Limba followed the British creation of the office of chief.

---

[7] Christopher Clapham, *Third World Politics: An Introduction* (Madison: University of Wisconsin Press, 1985), p. 22.

[8] Rudolf von Albertini, *European Colonial Rule, 1880–1940: The Impact of the West on India, Southeast Asia, and Africa* (Oxford, England: Clio Press, 1982), p. 315.

[9] Ruth Finnegan and David J. Murray, "Limba Chiefs," in Michael Crowder and Obaro Ikime, eds., *West African Chiefs* (New York: Africana, 1970), pp. 416–19.

First, Western rule broke the older hierarchy of political governance. The British replaced the existing hierarchy of three main overlords, who had been accepted by lesser local leaders, with a system of fourteen equally ranked chiefs. Suddenly, formerly subordinate localities had chiefs claiming rule over these territories as self-governed chiefdoms. Second, power had previously rested on a leader's ability to gain sway over subjects. British involvement now meant one's domain was limited strictly by the new territorial boundaries imposed by the colonialists. Third, and probably most important, the local leaders' power grew immensely through the British formalization of chiefs' duties and privileges and through the resources the British lent to that process. "In contrast to the earlier situation, local rulers were now constitutionally recognised, their relations with each other and with their people laid down by law, and the officials around them defined. The chiefs of the 'new' chiefdoms in particular found that their positions were immensely stronger than those held by their earlier counterparts."[10] Chiefs now held formal rights to tribute and labor and could appeal to the district commissioner, if necessary, to exercise those rights. The new order established both the chiefs' power and the position of the elders on the British-created "Tribal Authority" in ways quite different from those of earlier periods.

A somewhat different pattern of change in social control took place among the Mende of Sierra Leone, one of two main tribes that emerged in the country, along with the Temne. Nevertheless, in one important respect, conclusions about British rule run strikingly close to those drawn from the Limba experience: "The present chiefdoms are not traditional entities."[11] As one chiefdom speaker put it, "There were then no chiefdoms [before 1896 among the Mende] as they are now termed. Great warriors had ownership over extensive areas. But after the 1898 rebellion the British Government thought it best to split up these areas into chiefdoms, thus ultimately creating a lot of chiefs."[12]

Among the Mende, British policy led to a rapid proliferation of chiefdoms. Nine Mende political authorities existed in 1880, the pe-

[10] Ibid., p. 417.

[11] Arthur Abraham, *Mende Government and Politics under Colonial Rule* (Freetown: Sierra Leone University Press, 1978), p. 214. Abraham takes issue with the "Colonial thesis": "the country being divided up into the numerous chiefdoms we know today, independent and having no common allegiance" (p. 170). Also, see K. L. Little, *The Mende of Sierra Leone: A West African People in Transition* (London: Routledge and Kegan Paul, 1951), pp. 175–77.

[12] Abraham, *Mende Government*, p. 174.

riod prior to the protectorate; in 1889, twenty-seven chiefdoms existed; in 1912, eighty-two; and by 1924, well over one hundred. Some amalgamation took place thereafter, reducing the number to just under a hundred after World War II.[13] Whether or not the precolonial Mende political structures had the breadth and depth of authority and control that Arthur Abraham suggested, it is certainly true that British constraints and requirements constitutionally changed the basis of leaders' rule. Drastic changes in the basis of social control were bound to occur if only because previously much of the chief's power had rested on his role as warrior and military protector of his people. The ultimate recourse of each chief to British power in itself substantially transformed the nature of social control. Chiefs who had had no former claim on leadership roles relied heavily on British backing and support.

Even for those who had exercised significant power before British rule, the new conditions changed the nature and strength of their leadership. The ultimate reliance on British authority and resources gave new bases for establishing indigenous social control and, at the same time, imposed important territorial and other limits on the chiefs. For example, T. J. Alldridge, British traveling commissioner, described chief Nyagua as a leader who exceeded British limits. Nyagua, wrote Alldridge, was "a most arrogant man, insufficiently courteous to the British government, and requiring much ceremonial treatment himself."[14] In the wake of the Hut Tax War, Nyagua's reputation among the British led to his arrest and exile. The connection between the maintenance of social control by indigenous leaders and cooperation with the British was unmistakable. Chiefs ruled at the pleasure of the colonial administration, but British influence in turn rested heavily on the chiefs' social control.

Compared to the later constitutional arrangements, the British granted the chiefs only circumscribed powers at the end of the nineteenth century and beginning of the twentieth. The chiefs were responsible for security, tax collection, labor recruitment for public works, and other minor tasks. Whatever the chiefs did receive, however, was critical in these decades coinciding with the dislocation caused by growing trade. Even prior to 1896, it is true, traders changed people's lives in the hinterland. "Many bushels of palm kernels," wrote Governor Rowe in 1879, "are collected by native women

---

[13] Ibid., p. 175.

[14] Quoted in Arthur Abraham, "Nyagua, the British, and the Hut Tax War," *International Journal of African Historical Studies* 5 (1972): 95.

that they may buy the handkerchief and the looking-glass brought to their village by the Sierra Leone adventuress [Creole women traders from the Colony]."[15] (The Creoles were the descendants of the freed slaves who settled in Freetown.) A potpourri of European, Creole, and even Syrian traders hawked their wares up-country, as the interior was called, and took out palm kernels and ground nuts in the decades preceding the establishment of the protectorate.

But these economic relations of the late nineteenth century did not nearly demand the new forms of production, migration, and class relations comparable to those stemming from the surging economic activity in the two decades prior to World War I. With the disruptions of the Hut Tax War in 1898 behind them, British traders poured into the protectorate. Contractors oversaw the furious laying of railway lines from the end of the war until 1908. Traders doubled the 1904 export figure by 1909 and tripled it in 1912. Customs duties nearly tripled between 1900 and 1912, and Hut Tax revenues grew steadily at a rate of about £2,000 a year.[16] The Creole-mediated relationship with the world market for the up-country producer became rarer and rarer. "The trains that opened up the Protectorate," wrote Fyfe, "brought Creoles competition of a new kind. European firms, once content with factories on the river-banks which enterprising Creoles could cut out by pushing inland, began opening agencies along the line."[17] The international market's deepening penetration inexorably moved the economy from subsistence agriculture. A workforce now ranged far from home villages, toiling not only in farming but in mines as well. In the swirl of such dizzying changes, the chiefs judiciously used even the limited sources of authority the British granted them to consolidate their social control in the midst of extensive social dislocation among the peoples of Sierra Leone.

The British, however, found their mediated rule through the chiefs less than satisfactory. By World War I, enough social and economic change had occurred to make the British feel the existing arrangements were inadequate mechanisms for effective governance. Colonial officials feared the rapid changes had made the chiefs' limited official

[15] Quoted in C. H. Fyfe, "European and Creole Influence in the Hinterland of Sierra Leone before 1896," *Sierra Leone Studies* 6 (1956): 120–21.

[16] Christopher Fyfe, *A History of Sierra Leone* (Oxford: Oxford University Press, 1962), p. 612.

[17] Ibid., p. 613. Signs of important cleavages and discontent resulting from British activity were already emerging. "Trade was booming, revenue coming in as never before, but the Colony's inhabitants [the Creoles] found themselves growing steadily poorer, without prospect of recovering their commercial prosperity" (p. 614).

functions—little more than collecting taxes, suppressing slavery, and preventing open disorder—unsuitable for the times. Within the loose framework laid down by the British, chiefs had considerable latitude in demanding levies, tribute payments, and forced labor. From time to time, other tasks devolved to specific chiefs, but these roles were of only minor significance through the mid-1930s. For example, a chief could be designated a "health authority" to perform certain public health tasks.

The concerns of the British for effective government led almost from the beginning to reform and then reform of the reforms. In every decade of British rule in this century, colonial officials tinkered administratively, creating and recreating districts, in endless attempts to rationalize government. They alternately expanded and contracted the range of powers they bestowed on the chiefs.

The most serious expression of concern came in a report in 1935 by the Senior District Commissioner, J. S. Fenton.

> In the face of modern conditions (education, effects of mines, etc.) it appears the native institutions of the chiefdoms are no longer secure. . . . Native institutions are likely to be more heavily attacked in the near future. Increasing ease of travel and the attraction of mines means the influx of strangers into the chiefdoms, strangers who know what is done elsewhere, who criticize and despise a weak native government, or one which tends to be reactionary or oppressive.[18]

Following Fenton's report, the most notable British reform in government established the Native Administration or Native Authority system. Imported from Nigeria, where noted colonial governor, Frederick Lugard (later Baron Lugard), had first implanted it, the Native Administration system elevated the power of Paramount Chiefs in designated "Tribal Authorities." The Paramount Chiefs headed financial institutions called Chiefdom Treasuries, received new taxing authority (from the taxes the Paramount Chiefs collected came half the government's revenues), and gained legislative and executive authority with respect to social services and so-called development.

The Paramount Chiefs' roles in finance, revenue collection, law making, social services, and development gave them resources and opportunities for accumulating power as never before. The impact of

---

[18] Quoted in Martin Kilson, *Political Change in a West African State* (New York: Atheneum, 1969), pp. 20–21. Note the implied criticism of a system of rule that was, in fact, many different sets of rule.

British policy thus went far beyond maintaining existing social organization, as they so often claimed. In the wake of the most profound changes in living habits and social structure of the population, the British gave the chiefs tremendous *new* authority and resources with which to exercise social control. The Native Administrations "invariably expend[ed] 50 per cent and more on personal emoluments of Chiefs and other hereditary officials."[19] Clapham noted,

> By building up the chiefdoms as the principal units of "native administration," the British had made them, and especially the chieftancy, itself, prizes worth coveting; and by confining the chieftancy to representatives of specified families within each chiefdom, they had created a group of local patrons with their own clienteles within the chiefdom and a built-in basis for competition between them.[20]

In choosing the chiefs, the British consciously ruled out the alternative, the educated elites whom one British official in the Gold Coast referred to as that "self-selected and self-appointed congregation of African gentlemen" or whom Lugard in Nigeria called that "arrogant" educated elite.[21]

Once the chiefs further increased their social control with the aid of the new authority granted them in the Native Administrations system through the expeditious use of their salaries, tribute, and other incidental payments, the British found it extremely difficult to reverse the process. When wartime needs in the 1940s, for example, suggested schemes to increase food production and timber supplies, the chiefs proved totally inadequate as executors of the government's new policies. After World War II, in the 1950s, the British attempted new remedies to correct the situation by reversing the extensive control of the chiefs. Colonial officials first designated district councils and later government field staff to execute policies instead of the chiefs, but the costs of bypassing the chiefs soon became obvious. New British commissions levied criticism on the altered administrative practices, including claims that they failed to establish contact with the mass of the people.[22] The councils and the field staff found it difficult to establish

---

[19] Ibid., p. 212.

[20] Christopher Clapham, "The Politics of Failure: Clientilism, Political Instability and National Integration in Liberia and Sierra Leone," in Clapham, ed., *Private Patronage and Public Power: Political Clientilism in the Modern State* (London: Frances Pinter, 1982), pp. 84–85.

[21] von Albertini, *European Colonial Rule*, p. 331.

[22] See, for example, *Report on the Commission of Inquiry into Disturbances in the Provinces*

ties with the population, at least in part because of the degree of social control already exercised by the chiefs.

The British were caught in the dilemma of "how far the chief's office [could] be divested of its traditional significance without undue loss of the popular respect which . . . [was] its most valuable asset."[23] By the last few years of colonial rule, the British reverted to a heavier reliance on the chiefs, opening the way for these indigenous leaders to augment their powers beyond revenue collection and other sorts of administration through important roles in the new electoral system. Although the chiefs first ruled at the pleasure of the colonial authorities, before long the colonial authorities became limited by the control of the chiefs.

Many of those below the chiefs openly resented the advantages that accrued to these rulers in the form of the highly prized resources so important in the new money economy. They also resented the role of the chiefs as administrators for the colonial authorities.[24] In 1955–1956, in fact, antichief riots broke out in the north of the country. Many of the small but significant minority whose increased physical and social mobility effectively removed them from the sphere of the chief's control deeply resented the position the British afforded the chiefs. This minority included the few with university education, some entrepreneurs (and even workers) in the private sector, and indigenous members of the colonial administration. The educated elite's conflicts with the chief were many and grew with time. In Sierra Leone, where the mobile Creoles filled many of these roles (as they did, incidentally, in other West African colonies to which they migrated), the tension between chiefs and educated natives was especially intense.

Nevertheless, the new authority and the new sources of income generally enabled the chiefs to strengthen their rule as they adapted to the changing environment. Those whom the British recognized as chiefs more than compensated for the resentment as well as for the diminishing value of former bases for social control—slavery, war making, customary rights of tribute, land rights, and so on. All these old sources of power had either disappeared or become absorbed into the British administration of Sierra Leone.[25]

In brief, while the old foundations of social control withered and

---

(Freetown: Crown Agents for Overseas Governments and Administrations on Behalf of the Government of Sierra Leone, 1956).

[23] Little, *The Mende of Sierra Leone*, p. 210.

[24] Wallerstein, *Africa*, p. 42.

[25] Kilson, *Political Change*, p. 65.

old strategies of survival crumbled, colonialism provided the basis for new bonds of dependency. Often, the new social control of a chief far outstripped what he had maintained before. British rulers further strengthened the new bonds by regarding the population as members of social organizations led by chiefs rather than as people with individual rights and needs. Any concern with economic development in such a context demanded using the chiefs, inefficient as they were, as conduits to the population. In these circumstances, the strategies of survival adopted by most of the population necessarily started with the chiefs' organizational base, the tribe. The tribe was a key organizational ally of the colonial state, and it is impossible to understand the changing nature of the tribe in the twentieth century without noting its relation to the state. Using the tribal organization, the chief controlled key resources, including material goods, jobs, violence, and defense; some of those resources, chiefs received from the state. In addition, the symbolic importance of tribe was stressed by chiefs as they sought to build the basis of enduring social control. The tribe catapulted forward as a key structure in the modern world.

THE PLURAL INTERESTS OF THE BRITISH

Divergent, sometimes even discordant, interests underlay the policies of the colonizing state, in this case Great Britain, as it fragmented social control among the numerous chiefs. These differences among the British were to have longlasting effects on the reestablishment of social control in Sierra Leone in the wake of the disruptions caused by spreading capitalism.

Whitehall officials expressed one perspective mainly through the Colonial Office. They saw Sierra Leone, and all of West Africa for that matter, as only one small part of Great Britain's global imperial ambitions. At the same time, British officials in Sierra Leone itself acted upon a second and often quite different set of perceived state interests. Their view stressed the importance of local and regional events in West Africa to Britain's overall strategic position. Finally, British traders brought substantial pressure to bear on public officials both in London and in Freetown, reflecting yet another series of considerations. After all, these Victorian entrepreneurs reasoned, British enterprise, not the British state, was the main engine of British global expansion.[26]

[26] See Ronald Robinson and John Gallagher, *Africa and the Victorians* (New York: St. Martin's Press, 1961), p. 3.

Sierra Leone, in fact all of West Africa, held almost none of the strategic value for policymakers in London that they found, for instance, in Egypt and the Sudan, let alone India, in the last decades of the nineteenth century. The 1865 Parliamentary Select Committee went so far as to advise total withdrawal from West Africa.[27] Earl of Kimberly, colonial secretary, wrote in 1873 that he hoped no British government would "ever be mad enough to embark on so extravagant an enterprise" as the establishment of a West African empire.[28] Into the 1890s, reticence and inertia marked the Foreign Office's policy towards West Africa, a region that held neither the potential wealth of the Sudan, although West Africa certainly compared favorably to other parts of East Africa, nor the strategic locations of either the Sudan or Egypt with respect to routes to India. "Nothing is more striking about the selection of British claims in tropical Africa between 1882 and 1895 than the emphasis on the east and the comparative indifference to the west."[29]

Any active concern with West African affairs that the Foreign Office did evince stemmed from the nettling hindrance of French expansionism in the area. And, even given that concern, British officials in London preferred to resort to diplomacy as the means to temper French ambitions and assure access to British merchants. London-based officials feared that conflicting claims in areas as inconsequential as Sierra Leone and West Africa generally could lead to a rapid deterioration of Anglo-French relations. Until 1892, diplomatic measures seemed adequate enough. In the face of French-German entente, for example, the British basically conceded their monoply of imperial control over Africa at the Berlin Conference on African problems in 1884–1885, which set the rules for the appropriation of African territory. Only as tensions grew with the French over the Nile and the French forces continued expansion in West Africa did the British finally decide to expand the formal empire there in the 1890s.

Colonial Secretary Lord Knutsford made the initial strides, sanctioning new treaties with chiefs in the interior from 1890 on. The appointment of new Colonial Secretary Joseph Chamberlain in 1895, however, led to the logical extension of the decisions taken at the Berlin Conference, a new aggressiveness in British colonial policy including the acquisition of empire for its own sake. Chamberlain's concep-

[27] See Gustav Kashope Deveneaux, "Public Opinion and Colonial Policy in Nineteenth-Century Sierra Leone," *International Journal of African Historical Studies* 9 (1976): 56–58.
[28] Quoted in Brian L. Blakely, *The Colonial Office 1868–1892* (Durham, N.C.: Duke University Press, 1972), p. 41.
[29] Robinson and Gallagher, *Africa and the Victorians*, p. 393.

tion of empire discarded the earlier Victorians' disdain for the state compared to private entrepreneurs, and instead he saw the state as the Pied Piper of those Britons concerned with affairs overseas. With the new emphasis taking root in London, Cardew could finally get the official go-ahead to tighten his grip in Sierra Leone's hinterland through the creation of the protectorate in 1896.

Even among the policymakers in London, contending perspectives of the state's interest in expanding its empire were evident. Chamberlain's seat in the Colonial Office led him to different estimations of West African affairs from those of his government colleagues. "The Prime Minister [Salisbury] and several members of the Cabinet regarded the west African issues as trivial brawls over expendable places."[30] Larger global tensions with France in the last years of the nineteenth century afforded Chamberlain a stunning opportunity to act boldly on his views and substantially change Britain's role in West Africa.

The colonial secretary's success in his daring acquisition of territory depended on previously laid groundwork, which reflected an even wider rift in British state interests than that between Chamberlain and his fellow ministers. While caution and reticence had characterized London's approach towards imperial aggrandizement in West Africa during the last third of the nineteenth century, British overseas officials had taken a much different view. They adopted policies in the field formalized only later by Chamberlain's bold strokes. Despite official Whitehall policy in the 1860s, 1870s, and even 1880s opposing expansion in the hinterlands of West Africa, on-the-spot colonial authorities periodically extended the British domain. One description depicts the consternation that these officials in the field could cause among the cautious Whitehall contingent.

> Under the governorship of Samuel Rowe, an aggressive man who wanted to extend the commercial orbit of Freetown as far north and northeast as possible to thwart French expansion, from the mid-1870s the colony entered into numerous treaty arrangements with local rulers despite instructions from London to the contrary. The implications of some of Rowe's alliances caused serious embarrassment in London, where officials were studiously working to avoid open conflict with France. In one case, that of a treaty with the Baga north of the Mellacourie, the Colonial Office disavowed the treaty outright.[31]

[30] Ibid., p. 408.
[31] Deveneaux, "Public Opinion and Colonial Policy," pp. 57–58.

For officials in Freetown, French posturing around Sierra Leone loomed much more threatening and potentially destructive than for those in the far-off Foreign or Colonial offices in London. The French success in gaining control of trade in Niger at the expense of the British raised the fears of Freetown officials considerably. The instability in the hinterland caused by warring chiefs seeking control of inland trade had precipitated Freetown officials to interfere for decades; the added threat of the French taking advantage of such stirrings by supporting their own candidates led to more and more intervention in the hinterland in the years leading up to the declaration of the protectorate. Punitive British expeditions up-country against recalcitrant chiefs became commonplace after the mid-1870s. Whenever they could, British officials installed their own choices as chiefs. Nonetheless, by 1882, the French had won control of all the northern rivers. The cumulative effect on Britain's position of seemingly insignificant acts by the French (at least seemingly insignificant in out-of-touch London) badly frightened British officials in Africa.

The thought that French forces might disrupt British trade to the interior even further by promoting squabbles and tactical shifts among hinterland chiefs led to increased involvement by the Crown Colony officials beyond the colony's boundaries. Cardew's reorganization of the frontier police was one means of extending control deep into the hinterland. In those final years leading up to the protectorate, wrote Abraham, "a loud anomaly was that 'we exercise all the authority incidental to a Protectorate without venturing to declare that it is one.' "[32] What was accomplished de jure with Chamberlain's efforts had been effected de facto by the officials in Sierra Leone itself years before. "The shift from informal empire to effective colonial control," wrote von Albertini, "was so gradual it was hardly perceived. The initiative came not from London but from the men on the spot, the consuls and governors in West Africa."[33]

Those Britons who ruled in Sierra Leone had little patience with the kinds of policies devised in London that led, for instance, to the short-lived British-French boundary agreement in 1889. As political rulers in Africa, they acted to achieve as secure and stable local conditions as possible, based on their understanding of true British interests. What is more, they felt their careers depended upon this sort of decisive action. They believed that for all their superiors' talk about not increasing British imperial commitments, the London-based officials

[32] Abraham, *Mende Government and Politics*, p. 115.
[33] von Albertini, *European Colonial Rule*, p. 305.

were in fact more interested in simply not having to deal with any ruckuses occurring in out-of-the-way places, such as West Africa. From the 1830s on Sierra Leone governors worked to gain sufficient control to create security and stability to prevent such ruckuses, even under the specific injunction from London not to extend the colony territorially.

Like good bureaucrats anywhere, they sought to create an environment that would preclude the transmission to their superiors of information suggesting their inability "to handle" the local situation. Their tactic was to sign treaties of friendship with up-country chiefs to ensure influence and the security of trade and to gain leverage in the most destabilizing process of all—chiefs' conflicts with one another over gaining trade advantages. The security of trade was so important because the British traders whose feathers had been ruffled were most likely to transmit any negative information to these civil servants' superiors. In the final decades before establishment of the protectorate, when some chiefs had the additional option of contact with the French, governors escalated their involvement through new military expeditions and an expanded frontier police.

British merchants had concerns about Sierra Leone and conceptions of what British interests were that diverged, at times, from those of Whitehall and, at times, from those of local colonial officials. Prime Minister Salisbury had indicated as late as 1892 that the value of trade with Sierra Leone amounted to so trifling a sum as to preclude any thoughts of further territorial ambitions there.[34] The British merchants trading there had come to believe otherwise, although their pressure to further the British imperial domain lagged decades behind the aggrandizing schemes of the local colonial officials. Nonetheless, following the 1880s, the business interests pressed the government to extend empire. Their change of heart in seeking the umbrella of British rule arose from the growing internal squabbling among chiefs in Sierra Leone and the alarming French advances, eating into their commercial monopolies. Also, they finally came to believe "that only railways, taxation, and close administration would induce west Africans to take up farming for export."[35] The "Coasters," as these entrepreneurs came to be known, urged the government to create the necessary infrastructure for secure and profitable investment through the framework of an expanded empire.

[34] Robinson and Gallagher, *Africa and the Victorians*, p. 383.
[35] Ibid., p. 394.

In 1884, Liverpool entrepreneurs with interests in the area formed the African Trade Section. "Underlying the protests they addressed regularly to government," wrote Fyfe, "was the assumption that Africa and its trade should by rights be British, and that if foreigners intruded, Colonial and Foreign Office were to blame."[36] Into the 1890s, their feeling (along with many in the Colonial Office) was that Salisbury appeared to prefer placating the French to winning votes in Liverpool or Manchester.[37]

In short, from a position of deep Victorian suspicion about the role of the state in advancing empire that they had shared with London policymakers, these "heroes of commerce" (as one defender called them) or "palm oil ruffians" (as they were more commonly named) switched to positions much closer to those of the local colonial officials, who saw the serenity needed for successful commerce resulting only in the wake of their own successful governance. The merchants, however, never gained the kind of clout, with either London or local officials, that traders in some other areas had, perhaps due to the fairly limited volume of West African commerce throughout the nineteenth century.

British Reliance on the Chiefs

In the case of West Africa, local officials proved the dominant British actors. But their efforts to shape indigenous social control remained halting and tenuous until the merchants upset existing social patterns with their big commercial thrust at the end of the century. And only when London established the legitimacy of their governance in 1896 did these officials have the wherewithal to shape directly new patterns of social control. In brief, the new social structure and social control in twentieth-century Sierra Leone resulted in part from the odd mix of British interests and their link to particular indigenous groups.

After 1896, local British governors proceeded to adopt policies aimed at ensuring the security and stability of their rule in what they thought would be as least costly a manner as possible—tranquil rule on the cheap. The Protectorate Ordinance itself stressed the ideas of "Security, Peace, and Order." These officials saw their advancement in the British Civil Service as coming through colonial rule that unobtrusively paved the way for expanded trade while paying for itself.[38]

---

[36] Fyfe, *A History of Sierra Leone*, p. 500.

[37] Ibid., p. 503.

[38] Cardew himself had a more ambitious vision than most other officials. He foresaw a move from mere protection of trade to public outlays directed toward the promotion of production and trade.

Their professional reputations and careers would suffer due to any miscalculations. Civil servants in the London Colonial Office, already having a rather low opinion of officials in the colonies, rated these officials on their ability to stay out of "scrapes."[39]

A gross blunder did occur in Cardew's relentless drive to gain the revenues needed for administration through the Hut Tax, which led to a costly insurrection. It also sparked an investigation by a royal commissioner, Sir David Chalmers, an event hardly welcomed by Cardew and the other local colonial officials. Even though Cardew's views, rather than Chalmers's, were ultimately accepted by the Colonial Office, the point was probably not lost on Sierra Leone's rulers that their miscalculations had brought not only close scrutiny of their actions by London but also an embarrassing repudiation of their regime locally as a crowd of thousands gave Chalmers a tumultuous welcome upon his arrival in Sierra Leone.

Chalmers's conclusion that the uprising was due to the officials' insensitivity about the question of the Hut Tax and the methods to collect the levy also served as a rallying point for the petty grievances of British business interests in Sierra Leone against the officials. Unhappy with the administration's expenditures, taxes on them, and unwillingness to make public outlays on their behalf, they complained to Chalmers and even went so far as to selflessly suggest replacing the existing colonial rule with a council nominated by the English Chambers of Commerce.[40] These merchants would have laughingly scoffed at the notion that British state policies in Sierra Leone amounted simply to an expression of their commercial interests.

Given the additional burdens after the Hut Tax War of increased scrutiny from London, local colonial officials were even more eager to reestablish the stability and security they valued so highly. Ignoring the clear implications of the nearly universal participation of the chiefs in the insurrection, the colonial officials went assiduously about the task of establishing their rule through the chiefs. Such rule minimized costs by relying on the chiefs as legislators, judges, and administrators, while it attempted to ensure against concerted rebellion through policies that fragmented indigenous social control. Commenting on this fragmentation as late as 1951, Little stated that "today the picture in the Protectorate is of some 200 separate chiefdoms of equal political status. Each of these is an independent 'state' on its own and entirely self-contained, so far as administration is concerned."[41]

---

[39] Blakely, *The Colonial Office*, p. 118.
[40] Fyfe, *A History of Sierra Leone*, pp. 590–93.
[41] Little, *The Mende of Sierra Leone*, p. 206.

These colonial officials set the stage for a continued environment of conflict. They rapidly expanded the power and number of chiefs while simultaneously exacerbating tensions between rival factions.[42] They aimed to create as weblike a society for the twentieth century as had existed previously. The resources committed to the creation, or in some cases the resurrection, of the chiefs' powerful roles in a framework of fragmented administrative entities, each with a somewhat different set of rules governing people's lives, were the most important factors in shaping the distribution of indigenous social control in Sierra Leone through independence and beyond. At the moment when the rapid, deep penetration of the world market had so disrupted existing patterns of social control and people's strategies of survival, these officials used the resources at their disposal to determine the future social patterns. It seems doubtful that British officials were aware of the interaction of the disrupted old social patterns and their new administrative arrangements. As Kup put it, "Society was being restructured on all sides, a fact of which the colonial government . . . seemed almost oblivious."[43]

Decisive British action came in the 1890s when local officials, London officials, and merchants reached a modicum of consensus on what British interests in West Africa really were; the agreement came within the framework of the new protectorate, sanctioned in London. And the policies were enacted by the officials actually governing Sierra Leone who interpreted state interests as maintaining as inexpensive and secure a rule as possible there.

Relying on the chiefs posed all sorts of problems. As noted earlier, any British attempts at serious mobilization of people or material resources flagged badly. Although the chiefs provided tranquillity, colonial officials felt permanent British rule would ultimately depend on the introduction of British political values and the rule of law. Short-run expediency, however, may have put long-run goals out of reach. C. S. Whitaker wrote eloquently of a similar dilemma for the British in nearby northern Nigeria:

The nub of the difficulty was that the British proposed to rely on the continuing efficacy of the very system they sought to transform. Ultimately British administration meant to impose its own standards, but immediately it had to support traditional norms and tech-

---

[42] Abraham, *Mende Government and Politics*, p. 172; also see George Balandier, "The Colonial Situation," in Pierre Van den Berghe, ed., *Africa* (San Francisco: Chandler, 1965), p. 42; and Crawford Young, *The Politics of Cultural Pluralism* (Madison: University of Wisconsin Press, 1976).

[43] Kup, *Sierra Leone*, p. 192.

niques of traditional government, for these imparted the required stability and popular compliance. . . . In their dealings with emirs [chiefs], British officials had to be alternatively censorious and permissive, to applaud alike orthodoxy and innovation, to expose emirs favorably to alien values while confirming the essential preferability of traditional culture, to encourage Native Administrations to become responsible organs of government, but to insist on control remaining indefinitely in the hands of the colonial government, to allocate resources and rewards on the principle of functional rationality and yet uphold ancient privileges, to defend the surveillance over the Native Administrations on grounds of the welfare of the peasantry, but to discourage direct contact between commoners and British officers.[44]

In Sierra Leone, this same dilemma precipitated almost constant tampering with the administrative system. Once the chiefs had used British resources to reconstitute social control, however, the British found it exceedingly difficult to loosen these strongmen's grips. Officials encountered innumerable roadblocks to meet demands for more resources that filtered down to them during World War II. They designed policies to promote production and export, especially of food, but their schemes came to little avail. Attempts at amalgamation of chiefdoms, which sometimes covered only a few square miles, in order to foster more rational administration as a prerequisite for development met with only minimal success. British officials tempered their wish to undermine the prerogatives of the chiefs because ultimately they understood that secure, inexpensive British rule in Sierra Leone depended upon the social control exercised in the fragmented chiefdoms. Fragmentation was to have an enduring impact; in the postcolonial era it affected not only the capabilities of the Sierra Leone state but its character and policies as well.

WHY COLONIAL OFFICIALS DID NOT SEEK TO CENTRALIZE SOCIAL CONTROL

The creation of these fragmented loci of power in Sierra Leone, in fact, resulted from the convergence of several sets of circumstances. The rapid increase of world trade between the West and non-Western areas in the late nineteenth century affected the Sierra Leone population as deeply as peoples in other regions, although the value of

[44] C. S. Whitaker, *The Politics of Tradition: Continuity and Change in Northern Nigeria 1946–1966* (Princeton, N.J.: Princeton University Press, 1970), pp. 40, 46.

commerce with Sierra Leone was an insignificant portion of all British overseas trade. New seasonal and permanent migrations in Sierra Leone, as well as new ways of organizing people for production, precipitated fast rising exports of agricultural and mineral commodities. New relationships to the export economy made people's existing strategies for survival and the institutions offering those strategies more and more irrelevant to their needs.

At that time the British colonial administration injected whole new sets of resources with which new or renewed strategies and institutions could be built. A number of factors induced the British governors to shower their tangible and intangible resources on both old and newly created chiefs. These included a pressing need for cheap and effective social control, the fear of giving any indigenous leaders a potentially threatening oligopoly of control, experience elsewhere in Africa, and the nature of the previous societal institutional arrangements in the territory.

Through their own cultural lenses, the British saw the persuasive symbols they believed the chiefs could draw upon in constructing appealing strategies for survival. Oblivious to rapidly falling levels of social control by many indigenous leaders, the British focused on ostensible patterns of stratification. The indigenous leaders did have, after all, existing social organizations the British could use in constructing a foundation for their rule. The symbols and organizations the British relied upon for the reconstruction of social control help account for Sierra Leone's special culture in the twentieth century. The previous beliefs and social structure thus had new avenues to continue playing important roles into the future. For all its uniqueness and for all the culture's continuing impact, the society also faced constraints and conditions not at all atypical in Africa and Asia; an expanding market was gobbling up the population as producers of primary goods to be used elsewhere in the world, and a hegemonic power was purposely directing resources to a host of indigenous leaders, each with his own set of rules.

Colonial powers sought to operate through such heterogeneous groups of indigenous leaders for several reasons. At the top of the list was the weakness of the colonial power itself. Spread thin over rambling imperial domains, Britain and other powers were severely handicapped in achieving what they had so fervently accomplished at home—the delegitimization of social organizations with other sets of rules and the mobilization of the population directly into the state's own institutions. The great European imperial rule rested heavily on indigenous leaders because the amount of human and material resources expended by the European states was far from sufficient to create a system of centralized rules and procedures. The Europeans were too weak in most colonies to devise their own effective strategies of survival and exercise social control through centralized institutions.

The results of such weakness and of working through indigenous leaders were often quite different from those anticipated. Robinson, in his path-breaking work on imperialism, correctly stressed the indispensable role "of its victims' collaboration or non-collaboration—of their indigenous politics" in shaping the nature of imperialism.[45] The account above differs from the Robinson school in its emphasis on the key role of the imperial power in influencing who could and would be collaborators and noncollaborators.

The colonial powers' proclivity to work through fragmented groups and leaders, however, stemmed from more than just their weakness. British interests extended beyond investment and trade to include the complex operation of the British state itself. Two groups expressed the state's interests—London officialdom (the government and more specifically the Colonial Office) and the governing officials in the overseas territories. Once again, Robinson and his own collaborator, John Gallagher, contributed greatly to our understanding of imperialism by expanding scholars' fields of vision beyond London to the important people and events in the colonies. They pointed to the universe outside England and to a process of expansion more complex than single-minded concern with the issue of protected versus free trade. An overriding concern of London officials was strategic, but this preoccupation did not automatically lead to extension of the empire. Rather, British expansion, as Robinson and Gallagher argued in their *Africa and the Victorians*, resulted from a combination of the concern with strategic security, mainly relating to India, and the impact of local African crises that officials thought threatened such security.

Unfortunately, the Robinson-Gallagher thesis views the state too narrowly and posits an unnecessary degree of serendipity into the issue of expansion. The British state included more than the grand overseers of empire, who thought about overall strategy; other elements of the state also played a role in expanding empire in response to local crises. These crises, far from random, were not totally out of the realm of influence of British officials. The random crises Robinson and Gallagher point to may be better understood as molded by the

---

[45] Ronald Robinson, "Non-European Foundations of European Imperialism: Sketch for a Theory of Collaboration," in Roger Owen and Bob Sutcliffe, eds., *Studies in the Theory of Imperialism* (London: Longman, 1972), p. 118.

calculations of British officials in the field. These local officials had another whole set of concerns quite different from global strategic issues: they viewed local political and social stability as necessary for their own advancement through the civil service; they helped shape state policy often in opposition to the desires of both London officialdom and British commercial interests.

More than British weakness motivated the desire of British officials in Africa to rule through a fragmented, indigenous leadership, although that certainly was a prime constraint. These local officials simply did not have the same incentives as European rulers had had domestically to delegitimize existing social organizations and mobilize the population directly. In Europe, the motivation for such action in past centuries had frequently originated in the threats to rulers, as other strong, avaricious states cropped up on their borders. Consolidation of domestic social control could translate into the ruler's survival by making vast new material and human resources available. But the situation in the colonies differed. The extensive state resources local officials could call upon from outside in a local crisis, as evidenced in the Hut Tax War, assured local rulers that the costly, possibly destabilizing recourse to consolidation of social control within the ruled territory was unnecessary, perhaps even dangerous. Their goals of stability and security could be better achieved through policies that created and perpetuated a fragmented, weblike society with numerous poles of power, even though such a society posed formidable constraints on mobilization of human and material resources.

A Glance Aside at Egypt

Even where colonial states were not formed as capriciously as in sub-Saharan Africa or even where much more cultural homogeneity had existed, colonial policies could have similar fragmenting effects on social control. Egypt, with its long political history and its relatively homogeneous culture, demonstrates how imperial powers could cause considerable fragmentation of social control in a society much less diverse than Sierra Leone.

The Egyptian case is complex and interesting. In the face of near bankruptcy of the Egyptian state and the unsettling revolt of junior officers in the Egyptian army, the British hesitantly, even reluctantly, occupied the country in 1882. The Council of Foreign Bondholders, a private British group, urged the unenthusiastic Liberal government of Gladstone into intervention to protect investments of the British creditors. But, argued Tignor, "Egypt was occupied because of India, not because of the bondholders. The subsequent policies of reform and control in Egypt reflected the defensive nature of the occupation. The primary concern of the administrators in Egypt was to maintain the tranquility of a country considered important because of its strategic location."[46]

Part of the complexity in the Egyptian case lay in the conflicting aims of the British rulers to effect real administrative reform, which could lead to an early British exit, and to maintain tranquillity in the least costly way possible. The urge to reform undercut the local authority of village umdas (chiefs) and shaykhs (notables). Although their social control and wealth had waxed and waned under different rulers in the nineteenth century, they had fared exceedingly well in the period leading up to the British occupation. British rule changed all that very quickly. Not only did their wealth decline, but the British also transformed the umdas into the end links on an administrative chain. As Gabriel Baer noted, "Many were the functions which had constituted the foundation of the village shaykh's power and rule in the past and of which he found himself shorn in that period; as against this, burdensome new administrative duties were piled on him; the organization of justice deprived him of the discretionary power of which he had made free use with regard to the peasants."[47]

This impulse toward reform led to the weakening of past purveyors of survival strategies in the countryside. Reform also resulted in the development of some judicial and executive infrastructure, which could serve as the foundation for exercising a degree of centralizing control—certainly much more of a basis than the British fostered in Sierra Leone. The impulse toward reform that could have resulted in central social control in Egyptian society, however, ran headlong into the other British aim, the desire to maintain low-cost domestic tranquillity. What the British governors saw fit to take from Peter, they also seemed content to give back to Paul.

Especially after the first flush of the occupation, the British found new shoulders upon which to rest social control, maintaining stability in Egypt and securing the Suez Canal without the dangers and costs of centralization. The local benefactors were the large landowners. By the 1890s, they enjoyed the fruits of British policies, expanding cultivatable land and extending the infrastructure for cotton export. Just as important for the creation of new bases for fragmented social control, the British created new institutions—village councils, provincial

---

[46] See Robert L. Tignor, *Modernization and British Colonial Rule in Egypt, 1882–1914* (Princeton, N.J.: Princeton University Press, 1966), p. 24.

[47] Gabriel Baer, *Studies in the Social History of Modern Egypt* (Chicago: University of Chicago Press, 1969), p. 58.

councils, and local probate courts[48]—which channeled critical authority and resources to the landowners without significant control on the part of central authorities. The mechanisms for the strategies of survival that would take the Egyptian fellah into the twentieth century were in place.

In short, even where history, geography, and religion worked in the direction of a large dominant, homogeneous culture group, as in Egypt, rather than numerous communal or ethnic groups, colonial policy could still induce social fragmentation. In Egypt from the 1880s on British policy encouraged the emergence of a fragmented social organization: landlords applied their own systems of justice, their own strategies for peasant survival, within the villages they controlled. Umdas and wealthier peasants became the day-to-day managers for the landowners. Although the difficulties the Egyptian state has faced in recent decades in its attempts to centralize social control have not been nearly as untractable as those encountered by Sierra Leone's state leaders (see Chapter 5), the barriers have not been qualitatively different.

THE IMPACT OF THE NEW SOCIAL STRUCTURE ON POSTINDEPENDENCE POLITICS

By the time Sierra Leone achieved independence in 1961, its people had come to be organized into eighteen distinct ethnic groups. Two of the tribes, the Mende and the Temne, now make up almost two-thirds of the population. For Sierra Leone, as for peoples elsewhere, tribal or other group identities proved not immutable and everlasting but subject to flux and change.[49] J. Clyde Mitchell in his classic anthropological work on southern Africa, "The Kalela Dance," demonstrated how urbanization reshaped the boundaries of tribal identity and brought new expressions of group solidarity.[50] The combinations of colonial rule and incorporation into the world economy, along with a series of other factors such as Christian missionary activity, had a pro-

[48] See Eric Davis, *Challenging Colonialism: Bank Misr and Egyptian Industrialization 1920–1941* (Princeton, N.J.: Princeton University Press, 1983), p. 54.

[49] See, for example, Young, *Politics of Cultural Pluralism.* Also Charles F. Keyes, ed., *Ethnic Adaptation and Identity: The Karen on the Thai Frontier with Burma* (Philadelphia: Institute for the Study of Human Issues, 1979). Keyes notes in his introduction, "In sum, ethnic identities serve as adaptive strategies for people faced with certain types of social experiences" (p. 6).

[50] J. Clyde Mitchell, "The Kalela Dance: Aspects of Social Relationships Among Urban Africans in Northern Rhodesia," The Rhodes-Livingstone Papers, No. 27 (Manchester: Manchester University Press, 1956).

found impact on group identities in Asia and Africa during the nineteenth and twentieth centuries.

In sub-Saharan Africa, where the new colonial boundaries frequently lacked firm 'historical or cultural criteria, people faced a flood
of new experiences that presented them with new reference groups
and upset old patterns of stratification. The continent became a cru-
cible of shifting relationships and changing identities. With the resources they poured into particular administrative arrangements, into
selected leaders and their organizations, the colonialists held great
sway over the emerging structure of social life, the changing boundaries of tribes, and the identity of individuals as tribesmen.

By supporting the viability of some strategies of survival and not
others, the colonialists deeply influenced how individuals would order
their universe. Tribes, linguistic communities, and ethnic groups
changed dramatically in the late nineteenth and early twentieth centuries, in large part because of the colonialists' support of certain
forms of social organizations. The new tribes maintained a relationship to the past; they picked up old symbols and resurrected previous
organizational forms. New social fragmentation within the boundaries
of the colonial state, then, built upon some of the old social divisions,
hierarchies, and separations from the precolonial era. Chiefs, who
now used new sorts of material rewards and sanctions to gain social
control, refashioned tribal symbols and built alliances with other tribal
leaders to reinforce their organizational dominance. The new social
fragmentation, it is important to emphasize, did not depend entirely
on old tribal symbols and ties. As the spread of the world economy
undermined old strategies of survival, the purposeful policies of colonialism helped shape the new distribution of social control by directing
the flow of authority, force, and material resources in the society.

The social legacies of the colonial period have lived on in the postindependence era. "Twenty years after independence . . . ," one author
wrote, "the rancor of tribalism has persisted in posing an undue obsta-
cle to the integrated efforts for national development. . . ."[51] For the
people of today's Sierra Leone, these British policies in the dim past
have had an enduring impact upon social and political life, as have
similar policies in other former colonies. Such policies influenced the
very structure of society, including the distribution of indigenous social control and the strategies of survival that could emerge. And that
structure of society, in turn, has had a profound impact on the twen-

[51] George O. Roberts, *The Anguish of Third World Independence: The Sierra Leone Experience* (Washington, D.C.: University Press of America, 1982), p. 9.

tieth-century domestic politics and capabilities of the Sierra Leone state.

The dawn of independence in Sierra Leone brought the first clear signs of how the social structure that emerged over the previous century would deeply affect the capabilities and character of the new state. Prior to independence some efforts had been made toward a basis for postindependence unity. For example, a leading Creole activist, I.T.A. Wallace, organized the West African Youth League in 1938, aiming to bridge the gap between Creoles and the peoples of the protectorate. Wallace's efforts were part of a long line of efforts by the Creoles to civilize and educate provincial children.[52] By the date of Independence, however, these efforts had long since receded into dim memory, and the threat of Creole secession loomed as very real. Dr. Milton Margai, the first prime minister, began the process of shaping the state in response to this and other potentially destabilizing forces in society. He simply stacked the cabinet with a number of Creole leaders and promoted others into the highest ranks of the civil service. "In fact," noted Roberts, "the majority of civil service executives, such as heads of departments and Permanent Secretaries, were Creoles, as they continue to be, even today."[53]

Creole ascendancy brought institutional responses from those concerned about their inferior position. Chiefs in the former protectorate used tribal ties as a means of associating themselves and their constituencies in coalitions or blocs large enough to combat perceived domination by other groups, specifically the Creoles. They also used the tribe as a means to link their constituencies with a set of symbols that transcended the chiefs' narrow, seemingly vulnerable territorial control. Tribal boundaries, then, changed as a result of shifting circumstances—the ascendancy of one group or another, the movement of peoples into new territories—and the need for chiefs and constituencies to create or locate viable blocs in light of these circumstances.

Shortly after independence, the domination of the Mende induced further changes in coalitions and attempts by state leaders to influence the coalition making in their favor. Tribal tensions between Margai's Mende tribal group and the fearful Temnes portended ominous dif-

[52] Leo Spitzer, *The Creoles of Sierra Leone: Responses to Colonialism, 1870–1945* (Madison: University of Wisconsin Press, 1974), ch. 6.

[53] The role of the Creoles is a fascinating one that goes well beyond this study. On the Creoles see Spitzer, *The Creoles of Sierra Leone*; and Abner Cohen, *The Politics of Elite Culture: Explorations in the Dramaturgy of Power in a Modern African Society* (Berkeley: University of California Press, 1981). On Wallace, see Roberts, *The Anguish of Third World Independence*, p. 99.

ficulties for the new state. Milton Margai, even in the 1950s, had assiduously attempted to balance tribe and region. He coopted the support of chiefs by offering them protection against rivals, freedom from investigations of their practices, government loans, and more. As Clapham put it, the central government gained a fair degree of leverage, even though social control of the local population remained with the chiefs. Margai was adept at using the power of appointment as a prize to increase his leverage.

> The main such prize was the paramount chieftancy, but there were others too: chiefdom court chairmanships, location of chiefdom headquarters, boundary disputes between neighbouring chiefdoms, and the multitude of intra-chiefdom disputes that arose when two formerly separate chiefdoms were amalgamated. Such prizes, competed for between local factions, inevitably divided the area and inhibited the emergence of any ethic of local solidarity. This gave the centre considerable freedom of action in manipulating them—a form of politics at which Milton Margai was highly adept.[54]

The above quotation must be taken quite literally: Margai's freedom of action lay in appointments and manipulation, but beyond those he was severely restricted. He had to be quite cautious about tinkering with the system of chiefs or even about deposing individual chiefs. With social control of the population largely vested in the chiefs' organizations, Margai "bought" social stability and security of his own tenure by refusing to attack the prerogatives of the chiefs. His sole substantive reform of the system came shortly before independence when he created the role of court president, which took many judicial responsibilities from the chiefs. Otherwise, the array of rewards and sanctions in the hands of the chiefs to maintain their social control remained very impressive. Chiefs adapted to the circumstances that independence demanded of them to keep control. More than twice as many were literate at the time of independence, for example, than in the period immediately following World War II.

In addition, the chiefs learned how to use their roles as interlocuters between their constituents and the state to great advantage. A 1968 survey in Sierra Leone showed 42 percent of the respondents citing the Paramount Chief as the man who initiated local projects compared to 1 percent who cited the MP, and another 32 percent named the section chief or town chief. The chiefs gave their constituents, too, some sense of being involved with their destinies. In the same survey

---

[54] Clapham, "The Politics of Failure," p. 86.

seven of sixty-four farmers felt they had some chance to change an unjust national law, while fifty-one felt they had an opportunity to change an unjust chiefdom law.[55]

Milton Margai and his successors could attack the chiefs only at great risk since the mobilizational capabilities rested with these strongmen. They maintained effective social control although using state resources. As Cartwright noted, "The range of strategies open to a Sierra Leonean national leader in his dealings with the chiefs was severely circumscribed."[56] Margai's position depended on his skills of appointment and "buying" the proper support of chiefs. But others could play similar games; opposition figures courted chiefs from tribes where people felt slighted by Milton Margai. They also recruited those opposed to the chiefs' control, especially from the educated elite. By 1964 and Milton Margai's death, then, political competition for control of the state turned into little more than a series of factional disputes in which the upper hand sometimes was with one group of leaders courting chiefs and followers from one set of tribes, sometimes with another. Only a takeover by the military in 1967 brought a temporary halt to the factional conflicts for state control.

The crackdown by the military, itself dominated by Mende tribesmen, may have clamped down on capital city tribal competition, but it did not solve the basic dilemma facing any group or faction that gained state control. Nor did a second attempted military coup in 1971, led now by a Temne command, offer radical solutions. State control proved inadequate to undertake policies that could transform the lives of the vast majority of the population. Moreover, it was insufficient to mobilize a good portion of the population, which in turn could have provided a basis for far-reaching policy changes, because the continuing and persistent social control of the chiefs made them the conduit to the rural masses, even as their power in the capital city waxed and waned. Dr. Margai's "reliance on chiefs at the local level meant not upsetting them. Local government was left virtually unchanged between 1956 and his death in 1964, even though more than half the revenue still went on chiefs' emoluments and administrative costs."[57] The Sierra Leone People's Party (SLPP), the leader of the nationalist movement during the colonial period and the dominant political party at independence, had almost no independent organizational means to reach the population. It became dependent on the

[55] John R. Cartwright, *Political Leadership in Sierra Leone* (Toronto: University of Toronto Press, 1978), pp. 126 ff.

[56] Ibid., p. 132.

[57] Kup, *Sierra Leone*, p. 214.

chiefs during the colonial era and thus on the entire Native Administrations system.[58]

Dependence of the SLPP upon the chiefs moderated the nationalist movement in Sierra Leone. The party never became a "para-statal" alternative to colonial rule (to borrow a phrase from "Scipio"); that is, it did not provide services, either rewards or sanctions, such as loans, marketing crops, and police forces, frequently associated with states.[59] It developed a mediated relationship to the population, just as the British had. Party ties were through the chiefs, not with individuals.[60] Even in the urban areas, tribal associations adapted to the new setting, and the SLPP spread its influence in the towns through these tribal associations.

In short, the SLPP, attempting to establish a new set of dominant values and beliefs in the society by beginning with an ideology of nationalism, was different from those organizations that developed effective social control in the society, the chiefs. The chiefs, with their local circumscribed bases of power, both before and after independence tended to the needs and problems of the population and employed coercive methods. In Sierra Leone society, then, the chiefs had the mechanisms to demand the population's compliance and participation even if they could not gain widespread support and legitimacy. The state—colonial and later independent—could muster only the most limited sorts of mobilization of people and resources.

Formal independence did not suddenly give the state organization the institutional wherewithal to gain the population's compliance. The fragmented authority of the chiefs throughout the country continued to dominate the political landscape, although in a manner far less obvious to the naked eye than the factional disputes in Freetown. Kilson wrote several years after independence, "The Native Administrations continued to exist down through Sierra Leone's attainment of independence in 1961 and will be a part of the political landscape of Sierra Leone for some time to come."[61]

[58] Moreover, many of the nationalist party leaders were kin of prominent chiefs. This relationship is not surprising, since chiefs were garnering the resources to finance their sons' trips abroad and university educations—experiences that characterized the new elite. Right before Independence in 1961, as many as 35 percent of the SLPP's national officers were either sons, grandsons, or nephews of chiefs. See Kilson, *Political Change*, p. 232.

[59] Scipio, *Emergent Africa* (Boston: Houghton Mifflin, 1965), pp. 46–47, 55.

[60] See Kilson, *Political Change*, p. 264; and Christopher Clapham, *Liberia and Sierra Leone* (New York: Cambridge University Press, 1976), p. 121.

[61] Kilson, *Political Change*, p. 202.

THE STATE AND THE NEW ELITE

Certainly, there were tendencies in Sierra Leone counter to the creation of a society of fragments—each fragment with its own forms of social control, its own array of rules, rewards, sanctions, and symbols. Missionary education, for one, was a first step in creating the educated elite, whose interests and concerns transcended local boundaries. Edward Shils first called the members of such groups in postcolonial societies the intellectuals; I. L. Markovitz later referred to them in Africa as the "organizational bourgeoisie."[62] They have been the ones in Sierra Leone and elsewhere in the Third World who have manned industries, the army and police, and the growing bureaucracies; in short, they formed the new state and its organizational allies. Most had some Western education, and many went almost automatically into the civil service. The Creoles constituted a sizable proportion as did sons or nephews of chiefs. Their roles in the new state only added to their already significant advantages and privileges; no state exists that does not accrue for those in its upper reaches special status in the society.

In preindependence Africa, the ongoing sniping between this literate group and the seemingly archaic chiefs seemed the essence of native politics. And many observers believed that for all the British support for the chiefs the organizational bourgeoisie would triumph after independence while outmoded chiefdoms would simply fade away. The educated elite's success, many believed, would stem from its role in state administration and its unified stance. Markovitz called the organizational bourgeoisie "a combined ruling group,"[63] imputing to it a unity of purpose and organization wholly absent among the chiefs. The strongmen's alliances were circumscribed within a region or a tribe, but the organizational bourgeoisie's ties and interests were countrywide.

At first look, this elite has indeed triumphed. Since independence,

[62] Edward Shils, "The Intellectuals in the Political Development of the New States," *World Politics* 12 (April 1960): 329–68; Irving Leonard Markovitz, *Power and Class in Africa: An Introduction to Change and Conflict in African Politics* (Englewood Cliffs, N.J.: Prentice-Hall, 1977). There has been interesting literature developing on the question of a new class in Africa. See, for example, Ruth Berins Collier, *Regimes in Tropical Africa: Changing Forms of Supremacy, 1945–75* (Berkeley: University of California Press, 1982).

[63] Markovitz, *Power and Class in Africa*, p. 208. An expert on Southeast Asia makes similar claims of the solidarity of this literate group, especially those controlling the state. Benedict Anderson writes of the "transformation, step by step, of the colonial-state into the national-state, a transformation made possible not only by a solid continuity of established personnel but also by the established skein of journeys through which each state was experienced by its functionaries." Anderson, *Imagined Communities: Reflections on the Origin and Spread of Nationalism* (London: Verso, 1983), p. 105.

it has dominated capital city events and engaged the attention of Westerners. No one can doubt "the rising costs of maintaining political officialdom at ever higher levels of 'comfortable' living."[64] The state they rule in Sierra Leone, as those in other parts of Africa, has turned out to be quite a formidable organization. In sheer size and resources, it dwarfs any other formal organizations in society. "As a result of the pervasiveness of the role of the state in social and economic life, the majority of wage earners in most African countries, including Sierra Leone, are employed by government or parastatal organizations."[65]

Indeed, an academic debate has centered on the question of the "overdeveloped" postcolonial state.[66] In Sierra Leone, the state's prominence could be seen in its large bureaucracy and its increasingly authoritarian, coercive actions, especially after 1968 under President Siaka Stevens and his party, the All Peoples Congress (APC). As in many other states in tropical Africa, the postindependence democratic institutions were followed by "a period of political jockeying and institutional experimentation as political elites sought to establish various types of authoritarian regimes which would allow them to consolidate power and prolong their rule."[67]

It is no wonder, then, that control of the state has been a prize for which groups have competed fiercely. The dominant political fact in Sierra Leone, notes Riley, has been "the existence of a post-colonial state, which was extractive, coercive and significant both as a major employer and as an arena where factional conflict is articulated and power competition takes place."[68] In Africa and elsewhere, the simultaneous appearance of a powerful urban elite, some would even say a powerful "class"—the organizational bourgeoisie—and a so-called "overdeveloped" state seemed to determine the manipulation and distribution of social control for the foreseeable future.[69]

Nonetheless, there was something quite hollow for those who assumed the coveted offices in Sierra Leone after independence. As an

---

[64] Markovitz, *Power and Class in Africa*, p. 207.

[65] David Fashole Luke, *Labour and Parastatal Politics in Sierra Leone: A Study of African Working-Class Ambivalence* (New York: University Press of America, 1984), p. xv.

[66] Hamza Alavi, "The State in Post-Colonial Societies: Pakistan and Bangladesh," *New Left Review* 74 (July/August 1972): 59–81; and Colin Leys, "The 'Overdeveloped' Post Colonial State: A Re-evaluation," *The Review of African Political Economy* 5 (January–April 1976): 39–48.

[67] Collier, *Regimes in Tropical Africa*, p. 2.

[68] Stephen Riley, "Sierra Leone Politics: Some Recent Assessments," *Africa* 52 (1982): 106.

[69] Certainly, books such as Collier's *Regimes in Tropical Africa* made much of this wedding of class and state.

organization, the state did not live up to its advance billings. Social control, quite unexpectedly, has remained embedded in social organizations apart from the state. Urban elites including state officials, members of the organizational bourgeoisie, have found the solidarity of their so-called class weak and the power of state organs illusory. Politics has been neither the expression of state autonomy nor the dominance of a single class, but it has been a display of disparate acts of "accommodation and persuasion."[70] Appointments and manipulation, not social control and mobilization, remain the outer limits of state capabilities. The ability to enforce faithfully many types of social policy down to the level of the individual has persistently eluded those who have staffed state ministries. The military could bring "discipline" to politics as could subsequent single party rule by clamping down on factional strife and the open contest for control of the state. But armies and parties could not shift significantly the distribution of social control fragmented through the society. The rich diamond deposits in Sierra Leone could bring badly needed revenues, about half the export earnings now come from the major mining enclaves. But that could not substitute for the ability to regulate social behavior and mobilize the population.

The organization of society that emerged in the late nineteenth and early twentieth centuries, so deeply affected by the spreading world market and the machinations of the British state, has had a remarkably lasting impact. Those diffused fragments of society have stayed strong, even if they are far from centerstage. It is so tempting for researchers to give scant attention to the role these elements in the periphery have on power and politics; centerstage seems so dominating, so decisive in its own right. Note Thomas Cox's fixation on centerstage in his book on civil-military relations in Sierra Leone:

> In Freetown—as presumably in Lomé, Kigali, Bangui, and Contonou—some of the principal props of a coup d'état like the radio station and the presidential palace can be easily found within an area of a few square miles. Here too are the spacious homes belonging to government ministers, permanent secretaries, and high ranking army officers. Being restricted to such a limited physical area, civil-military relations are not unlike normal political relations involving civilian elites living in the capital.[71]

[70] Quoted in Riley, "Sierra Leone Politics," p. 107.

[71] Thomas S. Cox, *Civil-Military Relations in Sierra Leone: A Case Study of African Soldiers in Politics* (Cambridge, Mass.: Harvard University Press, 1976), p. 220.

I have tried to show that understanding where social control lies and what limits in capabilities state leaders face—the results, in part, of British colonial policies—can come only by looking far beyond center-stage at the relationships between the local population and the seemingly petty chiefs in far-flung urban slums, market towns, and villages. To be sure, no single chief can stand up to the strength of the state's leaders, but the sum total of all the chiefs' quiet control in remote parts of the country can have a crippling effect on state leaders' attempts to increase state capabilities. In Chapters 6 and 7, I will look at the relationship between fragmentation of social control and the capabilities and nature of the state much more closely. But here, in a preliminary fashion, I can say that the state has become a kind of great benefactor without the control or power one might think should stem from beneficence.

Drastic actions can be taken by the state, chiefs can be replaced, and certain policies can be pursued relentlessly. But such actions are risky because the state's mobilizational capacity is so limited. With effective social control in the hands of the chiefs, such drastic actions can be used only rarely or very selectively, usually in extreme situations. In everyday affairs, funds find their way into private hands—those of the chiefs or members of the new organizational bourgeoisie—and reinforce competing sets of rules, not those propounded by state institutions.[72] It is no wonder that recent titles of works on Sierra Leone are so downbeat—"The Politics of Failure" or "The Anguish of Independence."

Observers have placed the failures of Sierra Leone's state at the doorstep of its leaders. Roberts, for example, accused them of nepotism, cronyism, corruption, and arrogance.[73] There is no doubt all these have existed, in abundance, in Sierra Leone and elsewhere. In Chapters 6 and 7 I hope to complete the development of the theory of this book, explaining the strong connection between such traits in state leadership and fragmented social control. The theory will also explain the symbiotic relationship that has evolved out of the environment of conflict—a relationship in which presidents and chiefs have learned to accommodate one another. For the moment, I will simply note that corruption and arrogance are mere symptoms of a complex relationship between state leaders and local strongmen. Kup has summarized the situation for Sierra Leone:

[72] See Christopher Allen, "Sierra Leone," in John Dunn, ed., *West African States: Failure and Promise: A Study in Comparative Politics* (Cambridge: Cambridge University Press, 1978), pp. 196 ff.

[73] Roberts, *The Anguish of Third World Independence*, p. 103.

Politicians in Africa have proved fragile, even ephemeral, but chiefs have remained steadfast, watching, often unmoved, the rout of those they once voted for—and got their people to vote for. . . . No really satisfactory form of local government other than that involving chiefs has been found in Sierra Leone. Chiefs resent party offices in their towns, but in fact no party has as yet managed to establish anything even remotely resembling a grass-roots organization. . . . The president therefore needs the chiefs. They, too, need him.[74]

The continuing sway of chiefs, the political force of ethnicity and tribalism, are not simply artifacts of a distant past. British colonial policies, coupled with the dislocation caused by an expanding world economy, helped answer the question of who would reconstitute social control in Sierra Leone. Words such as tribe, party, and chief draw meaning today from the strategies of survival the people find most cogent. British rule went far in influencing which strategies would gain meaning in twentieth-century Africa.

COLONIALISM, SOCIAL FRAGMENTATION, AND WEAK STATES

An answer has begun to emerge to the central question posed in this book: How does one understand the varying capabilities of states? In particular, why have so many Third World states become organizations that no one in society can ignore—for example, the biggest employers or the conduit for huge revenues—while at the same time those states have failed to supply and authorize the rules dictating daily behavior in their societies? Our answer began in Chapter 1 with a heuristic device, a signpost of where and how to look for an explanation. All states have existed among a potpourri of other organizations in their societies. Where societies have been weblike and where social control has been fragmented among numerous organizations states have faced formidable barriers in seeing their policies through. Skillful state rulers, managerial prowess in the ministries, complex machinery and resources are in themselves insufficient bases for the state to make social policies that stick. An exclusive focus on these factors, on centerstage, without understanding other peripheral social organizations' influence on the state and its capabilities can be grossly mis-

---

[74] Kup, *Sierra Leone*, p. 221. A related point was made by Cartwright when he noted that even after the military took over "the chiefs still remained the principal channel of government communication to the villages." John R. Cartwright, *Politics in Sierra Leone 1947–67* (Toronto: University of Toronto Press, 1970), p. 255.

leading. Our signpost directs us to look beyond the capital city at how social control is actually distributed through the society.

Beyond models or heuristic devices, our answer points to why some societies have had fragmented social control and others have .not. Deep social dislocations that undermined people's existing strategies of survival universally preceded the emergence of states after the fifteenth century. Indeed, they are a precondition for the creation of strong states. In Europe, the catastrophes of the fourteenth century, reinforced by the crises of the first half of the seventeenth century, subverted the strategies of feudalism. For most societies in Asia, Africa, and Latin America, the destruction of old strategies came in the wake of the tremendous pressures extended by the European-dominated world system, as we saw in Chapter 2. Especially after 1850, rapid European and U.S. industrialization drove an expansion of the world economy, led by key policies of hegemonic states. In both Europe and outside, the result was similar: a rapid deterioration of existing bases of social control and strategies of survival.

The destruction of old strategies, whether in Europe or elsewhere, did not determine what new ones would replace them. Again, forces from the world system affected mightily all sorts of societies in their reconstitution of social control and viable strategies of survival. For a number of European societies, for example, the threats posed by neighboring political units in the emerging system of states induced leaders to take major steps and risks to mobilize populations and their resources directly, if only to guard the leaders' personal and political survival. To gain direct access to the population's manpower and revenues, princes initiated pitched battles against those who sought to maintain social control in a fragment of society. They built armies, police forces, revenue-collecting agencies, and courts to gain central control in the territory by a single state organization. The ability of the prince to organize such agencies was important, as was the existence of sufficient, talented, and loyal manpower to staff such agencies. The question of loyalty was paramount, for it implied people sufficiently dissociated from the old organizational bases of society to see their personal lot depending foremost on the success of the prince's grand scheme. In parts of Europe, such manpower developed in the free cities of late medieval Europe.

For African, Asian, and Latin American societies the reconstitution of social control took place in the context of a world with already existing, simply overpowering states. In the context of the severe dislocation caused by the spreading world market in the late nineteenth century coupled with a global environment of already-present strong states, only Japan among the non-European societies emerged at that juncture with its own strong, centralized state. For societies such as Sierra Leone, colonial rulers used their advantage in power to direct resources and authority and to enforce sanctions in ways that deeply affected how indigenous forces reconstituted social control. They gave scattered strongmen the wherewithal to build their social control in fragments of the society.

The British imperial officials rejected other possible paths. For example, they considered far too extravagant building a colonial state strong enough to either bypass indigenous forces altogether or absorb them into a single system of rules. They also offered little more than the back of their hands to the growing corps of cosmopolitan, literate indigenous elites concentrated mainly in urban centers. These were precisely the people who possibly could have provided the manpower for creating agencies to consolidate social control in the society.

In any case, the fragmentation of social control—the heterogeneity of rule making in society—greatly restricted the growth of state capabilities after independence. Even with all the resources at their disposal, even with the ability to eliminate any single strongman, state leaders found themselves severely limited. Any serious campaign to increase their capabilities—to penetrate, regulate social relations, appropriate resources, extract more from their societies—would necessarily undercut the prerogatives and bases of social control of the strongmen. Many state leaders realized that their tenure depended on the social stability the strongmen could offer through their social control; the strongmen had direct access to most of the population, and they could mobilize people for specific purposes. The paradox, which we will later delve into more deeply, is: while the strongmen have become evermore dependent on state resources to shore up their social control, state leaders have become dependent on strongmen, who employ those resources in a manner inimical to state rules and laws. In short, then, our preliminary answer to why some Third World states have been at such pains to increase capabilities is that colonial rule helped induce a fragmentation of social control, an environment of conflict, during that historical window of opportunity when the population sought new strategies of survival.

CHAPTER FOUR

Laying the Basis for a Strong State: The British and Zionists in Palestine

VARIATION IN THE RECREATION OF SOCIAL CONTROL

The recreation of social control following the tremendous expansion of the world market and of European state power starting in the mid-nineteenth century took on different hues in various societies of Asia, Africa, and Latin America. Centralized control of Zionists in Palestine, as we shall see, contrasted sharply with the fragmentation in Sierra Leone. Fragmentation of social control and the eventual creation of an extremely weak state were not *necessary* outcomes of colonialism, even in already heterogeneous societies. Direct colonial rule, such as that of French or Portuguese colonialism, channeled resources some-what differently from British techniques, leading to different distri-butions or amounts of social control in the indigenous societies. Even within the British empire, the type of rule varied considerably with wildly different results.

Although Sierra Leone may be a prototype for many former British colonies, all former colonies have by no means shared its experiences of continuing fragmentation of social control. Different types of col-laboration yielded varying results. States of different strengths do ex-ist, even some emerging from British *imperium*, and some are much stronger with respect to their populations than that of Sierra Leone. If the analysis offered in the last chapter on Sierra Leone is on target, these variations in strength should be explicable, in no small measure, by differences in outside influence on the organization of society dur-ing that historic window of opportunity when so many societies' old strategies of survival failed.

In India, for example, British actions had a much more contradic-tory effect than in Sierra Leone, sometimes tending toward fragmen-tation and other times toward consolidated control. Creation of the vaunted Indian Civil Service led the list of actions that spurred the creation of an all-Indian, unified elite. Civil servants, as Rothermund indicated, were in a position to act as "umpires" for a unified set of rules.[1] British influence in establishing a cohesive Indian army and a

[1] Dietmar Rothermund, "The Legacy of the British-Indian Empire in Independent

new legal system (with the proliferation of Indian career officers, as well as lawyers and judges, respectively) also created strong institutional and human bases for a formidable state after independence. The new educational system did much the same. At the same time, the diversion of British authority and resources first to various *rajas, zamindars*, and other lords and later to rich peasants recreated a foundation for numerous strongmen to exercize fragmented social control throughout the country. Much of the essence of Indian state-society relations since 1947 has been the accommodation and struggle between a state with significant mobilizational capacity, compared to Sierra Leone, and the rich peasantry with its tenacious hold over aspects of rural life.[2]

The Israeli state offers a case at the opposite end of the spectrum from Sierra Leone's, a case in which strongmen with fragmented social control did not at all become a major part of the state-society relations. Israeli society—even only the Jewish portion of Israeli society—was extremely heterogeneous. Yet, the state's ability through social policies to change its population's daily habits and to preempt and delegitimize contending social organizations from exercising autonomous social control has placed it among a handful of new strong states.

Background to Creation of Jewish Society in Palestine

The world system's forces that so drastically changed the face of Palestine in the twentieth century first took root far from that country. The Jews of Europe, especially Eastern Europe, faced head-on the unsettling political and economic winds that buffeted the European continent throughout the nineteenth century. New symbols, which cemented the revised strategies of survival among the peoples of Europe, left the Jews open to grave dangers. The latter part of the nineteenth century witnessed rapid growth in the importance of these symbols, particularly those contained in new aggressive nationalist ideologies, which effectively excluded the Jews. The strategies of the Gentiles now put the differentness of the Jews in a new light. In Rumania, to take one example, "Jews *as such* were denied citizenship even where their families had lived in the Principalities for centuries."[3] Vital

India," in Wolfgang J. Mommsen and Jürgen Osterhammel, eds., *Imperialism and After: Continuities and Discontinuities* (London: Allen and Unwin, 1986), p. 141.

[2] See, for example, Akhil Gupta, "Technology, Power and the State in a Complex Agricultural Society: The Green Revolution in a North Indian Village" (Ph.D. diss., Stanford University, 1987).

[3] David Vital, *The Origins of Zionism* (Oxford: Clarendon Press, 1975), p. 89.

quoted a Rumanian court decision of 1877, which stated that "the Jews do not have a country of their own and therefore do not belong to any state."[4]

The growth of a world economy based in Europe and the consolidation of new states on that continent upset the Jews' bases of social control and existing strategies of survival as much as any group's. What became known as the "Jewish problem" was the combination of this dislocation with the exclusion of the Jews from participation in the new strategies that took hold in the countries of Europe. Jews faced growing anti-Semitic sentiments, open attacks, and hostile state policies at the very moment in their history when many of them considered the elements of their old strategies of survival—adherence to rabbinic codes, communal organization, alliances with princes, and more—irrelevant to their new needs.

Jews responded to the Jewish problem with a tremendous burst of creativity in at least four sorts of solutions. They tried, where possible, assimilating into Christian European societies, assuming the mores and habits of their non-Jewish neighbors with unbridled enthusiasm. Second, they created new Jewish institutions, such as Reform temples, which could change Jews sufficiently to fit into new European societies, without losing their identity as Jews. Third, they left Europe in massive numbers, mainly for the United States but also for many other countries. Finally, they proposed radical transformations of society— either general society or Jewish society or both—to eliminate altogether the bases for the Jewish problem. Anarchists, Communists, Socialists, Bundists, and others set out the schematic contours of future societies in which the underpinnings for any sort of Jewish problem would be entirely absent; they participated in movements and organizations, heavily populated by Jews, to work toward their goals.

Zionism was one such proposal to transform society radically. Its creators, led by the stately Viennese Jew, Theodor Herzl, envisioned a social transformation in which Jews no longer would occupy selected, vulnerable niches in other societies. Instead, they would fill the whole range of "normal" social roles in their own Jewish society located in their own territory. Herzl wrote:

We have sincerely tried everywhere to merge with the national communities in which we live, seeking only to preserve the faith of our fathers. It is not permitted us. In vain we are loyal patriots, sometimes superloyal; in vain do we make the same sacrifices of life and property as our fellow citizens; in vain do we strive to enhance the

[4] Quoted in ibid., p. 90.

fame of our native lands in the arts and sciences or their wealth by trade and commerce. In our native lands where we have lived for centuries we are still decried as aliens, often by men whose ancestors had not yet come at a time when Jewish sighs had long been heard in the country. The majority decide who the "alien" is; this, and all else in the relations between peoples, is a matter of power.[5]

After some arguing within Herzl's movement, by the early twentieth century the Zionists agreed that the territory of the Jews would be Eretz Israel, Palestine. No other place had the symbolic overtones for the socially dislocated Jews, whom the Zionists so desperately sought to recruit to their cause. In addition, Palestine had always maintained a Jewish population, and after the 1880s the settlement grew fairly quickly. Its numbers swelled from about 23,000 in 1881 to 85,000 by the outbreak of World War I; however, this was still considerably less than 20 percent of the country's total population. Probably close to 100,000 Jews immigrated to Palestine in those years, but more than half left shortly after their arrival in that desolate Asian outpost.

Zionism certainly did not yet offer sufficient components for strategies of survival for a society of Jews in Palestine. By 1914, it did little more than propose a set of symbols—or more accurately, a number of competing sets of symbols from its various factions—which could eventually be incorporated into such strategies. Zionist organizations lacked the rewards and sanctions those symbols could tie together and provide the material base for effective strategies of survival. Jewish society, growing alongside the more established Muslim and Christian Arab society in Turkish-ruled Palestine, was still very much in the making. What sorts of social control would be created at this historical moment when Jews were migrating into the country seeking viable strategies of survival was an open question.

Jewish experience in reconstituting social control in Palestine was clearly an exceptional case. After all, the demise of their old strategies included transplantation to a faraway land. Such migration, however, has many analytic similarities to the spread of the world market in the late nineteenth century. Migration, as I shall discuss in Chapter 8, is one of the most powerful means of shattering old forms of social control. Together with the effects of the new world economy on the Jews as well as the aggressive nationalism in Eastern Europe, migration had a severely dislocating impact on Jewish society. Breaking old patterns of social control among Jews was not terribly different from destroying existing forms of social control among other societies.

[5] Theodor Herzl, *The Jewish State* (New York: Herzl Press, 1970), p. 110.

Other aspects of the Jewish case were also exceptional. Most of the original Jewish settlers, for example, were from Europe, not the Third World. Jewish society in Palestine, the *Yishuv*, grew in a bicommunal setting in the midst of established Arab society, and the two were deeply divided. Also, among many new Jewish settlers, there were both high motivation to achieve a unified political entity and deep commitment to certain shared symbols derived from Jewish history and religion. In these and other important ways, the Yishuv was a singular experience.

Nonetheless, it has been argued quite convincingly, both generally and in the particular instance of the Yishuv, that the exceptional case can shed light on the general phenomenon.[6] In the matter of the reconstitution of social control in the wake of socially dislocating forces, the Yishuv and later Israeli society provide some stark lessons about the impact of outside forces on this process and the ultimate creation of a strong state. Dan Horowitz, who felt the Yishuv could be very instructive in understanding some general issues of social change, posed the question before us in this way: "Despite these cultural and ideological splits and despite the great potential for conflict embodied in them, how did the 'centripetal' propensities in the Yishuv overcome the 'centrifugal' propensities; for the history of the Yishuv during the Mandate can be portrayed as an almost continuous process of growth, integration, and deepening of communal autonomy."[7] The battle between centripetal and centrifugal forces, as I shall elaborate more fully in Chapter 6, lies at the heart of the political process throughout the Third World. Israel's experience in how these forces confronted each other is illuminating for understanding other countries whose histories have differed considerably in other ways from those of Israel.

THE BRITISH PROPOSE A JEWISH AGENCY

The Ottoman Empire's defeat in World War I and the British succession to power in some of the Ottomans' former Middle Eastern provinces sent shockwaves through the local populations, especially in Palestine. For Palestinian Arabs, the new status of Palestine as a united country, separate from the rest of the Arab and Muslim world and ruled by an alien Christian power, raised an even further level of anx-

---

[6] On the general methodological issue, see Arend Lijphart, "Comparative Politics and the Comparative Method," *American Political Science Review* 65 (September 1971): 682–93; on the specific case, see Dan Horowitz, "The Yishuv and Israeli Society—Continuity and Change," *Medina U'Mimshal* (1983): 31–67 (text in Hebrew; title translated).

[7] Ibid., p. 46 (my translation).

iety many felt due to the emerging threat of Zionism.[8] Jews in the country faced seemingly more sanguine prospects, a ruling power committed to promoting in Palestine the establishment of a Jewish national home where the Zionists could realize their dream of an autonomous Jewish society.

Even before the British marched into Palestine in 1918, their Secretary of State for Foreign Affairs Balfour wrote to Lord Rothschild, on November 2, 1917, that "His Majesty's Government view with favour the establishment in Palestine of a national home for the Jewish people, and will use their best endeavors to facilitate the achievement of this object." This simple statement turned the Middle East topsy-turvy: Jews rejoiced; Arabs have mourned and demonstrated each November 2, until this very day. The Balfour Declaration became a cornerstone for the subsequent establishment of British rule in Palestine.[9] In fact, the preamble to the Mandate for Palestine, approved by the Council of the League of Nations, stated that the Allies "agreed that the Mandatory should be responsible for putting into effect the declaration originally made on November 2nd, 1917."

The new system of mandates resembled colonialism because it involved the direct appropriation of the highest formal decision-making posts in the society by the outside power. Unlike the building of empires in Africa, however, the new mandates were not intended to establish the hegemonic power's rule into the indefinite future. Article 22 of the Covenant of the League of Nations recognized explicitly the temporary and provisional character of all mandates. The antiimperial legacy of World War I, in fact, initiated a half-century of what has been called "imperial sunset."[10] The mandatory powers sought ways to build local forces that could secure their interest in the region without a permanent colonial presence.

In Palestine, the mandate was unusually specific about the need for the ruling British to share power with local Jewish forces: "Article 4. An appropriate Jewish Agency shall be recognized as a public body for the purpose of advising and cooperating with the Administration

---

[8] See Joel S. Migdal, *Palestinian Society and Politics* (Princeton, N.J.: Princeton University Press, 1980).

[9] For the events leading up to the Balfour Declaration and the immediate reaction to it, see Leonard Stein, *The Balfour Declaration* (London: Vallentine, Mitchell, 1961). On British motivations in issuing the declaration, see Esco Foundation for Palestine, *Palestine*, vol. 1 (New Haven: Yale University Press, 1947), pp. 114–18. Also, see Ronald Sanders, *The High Walls of Jerusalem: A History of the Balfour Declaration and the Birth of the British Mandate for Palestine* (New York: Holt, Rinehart and Winston, 1983).

[10] Max Beloff, "Britain's Liberal Empire 1897–1921," vol. 1 in *Imperial Sunset* (London: Methuen, 1969).

of Palestine in such economic, social and other matters as may affect the establishment of the Jewish National Home and the interests of the Jewish population in Palestine."[11]

The British decision in the early 1920s to encourage the creation of a Jewish Agency, with an active role in the economic and social affairs of the Yishuv, was a critical element in shaping the nature of Jewish society and the entire future of Palestine. It also had much greater repercussions than the British foresaw or with which they could cope. When the British attempted to include the Arabs of Palestine as local forces participating in ruling, they found the Arabs simply unwilling to accept power sharing based on the premises of the Balfour Declaration. In fact, Arab leaders rejected any official participation in the administration of the mandate, including the option of an "Arab Agency" alongside the Jewish Agency, because it included the Balfour Declaration with its promise of a national home in Palestine for the Jews. Britain's inability from the start to reconcile the growing animus between Arabs and Jews—so painfully obvious with the first outbreak of anti-Jewish Arab rioting in April 1920—led the British officials to conclude that a unified political framework in Palestine was unattainable. Although they continued to speak officially about the goal of unity through the 1930s, they basically lost hope in such a framework by the early 1920s.

For the British, this realization constituted a profound disappointment. From the strategic view of London-based Foreign Office civil servants, control of Palestine and other parts of the fertile crescent had been extremely important at the end of World War I. It gave the British unimpeded access to the northern overland route to the Persian Gulf and from there to India, in addition to their control of the southern waterway route to the Indian Ocean through the Suez Canal. Fear of spreading Bolshevism magnified Foreign Office concerns at the end of World War I. Alarm over the possibility of a Turco-Bolshevik threat to India through the Middle East only increased the strategic value the British placed on the region and their hold on Palestine.[12]

[11] Zionist leader Chaim Weizmann presented the idea of an agency to the Council of Ten at Paris during the peace conference in 1919. He spoke of a Jewish council or agency—representative of Jewish Palestine and world Jewry. His ideas echoed other Zionist proposals asking for a maximum degree of self-government for the Jews. See *Palestine*, vol. 1, pp. 156–64.

[12] Aaron S. Klieman, *Foundations of British Policy in the Arab World* (Baltimore: Johns Hopkins University Press, 1970), p. 25. One British document, written during the mandatory period, described the strategic value as follows: "Palestine is the bridge connecting

Prior to actually setting foot in Palestine, they had believed that a unified mandatory state working toward a Jewish national home and protecting the rights of the Arabs could provide a British strategic presence in Palestine. Through power sharing they felt they could avoid the high costs of governing the territory directly. The arrangement could also lead to a stable regime even after a formal end to the mandate, ensuring British interests. These hopes evaporated quickly after the implementation of the mandate. As early as 1920, former Foreign Secretary Balfour, who after all had authored the very document that had fired Jewish hopes, spoke of Palestine as "no great catch."[13] In 1922, debates were held in parliament on the question of abandoning the mandate altogether.[14] With the growing tension between Arabs and Jews in the 1920s and 1930s, the Foreign Office became less and less convinced of the strategic importance of Palestine and of the viability of an autonomous Jewish national home.[15]

Left with the responsibility of actually governing the territory and realizing there would be no reconciliation of Jews and Arabs within a unified mandatory state, Colonial Office civil servants sought some new political framework. Many powers in the territory, they concluded in the early 1920s, should be devolved to separate communal institutions of those Arabs and Jews, although some functions such as security and public works stayed within the mandatory state.[16] The implications for the reconstitution of social control among the local forces in Palestine were profound. Even though some of these implications, such as the growing British penchant to play Arabs and Jews off one another in classic divide-and-rule form, were ominous, there were also clear advantages to be gained.

For the Jews, the benefits reaped from the distribution of British resources did not stem from warm personal ties to mandatory officials.

Africa and Asia, part of the only practicable corridor between the Nile and the Euphrates. It is in a similar relation to the Suez Canal on the one side as is Egypt on the other, for it affords the possibility of defence against land attack upon the Canal from the North." Royal Institute of International Affairs, *Political and Strategic Interests of the United Kingdom* (London: Oxford University Press, 1939), p. 142.

[13] Quoted in Elizabeth Monroe, *Britain's Moment in the Middle East 1914–1956* (London: Chatto and Windus, 1963), p. 79. Balfour himself, nonetheless, never relinquished his belief in the Jewish national home.

[14] See Norman Bentwich, *England in Palestine* (London: Kegan Paul, 1932), p. 82. Bentwich, a Zionist sympathizer, was British attorney general of Palestine in the 1920s.

[15] See Michael J. Cohen, *Palestine: Retreat from the Mandate* (New York: Holmes and Meier, 1978).

[16] Bernard Wasserstein, *The British in Palestine: The Mandatory Government and the Arab-Jewish Conflict 1917–1929* (London: Royal Historical Society, 1978), p. 16.

In fact, Jewish leaders' relations with these civil servants ranged from outright antagonism, as in the case of the military administration in 1919, to strong suspicions and recurring tensions, as in the case of High Commissioner Herbert Samuel's regime from 1920 to 1925. The British habit of periodically restricting Jewish immigration and land buying in order to deal with Arab sensibilities and violent outbursts undermined for the entire mandate period the basis for a harmonious collaboration between British officials and Jewish representatives. Jews claimed such restrictions constituted a retreat from the promises in the Balfour Declaration and the mandate itself. However, it is important to stress that, although the collaboration between the British and the Jews was not harmonious, it was still collaboration.

The benefits the Jews reaped came from the authority the British allowed them in spite of, perhaps even partly because of, the existing tensions and antagonisms. Bernard Wasserstein wrote:

> Towards the Jewish National Home in Palestine Samuel pursued a deliberately passive policy: the task of the Government of Palestine in relation to Zionism was merely to create the conditions, political, legal, and (to a lesser extent) economic, necessary for the Zionists themselves to carry on their work; the government would facilitate rather than encourage or direct Jewish immigration and settlement. This had the advantage for the government of precluding the diversion of state revenue to investment in Zionist development.[17]

British despair of creating a viable unified political framework for Palestine worked to the Zionists' advantage, allowing them to create a basis for an autonomous Jewish community with relatively consolidated social control. Even British restrictions, such as those on immigration, assisted the central Zionist leadership to a degree when it controlled the distribution of the limited numbers of certificates for immigration. For the Arabs, the effect of British rule was precisely the opposite. By refusing on principle to collaborate with the mandatory power, the Arabs lost the opportunity to use British authority and resources to succor fledgling, countrywide Arab institutions. Arab-British collaboration existed, to be sure; no colonial rule was possible without it. Its bases, however, were personal (Arabs, for example, who worked as policemen, magistrates, or clerks) or local organizational (for example, village councils, which established official relations with the mandatory power). This sort of collaboration limited the amount

---

[17] Ibid., p. 87.

of resources and authority the British supplied to the Arab population and directed that limited quantity to reinforce fragmented control.[18]

In short, the resources the British proffered were not so much material as the authority to undertake tasks, which in Europe would normally have been performed by state agencies. Arabs intent on building national power hardly benefited from the offers of British authority because they refused to deal officially with the mandate that included the Balfour Declaration. For the Zionists, British policy contained disadvantages, mostly concerning their shortage of capital, but it also held great potential. The Zionists' assumption of statelike tasks was, at least in part, a sign of their slackening confidence in the mandatory government, but in the end it gave them the foundation to establish consolidated social control in the country. We will look at how the Jews seized the opportunity presented by the particular way the British chose to collaborate and offer resources. For the moment, we must still answer the question of which Jews benefited. Who were those who collaborated with the British, thereby garnering the resources essential for the establishment of effective social control?

THE STRUGGLE AMONG THE JEWS

Britain's proposal to recognize "an appropriate Jewish Agency" focused the struggles among the Jews to create social control in the Yishuv. The Jewish Agency, by the very latitude the British were willing to allow it, was to become the centerpiece of all Jewish communal institutions. The struggles to control it molded the character and capabilities of Jewish political organization, including the ability to resist British designs after 1939, when Zionist leaders felt the British had finally annuled the legitimacy of the mandate. This agency that the mandate singled out as the basis for British-Jewish collaboration, was the forerunner of a strong Jewish state, the state of Israel.

Article 4 of the Mandate for Palestine, had obliquely answered who would lead the Jewish Agency: "The Zionist organisation, so long as its organisation and constitution are in the opinion of the Mandatory appropriate, shall be recognized as such agency." The explicit recognition of the World Zionist Organization (wzo) in the mandate gave that organization the League of Nations's stamp of approval, enhancing its claims among Jews as the proper representative body to solve the Jewish problem. Article 4 took cognizance of two sorts of Jews. It

---

[18] Joel S. Migdal, "Urbanization and Political Change: The Impact of Foreign Rule," *Comparative Studies in Society and History* 19 (July 1977): 328–49.

spoke of both the Jewish population in Palestine (the Yishuv) and, implicitly, of the larger worldwide Jewish population for whom the Jewish national home would be a refuge. As it turned out, both Jews of the Yishuv and Jewish leaders from abroad constituted part of the struggle for dominance. Numerous groups and coalitions formed among Jews in Palestine and in the Diaspora in order to gain control of the Jewish Agency. They were led by some of the great names of Jewish life of that time: Louis Brandeis, Nahum Goldmann, Vladimir Jabotinsky, and others. The two coalitions led by Chaim Weizmann and David Ben-Gurion stood out. Their strategies differed markedly, although there was also close cooperation between the two coalitions at many important junctures. We can label Weizmann's tactics, the external strategy, and Ben-Gurion's, the internal strategy.[19]

Weizmann's External Strategy: Building a Global Consensus

In some ways, the very constitution in 1929, at long last, of a Jewish Agency, broadly accepted by Zionist and non-Zionist Jews, by Palestinian and Diaspora Jews alike, was the personal achievement of Weizmann. In 1904, he had immigrated to England at age thirty from Eastern Europe. Later, as a well-known scientist and Zionist, he had cajoled the British into issuing the Balfour Declaration, catapulting him to the head of the Zionist movement. His eyes were most often turned toward the international movers and doers of his age—the Lloyd Georges, Arthur Balfours, and Jews of great wealth and influence. His strategy involved endless statesmanship of cultivating British politicians and influential non-Zionist Jews in Europe and North America. Through his tireless negotiations, he laid the basis for his leadership of an autonomous Jewish community in Palestine, directed by a broadly-based Jewish Agency.

Even before the mandate was officially in place, while the British military still ruled Palestine through its administration, the Weizmann-dominated wzo urged the British to allow it to form a quasi-government in the territory of Palestine. As early as December 1918, the very month in which the British assumed actual rule in Palestine, these Jews had produced an "Outline for the Provisional Government of Palestine." In some ways, the British had encouraged such initiative. They had sent the Zionist Commission, what Wasserstein called the embryo of the future government of Israel, to Palestine in March 1918.[20] With Weizmann at its helm, the commission, consisting of Jews

---

[19] What I call in shorthand the Ben-Gurion strategy was, in fact, the product of a number of outstanding labor Zionist leaders in the Yishuv, including Yitzhak Ben-Zvi, Berl Katznelson, and Chaim Arlosoroff.

[20] Wasserstein, *The British in Palestine*, p. 24.

from several countries, was to carry out steps to help establish the national home and act as an interlocutor between British authorities and the Yishuv. The commission, however, went even further; it proposed that it would have to agree beforehand to every implementation of policy, a suggestion not received kindly by the British military administrators. And, throughout the 1920s, while Weizmann kept up his continuous dialogue with the British urging full implementation of the Balfour Declaration, he also hammered out the compromises necessary to win support from non-Zionist Jews for the entire Jewish enterprise in Palestine and especially the proposed role of the Jewish Agency.

The Zionist Commission was indeed the kernel of a future autonomous Jewish community. Weizmann took personal charge of it in 1918, but his interests were much wider than the commission's principal concern with day-to-day affairs in Palestine. By the time the commission had instituted departments to deal with education, technical matters, and agriculture and settlement in the Yishuv, Weizmann had handed over its leadership to others in order to pursue his global lobbying. His style was simply not attuned to the nuances of building strategies of survival and mobilizational capabilities in the Yishuv; his principal interests were not in using selectively the resources funneled through the Zionist Commission as a base for his social control in Palestine. This sort of organizational work held little attraction for him; rather, his passion was achieving compromises in principle and languages in order to reach a broad consensus among world Jewish leaders. His time was spent shuttling among them. Weizmann wrote:

> During all those years I spent the bulk of my time traveling, sometimes accompanied by my wife, sometimes alone. . . . I was actually at home only for short intervals between trips to America, Palestine, Germany, France, Holland and Belgium, not to speak of my attendance at various international conferences. I was trying to build up the movement, making contacts with governments and Jewish communities, and in the process acquiring a good many friendships in political, literary and scientific circles in different countries. I came to feel almost equally at home in Brussels or Paris or San Francisco.[21]

Weizmann, as president of the wzo, worked relentlessly through the 1920s to create an extended Jewish Agency. He beat off opposition from American Zionists, led by Brandeis, and from East European factions. Weizmann then forged alliances with non-Zionist Jewish

---

[21] Chaim Weizmann, *Trial and Error* (London: Hamish Hamilton, 1949), p. 407.

groups, which could supply badly needed capital and technical expertise in building the national home, and with Zionists, who would supply the ideological motivation behind the drive for sovereignty. His initiative led to the establishment of a basic fund, Keren Hayesod, which could attract the money of Jews personally unwilling to join the World Zionist Organization. In 1923, the congress of the wzo gave Weizmann the authorization to implement his plan for the extended Jewish Agency. It then took him six years to cultivate the non-Zionist leaders in the United States, Britain, and elsewhere and to work out the minute details in constituting it.

Ben-Gurion's Internal Strategy: Building Social Control in the Yishuv

Ben-Gurion's internal strategy for dominance of the Jewish Agency contrasted with Weizmann's external strategy. In the first few years after the British put forth the idea of the Jewish Agency, Ben Gurion and other socialists were heavily dependent on wzo capital for their activities in Palestine.[22] Very few of their enterprises were even close to being self-supporting. Ironically, Weizmann's defeat of Brandeis, who had demanded that the wzo devote funds on a businesslike basis only to profitable investments in Palestine, ensured an open tap to the enterprises initiated by Ben-Gurion and his colleagues. They undertook those enterprises for a number of reasons, most of which had little to do with sound economic criteria. The financial dependence came even as the labor parties could muster only about 20 percent of the vote for delegates of the wzo during the 1920s. They wielded very little influence in that organization.

Ben-Gurion's tactics for dealing with these financial and political weaknesses at first may seem a bit odd. Instead of spending his time on international lobbying, he focused his efforts principally on building the labor parties in Palestine and expanding their scope of control in the Yishuv itself. Peter Medding wrote: "From the very beginning of the resettlement in Palestine, these parties, in keeping with their all-encompassing ideological view of life, sought to cater to the needs and interests of their members in many spheres. They produced separate journals and organized separate labour exchanges, soup kitchens, loan funds, cultural activities and agricultural collectives."[23]

At first, the parties had competed among themselves to offer the components for viable strategies of survival for the tens of thousands

[22] Yonathan Shapiro, *The Formative Years of the Israeli Labour Party* (Beverly Hills: Sage, 1976), p. 74.

[23] Peter Y. Medding, *Mapai in Israel* (Cambridge: Cambridge University Press, 1972), p. 9.

of Jewish workers in Palestine, but the competition prior to the 1920s had involved small stakes, since the parties had so few material resources with which people could construct meaningful strategies. The only part of a strategy of survival the parties offered in abundance was symbols, and under such circumstances factions had developed over fine shadings of ideological meaning. All parties in Palestine prior to 1920 had been fairly unstable entities, with party membership and lists changing from year to year. The labor parties had been ahead of others in the beginnings of the development of a stable party leadership, but they, too, were more centers of hot rhetoric than much else.

Conditions did not change immediately after the British takeover. The military administrators, in the fine tradition of colonial rulers, did little that might enhance the creation of a consolidated Jewish leadership. They opposed London's policy of promoting a Jewish national home and refused, therefore, to promote the idea. By the 1920s, when the civilian administration had assumed power and High Commissioner Herbert Samuel's civilian regime had failed to create the basis of a unified political framework for Jews and Arabs, British rulers allowed the Jews an assertive role in taking on functions of public service themselves. It was to this British sufferance that Ben-Gurion and his party, Achdut Haavoda, addressed themselves.

The Achdut Haavoda party (forerunner of Mapai and later the Israel Labor Party), formed in 1918–1919, finally achieved preeminence among all the competing parties. It became the dominant indigenous Palestinian element in the incipient Jewish state. Even though its ideology was not widely accepted within the Jewish society in Palestine during that crucial decade following World War I, it triumphed in Palestine because of its brilliant use of the resources and opportunities offered by both the British and the wzo. The party offered the components for workable strategies of survival for many of the small but growing Yishuv population in the 1920s and 1930s by concentrating on two internal spheres.

The first, and far less important, was a representative political structure for the Yishuv alone, autonomous of the worldwide representative political structure embodied in the wzo. Without British opposition, Yishuv leaders established a set of national institutions referred to as Knesset Israel.[24] The first elected assembly of the Yishuv was constituted in 1920, with almost 80 percent of the eligible electorate voting. Despite some splintering on a religious and communal basis

[24] See Dan Horowitz and Moshe Lissak, *Origins of the Israeli Polity* (Chicago: University of Chicago Press, 1978), pp. 42 ff.

within the Palestinian Jewish community, Knesset Israel made strides in bringing the Yishuv's political life under a single umbrella. The Achdut Haavoda party was at the center of this process, as the largest party in the assembly, and came to hold the key positions in Knesset Israel's working arm, the National Council (*Vaad Leumi*). The mandatory government aided greatly by granting legal recognition to Knesset Israel based on the Religious Communities Ordinance of 1926.

Yishuv leaders, particularly those in the secular socialist parties led by Achdut Haavoda, bridled at the British conception of Jewish society as primarily religious (as the 1926 ordinance implied). They viewed the Yishuv as a *national* political community. Also, they resented the British policies of allowing individuals to withdraw from Knesset Israel's registry and of recognizing separatist groups, such as sections of the Jewish orthodox community, as autonomous religious communities. Nonetheless, legal recognition of Knesset Israel constituted an important step in Ben-Gurion's campaign to achieve increased autonomy for the Yishuv through his party's leadership.

Still missing were the material resources upon which people would build strategies of survival, so important because the Palestinian economy was so poor. A small part of this problem was solved in the 1930s when the British allowed Yishuv authorities and local community councils to collect their own taxes. But for the most part, Knesset Israel and its National Council were sideshows in the 1920s because they contributed so little revenue to the enterprises that constituted the backbone of Achdut Haavoda's efforts to create viable strategies of survival. The inducement to control the Jewish Agency with its connection to wealthy Diaspora Jews, then, was quite high.

Besides the comprehensive Yishuv political structure of Knesset Israel, the other internal sphere upon which Ben-Gurion and Achdut Haavoda concentrated their efforts in creating strategies of survival was the socio-economic arena. Here, they sought not a comprehensive structure but an institution for their main potential constituents, the Jewish workers. The General Federation of Labor, commonly known as the Histadrut, was created by labor parties in Palestine in 1920. By 1926, 70 percent of Jewish workers in Palestine belonged to the Histadrut.[25] In the Histadrut elections in the 1920s, Achdut Haavoda won more than half the votes and gained control over the labor federation's executive bodies.

This dominance in the labor federation was very important because of the wide-ranging functions the Histadrut performed. The British

[25] Shapiro, *The Formative Years*, p. 18.

regarded the Histadrut with suspicion but nonetheless did little to impede it. In fact, the British gave wide latitude to the central Jewish leadership to provide services through the Histadrut to the Jewish population. The services offered by the Histadrut included health care, labor exchanges, trade unions, education, workers' kitchens, and a bureau of public works. By the end of the 1920s, the Histadrut, under the direction of Achdut Haavoda's leaders, created bonds of dependency with a large part of the Jewish population in Palestine. New Jewish immigrants found in the Histadrut the primary basis for strategies of survival, including jobs, housing, and schools for their children. Ben-Gurion and his compatriots' initial tactic, then, was to enhance the labor leadership's social control in the Yishuv by using their limited resources carefully and selectively, in close conjunction with the symbols their Zionist socialist ideology provided, to offer viable strategies of survival. Their success was outstanding. As Howard Sachar wrote, "Nearly all phases of a man's life, and the life of his family, were embraced by the vast canopy of the workers' organization. By the eve of World War II, the Histadrut had become much more than a powerful institution in Jewish Palestine. For a majority of the Yishuv, the Histadrut was all but synonymous with Jewish Palestine itself."[26]

The Histadrut probably could not have blossomed without the wzo. There was, of course, the flow of revenues from the wzo to the labor federation to undertake the latter's social and economic tasks. In addition, the Histadrut gained by the recognition the British accorded the wzo, first through Article 4 of the mandate and later through actions by Samuel and subsequent high commissioners. British recognition of the wzo allowed the Histadrut to expand its services as a direct beneficiary of the Zionist organization. To be sure, tensions abounded on all sides. The British often rued their decision to include Article 4. One British official wrote, "An exception has been made in this country for which, I think, there is no precedent elsewhere, of associating with us in the administration of the country another body, the Zionist Commission." He went on to note "that H.M.G. was bound hand and foot to the Zionists."[27]

There were tensions, too, between members of the Zionist Executive (before 1920, called the Zionist Commission), which represented the world body, and the local Histadrut leadership. Histadrut representatives felt continually hamstrung by the limited funds they received

---

[26] Howard M. Sachar, *A History of Israel: From the Rise of Zionism to Our Time* (New York: Alfred A. Knopf, 1976), p. 159.

[27] Quoted in Wasserstein, *The British in Palestine*, p. 134.

from wzo. Zionist Executive members, for their part, uneasy with the independent social control being built by Ben-Gurion and other labor leaders, attempted to use their subsidies to the Histadrut to gain control over its operations in Palestine by demanding economic accountability on the party of Histadrut enterprises. Ben-Gurion countered by arguing that Zionism per se, not narrow economic criteria, should direct the flow of funds and, since the interests of labor expressed the true national interests, discretionary spending should be left in labor's hands. To a surprising degree, this argument won the day, even though workers were far from constituting a majority of the Yishuv population.

Formally the labor leaders depended on the Zionist Executive for both revenues and access to the British. The fact that the Histadrut had created such effective social control in the Yishuv, however, actually made the Zionist Executive, and later the Jewish Agency itself, dependent on the labor leaders. To further their goal of enhancing the autonomy of the national home, wzo representatives had to rely on Histadrut leaders, who had so effectively established social control in the Yishuv, and accept their argument that the interests of labor best expressed Jewish national interests. The labor organizations stood head and shoulders above other organizations in their ability to mobilize the Jewish population for common purposes.

The effectiveness of the Histadrut made the Zionist Executive into a conduit for revenues. The executive's Department of Colonization, which absorbed one-third of its budget, mainly channeled revenues for the Histadrut agricultural settlements; its Department of Labor supported all other Histadrut enterprises.[28] The wzo oversaw the actual distribution of funds in only the most minimal fashion and then only in the face of vigorous protests by Yishuv labor leaders. As Shapiro notes, the wzo leaders "soon realized that they could not build a bureaucratic organization of their own to handle all of the necessary functions—especially since most of the members of the Executive were foreign Jews."[29] wzo leader Arthur Ruppin explained the abdication of responsibility in favor of the Histadrut in this way: "Experience had taught us that, the settlements of ours go to pieces as the result of inner division, where there does not exist at least a kernel of individuals with a more or less unified outlook to give the tone, and to assimilate to their unified outlook the other members of the group."[30]

[28] Shapiro, *The Formative Years*, p. 72.
[29] Ibid., pp. 78–79.
[30] Quoted in ibid., p. 79.

Direct control of the Jewish Agency by the Yishuv labor leaders did not come until the 1930s, grounded in the firm internal social control they had established in Palestine. It also came only after Ben-Gurion took a new approach toward coalition building in the wzo. In the first years of British rule, the socialist Achdut Haavoda leaders viewed the Zionist Executive as the perpetrator of "a sinister design by the moneyed class abroad to control the laborers in Palestine."[31] The Yishuv leaders declined to enter into any political coalitions with these bourgeois elements, refusing to join the Zionist Executive and consigning themselves to a marginal role in the running of the wzo.

Only in the latter half of the 1920s did the Achdut Haavoda leaders change tactics and enter into political coalitions with middle-class leaders in the Yishuv and abroad. By that time, they had built the tools to create social control in the Yishuv. Ben-Gurion paraphrased the change in tactics as "from class to nation."[32] The first step was to gain representation on the Zionist Executive. wzo leaders, for the most part, welcomed the labor leaders' new role since "they had become convinced that only the laborers had an organized force in Palestine which could reach the Zionist goals."[33]

Next, the labor leaders used their firm base in the Yishuv to mobilize support for wzo elections. Ben-Gurion spent months in cities in Europe and North America in a major organizational effort. In 1933 at the Zionist Congress held in Prague the Palestinian labor parties made their major gains. They won 138 of 318 seats and, what is even more important, an absolute majority on the Jewish Agency Executive. By 1935, Ben-Gurion was chairman of the Jewish Agency Executive and his lieutenants ran the key "ministries."

Ben-Gurion was now in an ideal situation: control of the World Zionist Organization placed him in an indisputable position to be recognized by the British as the national leader of the Jews. Not only did his party control the Histadrut with its strong social control, it led the very Jewish Agency the British themselves had proposed. In short, Ben-Gurion's internal strategy had paid off handsomely. The keys to his success lay first in the exploitation of the opportunities presented by the British; these included the proposal for a Jewish Agency and

---

[31] Ibid., p. 37.

[32] See David Ben-Gurion, *From Class to Nation* (Tel-Aviv: Am Oved, 1974) (text in Hebrew; title translated).

[33] Shapiro, *The Formative Years*, p. 233. The newfound position of the labor leaders was threatened in 1927 when an efficiency-minded executive under British Zionist, Harry Sacher, took a much more aggressive supervisory stance. By 1929, the laborers had established their preeminence.

the subsequent British inclination to devolve communal responsibility to that agency upon their failure to reconcile Jewish-Arab differences within the context of the mandatory regime.

Ben-Gurion's rise to the status of preeminent leader of the Zionist movement in place of Weizmann and, ultimately to the post of prime minister of Israel, stemmed directly from his tactics exploiting the opportunities the British presented for the consolidated control of the national home through a single agency. Those tactics were to concentrate initially on building the organizational bases for offering components for workable strategies of survival to the immigrant population. Until the latter years of the 1920s, he largely eschewed Weizmann's globe-trotting, especially after one unproductive episode in London.

Instead, he stayed at home in Palestine, combining his unusual organizational talents with the energies of a group of young immigrants from Russia. For them, Ben-Gurion was the prince, whose vision and plan of action could shape the very essence of this new society with them as the point men in execution. Their rebellion against the old construction of Jewish society, especially in Eastern Europe, put them in a perfect position to support the preeminence of the party and its allied organizations without conflicting loyalties to specific groups in Jewish society. They strengthened the labor party and then, with Ben-Gurion as general secretary of the Histadrut, offered workers a set of comprehensive services. Only once control in the Yishuv was secure did he use that base in a worldwide effort to gain direct control of the Jewish Agency.

Weizmann's strategy successfully mobilized capital for the national home, but it failed to build the means to use that capital to increase control in Palestine for his wzo. His talents were in mediation and conciliation, not in organization. He neglected to use the new talent pouring into the Yishuv in the early 1920s; he ignored those young men freed from the moorings of the old world and willing to build frameworks that transcended the ethnic and language differences differentiating the Jews of Palestine.

A fortuitous factor that aided Ben-Gurion in his campaign to gain control over the Jewish Agency stemmed from a British decision. The London-based wzo lobbied British officials constantly throughout the 1920s, pushing for full implementation of the national home. To escape this pressure, the Colonial Office decided at the beginning of the 1930s to transfer the locale of Jewish-British negotiation from Britain to Palestine. At that time High Commissioner Arthur Wauchope became the key link for the Zionists instead of the London-based Colonial Office. Just as the labor leaders' activities in Knesset Israel, the Histadrut, and the wzo were beginning to pay handsome organizational dividends among the Jews, these Yishuv leaders were now also much more strategically located than the non-Palestinian Jewish leadership to deal with the British on issues of importance and to influence British policy.

In the two decades of British rule until 1939, the labor leaders and foremost the indomitable Ben-Gurion exploited every activity the British sanctioned, from distributing certificates of immigration to collecting taxes. One of the activities that the British intermittently put restrictions on, Jewish land purchases, became the most important of all in consolidating the Zionist leadership's control in the Yishuv. As Kimmerling has pointed out in his innovative book, *Zionism and Territory*, the existence of a very limited frontier became a tool in the hands of Ben-Gurion and his fellow Yishuv leaders.[34] As the Jews drove up the price of land, the Zionist organization came to control more than 50 percent of all Jewish-owned land through its arm, the Jewish National Fund. The JNF bought lands with resources raised almost exclusively among Diaspora Jews. The distribution of the land in long-term leases to selected Jewish groups and individual Jews was critical in the establishment of central social control. The marshaling of resources from the British along with those from world Jewry enabled Zionist leaders in the Yishuv to create a pattern of social control among Jews already in Palestine and, later, among European Jewish refugees in the 1930s who constituted the largest wave of Jewish immigration to that point.

Colonial forces could push in precisely the opposite direction from that in Sierra Leone. In Palestine, the reconstitution of social control—putting Humpty Dumpty together again—involved consolidation much more than fragmentation. Article 4 and the British decision to devolve an unusual amount of responsibility for delivering public services to the Jews allowed the labor leaders to use the British-proposed Jewish Agency as a springboard for centralized social control. Consolidation of the incipient state was truly impressive. Among the branches of the Jewish Agency were Labor, Financial, Trade and Industry, Agricultural Settlement, Organization, Statistics, and Political departments. The latter even served as a kind of Foreign Office. Labor leaders controlled the most important of these departments. As J. C. Hurewitz commented, these bureaus were providing valuable ex-

[34] Baruch Kimmerling, *Zionism and Territory: The Socio-Territorial Dimensions of Zionist Politics* (Berkeley: Institute of International Studies, University of California, 1983).

perience in self-rule as well as a core of trained civil servants.[35] Probably most important were the bonds of dependency, the social control, that grew from the new organizations. Medding wrote:

> The Jewish community thus enjoyed fairly wide self-governing functions: the Elected Assembly [Knesset Israel] and the National Council (its executive body) represented the Jews of Palestine before the British government in matters of civil and legal rights, and were responsible for economic activities, health facilities and, after 1931, education. The Jewish Agency Executive in Jerusalem, the local representative of the World Zionist Organization, was given charge of all settlement activities, immigration, foreign affairs, education (until 1931), and defence. By 1935, Mapai [the labor party] led all the main bodies of Palestinian Jewry.[36]

Weizmann Ensures Ben-Gurion's Success

The success of Ben-Gurion's strategy depended on skillfully using the opportunities presented by Article 4 and the nature of British rule. It was not determined simply by the world conditions that created the Jewish problem and the severe social dislocation of Jews in the late nineteenth and early twentieth centuries. Weizmann, too, understood the importance of Article 4, but his strategy failed finally because he paid more attention to the Jewish problem than to the Jews with problems. With his lack of social control plaguing him and his party, the General Zionists, and his position in the wzo slipping, Weizmann had to make a fateful choice at the seventeenth Zionist Congress in 1931. Two other blocs existed to which he could throw his support after a vote of no-confidence in his policies had effectively removed him from the wzo presidency: one, of course, was labor; the other was the Jabotinsky-led Revisionists.

In substance, Weizmann may actually have been closer to the Revisionists. He was not a socialist, after all. Also, the Revisionists put much greater stock in international diplomacy and paid much less attention to the organization of daily life in Palestine. But, in the end, Weizmann cast his lot with labor. In part, that may have come about because differences in tone are frequently as important as differences in substance. Jabotinsky's militancy, as eloquent as he was, grated against Weizmann's most basic instincts. Weizmann, too, was deeply wounded by Jabotinsky's charges that he was not forceful enough in his dealings with the British. His support of labor, however, also came

[35] J. C. Hurewitz, *The Struggle for Palestine* (New York: Schocken Books, 1976), p. 41.
[36] Medding, *Mapai in Israel*, p. 10.

from an understanding that the Revisionists had exceeded even his own failing of not taking advantage of the opportunity the British gave the Jews in Article 4. The Revisionists had steadfastly maintained during the prestate era that it was the mandatory government's responsibility to provide the Jews with services. They scorned the opportunity for Jewish autonomy within the framework of the mandate. The position of the Revisionists left them without access to a tap controlling the rewards and sanctions that made labor's strength possible.

Shaken by the wzo's rejection of him—"the feeling came over me that here and now the tablets of the law should be broken," he wrote without undue modesty—Weizmann understood the importance of Ben-Gurion's success in the Yishuv.[37] Surveying the choice before him, Weizmann wrote,

> It was the conflict between those who believed that Palestine can be built up only the hard way, by meticulous attention to every object, who believed that in this slow and difficult struggle with the marshes and rocks of Palestine lies the great challenge to the creative forces of the Jewish people, its redemption from the abnormalities of exile, and those who yielded to those very abnormalities, seeking to live by a sort of continuous miracle. . . . I felt that all these political formulas would be no use to us. . . . It was not lack of respect for governments and parties, nor an underrating of the value of political pronouncements. But to me a pronouncement is real only if it is matched by performance in Palestine. . . . If there is any other way of building a house save brick by brick, I do not know it. If there is another way of building up a country save dunam by dunam, man by man, and farmstead by farmstead, again I do not know it.[38]

With Weizmann's support, the labor bloc went on to become the dominant force in the wzo and Zionism.

JEWISH AUTONOMY AND BRITISH COMPLICITY

The autonomy that the Jewish Agency and Histadrut achieved was remarkable for a colonial-type situation. Britain's role in this extraordinary consolidation of the means of social control by Ben-Gurion and his cronies was more in what it permitted than in what it gave or did. The mandatory government allowed the growth of social services and

[37] Weizmann, *Trial and Error*, p. 42.
[38] Ibid., pp. 418–19.

political functions under a central Jewish leadership because of its own unwillingness to assume those tasks.

In cases, such as India, where certain policies on the part of the colonial state did push toward consolidation of control, they took place in the face of other, even stronger policies pushing toward fragmentation. Also, even those forces pushing toward consolidation in India took place either within the context of the colonial state itself, especially creating a small army of civil servants trained in British techniques, or within organizations directly opposed to the colonial state, most important of which was the Congress party. In fact, Gandhi dubbed the Congress party a parallel state.

In Palestine, there were such Jewish civil servants working directly for the mandatory state, but they were a negligible factor in the ultimate struggle over social control. The Jewish Agency, although frequently in conflict with the British, essentially grew as an organization promoted and sanctioned by the colonialists and used by them to lessen their own burdens of ruling. Thus, the disadvantages of multiple loyalties, which Indians in the British civil service frequently felt, or of building autonomy under difficult, clandestine circumstances, which plagued many nationalist movements, were not as serious impediments to Ben-Gurion and his cohorts.

The Zionists certainly had other important advantages, too, in working toward consolidated social control. For many Jewish immigrants, especially those who chose Palestine over other options (after 1930 or so, refugees often landed in Palestine because of lack of other choices), Zionist myths and symbols were already well assimilated. Many came to Palestine because of their deep-seated belief in the Zionist solution to the Jewish problem. Establishing social control under these conditions was easier than "selling" Zionist symbols to a skeptical public. Even for Jews whose understanding of those symbols differed from that of the labor leaders, the shared attachment to Jewish religious symbols, even when used in new contexts of a secular civic religion, gave a common ground to those seeking social control and those piecing together strategies of survival. Also, the Zionist leaders benefited in their drive for consolidated social control by the devastating effect immigration had on the viability of people's old strategies (see Chapter 8).

With the first outbreak of widespread Arab rioting in Palestine in 1920–1921 and with every major incident thereafter, especially those in 1929 and 1936–1939, the British reexamined their policy of creating a Jewish national home. As the first British illusions about the viability of a unified political framework for Palestine shattered, important differences in the conception of Britain's role opened up among British officials. As in Sierra Leone, policy was not of a cloth, the product of a single accepted understanding of British interests, nor did policy always have the effects its implementors intended.

The actual governing of Palestine was the responsibility of the Colonial Office. It adopted its familiar pattern of devolving much of the actual day-to-day local control into the hands of its officials placed in Palestine, especially after 1931 during the term of Wauchope.[39] Not surprisingly, the various high commissioners and their staffs had a penchant for ruling as securely and cheaply as possible. And, obeying the universal cardinal rule of bureaucrats, they did everything in their power to prevent ruckuses from reaching upward to London. They set about devising scheme after scheme to contain Jewish-Arab tensions without jeopardizing security. In the end, those schemes took much of the actual governing from them. Authoritative positions in the central government and in districts, to be sure, remained in their hands, but they devolved many administrative responsibilities to the two communities; they gave more to the Jews, who accepted them readily.

Unfortunately, despite their schemes, the high commissioners were incapable of containing disturbances sufficiently to keep London officials from willy-nilly becoming involved in Palestinian events. The 1929 Arab riots brought one commission, and the 1936 Arab general strike and revolt brought another, the latter at the initiative of an exasperated Wauchope. It is not startling to find contempt for Wauchope in London once he admitted defeat and placed the unpleasant issues in the hands of London officials. The War Office concluded "that the method adopted by the High Commissioner was entirely ineffective."[40] The head of the Colonial Office, W.G.A. Ormsby-Gore, spoke of Wauchope as "a dear little man, admirable while the going is good, but hardly the character to ride out a storm."[41] Another superior noted, "Sir Arthur Wauchope loves greatly, administers with knowledge and imagination, but he does not rule."[42]

The Colonial Office in London, though, had scarcely more success than Wauchope and its other civil servants in Palestine. Its officials in London continued to search for some plan that would satisfy both of

[39] Aaron S. Klieman, "The Divisiveness of Palestine: Foreign Office versus Colonial Office on the Issue of Partition, 1937," *The Historical Journal* 22 (1979): 425.

[40] Quoted in Cohen, *Palestine*, p. 15.

[41] Quoted in ibid.

[42] Quoted in ibid., pp. 15–16.

its irreconcilable clients, the Zionists and the Palestinian Arabs. The plan they finally came to back was based on the 1937 proposals of the Royal Commission, the so-called Peel Commission Report, which recommended the partitioning of Palestine. Colonial Office civil servants, led by Ormsby-Gore, supported the idea of partition, while the Foreign Office, under the direction of the formidable Anthony Eden, was loathe to see the plan implemented.

The Foreign Office's opposition to the partition of Palestine between Arabs and Jews grew out of its particular vision of British interests. Unlike Colonial Office personnel, whose field of vision had narrowed in this period of the sunset of empire to the tragedy of Palestine itself, Foreign Office officials regarded Palestine as only one part of their global strategic concerns. With the emergence of independent Arab states in the Middle East, Foreign Office officials feared that continued support for a Jewish national home, even in a partitioned Palestine, would gravely affect Britain's interests and standing in the region. As Aaron Klieman wrote,

> The lines could not possibly have been drawn any clearer: the eastern department [of the Foreign Office] saw partition as a betrayal of the Arabs; the Middle East department [of the Colonial Office] saw its cancellation as betrayal towards the Jewish people. Of interest for bureaucratic politics in general is the fact that both perceived of each other's position as damaging British national and imperial interests.[43]

In the end, the Foreign Office and Eden simply outweighed their competitor. Ormsby-Gore and the whole idea of partition supported by the Colonial Office could not stand up in the government to the more powerful sister ministry, the Foreign Office. In 1939, the British issued its renowned White Paper on Palestine. It outlined a new policy, which the Zionists considered formal abdication of the Balfour Declaration and its support for a Jewish national home by the British. The White Paper indicated the British intention to create an independent Palestine state with an Arab majority within ten years, limit Jewish immigration to a trickle for five years and then to prohibit it entirely without Arab consent, and to forbid all land sales to Jews. This document, not surprisingly, led to a rapid deterioration in British-Jewish relations and to open animosity, much still neither forgotten nor forgiven.

The British rediscovered in the 1940s what had become apparent in

---

[43] Klieman, "The Divisiveness of Palestine," p. 438.

the early 1930s, namely, that they had created something of a Frankenstein. In the 1930s, too, the British had attempted on a smaller scale to hamper Jewish activities in areas where the Jewish Agency or its allied institutions had dominated, such as agricultural settlement, land purchases, and immigration. Just as then, British officials found Jewish leaders, strengthened by their control over activities that had been bequeathed to them by the British themselves, able to circumvent many British regulations and restrictions.[44] Even after the White Paper was issued the mandatory state refrained from excessive meddling into the social services and political functions the Jews had assumed. As in the early 1930s, British officials felt that their own performance of such tasks among the Jews might only further harm their relationship with the Arabs.[45] Moreover, the mandatory state simply lacked the capabilities at that point to provide those services.

It would have taken an extraordinary effort by the British, who were by late 1939 concerned primarily with European affairs, to reverse the social control the Jewish labor leaders had consolidated in Palestine. Even earlier in the 1930s, there were moments when the existence of a consolidated Jewish leadership had been so loathsome that the British had adopted some subtle and not-so-subtle policies to weaken labor's control. The voting regulations for Knesset Israel's Elected Assembly in 1932, for example, provided for separate ethnic groupings. Jewish parties then had proposed candidates for three groupings, Sephardic, Yemenite, and Ashkenazic.[46]

Even with the shared hopes that many immigrants harbored due to their belief in the Zionist program as a solution to the Jewish problem, the potential for social and political organization of the Yishuv along ethnic lines or, for that matter, according to language groupings, countries of origin, or religious differences was certainly always very much present. Jews from every continent converged in Palestine with almost no organizational ties among them. Even cultural affinity—their very Jewishness—paled next to the differences in dress, language, forms of worship, and more.

The remarkable result, however, was that Britain had not been able to exploit these differences: they did not become highly politicized. Social groupings with the ability to enforce their own rules of the game did not achieve any notable success among the Jews. For the most part, the labor leaders channeled the very real tensions among

---

[44] See, for example, Kenneth W. Stein, *The Land Question in Palestine, 1917–1939* (Chapel Hill: University of North Carolina Press, 1984).

[45] Horowitz and Lissak, *Origins of the Israeli Polity*, p. 45.

[46] Ibid., pp. 42–43.

the diverse Jews into the political and social institutions they themselves dominated. The labor leaders dictated the rules of the game.
When the Sephardim, along with the Revisionists, boycotted the 1944
elections, they found their basis for opposition undermined by the
turnout that labor and the other parties could generate.

In the 1920s and early 1930s British policy had opened the doors
too wide to the Jewish Agency for the British now to destroy the agency's control and refashion the society. Hundreds of thousands of Jews
had already settled onto Zionist-owned land and bought into the educational, health, and other services that labor leaders had spun into
strategies of survival. Perhaps a wholesale withdrawal of authority
from the Jewish institutions and a move to assume the provision of
these services by the mandatory state itself could have undone the social control built by Ben-Gurion and his fellow labor leaders. But even
this drastic an action probably would not have been effective at this
point given the growing strength of labor's symbols among the Jews.
Such a withdrawal, however, is but idle speculation because the British
were unwilling. Even when labor undertook armed resistance against
British rule after World War II, the Jewish Agency and its affiliated
organizations continued in many spheres to work as collaborators with
the British in ruling the Yishuv.

Only in one area did Jewish autonomy in Palestine develop mostly outside the sphere of British complicity—security and defense. Jewish
self-defense units, called Hashomer (The Watchman), had existed as
far back as the beginning of the century in Palestine, but the British
put a firm clamp on their reemergence in the immediate aftermath of
World War I. The Arab riots of 1920–1921, however, posed the
strongest sort of threat to Jewish settlement in Palestine. British intervention against the rioters proved so paltry that the labor Zionists
opted to develop a clandestine force, the Haganah. The labor Zionists
were not the only Jews attempting to organize defense. Jabotinsky
tried to activate units during the riots of 1920, but he met with little
success. In fact, control of defense and security policy and forces became a major source of struggle for social control in the Yishuv
throughout the mandatory period.

From the time of the founding of the Histadrut, labor leaders
sought to add defense to the host of services they offered Jewish immigrants. The threat of Arab violence was perceived as all too real to
trust what the labor leaders considered an indifferent British administration or to leave security issues to Jewish organizations outside
their control. Labor leaders put the Haganah under Histadrut political auspices and then set out to attract Hashomer members into both

the new Haganah and their political party, Achdut Haavoda. Various ploys were then used to control former Hashomer personnel.

At times, the Haganah was an underground force, operating illegally and, at other times, it was a semilegal organization allowed by the British to perform tasks they were unwilling or unable to undertake. For example, for much of the period the Haganah illegally imported arms and, after World War II, even mounted raids against British installations. In 1936, however, the British created and armed Jewish guards, whose actual membership in the Haganah the British accepted.

Challenges to labor's control of the Haganah came within the Jewish community, too. The wzo, for a time, was reluctant to fund a defense organization intended for the entire Jewish community but so completely dominated by one segment, labor. One Yishuv party wanted the Haganah under the control of the National Council and not the labor federation, the Histadrut. Jabotinsky successfully organized an additional armed group, the Irgun (Irgun Zvai Leumi), which broke labor's monopoly on control of violent means among those in the Yishuv. Another group, Lehi (the Stern Gang), undertook terrorist acts and daring raids against the British. As in no other area, labor faced intense competition. Even within the Haganah itself, there were indications of military leaders smarting under the control of Histadrut leaders.

The labor leaders, for their part, felt their social control could be imperiled by allowing independent military forces to organize in the Yishuv.[47] At times, they coordinated efforts with the Irgun and Lehi, and, in other instances, actually turned members of these forces over to the British when they felt these groups were working contrary to the best interests of the Yishuv. Ben-Gurion, probably more than any other leader, was guided by a central principle: the potential of Arab violence was so great as to make control of defense, no matter what the costs he might have to pay in maintaining Jewish consensus, something labor simply could not give up if the Yishuv was to survive and labor was to maintain its social control.

ISRAEL AS A STRONG STATE

Despite the repeated blasts to the conception of a self-governing Jewish national home—culminating in the most forceful blow of all, the White Paper of 1939—the earlier actions of the British proved to have the longest and deepest impact on the Yishuv's social and political or-

---

[47] Shapiro, *The Formative Years*, p. 31.

ganization. The early recognition of a single Jewish Agency and the appropriation of broad responsibilities to it provided the outlines for the new distribution of social control in Palestinian Jewish society. An irony of the entire situation was that the policies of the Colonial Office devolving so much autonomy to the Jews, though they eventually were rejected by the government, were able to have the most enduring effect on the future of Jewish society and, indeed, the entire Middle East. With the continuing fragmentation of Palestinian Arab society during the mandate, the central Jewish organization came to be far and away the strongest local base for social control in the entire country.

The test of the strength of the Israeli state, which grew out of the Jewish Agency, came immediately upon the declaration of independence in May 1948. By that time, events had long since overtaken the policy of the White Paper. Palestine's future was decided by a UN resolution and the outcome of war, not by the British, who found themselves increasingly powerless to control events after 1945.

For the new state, the test in 1948 was twofold. The first was the Arab-Jewish civil war for control of Palestine and the accompanying interstate war between Israel and its Arab neighbors. Innumerable popular and scholarly accounts have documented the 1948 war. Of interest here is that despite the vast population, which the Arab states and Palestinian Arab leadership had to draw upon, the Israeli state leaders, ruling a society of considerably less than a million people, were able to use the social control they had garnered in a tremendous mobilizational effort. Their forces tripled from 30,000 soldiers in May to over 90,000 in October. By that time, they had accomplished an astounding defeat of the combined Arab armies. The advantage in mobilization that the Jews had in the 1948 war grew directly out of the painstaking social control they had developed in delivering mundane services such as housing, jobs, and education.

The second threat to the Israeli state came in the internal Jewish challenges to Ben-Gurion's leadership and organizations. I discussed that threat above, in the introduction to Part II of this book. Suffice it to say here that the social control built in the 1920s and 1930s created the basis for a state able to withstand challenges from disaffected military leaders in the Haganah and from Menachem Begin's autonomous military force, the Irgun.

The British had divided their collaborative efforts between the two competing communities of Arabs and Jews. Arab rejection of a British offer to back a counterpart to the Jewish Agency was at the center of a number of factors fragmenting social control. Elsewhere, I have discussed that fragmentation of control among the Palestinian Arabs that resulted from British rule.[48] In the ultimate test of war against the Zionists, Arab fragmentation led to disaster. Arab political institutions collapsed, the Israeli forces advanced, and Palestinian Arabs fled or were driven from their villages and cities. Only slightly more than 10 percent of the Arab population of Palestine remained within the territory controlled by the Israeli state at the end of the war. What had started as organizations to establish social control exclusively among the Jews of Palestine now became the basis of a state exercising such control over Jews *and* the Arab remnant population alike.[49]

Since the tumultuous events of 1948, Israelis have survived from crisis to crisis. Much of the social control built in Yishuv institutions has, with some fits and starts, been shifted to the agencies of the state.[50] On many indicators reflecting the relative strength of states in respect to their societies, the Israeli state is very high, especially for a new state. In 1979–1980, it collected 36 percent of GDP in taxes, higher than any OECD state; it offered nearly universal education through elementary school and high school; it devoted almost one-quarter of GDP to defense expenditures; it demanded universal military service for Jewish males, service from a high percentage of Jewish females, and service from some Arab males; it adopted a housing policy so that virtually no Jewish family lived more than four to a room.[51] The Israeli state has created extensive policy networks, simultaneously making it one of the most militarized states in the world and among the most extensive welfare states.

The legacy of labor's rule—the Israel Labor Party was turned out of office only in 1977—also contains some elements that have eroded the consolidated social control of the state. The primacy of politics over economics has led to a tendency for the state to promise far more than it can deliver, especially with the severe resource limitations faced in Israel. Even after the creation of the state, the Jewish Agency and Histadrut continued to exist, with modified functions, making policy coordination difficult. Labor leaders' concern with building a constituency among former East European Jewish workers left other groups, by the 1980s the clear majority of the population, open to disaffection and other parties' recruitment. Deepening social cleavages and a near-electoral stalemate in Israeli politics have resulted. With the shift from

[48] Migdal, *Palestinian Society and Politics*, ch. 2.

[49] See Ian Lustick, *Arabs in the Jewish State: Israel's Control of a National Minority* (Austin: University of Texas Press, 1980).

[50] Asher Arian, *Politics in Israel: The Second Generation* (Chatham, N.J.: Chatham House, 1985), pp. 226–32.

[51] See Ira Sharkansky, *What Makes Israel Tick? How Domestic Policy-Makers Cope with Constraints* (Chicago: Nelson-Hall, 1985).

"class to nation" came broad coalitions and concessions to small parties, diluting ideology (effective symbols) and creating numerous ministries to accommodate all. Again, policy coordination has been a victim.

Despite all these factors, the Israeli state's strength relative to other new states is impressive. Waves of immigration helped swell the numbers of Jews in Palestine from about 50,000 at the beginning of the century to about three and a half million today, introducing forces with tremendous divisive potential. Immigrants came with vastly different backgrounds and needs. Labor leaders seized the opportunity the British afforded to develop central political and social institutions through the Jewish Agency. The vast array of services monopolized by the incipient state, and later the state itself, made it extremely difficult for localistic social organizations to offer meaningful rewards, sanctions, and symbols to the individual. Attempts to this day to build political organization on a different basis have met with little success.

The Conditions for Creating a Strong State

Let us return to Horowitz's question quoted earlier in this chapter, how did the "centripetal" propensities in the Yishuv overcome the "centrifugal" tendencies? Among the most important factors are:

1. The emerging Jewish society in the Yishuv until the end of World War I was weak. Economic dislocation in Europe, the growth of the "Jewish problem," and migration itself produced a society in search of new strategies of survival. Old social control had crumbled.

2. The Mandate for Palestine created the opportunity for consolidated social control through the latitude given to the Jewish Agency and allied organizations.

3. There existed a skillful leadership. Weizmann and Jabotinsky had faced the same challenge as Ben-Gurion, but they failed to see the advantages in concentrating on the building of viable strategies of survival through an artful blend of rewards, sanctions, and symbols. Not only must that leadership discern the proper path, but it must also have strong organizational capabilities. Weizmann's talents simply did not run in that direction. Ben-Gurion's colleagues prized him as an exceptional organizer, as much as thirty years before he became prime minister of Israel.

4. The top labor leaders had available a group of talented young "pioneers," as they were called in Palestine, freed from the moorings of the old world. They saw their personal fulfillment in the suc-

cessful implementation of the top leaders' visions and plans. And, they were willing and able to build an autonomous set of organizations that transcended parochial ethnic and language ties among the Jews. Their strength lay in implementing the policies that would create strategies of survival for the population, not in devising those strategies from scratch.

5. The military threat posed by the Arabs made Ben-Gurion and his colleagues accept the risks of challenging any fragmented power bases, such as the Irgun, that had arisen. It was too risky *not* to consolidate social control; the very survival of the leader and his carefully nurtured organizations, the new state, depended on it.

The emergence of a strong, autonomous state is by no means a natural outcome of the social transformations associated with the modern era. The empirical question is who could take advantage of the new circumstances and reestablish social control? In Part II I have outlined two necessary conditions for the success of those about to consolidate social control, eventually in a strong state. One is rapid and universal dislocation, which I discussed in Chapter 2. The other, relevant to societies that experienced direct, outside hegemonic rule, is the channeling of resources to indigenous organizations capable of extending social control throughout the society. Sierra Leone fit the first condition but not the second; Jewish society in Palestine fit both. Ethnic identities there did not disappear altogether, but for most of the history of Palestine and Israel since World War I, they have been irrelevant among the Jews to the exercising of social control. Primary identity for Jews came to be Israeli, not Moroccan or Sephardi or orthodox. For most, although certainly not for all Jews in Israel, the state's social control has reached the level of legitimacy. They not only comply with state rules to an impressive degree, but they also accept the rightness of the state's making the rules of the game. For Arab citizens of Israel (about 17 percent of the population), social control has mostly been at the level of participation. They take part in the education, health, and other systems of services, but they have not accepted the major myths the state has propounded. Those symbols have mostly been irrelevant to their identities and strategies of survival.[52]

[52] For Arabs, firm control has been maintained but without reaching the level of high legitimacy and without personal identification as Israelis outweighing other identities. See Migdal, *Palestinian Society and Politics*; and Lustick, *Arabs in the Jewish State*. On identity of Jewish Israelis, see Uri Farago, "Stability and Change in the Jewish Identity of School-Age Youths in Israel (1965–1974)" (Paper distributed by Levi Eshkol Research Institute for Economics, Society and Policy in Israel, Hebrew University, 1977).

PART THREE

The Continuing Impact of an Environment of Conflict on State and Society

LEADERS of new and old states in the post–World War II era, puffed with pride and ambition, have aimed to establish their unequivocal rule over societies in Asia, Africa, and Latin America. But these societies, newly restratified and indeed restructured, in the last century are already ruled. Patterns of social control in the towns and countryside, painstakingly constructed with the mortar of resources, opportunities, and property rights available in the late nineteenth and early twentieth centuries, did not hopelessly dissolve with the proclamations of resolute state leaders establishing a new order. Too many have had too much of a stake in the existing patterns of social control to allow state leaders to impose their rules uncontested.

It has now been more than a generation, almost two, since the creation of the new international institutions, especially those of the United Nations, which have outlined what is expected of states in the postwar world. Also, more than a generation has passed since the rush of decolonization drew to a close and the leaders of new states began trying to rule their societies independently. Many observers have been genuinely surprised that during this period those at the helm of states have not made more headway in establishing unified, effective rule.

And that surprise comes with good reason. After all, in their battle for social control, states have usually not faced the opposition of fortified, large armies, but scattered, small social organizations jealously protecting enclaves of social control. One would have imagined an easy triumph of the state over such seemingly feeble opposition. Also, the state has armed itself well for battle. Almost everywhere in the Third World state bureaucracies have grown rapidly. That growth has meant more people to apply state rules and offer rewards, such as education, housing, special allowances, and the like. More civil servants have also produced a steady, although sometimes painstakingly slow, increase in state tax revenues, both in absolute terms and as a percentage of GNP.[1]

In addition, states have not lacked instruments to enforce their

[1] Alex Radian, *Resource Mobilization in Poor Countries: Implementing Tax Policies* (New Brunswick, N.J.: Transaction Books, 1980), pp. 12–13.

rules, Third World states have beefed up both military and police forces substantially, and they have garnered increased outside aid, manpower, and budgets for those forces. The United States alone poured over $70 billion in military assistance into Asia, Africa, and Latin America in the thirty years following World War II.[2] Major arms suppliers—the United States, USSR, United Kingdom, and France— sent more than 12,000 aircraft, 800 naval vessels, and 38,000 tanks and armored carriers into Third World states in the decade from 1967 to 1977.[3] To be sure, these armaments and those sent in other periods have not been distributed evenly throughout the Third World. Even so, hardly a state exists that has not built up an impressive array of foreign armaments, arsenals quite remarkable for purposes of internal control. Countries such as Israel, Egypt, India, and Mexico have also taken giant strides in domestic production of weapons.

There is no shortage of manpower to enforce state rules and undermine those attempting to guard contradictory sets of rules. In 1965, a sample of ninety countries from Asia, Africa, and Latin America showed an average of 11.2 people in the military for every 1,000 in the working age population. Although this is low compared to the figure of 23.4 for a sample of twenty-five European countries plus the United States and Canada, on any historical scale it is impressive indeed. Even more striking is the growth of internal security forces. The average number of such forces per thousand working age population in ninety-three Asian, African, and Latin American countries in the early 1960s was 3.4. The comparable figure for the European countries plus the United States and Canada was only slightly more, at 3.8.[4] In summary, no dearth of manpower or arms to apply and enforce the state's rules of the game against those in scattered enclaves of the society has limited state effectiveness in many societies.

Nor does the continuing weakness of states stem principally from crippling budgets. Although state leaders never cease to complain of shortages of capital, compared to those other social organizations struggling for social control the postwar state has been positively flush.

---

[2] Michael T. Klare, *Supplying Repression: U.S. Support for Authoritarian Regimes Abroad* (Washington, D.C.: Institute for Policy Studies, 1977), pp. 31–33.

[3] Michael Mihalka, "Supplier-Client Patterns in Arms Transfers: The Developing Countries, 1967–76," in Stephanie G. Neuman and Robert E. Harkany, eds., *Arms Transfers in the Modern World* (New York: Praeger, 1979), p. 60. Also, see Uri Ra'anan, Robert L. Pfaltzgraff, Jr., and Geoffrey Kemp, eds., *Arms Transfers to the Third World: The Military Buildup in Less Industrial Countries* (Boulder, Colo.: Westview Press, 1978).

[4] Adapted from Charles Lewis Taylor and Michael C. Hudson, *World Handbook of Political and Social Indicators*, 2d ed. (New Haven: Yale University Press, 1972), pp. 38–47.

Besides rents and revenues collected directly from the population, most states have also had access to foreign capital often unavailable to the landlords, chieftains, and others who manage to continue to hold sway in many areas. In 1970, OECD states, Socialist states, and multilateral agencies disbursed almost $8 billion in aid. By 1980, the figure topped $27 billion, not including loans and equity investments (more than $14 billion in 1980) channeled largely to the state organizations in Third World countries. Also, states secured a large share of private foreign capital flowing into their countries, more than $40 billion in 1980.[5] Third World states owed sums approaching a trillion dollars to foreigners in 1986. As with military assistance, capital from loans, nonmilitary aid, and other foreign capital flows have not been distributed at all evenly, but all Third World states have tapped into the world capital market and found donors and lenders. Resources for states engaged in domestic battles for social control have been available to one degree or another; for some states they have been positively bountiful.

Why, then, have so many states gained so little during the last generation in their leaders' quest for unified rule? Why have so many states in the Third World failed to predominate in their societies? The asymmetry in the arsenals on each side of the battle for social control does cause surprise over the endurance of the environment of conflict. Part III explores several questions: Why have some states found it so difficult to overcome those forces in their own societies that continue to maintain rules quite different from those of the state? Why does social control remain highly fragmented? Why do so many Third World states stay weak? Although states in the Third World have rarely achieved the heady goals their leaders staked out for them a generation ago, it would be a terrible mistake simply to dismiss the battle for social control as a victory for the fragmented social organizations or even as a standoff, and leave it at that. All states *have* been a major presence in their societies; they have precipitated major changes among their populations. With all the resources available to states, how could it be otherwise? And those resources have led to changes and adjustments in society. To the regret of many state leaders, those changes have not always been in their intended direction, but they still have been substantial enough to make us ask how these

[5] On the figures for net resource flows to Third World countries from foreign sources, see Organization for Economic Cooperation and Development (OECD), *Development Cooperation: 1981 Review* (Paris: OECD, 1981), Table A.1.

societies have adjusted to the ambition, wealth, actions, and sheer mass of their states.

What is not so self-evident is that states themselves have had to change and adjust as a result of their encounters with other social organizations able to maintain their own social control. Too often, especially in the new social science literature reviving the states as a major actor and unit of analysis, the state has appeared as a given—autonomous, impenetrable, the ultimate independent variable. That view ignores too much of the dynamic of state-society interactions, certainly in Asia, Africa, and Latin America. The impact of society on the state is as important as the effect of state on society for understanding the sometimes surprising patterns of continuity and change in the Third World. In Part II, we saw how the spread of the world economy and powerful states out of Europe gave the opportunity for new distributions of social control in Third World countries. Many societies, such as that in Sierra Leone, ended up with highly fragmented control. Now, in Part III, I extend my analysis about the capabilities of states by asking why independent Third World states in the postwar era have not succeeded in terminating the social control of strongmen and in ending fragmentation. Part III poses an additional question: what impact does the inability to consolidate control—the continuing weakness of the state—have upon the political life and the administration of the state organization itself?

CHAPTER FIVE

The Egyptian State Attempts to Transform Egyptian Society

THE IMAGE OF SOCIETY AFFECTING THE STATE

The concepts of center and periphery continue to shape much current thinking about state-society relations in the Third World, especially the direction of change—from center to periphery, not the opposite. In most accounts, events hundreds or thousands of miles from state capitals or even in the slums of those very capital cities have had little apparent impact on the style and substance of state organizations. In particular, outside observers have portrayed the remotest, weakest groups in society much as people in these groups see themselves, as marginal to the real stuff of politics. The standard image is still as Edward Shils portrayed it more than a generation ago: centers are active and creative while peripheries are passive and malleable.[1]

The experiences of the last decades suggest a much more interesting picture of the relationship between states, centered in capital cities, and their widely scattered societies. As we shall see, strategies adopted by even the weakest groups in society, the masses of poor peasants and workers, have helped determine the ultimate power of the state—its ability to get people to behave in certain ways and its success in mobilizing resources from the population. In the final analysis, the ability of the state to garner support through a multitude of institutional channels decides the fate of state leaders and their often ambitious policy agendas.

To develop this line of reasoning, where the society shapes the state even as the state deeply influences the society, I must qualify further two concepts introduced earlier in the analysis. The first is the environment of conflict, which up to this point has denoted totally antagonistic relations between states and other organizations with opposing rules of the game. Second is the state itself, which I have so far presented as a more or less monolithic organization, a single actor, without significant differentiation of parts. Part III illuminates state-society relations by disaggregating the state to a limited extent without, I

---

[1] Edward Shils, *Center and Periphery* (Chicago: University of Chicago Press, 1975).

hope, losing too much of the parsimony in the model portraying the state as one social organization among many. Such disaggregation allows the analysis to go beyond unrelenting antagonism in the environment of conflict to situations of accommodation between parts of the state and social organizations with opposing rules of the game; and in Chapter 7 I even talk of the capture of parts of the state itself by other organizations in the society.

New innovative works, largely still unpublished, on a number of major countries are now demanding that we understand state-society relations in the Third World in ways quite different from those offered in existing theories.[2] They provide ample evidence to draw out important issues about the continuing difficulty of states, even with all their resources at hand, to centralize social control and about the subtle impact of remote groups on the character of the state. Evidence on a variety of countries in some older works, particularly those on patron-client relations, can also be reinterpreted to support a new approach to state-society relations.[3] In Chapters 6 and 7, I will outline in general form a new theory that can account for the continuing weakness of many states and the effect of such weakness on state character. For now, I want to focus on a single country, working through the sort of evidence mentioned above. Although this chapter could just as well have been written about Mexico, India, or other countries, I have chosen the very instructive, rich case of Egypt following the 1952 Revolution of the Free Officers to lay the groundwork for the more general material that follows. Egypt's new state leadership was intent on restructuring society. One of the main tools it chose—the one we will look at in this chapter—was an extensive agrarian reform, attacking the very property rights that bolstered some of Egypt's most dominant social organizations.

Nowhere does the influence of so-called peripheries on the state seem more unlikely than in Egypt. Its lifeline, the Nile River, along whose banks almost all its population has lived, has created a society far more bureaucratized, far more homogeneous, than most other societies in history. The standard caricature of Egypt has portrayed its society as one with highly concentrated power in which central political organizations have dictated the tenor of social life to a passive peas-

---

[2] See footnote 5 in Prologue.

[3] A good sampling of the patron-client literature is found in Steffen W. Schmidt, Laura Gvasti, Carl H. Landé, and James C. Scott, eds., *Friends, Followers, and Factions: A Reader in Political Clientilism* (Berkeley: University of California Press, 1977). This literature, unfortunately, has all too often given only slight attention to the connection between these societal relations and the state, enmeshing itself instead in the intricacies of local affairs.

antry.[4] The post-1952 state has been all this and more. Its bureaucracy, army, and sheer resources supercede anything Egypt had ever seen previously. Moreover, its leadership in the generation after the Free Officers seized control was imaginative and innovative.

Despite all these assets, the post-1952 Egyptian state in the end failed to concentrate the social control it sought. It failed to achieve predominance by eliminating other social organizations applying conflicting rules of the game. This chapter analyzes why success in creating a strong, predominant state was beyond its leaders' grasp and studies the impact of such failure on political life in Egypt.

NASSER AND THE EGYPTIAN LAND REFORM

Gamal Abdul Nasser, who ruled in Egypt from the overthrow of the monarchy in 1952 until his death in 1970, was one of the most intelligent and capable state leaders of the postwar era. Brimming with grand ambitions and plans, both domestic and international, he felt at times an almost unconstrained ability to remold Egyptian society. The precise goals he harbored were not always totally clear to others, but almost twenty years of governmental action and programs testified to the extent that Nasser aimed to transform Egyptian society. He was undaunted, at least until the late 1960s, at how monumental were the tasks he set out for himself and the Egyptian state. Nasser linked his vision of a transformed Egyptian society to his aspirations for changes in the larger milieu, all on the back of a reinvigorated Egyptian state.

> For some reason it seems to me that within the Arab circle there is a role, wandering aimlessly in search of a hero. And I do not know why it seems to me that this role, exhausted by its wanderings, has at last settled down, tired and weary, near the borders of our country and is beckoning to us to move, to take up its lines, to put on its costume, since no one else is qualified to play it.[5]

Nasser used the mantle of leadership, which rested so comfortably on his shoulders, as the impetus for the state first to reshape Egyptian society and then the larger circles within which Egypt existed. "At the heart of the Nasserist vision of Egypt's destiny," wrote Raymond Baker, "was a grasp of the necessary linkage between domestic and

[1] For a sympathetic view of such ways of looking at Egyptian society, see Nazih N. M. Ayubi, *Bureaucracy and Politics in Contemporary Egypt* (London: Ithaca Press for the Middle East Centre, St. Anthony's College Oxford, 1980).

[5] Gamal Abdul Nasser, *Egypt's Liberation: The Philosophy of the Revolution* (Washington, D.C.: Public Affairs Press, 1955), pp. 87–88.

international politics."[6] Inside and outside Egypt, from North Africa to Pakistan, millions of people regarded Nasser as a hero, a savior.

Nasser did not separate the question of his aims from that of the practical issue of means. He immediately followed his question of "what is it we want to do?" with another query of "how is it to be done?"[7] Frankly, he admitted, the second question was far more troublesome and divisive than the first. How did he set about achieving his ambitious goals? The answer lies in the reorganization of the Egyptian state that Nasser and the Free Officers began to undertake after their lightening coup d'état.

When one of the officers, Anwar el-Sadat, broadcast news of the successful uprising on the morning of July 23, 1952, Egypt's old politicians had no inkling of how profound the changes in the state organization would be. The new military leaders compelled almost all the old political guard to exit from state posts. Even more significantly, they slated the institutions of the state for overhaul or, in some cases, for complete elimination. New state structures proliferated. It could not be otherwise if Nasser and the Free Officers hoped to achieve even their first major proposed change of Egyptian society.

That change, which in the end would be among the most important of all domestic state policies in the Nasser era, involved a sweeping agrarian reform. It addressed one of the most remarkable features of Egyptian society before 1952, the striking inequality in land ownership. Less than one-half of 1 percent of the landowners, those with holdings of fifty feddans or more, had title to 35 percent of all the cultivated land.[8] A bit more than 5 percent of the holders, with plots ranging from five to fifty feddans, owned another 30 percent of the farmed land. That left the final 35 percent of cultivated land for almost 95 percent of the landowners.[9] For this group with postage stamp parcels, the situation had worsened steadily for the half century prior to the Revolution. The number of peasants, or fellahin, with less than five feddans tripled, and their average plot shrank in half. Even more alarming, the numbers and proportion of rural families with no land at all grew dramatically. A generation before the revolution, they

[6] Raymond William Baker, *Egypt's Uncertain Revolution under Nasser and Sadat* (Cambridge, Mass.: Harvard University Press, 1978), p. 44.

[7] Nasser, *Egypt's Liberation*, p. 49.

[8] One feddan equals 1.04 acres.

[9] Eprime Eshag and M. A. Kamal, "Agrarian Reform in the United Arab Republic (Egypt)," *Bulletin of the Oxford University Institute of Economics and Statistics* 30 (May 1968): 76.

had made up barely one-quarter of the total number of rural families; by 1952, they were approaching one-half.[10]

The revolutionary land reform addressed this severe inequality of land ownership in Egypt. After the reform, that distribution changed, as did the distribution of social control in society as a whole. The state indeed transformed the society. As I shall discuss in the following account, however, the results of the reform were not as Nasser and his dozen cohorts had anticipated them. State leaders failed to concentrate social control in the state organization. The prerevolutionary social structure came to influence deeply the disposition of land and other benefits of the reform. In the end, this social structure limited the growth in state strength and helped shape the nature of politics within the institutions of the state. Thus society transformed the state.

The new state executive enacted the first land reform law only six weeks after the coup d'état in 1952. Its purpose was not palliative. Nasser was out to break the biggest, richest landowners, who concentrated much of the social control in Egypt in their hands. With the stakes so high, it is small wonder that political turmoil surrounded the adoption of the reform. Such measures had been proposed before in Egypt, in 1945 and 1950, but the powerful landlords had been able to stem the tide of land reform then. Now, the civilian cabinet still in existence resigned two days before the law was passed. The Free Officers issued accompanying decrees to forestall opposition. For example, they reorganized political parties and arrested about ninety palace officials and party leaders.[11] And five days after they issued the law, they retired high-ranking civil servants and about 450 army officers.[12] The battle for social control began.

The law itself was rather simple. It placed a 200-feddan ceiling on individual landholdings, with another maximum of 100 for wives and children. Amendments later lowered the limit to 100 feddans per family in 1961–1962 and then to 50 feddans per individual, still 100 per family in 1969. Landowners had to sell off any land above the limit within a short time, or the state requisitioned it for redistribution to small farmers, tenants, and laborers. The state paid compensation in the form of bonds equaling about half the value of the land to all ex-

[10] Mahmoud Abdel-Fadil, *Development, Income Distribution and Social Change in Rural Egypt 1952–1970: A Study in the Political Economy of Agrarian Transition* (Cambridge: Cambridge University Press, 1975), pp. 3–5.

[11] P. J. Vatikiotis, *The History of Egypt*, 2d ed. (Baltimore: Johns Hopkins University Press, 1980), p. 378.

[12] Ibid., p. 379.

propriated landowners except members of the royal family. It committed itself to redistribute land to those with 5 feddans or less of land; the practice was first to sell requisitioned land to tenants actually working the land and then to landless families in the same village.

Despite the controversy surrounding passage of the agrarian reform and the risks the Free Officers took in enacting it, the results have been quite mixed. The lower strata of Egyptian rural society has benefited from it only to a limited degree.[13] Probably its greatest successes came in three areas:

(1) the new tenancy regulations, which lowered rents and afforded legal protection to tenants;

(2) the destruction of the big landowners as a powerful class in Egyptian society; and

(3) the gains in productivity on those fields included in the reform.

The revolutionary state succeeded in achieving some major changes in Egyptian society.

The actual redistribution, however, brought only modest gains. In the 1950s, the state redistributed 8.4 percent of the cultivable land. By the 1970s, this figure rose to about 12.5 percent. All in all, approximately 9 or 10 percent of the rural population gained land as a result of the 1952 reform and subsequent reforms through 1970, the year of Nasser's death.[14] The average parcel of land distributed to beneficiaries amounted to less than 2.5 feddans. The average plot in Egypt is still barely larger than a single feddan, and two-thirds of the male agricultural labor force has no land at all or less than a single feddan. To the credit of the reform, inequality did decrease.[15] While the relative number of plots under 5 feddans continued to hover around 95 percent of the total, these small farms now encompassed more than one-half the cultivable land, as opposed to one-third before the revo-

---

[13] See, for example, Assem el-Dessouki, "Land Tenure Policy in Egypt, 1952–1969, and its Effects on the Re-formation of the Peasantry," in Tarif Khalidi, ed., *Land Tenure and Social Transformation in the Middle East* (Beirut: American University of Beirut, 1984), pp. 437–48.

[14] Waterbury wrote, "What we are left with, then, is a series of reforms that involved at most about 16 percent of Egypt's cultivated land, leading to the actual redistribution of 13 percent of that land to about 10 percent of Egypt's rural families." John Waterbury, *The Egypt of Nasser and Sadat: The Political Economy of Two Regimes* (Princeton, N.J.: Princeton University Press, 1983), pp. 266–67.

[15] The Gini coefficient, which measures the degree of inequality in wealth and income and here reflects the concentration of land ownership, decreased from 0.611 before the 1952 reform to 0.383 in 1965. Abdel-Fadil, *Development, Income Distribution and Social Change*, p. 9.

lution. At the same time, the new measure cut the share of land of those owning more than 100 feddans in half.

The results of this cornerstone of the revolution were, in short, disappointing. Discovering why the agrarian reform failed to achieve some of its architect's major goals will shed light on the constraints state leaders, such as Nasser, have encountered in their attempts to concentrate social control in the state—even given the popularity Nasser enjoyed and the resources at his disposal. The answer starts with Nasser's efforts to build a strong state and concludes with the difficult lessons he learned about the intertwining of state and society.

NASSER'S TWO-STEP PROCESS FOR BUILDING A STRONG STATE

Nasser confronted an arresting mix of problems as he began to think in 1952 about implementing the principles of the Free Officers' takeover, including the agrarian reform. The muscle needed to transform society had to come from somewhere. Existing state agencies' personnel were inadequate, if not downright opposed, to the challenge. The state was flaccid, filled with enemies of reform and revolution. Social control lay in the hands of those with aims and rules of the game dramatically opposed to the Free Officers' programs. Backing in the form of popular mobilization also appeared chimerical. Nasser had been deeply disappointed that the military putsch had not sparked major demonstrations of support by the Egyptian masses. If peasants and workers were ever to serve as the lever for the regime to effect change, Nasser and his colleagues would have to build the vehicles to motivate and sustain their mobilization; that certainly was not going to come spontaneously.

Where, then, could Nasser find the muscle necessary to transform Egyptian society? His answer included two steps. First, as a stopgap solution, he relied heavily on the military. Second, he elaborated the state agencies and related institutions that would deliver the new strategies of survival—the rewards, the sanctions, and the symbols—to take the place of those of the old social organizations.

The stopgap solution drew upon former army colleagues to fill important state roles, allowing them considerable autonomy in leading the state's major agencies.[16] "Having come to power without ideologi-

[16] On the Egyptian military in post-1952 politics, see Anour Abdel-Malek, *Egypt: Military Society* (New York: Random House, 1968); Eliezer Be'eri, *Army Officers in Arab Society and Politics* (New York: Praeger, 1970); P. J. Vatikiotis, *The Egyptian Army in Politics* (Bloomington: Indiana University Press, 1961); Mahmud A. Faksh, "Education and Elite Recruitment: An Analysis of Egypt's Post-1952 Political Elite," *Comparative Education Re-*

cally motivated cadres from whom he could draw for appointments," noted Baker, "Nasser assigned key responsibilities to individuals (technically qualified, if possible) who enjoyed his personal confidence."[17] For the most part, the army was the well from which Nasser drew.

Baker compiled some interesting statistics on the extent to which Nasser relied on the military in gaining control of the state. After the initial purge of the army following the coup d'etat, 3,500 men were in the officer corps. About two-thirds continued in the military, and about 1,000 took posts in other state agencies over the years. In 1961, approximately 300 exofficers worked in state ministries, and, in 1964, at least 22 of the 26 provincial governors were officers or former officers.[18] All these appointments in themselves would not bring the "revolution from above" of which Nasser dreamed—that required far more substantive institutional change—but they did provide loyal cadres within the organs of the state who could guard against reaction and initiate such institutional change.

Another more obvious role for the military in Nasser's stopgap solution lay in the area of security. Nasser and the Free Officers were tested only weeks after the July 23 takeover. More than 10,000 textile workers joined a violent strike. Strikers set a factory on fire and clashed with police. The army quickly stepped into the fray, battling workers, killing and wounding many. In the aftermath, a special military tribunal tried the leaders of the strike, and two workers were later hanged.

Little doubt remained that the regime would rely heavily on the army to maintain the security necessary to ensure its survival and introduce its reforms. It is hardly surprising that, as Anwar el-Sadat recounts in his memoirs, old party politicians now attempted to gain influence in the army.[19] The Free Officers moved quickly to thwart these efforts and to maintain the army as unsullied by other institutional or personal ties. They arrested politicians, court-martialed some officers, and finally disbanded all political parties. By 1961, the role of the army in internal security was paramount. More than three-quarters of the people working in the all-important Ministry of the Interior were either active or retired military officers.[20]

---

view 20 (June 1976): 140–50; and R. Hrair Dekmejian, *Egypt Under Nasir: A Study in Political Dynamics* (Albany: State University of New York Press, 1971).

[17] Baker, *Egypt's Uncertain Revolution*, p. 55.

[18] Ibid.

[19] Anwar el-Sadat, *In Search of Identity: An Autobiography* (New York: Harper and Row, 1977), p. 124.

[20] Baker, *Egypt's Uncertain Revolution*, p. 75. Also, see Dekmejian, *Egypt Under Nasir*, p. 220.

In the long run, however, the military alone could not build new strategies of survival to challenge the old bases of social control. Nasser concluded early in his role that effective ministries and a political party under his control would ensure the success of the revolution. His second step in creating a foundation for sustained mobilization and support, then, involved building effective state agencies and a mass party.[21] He had learned an important lesson in his encounter with the large landowners in 1952, reinforcing this conclusion: the state could not simply displace existing social arrangements; it had to offer a viable substitute of its own. Landlords were able to dictate social behavior of the peasants, Nasser grasped, because they offered the elements for people's strategies of survival; if the state were to dictate behavior instead and mobilize the peasants, it and its allied party had to deliver the components for viable strategies for the population.

The success in bringing about the demise of the powerful class of large landlords through the reform was resounding, but Nasser came to understand that landowners had played important roles in maintaining the social and economic stability of Egypt's villages through the social control they had exercised. In some villages, single absentee landlords had owned all the village lands and had ruled through middlemen, many of whom were middle peasants who rented lands from the owner and, in turn, leased parcels out to other villagers. In other villages, the order was more varied. Some absentee arrangements existed, but other big landlords exercised direct control in the villages as did rich peasants, who in addition to hiring labor for their own lands acted as middlemen for parts of larger estates. The big landowners in the village, along with the middlemen and rich peasants, maintained their own enclaves of social control in a host of such enclaves—with their own rules of the game and sometimes even with their own little armies. They kept order by dictating behavior, using the rewards and sanctions at their disposal as leverage.

Thus, a major challenge faced the new regime. Nasser had to ensure a substitute for the order the landlords' social control had created in the countryside by offering components for effective alternative strategies of survival. He and other state leaders had to devise a new set of rules, a new order, as a basis for social control to further the

[21] There was a strong interlocking of state and party. Dekmejian gives some interesting tables on personnel in both state agencies, particularly the military, and the top leadership of the party. He adds, "The twelve members of the former Presidential Council and six of the former Executive Council constituted the total membership of the ASU Supreme Executive. An interlocking relationship thus existed at the top between the governmental and party structures." Dekmejian, *Egypt Under Nasir*, p. 149.

purposes of the state. He needed immediately a set of state institutions with staying power to suffuse Egypt's 4,000 villages; those institutions could be the vehicles to motivate and sustain the peasant mobilization that would provide the state with the muscle necessary to initiate still further changes. In 1952, the problem was how to begin the process of change at all when almost no such backing existed outside the military.

Nasser needed a set of institutions he could count on to replace all the opponents of the state in the environment of conflict. Only effective agencies, not individual army officers with unbounded loyalty, could guarantee a staying power to manipulate rewards, sanctions, and symbols effectively; only they could induce a permanent shift of social control toward the state. But in the creation of state institutions to replace expropriated landowners Nasser and his colleagues stumbled.

THE STATE'S AGENCIES FOR CONCENTRATING SOCIAL CONTROL

The construction of state agencies and a complex party organization certainly began ambitiously enough. Nasser's strategy, not unlike F.D.R.'s had been in the United States, was to overcome the bureaucracy's inertia by creating new state bodies or shoring up old ones, thus bypassing or rivaling the established routines. Following the agrarian reform, new institutional structures or old ones with new forms and purposes inundated Egypt's villages. Their mandate was to circumvent, or sometimes confront, established local organizations with a new set of rules, carrying out many of the functions formerly performed by large landowners and their underlings. The ultimate success of the Revolution, especially its ability to mobilize the rural population as a future lever for change, hinged on the success of these structures. The key institutions to channel energies for the benefit of the state were the agricultural cooperatives, the local councils, and the Committees of Twenty.

Agricultural cooperatives were not unknown in Egypt prior to 1952. They had gained ground in the first half of the century, especially during World War II, and by the time of the revolution included three-quarters of a million farmers. Now, the state overhauled the cooperative movement and used it as a means to increase state control through selective rewards to farmers. The regimes designed cooperatives to supplant the old social organizations as economic brokers for the peasants, especially in supply of credit, marketing of crops, and provision of seeds and tools. Other state-directed, service adr   istrative structures, including the Combined Units that supplied health care, education, and social services, supplemented the activities of the cooperatives. All these agencies supplied critical services to be used judiciously by state administrators as the building blocks of new strategies of peasant survival. The movement's membership expanded rapidly. The state required all those who received redistributed land to join cooperatives.

These multipurpose cooperatives distributed agricultural inputs (seeds, fertilizers, machinery, livestock, pesticides) and marketed outputs (especially cotton). They vested tremendous leverage in the state, especially through its pricing policies on both the input and output sides. The pricing policies had the long-run effect of transferring tremendous wealth out of agriculture generally and into urban-oriented subsidies and projects. In the local rural area, the appointed supervisor of each cooperative served as a key figure in distributing rewards intended as the backbone of the new strategies of survival, which the state fashioned for the agricultural population. He could dictate the sorts of inputs bought by the farmers, the methods of farming used, and the sale of the major crops. Loans and credit, previously dispensed largely by the big landowners as a major tool in maintaining social control, now became a concern of the cooperatives. The promise of low- or no-interest loans induced practically all fellahin to join cooperatives in the 1950s; later, the state made membership compulsory for the few still left outside. Although credit served as the most attractive feature of the cooperatives, their marketing activities proved quite successful. There was also extensive cooperative mechanization and coordinated crop rotation among members.

Local councils also predated the revolution, going back as far as the Napoleonic conquest of Egypt. Nasser and the Ministry of Local Government presented the idea of revived village councils in 1960 as a means to unburden the central government, tailor programs to the individual needs of villages, and increase administrative efficiency. Decentralization was the new byword of development specialists around the globe at that time, and the Egyptian state endorsed the concept.

Through the councils, Nasser hoped to gain the same sort of responsiveness to local needs that the previous fragmentation of social control had achieved. If new state-oriented strategies of survival were to be attractive to fellahin, state agencies would have to reflect some knowledge about local issues and circumstances. The councils could help adapt the state bureaucracy to the contours of each locale. Their purpose was to coordinate governmental services with the desires and actions of the local populations, especially through self-help programs in which the communities provided the labor and the state contributed material and equipment. Each council represented about 15,000 people (usually between three and seven villages). Elected villagers, villagers appointed by the local government administrator, and state workers functioning in the area constituted the membership on the councils; they dealt with issues including health, education, housing, and development.

Each Committee of Twenty (*lajnat al-'ishrin*) served as the executive group at the village level of the single recognized political party, the Arab Socialist Union (ASU). Nasser founded the ASU in 1962, his third effort to build a mass-based political organization. He initiated it as the comprehensive "packaging" agency that would provide the critical symbolic content. Its purpose was to fashion the hodge-podge of rewards and sanctions provided by the agencies of the state so that the population could adopt coherent, integrated strategies of survival. It would be the vanguard in a way that Nasser or even all the Free Officers together could not: the ASU could be everywhere at once. "All in all, Nasser wanted the ASU to do everything: preempt all other political forces, contain the entire citizenry, and, through the vanguard, turn it into a mobilizational instrument with a cutting edge."[22]

The permanent presence of the ASU in the rural areas came through the Basic Unit, one for every major village, and its executive arm, the Committee of Twenty. Each committee was designed to integrate the village population into the various tentacles of the state. They sought to achieve this aim by focusing on the people themselves—creating "political awareness," developing "spiritual standards," urging increased production, and conveying information from above. And the goal also entailed a watchdog role for the committees, ensuring the bureaucracy's proper execution of its duties and neutralizing village exploiters.[23]

THE CRITICAL ROLE OF THE RICH AND MIDDLE PEASANTS

The new institutions changed the face of village life in Egypt. Iliya Harik offered one interpretation of the enormity of that transformation:

Agrarian reform as a broad package brought with it government hegemony over agriculture and rural society. Whether students fo-

[22] Waterbury, *The Egypt of Nasser and Sadat*, p. 322.
[23] See United Arab Republic, *Statute of the Arab Socialist Union*, pp. 25–28. Also, see James B. Mayfield, *Rural Politics in Nasser's Egypt: A Quest for Legitimacy* (Austin: University of Texas Press, 1971), pp. 134–35.

cus on village communities, regions, classes or the market community, they will find that in countries such as Egypt these sectors have incontrovertibly become integrated with the national system and can be understood best in that context. The fact of the matter is that rural people are no longer face to face with the landlord, the money lender, the merchant or urban population, such classical conflicts are no longer prominent. . . . The villager now lives within a larger context—the state. He is face to face with its officials, its teachers, doctors, police, its plans and rules, its designs and its intractability.[24]

This interpretation, like so many others on the Third World, misses an important side of the process of political and social change. In fact, the state's success has been much more mixed than Harik's words here convey. All the new institutions—the agricultural cooperatives, the local councils, and the Committees of Twenty—became dominated by people pressing rules for Egyptian village society different from those intended by Nasser and his associates in Cairo. The supreme irony was that the very agencies created to achieve state predominance in Egypt perpetuated an environment of conflict and fragmentation of social control. "To assume that the state is able to control the daily lives of peasant cultivators," wrote Richard Adams, "is to greatly overestimate the state's power of control over both its own officials and members of the rural sector. . . . The state remains quite incapable of determining the precise character and content of local-level interaction."[25] All the teachers, doctors, and police, all the plans and designs, did not establish the new rules of the game in rural Egypt.

In short, the new Egyptian state, as many others in the middle range of a spectrum of state strength in the Third World, seems an anomaly. Its presence, through its agencies, is almost overwhelming. Those agencies affect nearly every dimension of economic and social life. And yet social elements exist that somehow capture state resources and agencies for their own purposes, denying state leaders the ability to determine "the precise character and content of local-level interaction." The key groups thwarting the designs of the state's village-level institutions in Egypt's agrarian reform were the middle and rich peasants holding between five and fifty feddans of land.[26]

[24] Iliya Harik, "Continuity and Change in Local Development Policies in Egypt: From Nasser to Sadat," in Louis J. Cantori and Harik, eds., *Local Politics and Development in the Middle East* (Boulder, Colo.: Westview Press, 1984), pp. 84–85.

[25] Richard H. Adams, *Development and Social Change in Rural Egypt* (Syracuse: Syracuse University Press, 1986), p. 78.

[26] "Middle peasants" refers to those who own sufficient land so that they need not sell their labor to others to live but who also do not permanently hire others to farm their

These groups, to the surprise of some, had advanced handsomely through the reform. Many of those farmers gained new acreage from the large landowners through crash sales and private deals in the immediate wake of the new agrarian legislation. Accounting for only a small percentage of the Egyptian rural population and owning nearly half of the cultivable lands, they came to occupy the most important roles in exercising social control in rural Egypt. Leonard Binder commented that "the rural middle class, like lucky Pierre, always seems to turn up as a beneficiary of the system."[27] It emerged as the weightiest element in the countryside, certainly not the intended result of the state's reform program, which had aimed to bolster the largest groups in the village—the poor peasants with less than five feddans and those with no land at all.

Rich and middle peasants continued to dominate the state's village-level agencies as well as the local rural branches of the ASU for all but a short period. They turned the agricultural cooperatives into both vehicles for their own material gain and means for impressing their own rules of the game on village social life. "With their social and economic influence, they have succeeded in dominating the administration of the cooperatives and taking full advantage of them."[28] Adams

---

land. "Rich peasants" are those who farm their lands but also hire others to do the farming on a more or less permanent basis. In Egypt, anyone with a sizable plot—middle or rich peasants or landowners who do no cultivating themselves—are referred to as landowners, *al mullak*. In a number of works, the middle and rich peasants are referred to as the rural middle class. Some see anyone with more than five feddans as part of this class; others draw the line at ten feddans. Officially, the state came to define peasants as those with less than twenty-five feddans. A debate among scholars has raged over precisely who gained most from the reform. Abdel-Fadil, *Development, Income Distribution and Social Change*, p. 23, singled out those with twenty to twenty-five feddans. There has been some disagreement, given the paucity of figures, over whether these middle-range landowners continued to hold sway or sold out, discouraged by economic opportunities in Nasser's Egypt. The most forceful statement arguing the dissolution of this group is in Iliya Harik, *Distribution of Land, Employment and Income in Rural Egypt* (Ithaca, N.Y.: Rural Development Committee, Cornell University, 1979). Also, see Mohaya Saytoun, "Income Distribution in Egyptian Agriculture and its Main Determinants," in C. Abdel-Khalek and R. Tignor, eds., *The Political Economy of Income Distribution in Egypt* (New York: Holmes and Meier, 1982). Waterbury has convincingly cast skepticism on any premature assumptions about the waning role of middle-range landowners. *The Egypt of Nasser and Sadat*, pp. 270–72. He has argued, however, that the most dynamic group owns five to ten feddans. Waterbury may be right formally, but, in effect, these may be the same peasants who owned twenty to fifty feddans but who have transferred parts of their holdings over time to family members.

[27] Leonard Binder, *In a Moment of Enthusiasm: Political Power and the Second Stratum in Egypt* (Chicago: University of Chicago Press, 1978), p. 7.

[28] Baker, *Egypt's Uncertain Revolution*, p. 205.

describes a village of the 1970s that reflected the situation for many other villages a decade after the reform. Here the agricultural cooperative board consisted of twelve members; nine of these were poor peasants, all of whom were either relatives of the richest peasant in the village, who was head of the board, or his clients.[29]

Rich and middle peasants also took control of the local councils. Mayfield noted, for example, that the larger landowning families controlled the vast majority of village councils, at least until 1966. From 1966 to 1970, an "anti-feudal" campaign (see next section) temporarily wrested control from these families in some villages. Even in that period, however, he estimated that at least 40 percent of all councils could be classified as "reactionary."[30]

The biggest disappointment of all came in the role the rich and middle peasantry played in undermining the purposes of the ASU. It transformed the Committees of Twenty into further means to extend its influence. A predecessor of the ASU, the National Union, had already staked out a special, influential role for these villagers.[31] Binder's analysis offers evidence of a marked continuity in the role of the rich and middle peasants from the National Union to the ASU.[32]

The agrarian reform, the new and renewed institutions of the state, and the single party all greatly affected Egyptian village life. The state, in effect, transformed the society; through the institutions it built, the state also had a continuing strong impact on rural life. By setting prices for crops, especially cotton, at a low level relative to world prices, the state used the marketing function of the agricultural cooperatives as a means to tax peasants indirectly and regressively and to effect a major net outflow of resources from the agricultural sector.[33] In addition, the new institutions became the channel for key resources, such as credit, which entered rural communities.

The transformation of society, however, took on unexpected dimensions and deprived state leaders of the concentrated social control and mobilization capabilities they had sought. Despite all the resources and institutions apparently at the disposal of state leaders—especially

[29] Adams, *Development and Social Change*, pp. 84–85.

[30] Mayfield, *Rural Politics in Nasser's Egypt*, p. 206.

[31] See Binder, *In a Moment of Enthusiasm*, p. 305.

[32] Ibid., pp. 314 ff. Waterbury interpreted these data differently. *The Egypt of Nasser and Sadat*, p. 281.

[33] See Richard H. Adams, Jr., "Taxation, Control and Agrarian Transition in Rural Egypt: A Local-Level View" (Paper Presented at the Conference Sponsored by the Social Science Research Council on the Food Problem and State Policy in the Middle East, Rome, September 17–18, 1984).

when compared to the petty farmers who ended up setting the rules of the game in rural Egypt—state figures could not overcome the fragmentation of social control. The rich and middle peasants were at the center of the dashed hopes of state leaders and the sort of rural transformation that did occur.

Harik portrayed the impact of the state on rural society and the resilient role of rich peasants in his account of a single village in Egypt.[34] Prior to the revolution absentee landlords had owned most of the lands of Shubra (the name is fictitious). A single prince had owned fully one-third of all the village lands; two resident families, the Samads and the Kuras, also had significant landholdings and played important middlemen roles. All other villagers' plots together totaled less than 100 feddans. The Samads dominated village life on a day-to-day basis. Besides managing their own lands, they rented lands from the absentee owners and leased plots to other villagers, ran the village cooperative with generous loans from the state agricultural bank and other banks, and marketed almost all the crops grown in the village. Politically, too, they monopolized village life. The position of umda, village headman, was inherited in the family. Mustafa Samad, the last umda, collected taxes, settled disputes, maintained order with the aid of fifteen guards under his authority, dealt with village agricultural problems, and participated widely in provincial political affairs.

With the introduction of the new state initiatives in 1952, the Samads made every effort to maintain their positions under the new political format. Even as their middleman role waned in the wake of the expropriation of the absentee landlords for whom they had served as managers, they continued to dominate village political affairs for seven years after the revolution. No single family exercised as much control thereafter as the Samads had for the previous half-century.

After 1952, however, political competition was sharpened. More villagers began to take active parts in village politics. The other rich peasant family, the Kuras, came to play the leading role in this cyclone of political excitement. The biggest employers in the village, they dominated the mayoralty of the village, the village council, the local branch of the National Union, and later the Committee of Twenty of the ASU. The entire face of the village changed. Donating seven feddans of their own land, the Kuras speeded the construction of a Combined Unit, including a health clinic, a veterinary center, crafts center,

[34] Iliya Harik, *The Political Mobilization of Peasants: A Study of an Egyptian Community* (Bloomington: Indiana University Press, 1974).

school, and children's nursery. In addition, they instigated the construction of a new marketplace in the village and a road directly to it.

That rich and middle peasants came to lead new village institutions throughout Egypt in itself might not have been so bad from Nasser's point of view. After all, the state, through its agrarian reform, had succeeded admirably in deeply changing rural society: it had eliminated the most distinctive feature of village social life of the late nineteenth and early twentieth centuries, the tremendous gap between the fellahin and the absentee and resident giant landowners, who had concentrated so much social control in their hands and the hands of their agents. The new social structure surely did not reproduce that of the late nineteenth century.

Of great concern to Nasser, however, was that the new structure did not achieve the deeper goals he had harbored for his ambitious reform. The new rules of the game in rural social life were not those of the state. The rich and middle peasants used their sinecures in the new state institutions and the ASU for their own purposes, subverting the designs of the state leadership. Poor peasants most often suffered miserably by the principles of distribution the strongmen instituted, but those strategies of survival for the poor were better than none at all. Note the statement of one poor peasant: "*al-hamdu lillah* (praise to God) it is Ahmed and Mohammed (two rich peasants) who keep (me alive). When they have work in their fields, I work for them. When they have no work for me, I can usually borrow a little money from them (against future work periods)."[35]

The distribution of social control was substantially different after 1952, but an environment of conflict persisted. Egyptian society adjusted to and was transformed by the initiatives of the state, but the legacy of that nineteenth-century social structure continued to shine through. The newfound strength of the middle and rich peasants, their ability to exercise significant social control in the countryside, drew from their positions in the prerevolution order—especially in their service of absentee landlords—as well as from the needs Nasser and the state had as they attacked that order.

In the early 1960s, the state took steps to bolster the poor peasants—those it claimed had a natural interest in the state's socialist policies—to contain the rich and middle peasants. It issued a law requiring peasants with less than five feddans to constitute at least 80 percent of the

[35] Richard Hilton Adams, Jr., "Growth without Development in Rural Egypt: A Local-Level Study of Institutional and Social Change" (1981, mimeographed), p. 128.

boards of directors of the cooperatives. Again, results were disappointing. Some landowners transferred property to relatives to fall within the guideline; others simply used their social control to dominate the boards. By the mid-1960s, tales of how middle and rich peasants used the new institutions to further rules different from the state's began to appear in the Egyptian press. Some of the material that appeared was sensationalist, but it did demonstrate the vitality of these other sets of rules, of a mélange of social organizations maintaining their own way of doing things. Different from the old environment of conflict were the strongmen (rich and middle peasants rather than big absentee and resident landlords) and the degree to which they used state resources and institutions as the bases for their own social control; state capital and agencies were now crucial. Rich and middle peasants, the charges went, used the agricultural cooperatives virtually as private businesses. They appropriated funds without justification, appointed relatives to cooperative posts, dealt on the black market and more.[36] A 1968 newspaper account reported that one village family's members held the following positions:

> In the administration—the mayor, his alternate, and his four assistants, the chief of police and his assistants; in the Arab Socialist Union—the secretary of the committee, the vice-secretary, and eighteen out of a total of twenty members; in the village council—the chairman, the secretary, and ten members; in the village cooperative—the president, the secretary, and another member of the board of directors.[37]

Waterbury, in his outstanding book, *The Egypt of Nasser and Sadat*, may have underestimated the strength of the rich and middle peasants in their own enclaves because he found no pattern of active support for them by the Nasserist regime. It is striking, however, that these strongmen ended up using state resources and institutions to build significant control in opposition to the declared rules of the state even without the active support of the regime. As Ali Sabri, secretary-general of the ASU, wrote, those with more than twenty-five feddans "managed to establish links with the administrative, technical, and cultural organizations in the village with the aim of exploiting them uniquely for personal aims."[38] The key is not "the *active* support of the regime." The strongmen built their control, for reasons we shall explore, with

---

[36] Baker, *Egypt's Uncertain Revolution*, reports some of these findings, pp. 205–6.
[37] Story by Michel Kamel, an editor of *al-Tali'ah*, cited in ibid., p. 209.
[38] Quoted in ibid.

significant accommodation by the state to their activities. Waterbury noted this tendency when he wrote that this stratum

> was allowed to become the local overseer for much that the state undertook in rural areas. With the exception of the period 1966–1968, the regime turned a blind eye to its manipulation of official pricing arrangements, its violation of rent and wage laws and of landholding ceilings. It was allowed to control, directly or indirectly, much of the political infrastructure that Nasser introduced into the countryside.[39]

One fellah expressed the accommodation between strongmen and the state facing the lowest stratum in the village: "What poor peasant here would ever go and complain about 'Anwar's' (evasion) of land tenancy regulations? They are all too fearful of the government and too dependent on Anwar for agricultural work."[40]

The Attempt and Failure to Break the Control of the Strongmen

In 1966, Nasser stepped up efforts to break the fragmented social control maintained by the rich and middle peasants by organizing the Committee for the Liquidation of Feudalism. In that year and the next, for the only time in the course of the reform, state leaders failed to accommodate the new strongmen and sought to break their control. The forty-member committee intended to combat the remnants of the large landowning class that had circumvented the requirements of the reform *and* the rich and middle peasantry that abused the institutions of reform. It aimed to root out competing rules of the game and enclaves of social control. Although its chairman was the head of the military, the Arab Socialist Union inspired and supported its activities. In fact, the ASU sat at the very center of the frenetic "anti-feudal" campaign. Newspapers loudly proclaimed the attack on "agrarian feudalists" and printed all the lurid details of the abuses the committee uncovered. The successes were notable. Hundreds of village umdas lost their jobs; the Ministry of Agriculture dissolved about 300 boards of directors of agricultural cooperatives; the state recovered tens of thousands of feddans of illegally owned land; the ASU dissolved its Committees of Twenty and replaced them with new, appointed members to local Leadership Groups.

However, these achievements proved short-lived. The state, in fact, eventually returned all the seized land, and other charges dissolved as

---

[39] Waterbury, *The Egypt of Nasser and Sadat*, p. 277.
[40] Quoted in Adams, "Growth without Development," p. 124.

well. In the spring of 1968, Nasser took what on the surface appears a most puzzling step; he effectively ended the state's attack against the rich and middle peasants. He admitted in the March 30 Declaration, which became a "basic document" of the revolution, that the ASU had been ineffective as a representative of the people. Nasser's statement, in essence, undermined the very institution he had designated to lead the combat against the continuing fragmentation of social control. From that moment until his death, he subverted the ability of the ASU to play a serious role in either mobilizing the poor peasants or concentrating social control. He dissolved the ASU Secretariat, halted the activities of the ASU Youth Organization, rid the party of its leftist cadres, and, finally, arrested Secretary-General Ali Sabri.

NASSER UNDERMINES HIS OWN AGENCIES

Why did Nasser engage in such seemingly pathological behavior, destroying his own creation, the primary channel the state had for the mobilization and support of the population? Nasser could not hope to concentrate social control and dictate the effective rules of the game without complex state agencies and related institutions (such as the ASU); only those together could offer the elements for viable strategies of survival to the vast numbers of poor fellahin. Moreover, only such institutions could selectively offer the rewards and sanctions necessary for personal survival and mobility, and only they could package the strategies in symbols meaningful to the circumstances of the population. Nasser had charged the ASU with just such packaging plus an all-important watchdog role in monitoring the performance of state agencies in contributing their part to the rewards offered by the state. His own rhetoric and charisma could energize that process, but they could not substitute for it.

Now, near the end of his life, Nasser used his powers of appointment and his ability to manipulate the organizational makeup of the ASU to ensure failure of the important second step of his plan to concentrate control—building effective state agencies and a mass party. Nasser's problem was that the creation of a strong channel for mobilization, such as the ASU, in the absence of many other state channels with significant independent mobilizational capacities, posed serious threats to him. His other state channels did not have such mobilizational capabilities; in rural Egypt, the strongmen still held social control and mobilizational capabilities. No matter how much Nasser used his power of appointment to inject loyal military figures into the ASU, he found that once in their new positions these figures began to assume the distinct perspective of the ASU; often that varied with Nasser's own perspective. He began to fear the development of "power centers," as he called them (or what his successor amended to "nefarious power centers"), within the ASU, the military, and several other state agencies. He suspected the patron-client ties that developed in these institutions.

The nature of Egyptian society, still largely rural with fragmented social control, influenced how far Nasser was prepared to go in building powerful new institutions to mobilize the population. With social control still vested in rural Egypt in the rich and middle peasantry, Nasser had precious few alternative channels of mobilization to check the power centers. As the ASU moved in the mid-1960s from an amorphous mass movement to a more tightly knit organization, his concerns grew. "A dominant regime," wrote Harik, "is likely to have low tolerance for strong organizations that seek to free themselves from the subordinate position to which mass movements are condemned."[41] The more Nasser bestowed the authority and resources upon the ASU to challenge the rich and middle peasants, the more the ASU developed its own institutional perspective on the ills of Egypt and how to right them—and the more its mobilizational capability began to outstrip the combined remainder of the state's mobilizational capabilities. Waterbury summed up Nasser's dilemma:

> For two years Nasser laid aside his fears and hesitations and tried to make of the ASU an instrument that could promote his increasingly radical goals. He seemed genuinely to want to reach out to new, underprivileged constituencies to sustain the socialist transformation. At the same time he knew that if the ASU became such an instrument it could be turned against him.[42]

As one of the original Free Officers, Khaled Muhieddin, put it, the regime entrusted loyal individuals in key institutions with tremendous responsibilities, but it did so without yet having the institutional ability to monitor and check them.[43] Within the ASU, power had been concentrated in the Vanguard Organization. The main figures in it were trusted military men, particularly those who had dealt with intelligence and security issues. Nasser, however, knew how frail a reed such loyalty could be. As those within the ASU developed a distinctive per-

[41] Iliya Harik, "The Single Party as a Subordinate Movement: The Case of Egypt," *World Politics* 26 (October 1973): 105.

[42] Waterbury, *The Egypt of Nasser and Sadat*, p. 332.

[43] Baker, *Egypt's Uncertain Revolution*, p. 80.

spective and as patron-client ties formed within it, he grew increasingly suspicious of his own lieutenants and the ASU as a whole.

Nasser was without the benefit of a myriad of other agencies, each effective in delivering some components for strategies of survival offered by the state and together able to check the growth in power of any major single institution. These circumstances drove him in the early and mid-1960s to balance his two major institutions, the military and the ASU. The military from the time of the revolution until 1967 was under the command of Nasser's fellow Free Office, Abdul Hakim Amir. But the military, as the ASU, developed its own institutional perspective and remained a recurring source of anxiety for Nasser. As Baker noted, inevitably time strengthened Amir's identification with the particular interests of the military, and gradually he became the spokesman for these interests.[44] Nasser successfully used each institution, the military and the ASU, as a lever to contain the particularist tendencies inherent in the other. When the ASU's star rose, for example, with the antifeudal campaign, Nasser appointed commander of the armed forces Amir as the figure to head the Committee for the Liquidation of Feudalism.

In late 1967 and early 1968, however, Nasser's balancing act began to topple. First, the humiliating defeat in the June 1967 War against Israel discredited the military. Amir resigned in June, but Nasser rightfully feared his reemergence and a possible bid for top state leadership through a military coup. Nasser retired hundreds of officers, who were clients of Amir. In September, he placed Amir under house arrest and shortly thereafter announced Amir's suicide. All·this occurred after the period in which the ASU had taken its most forceful strides forward. It had undertaken witchhunts in support of the Committee for the Liquidation of Feudalism as well as attacks on the civil service and those running newly nationalized public enterprises. With its widening mandate and growing militant stance, the ASU had threatened, even before the June War, to undo the balance Nasser had maintained. Now, with his attack against the officer corps, Nasser eclipsed the military as a counterweight to the ASU. Waterbury wrote, "With Sabri at its helm, the ASU by 1968 was the only significant political force in the Egyptian arena and by that token a legitimate cause for Nasser's suspicion."[45] Also, part of Nasser's reason for keeping the ASU strong had now evaporated. The degradation of the military and the purge of its officers made the ASU less essential as a counterweight to the military.

[44] Ibid., p. 53.
[45] Waterbury, *The Egypt of Nasser and Sadat*, p. 329.

February 1968 caused Nasser even more to question the soundness of a strategy supporting the ASU's efforts to break the pattern of fragmented social control in the countryside. The announcement of relatively lenient sentences doled out to senior military officers for their part in the June 1967 debacle sparked riots in cities, factories, and universities in Egypt. Nasser subsequently demonstrated much anxiety about the effect widespread social instability could have on his rule. To placate the urban rioters, he promised resentencing of the military officers.

Nasser must have also realized in his own mind the issue of rural social stability. The middle and rich peasants assured such stability through their effective use of sanctions and rewards, even if they also maintained the ascendancy of conflicting rules of the game. To lend backing to the ASU's efforts to unseat rural strongmen held the danger of investing in long-term concentration of social control at the expense of short-term social stability. Nasser was not willing to fall prey to that danger. The month after the riots, he levied his harsh criticism against the ASU and reversed its course in Egyptian society. In effect, he announced his willingness to accommodate local strongmen and their fragmentation of social control in exchange for social stability in the countryside.

The Vicious Cycle of State Failure

There is little question that state policies and actions after 1952 led to rapid transformations in the Egyptian countryside. These transformations reflected the hand of a formidable state organization, such as those found in India and Mexico as well as Egypt. It is inconceivable that a much weaker state—Sierra Leone's, for example—could have wrought such deep changes. Egypt's state institutions eliminated the class of large landowners. They channeled new state resources into the villages while transferring massive amounts of privately generated wealth out of the rural areas altogether. The new credit, health clinics, schools, social workers, marketing facilities, and more all made the Egyptian village of 1970 a far cry from that of 1950. Nasser's agrarian reform and accompanying measures certainly had a deep impact. In its ability to transform rural society, the Egyptian state appeared strong indeed. It continued and intensified Egypt's historical tradition of a strong centralized, bureaucratic presence in village life.

By the last quarter of Nasser's rule, however, he was deeply disappointed about these changes. State policies induced unprecedented changes in social structure but not at all what top policy makers had envisioned. Rich and middle peasants—not the poor peasants Nasser had considered the natural allies of socialism—benefited the most from the new reforms. Those villagers holding from twenty to fifty feddans, who often distributed their holdings to trusted friends and relatives so as to appear to own only five to ten feddans, dominated the new state institutions. They used the credit, marketing facilities, subsidized agricultural inputs, even the new social services, as means to build organizational bases to support principles of distribution very different from the Cairo guidelines.

Numerous amendments to the law did little to impose Nasser's vision of who-should-get-what on actual village life. The strongmen of the village built their fortunes (modest by most international standards but quite substantial in terms of Egypt's villages) by skillfully using the new institutional and material inputs of the state according to their own rules of the game. At best, they counted on the acquiescence or accommodation of the state authorities, not the active support of the regime. Social control remained fragmented.

A vicious cycle linked Nasser's aspirations for the state and this pattern of fragmented social control. This cycle goes far toward answering our question of why the state, with all its assets, failed to consolidate social control. Nasser faced a "Catch-22." Rural strongmen maintained social control and made the rules by offering the wherewithal for the survival strategies of poor peasants. Nasser's chance for concentrating control in the state depended upon building powerful agencies to bring the state's own rewards, sanctions, and symbols to the fellahin. In a conversation with non-Egyptian Arabs, he once said, "You imagine that we simply give orders and the country is run accordingly. You are greatly mistaken."[46] He knew the value of effective institutions in achieving his goals. But building powerful agencies when he had few other sources of social control and when that control still lay in the strongmen's enclaves threatened Nasser with Frankensteins. Here were powerful agencies, particularly the ASU, building cohesion and a particular perspective on Egypt's ills with only minimal tools at Nasser's disposal to monitor and contain them. He felt his own leadership at stake. Moreover, his tenure depended on his ability to buy social peace. In Egypt's villages, the strongmen shared Nasser's concern with social stability, and they had the means to achieve it.

He accrued other benefits from the existing distribution of social control, as well. After the agrarian reform, under the rich and middle

---

[46] Quoted in Malcolm H. Kerr, *The Arab Cold War: Gamal 'Abd al-Nasir and His Rivals, 1958–1970*, 3d ed. (London: Royal Institute of International Affairs by Oxford University Press, 1971), p. 61.

peasants' leadership, agricultural output and productivity exceeded Egypt's rapid population growth. This trend reversed the fall in output and productivity under the old regime. The extreme fragmentation also meant the state could effect a considerable net flow of resources from the rural sector as a whole while accommodating those who profited most from the existing order. As Egyptian society changed, new groups, practically all urban, clamored for state attention and resources, as their members created strategies of survival. Labor unions, professional organizations, and business associations all made demands upon the state. The transfer of resources from the rural areas, made possible in part by the accommodations with rural strongmen, gave the state leadership resources to make still other accommodations with these urban interests. Unleashing the ASU against the rural strongmen could threaten social peace in the countryside as well as a web of accommodations in the urban areas. Nasser chose, in these difficult circumstances, to subvert the very means he had nurtured to achieve consolidated social control and the imposition of the state's rules of the game.

What impact did the continuing fragmentation of social control have upon the administration and political life of the state? I will look more fully at that question in Chapters 6 and 7, but here I can note two important effects. First, the ministries of the state and their local institutions—the councils, cooperatives, Combined Units, and the like—continued to operate in Egypt's villages. Local strongmen, however, used public policies and the agencies charged with executing them to satisfy their own needs and benefits. The state resources and institutions became the mortar for organizational ties at the local level based on very different rules of distribution from those of the state. Second, Nasser, along with a cadre of aides, advisers, and clients, developed a political style of "preemption."[47] As "power centers"—the state's own agencies, enterprises, and affiliated party, as well as centers outside the state such as the Muslim Brethren—threatened Nasser's personal and regime survival, he relied heavily on police and intelligence agencies to thwart their cohesion before they could be used against him. What started as one of the most idealistic political revolutions in the postwar period ended in a rash of charges of torture, arbitrary arrest, and the like. "By the mid-1970s," wrote Waterbury, "there was an impressive body of literature on what had been one of the murkiest and most unseemly sides of the Nasserist experiment."[48]

[47] Waterbury, *The Egypt of Nasser and Sadat*, p. 333.
[48] Ibid., p. 338.

CHAPTER SIX

The Politics of Survival:
Why Weak States Cannot Overcome
Strong Societies and What Happens to Them
as a Result

STATE LEADERS AND STATE AGENCIES

In a single generation, new states of Africa and Asia have insinuated themselves so completely into their societies, even in the far corners of their countries, that in terms of formal institutions many of those societies are almost unrecognizable compared to what they were, say, at the end of World War II. Older states in the Third World, too, have managed to transform the political and social landscapes of their societies.[1] All sorts of state agencies, from agricultural banks to grade schools, have made the city, town, and village a far cry from what they had been only a few decades ago. These institutions have led irrevocably to new social relations throughout the Third World.

The state media in many countries have sought to reinforce the omnipresence of state institutions by representing the chief state leaders as the actual embodiment of the state. In Jordan, for example, rarely a day passes when the television news does not begin with the same words: "His Majesty King Hussein today. . . ." "In Zaire," wrote V. S. Naipul, "Mobutu is the news: his speeches, his receptions, the *marches de soutien*, the new appointments: court news."[2]

The relationship between state leaders and other parts of the state, however, is more problematical than such news reports would have us believe. A state leader's ability to go beyond mere patriarchal or patrimonial sorts of rule lies in the character of his ties with those state agencies that have so permeated society. Using those institutions to proper advantage can mean all the difference for the state leader in effectiveness and political survival. Of special importance is the extent to which he can use those institutions for security and mobilization.

---

[1] On Latin America, for example, see Merilee Serrill Grindle, *State and Countryside: Development Policy and Agrarian Politics in Latin America* (Baltimore: Johns Hopkins University Press, 1986).

[2] V. S. Naipaul, "A New King for the Congo," *New York Review of Books*, June 26, 1975.

Security agencies, of course, can preserve domestic social stability and defend the country against outside attack or deter potential attackers altogether.

Mobilization of human and material resources is also key for achieving the state leader's goals. "Much of what is traditionally meant by power *does* involve the government's capacity to mobilize resources."[3] Bureaus can mobilize such resources through direct and indirect revenue collection and through reorganization of manpower and production. Not only can effective institutions enhance state revenues for domestic purposes, but they can alleviate some of the severe pressures on state leaders from the international economy stemming from deficits in balance of payments and debt repayment. Mobilization also plays an essential role, as we shall see, in preventing the many parts of the state from acting at cross-purposes. In short, building strong state agencies, ones able to set the rules in their societies, is not simply an abstract norm for state leaders; there are clear imperatives coming from within the society and outside to build as strong an apparatus as possible.

And yet, bizarre as it may seem, state leaders with limited capacity to mobilize their public have themselves crippled the arms of the state, especially those organs that ultimately could have given the leaders not only mobilizational ability but also, as I shall show, enhanced security. In this chapter I explore the paradox. I argue that in societies with weak states a continuing environment of conflict—the vast, but fragmented social control embedded in the nonstate organizations of society—has dictated a particular, pathological set of relationships within the state organization itself, between the top state leadership and its agencies. In turn, these ties within the state organization have shaped the very nature of the insinuation of state institutions into society.

The Dilemma of State Leaders

The nub of society's impact on the state lies in the process of political mobilization. As the above quotation from Lamborn stressed, "Power *does* involve the government's capacity to mobilize resources." Societies with a mélange of social organizations, many having their own rule-making ability, have witnessed stiff resistance to leaders' efforts to use the state as a means of sustained political mobilization. Such mobilization demands much more than exhortations, charisma, or abstract

[3] Alan C. Lamborn, "Power and the Politics of Extraction," *International Studies Quarterly* 27 (June 1983): 126.

ideology; it entails the state's creation of circumstances whereby people feel that its symbols and codes of behavior are essential to their well-being, and it involves providing them with institutional channels to express their support. In brief, state leaders can seek sustained political mobilization only when they, in turn, have proffered viable strategies of survival to the populace.

Fashioning effective strategies of survival demands an elaborate set of institutions to dole out sanctions and material incentives, as well as to package state services and sanctions in a coherent, meaningful set of symbols. In societies in which social control has rested with a panoply of heterogeneous organizations, however, state leaders have been caught between Scylla and Charybdis, facing a baffling paradox: If domestic and international dangers can be countered through political mobilization, gained by constructing state agencies and viable strategies of survival, strengthening those state agencies may at the same time hold its own perils for state leaders.

We can understand and explore this paradox by using three simple models: a market model, a physical model of centrifugal and centripetal forces, and a model of risk taking.

Political mobilization is an effective tool for state leaders where there are many channels of support. As in a free market, where no single actor can change supply or demand sufficiently to affect the overall price of a good, here leaders seek sufficient channels of mobilization so that no single state agency can control so large a share of state mobilization capacity that it can affect the overall amount of support appreciably. In an oligopoly, a few economic actors control such a large share of demand or supply that they *can* affect the overall price of a good sufficiently. In an oligopoly of mobilizational capability, several agencies can influence the overall channeling of support to the top state leadership.

Why does such an oligopoly of mobilizational capability pose threats to state leaders? After all, these agencies are part of the state, and presumably their officials share preferences with state leaders. Dan Horowitz, quoted in Chapter 4, used a physical model to allude to the peril to state leadership. He asked, "How did the 'centripetal' propensities in the Yishuv overcome the 'centrifugal' propensities?"[4] Shapiro writing on the same subject noted Ben-Gurion's feeling that all activity must be controlled by one center. Even the institutions sponsored by the Jews' parastatal organization, Ben-Gurion stated, "pursue their

⁴ Dan Horowitz, "The Yishuv and Israeli Society—Continuity and Change," *Medina U'Mimshal* (1983): 46.

own interests instead of being guided by an overall national plan," and each could end up "ruled by itself and for itself."[5]

The unique perspective any state agency assumes creates in it centrifugal tendencies, pulling it from the views of other agencies and the executive state leadership. Such particular views are created and reinforced in any number of ways, including shared socialization (as in a military academy), the repeated representation of the agency's interests in wider forums (as in the competition for funds), daily personal interaction, the effective allocation of resources and status within the agency, and so on. These factors are found in any complex organization, and the centrifugal forces they generate are familiar to all students of bureaucracy. Matthew Holden, Jr., characterized this orientation among what he called administrative politicians, "This by no means implies that administrative politicians are pirates out for plunder. But it does imply that the most saintly idealist (if a saintly idealist ever could arise to such a high post) could not function if he abandoned the maxim of 'my agency, right or wrong!' "[6]

Top personnel in agencies seek to maintain or create clout for their bureaus by linking with a particular constituency and creating internal loyalty among the bureaucrats. These actions only reinforce the distinct perspective of those within the agency. The common, particular views in a given agency, which develop over time among its top officials about the purposes and functioning of the entire state apparatus, threaten the coherence and, indeed, the stability of the state.

All state leaders, then, must find centripetal forces to counteract the centrifugal tendencies of their agencies if they are to keep the state organization as a whole together, acting more or less cohesively. What can state leaders do in this regard other than make eunuchs of all their underlings? In states where there are many channels for mobilization of support, state leaders have much more ability to check centrifugal pulls. Their centripetal power stems from the fact that on almost any issue they can use those channels to mobilize support against any given agency that finds the particular issue of high saliency and differs on it from the state leadership. That given agency does not control so large a share of state mobilizational capacity that it can challenge the sum of support available to state leaders. Also, the issue is either not salient enough to other agencies to enable that agency to pull together a coalition of bureaus to challenge the leadership; or, if the issue is salient

---

[5] Quoted in Yonathan Shapiro, *The Formative Years of the Israeli Labour Party: The Organization of Power 1919–1930* (Beverly Hills: Sage, 1976), p. 56.

[6] Matthew Holden, Jr., " 'Imperialism' in Bureaucracy," *American Political Science Review* 60 (December 1966): 944.

to others, it is unlikely that the distinct institutional perspectives of the various bureaus would allow for a sufficient sense of common cause to launch such a coalition.,

Where social control is highly fragmented, however, a very different situation obtains; here we can see clearly the influence of society on the state. In circumstances of an oligopoly of mobilizational capacity—a few agencies with significant control on the total sum of support state leaders can generate—the centripetal forces are much weaker. Since the state's leadership in such countries has a limited reservoir of structural support upon which to draw and since so much social control remains with strongmen, the leadership finds it difficult to check the centrifugal forces that grow as a few, select agencies blossom. Threatening to state leaders are abiding loyalties in state organs or allied political parties in the absence of a multitude of effective, opposing centripetal forces. In countries in which such support is absent and costly to achieve, where a very few agencies have an oligopoly on mobilizational capabilities, the position of state leaders may be precarious indeed.

Thus, as long as strongmen continue to offer viable strategies of survival to those of their villages, ethnic groups, urban neighborhoods, and so on, states can marshal only limited public support; there is little motivation for the population to lend such support. A prerequisite for state leaders to substitute their own strategies of survival to peasants and laborers is a set of strong state agencies. There is also a need, however, to be able to mobilize significant support from the population so that these same state agencies will not themselves threaten the political survival of state leaders. Such political mobilization—and here is the catch—cannot be realized without already having channels to the population to induce mobilization through a viable mix of rewards, sanctions, and symbols; this is precisely why strong state agencies are needed in the first place. This paradox is the dilemma of state leaders.

This dilemma, fearing and undermining the very mechanisms leaders need to reach their own goals, has had reverberations in all societies with weak states. The degree to which it has hamstrung state leaders in appropriating power, in having their rules apply throughout the country, has varied from country to country. Where strongmen have been able to maintain tight grips on local resources, state mobilization of the population has been all the more difficult, and the dilemma of state leaders has been acute. The situation has been more fraught with danger for them because fear of domestic and international destabilizing factors forces leaders to concentrate coercive capabilities in no more than a handful of security agencies. These agencies, too, develop their own perspectives and pose obvious threats because of the means at their disposal. The effective counterweight a leader can hold against military and related security forces comes through the mobilizing agencies. Where mobilizing capabilities through these agencies are limited by fragmented social control in the society, the danger of a military takeover is even more acute.

The paradox state leaders face forces them, consciously or unconsciously, to engage in a risk analysis: they must weigh their need for effectiveness and security against the risks to their own political survival through creating agencies that can turn out to be what Nasser called power centers. One possibility is to plough ahead in building institutions, even where social control rests firmly in the grip of strongmen. State leaders do not then have sufficient support through a multitude of channels that they can draw upon to check the newly built institutions. This course exposes leaders to the specter of growing, unchecked centrifugal forces with the ever present possibility of loss of state cohesion and even their own overthrow. State leaders must then somehow resolve their inclinations to be risk averse (after all, what can they accomplish under house arrest?) against their desire to see their political agenda through.

One option is to seek other centripetal forces that can be brought into play; for example, balancing two or more strong agencies against one another or relying on specific social groupings might counterbalance a strong state institution. Such balancing acts have been most prevalent in cases involving military and security agencies, from which leaders have often faced their most serious challenges. I discussed how Nasser employed the ASU, for a time, to counter the Egyptian military. Other state leaders have gone beyond balancing existing agencies to counteracting the centrifugal tendencies of military forces by building two or more military forces to serve as counterweights to one another.

President Hafez al-Assad of Syria has created just such additional military agencies. Besides its regular armed forces, Assad's regime has spawned Defense Units, composed of between 12,000 and 25,000 troops, and Struggle Companies with another 5,000 or so men; both have acted as the regime's Praetorian Guard.[7] Assad has deployed the Defense Units in and around the capital, Damascus, rather than the regular armed forces. Throughout history loyalty has been critical in

[7] Hanna Batatu, "Some Observations on the Social Roots of Syria's Ruling, Military Group and the Causes for its Dominance," *Middle East Journal* 35 (Summer 1981): 331–44.

creating a Praetorian Guard; therefore, it is not surprising that in Syria the Defense Units, for most of Assad's tenure, have been under the leadership of his brother, Rifaat al-Assad. Adnan al-Assad, a cousin of the president, led the Struggle Companies. In addition, a special segment of the Defense Units has protected the Alawis, the ethnic group from which the al-Assad family comes. Jamil al-Assad, another brother, led this unit.

Even in a state confronting as difficult a security situation as Syria's—four major wars in the fifteen years from 1967 to 1982—its leaders have not sought simply to create as coherent and coordinated a fighting machine as possible. Isolation of units from one another, appointments and deployments on the basis of loyalty, and the creation of overlapping functions have all become central elements in military organization in Syria. Assad has had to play off his goal of building as effective a fighting machine as possible against the fears raised by building such an army without adequate other centripetal forces at hand; in fact, Syria has probably spent a greater percentage of national income on defense than any other state in the 1980s. Assad's choices seemed to pay dividends in May 1987, when Rifaat reportedly thwarted a plot against the president, leading to the execution of forty Syrian air force pilots.

In India, paramilitary police forces in the border security forces, the Central Reserve Police, and the Home Guards numbered about half a million in the mid-1970s. Weiner stated:

> A critical feature of these agencies is that they are not part of the military, and hence not under the control of the Defense Ministry. Nor are they under the control of the state governments, as are the state police. The paramilitary forces are directly under the control of the Home Ministry. This means that the prime minister has control of a quasimilitary force for dealing with domestic crises.[8]

It also reflects serious concerns by state leaders of centrifugal tendencies in the Defense Ministry and the state governments. A proliferation of state security and military agencies has meant more than an independent force in case of social unrest; it has represented a tangible counterweight to the regular military forces.

Another option, in addition to balancing large and threatening power centers against one another, especially military agencies whose

[8] Myron Weiner, "Motilal, Jawaharlal, Indira, and Sanjay in India's Political Transformation," in Richard J. Samuels, ed., *Political Generations and Political Development* (Lexington, Mass.: Lexington Books, 1977), p. 74.

services state leaders cannot easily forego, has been to dispense with major institution building and instead focus on lessening existing and potential centrifugal forces. In other words, where the dilemma of state leaders is acute, a top priority may become a set of actions designed to prevent, as much as possible, large concentrations of power from arising, especially those with their own mobilizational capabilities. It is a policy of preemption. Like Nasser in his attacks against his own agencies—the fast growing army and ASU—other state leaders have resorted to weakening potentially strong state agencies or, for that matter, any organization in society that seems to be building extensive mobilizational strength. Here the goal of achieving significant mobilizational capacity is put aside, with all the domestic and international risks that implies, as is the agenda for societal change the leader harbors. Instead, state leaders opt for lessening immediate threats to their political survival.

Since the era of decolonization there may have been a learning curve for leaders on how to survive in the churning waters of politics where states have had relatively little social control over broad segments of their societies. Leaders and future leaders of states may have noted the risks involved in rushing headlong into ambitious programs of social change. They may have witnessed the dangers inherent in pursuing full social agendas through their agencies to carry out far-reaching policies of change. Their own tenure has been brought into question by the Frankensteins—those bureaus they created—as long as widespread political mobilization has remained beyond their grasp. Learning can come from watching the precarious grip of those who preceded them; for example, the brief three-year rule of Algeria's independence hero, Ahmed Ben Bella, may have been very instructive to the man who deposed him, Houari Boumdiene. Also, mechanisms to deal with such threats and risks can be learned from events far beyond one's borders.

Society's impact upon the state has far exceeded the personal dilemmas of state rulers. Those societies with high fragmentation of social control among a mélange of social organizations and the consequent denial of mobilizational capabilities (centripetal forces) to state leaders have precipitated a particular political and administrative style in their states. The political style, which I will explore in this chapter, involves leaders' attempts to "solve" their dilemma by mitigating any possible centrifugal forces that could threaten their tenure. It is the "politics of survival."

THE POLITICS OF SURVIVAL

The politics of survival has involved some of the most distasteful aspects of life in societies with weak states. Often discussion of this side of political life has been relegated to newspapers, sometimes sensationalist, or used as a polemic against unpopular regimes. In other circumstances, it has been part of a praiseworthy informational-political campaign, led by Amnesty International, to lend a helping hand from outside the society to protect victims and potential victims. Academic literature, for the most part, has not gone beyond indictment of particular leaders and regimes. By putting the politics of survival into the context of society's impact on the state and the dilemma state leaders have faced, I hope to show the sociological roots of this political style. A number of different kinds of actions have characterized the politics of survival.

The Big Shuffle

The powers of appointment and removal from office in state leaders' hands have proved an important tool in preventing state agencies or state-sponsored political parties from becoming threatening conglomerates of power. The big shuffle is a set of preemptive actions taken by state leaders, using these powers, to prevent loyalties in potentially strong agencies from developing in the first place. These leaders have frequently replaced ministers of state, commanders of armed forces, party leaders, and top bureaucrats in order to prevent threatening centers of power from coalescing. At the apex of the state, the political style has frequently resembled a dizzying game of musical chairs. On December 31, 1985, for example, while clinging desperately and unsuccessfully to his presidency-for-life in Haiti, Jean-Claude "Baby Doc" Duvalier sacked his four most important cabinet ministers and immediately reappointed them all as ambassadors. In numerous other cases, too, the same people have appeared over and over in different key posts. Yesterday, one was the commander-in-chief of the armed forces; today, minister of the interior; tomorrow, ambassador to the United States or COE of a major state enterprise. In other instances, officials have disappeared altogether from the political scene.[9]

From the first years after the revolution of 1952 Egypt experienced

---

[9] In Bhutto's Pakistan, one observer reported the cabinet became "a revolving door, providing momentary but often precarious shelter for members of the party elite ousted elsewhere with Bhutto's support, or returning to favor and offering new alternatives for patrimonial selection, and new potential patrimonial selectees."

this sort of forced circulation of elites.[10] Here the most serious threat came from the military officers, whom Nasser appointed to positions of authority throughout the state apparatus. Baker reflected on the shuffling of these figures:

> Even the purges were remarkable for their lack of vindictiveness and their evident concern with avoiding disruption and alienation of the military. There have been numerous examples of potential dissidents eased, even promoted, out of positions where they could have been a threat. Service in the diplomatic corps, followed by generous retirement, has frequently been used to short-circuit a potentially dangerous career.[11]

When Anwar el-Sadat assumed the presidency of Egypt in 1970, he lacked any institutional base of support as vice-president. One of his first impressions as president was that none of the officials heading important state agencies and the Arab Socialist Union "ever paid any regard to the interests of Egypt and wanted nothing but to remain in power, seeking their own interests and motivated by hatred and jealousy."[12] One might put it more kindly: the agency heads understood the "interests of Egypt" differently from Sadat; their posts gave them particular perspectives on what was good for Egypt. Within a year after Nasser's death, Sadat attacked what he termed the "nefarious power centers" that threatened his rule, forcing out simultaneously six cabinet ministers and three party chiefs. All this came after a plot against Sadat was unveiled. Perhaps even more interesting for understanding the dynamics of the big shuffle is what happened to those who stood loyally by Sadat in the political crisis of May 1971, when so many top agency officials fell.

> Ashraf Marwan, married to Nasser's daughter, gave Sadat tapes that incriminated Sabri. He became Sadat's advisor on Arab affairs until 1978 and then was dropped. Muhammed Sadiq was arrested in late 1972. Mamduh Salim went on to be prime minister but then was given an honorific post of advisor after 1978. Hassanein Heikal was fired from the editorship of *al-Ahram* in 1974. 'Aziz Sidqi has had no public role since 1978. Hafiz Badawi, who became speaker of parliament, was dropped in favor of Sayyid Mar'ai. Dakruri, Dar-

[10] R. Hrair Dekmejian, *Egypt Under Nasir: A Study in Political Dynamics* (Albany: State University of New York Press, 1971), pp. 205, 217–19.

[11] Raymond William Baker, *Egypt's Uncertain Revolution under Nasser and Sadat* (Cambridge, Mass.: Harvard University Press, 1978), p. 54.

[12] Anwar el-Sadat, *In Search of Identity: An Autobiography* (New York: Harper and Row, 1977), p. 207.

wish, 'Abd al-Akhir, and Mahmud were all put on the Discipline Committee of the ASU; two went on to governorships and two to cabinet positions. All had disappeared by the late 1970s. 'Abd al-Salam al-Zayyat survived as an M.P., but was briefly arrested in 1980 and again in 1981. Hussain Shafa'i of the RCC [Revolutionary Command Council] was made a vice-president and then replaced by Husni Mubarak in 1975. Those who fared best were Mahmud Fawzi, who retired with honor, and Sayyid Mar'ai, who remained an influential but somewhat marginal figure in the early 1980s.[13]

Mexico's big shuffle began in the early years after the revolution.[14] The process by now has acquired an almost routinized character. Forced circulation of elites has occurred after every six-year presidential administration, the *sexenio*, rather than during the period of any single administration. As in states with a less orderly turnover, this practice has effectively ensured that state agencies have not developed deep internal ties over time. "On occasion the changes involve little more than switching jobs among a certain group of individuals; bureau chiefs change ministries, and state enterprise managers exchange seats."[15] Every sexenio "witnesses a turnover of approximately 18,000 elective offices and 25,000 appointive posts."[16] Those figures were estimated more than two decades ago; no doubt they are even higher today. In the dominant party and the bureaucracy, many of those displaced have filled new posts, but at the top many have left public office permanently. According to Peter Smith,

> There has been a constant circulation of elites, therefore, but not in the sense that Vilfredo Pareto used the term. In Mexico the process has involved the rapid rotation of individuals, but mostly of individuals within a single class, the middle class (and its component fractions). Circulation has not entailed the kind of social mobility, open opportunity, and extensive incorporation of lower-class elements which, in Pareto's view, would lead to institutional stability.[17]

[13] John Waterbury, *The Egypt of Nasser and Sadat: The Political Economy of Two Regimes* (Princeton, N.J.: Princeton University Press, 1983), p. 352n.

[14] See Nora Hamilton, *The Limits of State Autonomy: Post-Revolutionary Mexico* (Princeton, N.J.: Princeton University Press, 1982), p. 255.

[15] Roger D. Hansen, *The Politics of Mexican Development* (Baltimore: Johns Hopkins University Press, 1971), p. 178.

[16] Frank Brandenburg, *The Making of Modern Mexico* (Englewood Cliffs, N.J.: Prentice-Hall, 1964), p. 157.

[17] Peter H. Smith, *Labyrinths of Power: Political Recruitment in Twentieth-Century Mexico* (Princeton, N.J.: Princeton University Press, 1979), pp. 186–87.

Near the end of an administration in Mexico, jockeying for the next shuffle has become almost frenetic. "Every middle and upper level bureaucrat," noted Merilee Grindle, "knows that chances are very good that he will not continue in his present position after the next national elections; politicians are certain of their impending unemployment."[18] As one Mexican bureaucrat put it, "No one has a political future in this country. There is no such thing as a political career here. Someone can be strong and have lots of power and the next day he's out in the street; they sack him."[19]

At the core of all these manifestations of the big shuffle—in Mexico, Egypt, and elsewhere—lies the difficulty state leaders have had in using a multitude of channels as a source for political mobilization to check burgeoning power centers. The price these leaders have paid for this game of political musical chairs has been continuing turmoil in bureaus, wasted time in acclimation to new posts, and preoccupation of bureaucrats and politicians with fixing their next post and future security. The big shuffle is neither a one-time event, nor is it reserved for enemies; it is a mechanism of deliberately weakening arms of the state and allied organizations in order to assure the tenure of the top state leadership. The executive leadership protects itself through ample use of its most manifest power, the ability to appoint to and remove from office.

Nonmerit Appointments

The power of appointments in the hands of state leaders has involved more than merely dismissing people from positions and then reassigning them. Appointments have constituted the most important sources of patronage to loyal followers—emphasis on the word loyal—which could be doled out selectively to prevent the development of power centers within the state itself. Some Third World states, as a result, have taken on an almost familial character (for a few, one could just as well drop the "almost"), displaying many characteristics of much less bureaucratized patrimonial systems.[20]

Probably, the most popular method here has been to appoint top agency officials having deep personal loyalties to the state leaders. In India, Mexico, Egypt, Sierra Leone, and elsewhere, those with power

[18] Merilee Serrill Grindle, *Bureaucrats, Politicians, and Peasants in Mexico: A Case Study in Public Policy* (Berkeley: University of California Press, 1977), p. 49.

[19] Ibid.

[20] On neopatrimonialism, see S. N. Eisenstadt, *Traditional Patrimonialism and Modern Neopatrimonialism*, Sage Research Papers in the Social Sciences, Studies in Comparative Modernization Series, vol. 1 (Beverly Hills: Sage, 1973).

of appointment have continued to use kinship ties as an important criterion for recruitment to state posts. Other sorts of personal ties have also heavily influenced the makeup of state agencies: common regional origins (at times, limited to a single town or several villages); shared ethnic, tribal, or sectarian backgrounds; school connections. In Iraq, for example, many top officials have been from one family group, the Begat section of the Albu Nasir tribe, and primarily those members of the group from the small town of Takri in the northwest.

In those countries in which the structure of society has limited the ability of state leaders to generate centripetal forces—where strong-men have retained tight grips—appointment on the basis of personal loyalty has been a means of mitigating powerful centrifugal forces. In postrevolutionary Mexico, for example, the top elite has nurtured a series of reinforcing personal, political, and business ties. At the foundation of all these linkages has been membership in what Brandenburg called the revolutionary family. This family "is composed of the men who have run Mexico for over half a century, who have laid the policy-lines of the Revolution, and who today hold effective decision-making power."[21] At the highest level 20 or so men have monopolized the most important appointment powers in the state, including the nomination to the presidency; another approximately 200 people have been on a second level. Their loyalty has gained them access to the most coveted posts in the state and its related political party, the PRI (Partido Revolucionario Institucional).

Below these two levels, the small army of bureaucrats and politicos also have worked desperately to forge ties of loyalty to the revolutionary family. Kenneth Johnson indicated how wide the gulf could be between those with "legitimacy"—that is, inside the family—and those outside it. "Legitimacy is a jealously guarded political attribute in Mexico, an esoteric quality to which only members of an exclusive and large political 'family' have priority rights."[22] Because appointment to the bureaucratic posts and nomination to elective positions have most often been on a personal ad hoc basis, rather than on established merit criteria, people at the lowest level have sought to "buy" into the family by becoming loyal clients of individuals at higher levels. "The ambitious and the insecure in both politics and bureaucracy," wrote Grindle, ". . . tend to seek personal vertical attachments, for it is on individuals, not policy, ideology, or party loyalty, that their futures

---

[21] Brandenburg, *The Making of Modern Mexico*, p. 3.

[22] Kenneth F. Johnson, *Mexican Democracy: A Critical View* (Boston: Allyn and Bacon, 1971), p. 37.

depend."[23] The overall effect of such a system of political recruitment has been to limit severely the potential pool of appointees. Only those with proper credentials—similar class affinity, regional backgrounds, and the like—have been eligible for selection; these sorts of standards have taken precedence over technical competence. The use of loyalty as a means against the development of strong centrifugal forces has taken its toll on the capabilities of Mexico's agencies.

Egyptians have formalized ties of personal loyalty much more than people in most societies. There one finds the institution of *shilla*, an intimate grouping of about six people. Membership in each shilla has been unambiguous; there has been no question of who is part of the group and who is not. Each has formed on the basis of friendships made in school, the university, the army, and the like. Egyptians have often talked about the shilla as a kind of family.[24] In prerevolutionary Egypt, the military academy served as the setting for an important shilla whose members included Nasser, Sadat, Amir, and others. Political life in Egypt has continued to be rife with appointments based on shilla membership. The *dawrah* in Iran has served as a similar sort of informal group, which has created a hidden overlay to Tehran's formal political dealings.[25] As in Mexico, Egyptian state leaders have sought to overcome their dilemma—their limited capabilities of mobilization along with their fear of centrifugal pulls should they move to increase such capabilities—by relying heavily on personal, loyal relationships. Not only can such ties counteract the particular perspective of one's agency, but people also hope they may be a hedge if one does fall from power.

Another basis besides personal loyalty for appointment to state positions has been cooptation of those who might otherwise develop threatening power centers outside the state organization. Hansen commented on cooptation at the apex of Mexican politics. He noted that the personal gains have been both illegal (such as illegal landholding) and legal (such as special trucking contracts). In either case, "the co-opters and the co-opted who reach the top of the Mexican political ladder generally reap financial rewards that cushion their later years."[26]

Waterbury made a similar point for Egypt and noted additionally

[23] Grindle, *Bureaucrats, Politicians, and Peasants in Mexico*, pp. 49–50.

[24] Robert Springborg, *Family, Power, and Politics in Egypt: Sayed Bey Marei—His Clan, Clients, and Cohorts* (Philadelphia: University of Pennsylvania Press, 1982), pp. 98 ff.

[25] James Alban Bill, *The Politics of Iran: Groups, Classes and Modernization* (Columbus: Charles E. Merrill, 1972), pp. 44–49.

[26] Hansen, *The Politics of Mexican Development*, p. 126.

that the corruption tolerated by state leaders on the part of those they have coopted can be a further source of political control.

> For leaders like Nasser and Sadat, whose popular mandates to rule were always of dubious validity and whose trust in their peers was always minimal, corruption could be used to wed potential rivals to the regime. The elite would be allowed to play its crass material games, records would be kept of their activities, and were they ever to become politically threatening, legal action could be taken against them.[27]

The "crass material games" could do little to enhance the effectiveness of state agencies in Egypt, Mexico, or elsewhere. Cooptation could counter centrifugal forces in agencies by making the rule of present state leaders the personal interest of those at the top levels of state agencies. But the cost has been the subversion of those very rules of the game upon which state social control could be built. In Mexico, one exasperated observer lamented the ineffectiveness, even harmfulness, of provincial state government. "Our greatest problem in this state is that every four years we find ourselves obliged to turn out a rich governor. In the process of becoming rich, he bestows costly favors on relatives and friends, and he must also allow his subordinates to take at least enough to keep them quiet. . . . Would to God that a rich man would run for office!"[28]

Besides appointments motivated by personal loyalty and cooptation, a third nonmerit basis for recruitment into the public sector is "ethnic bargaining." This standard involves a special sort of cooptation based on group identity. Cynthia Enloe noted that state leaders have used appointments based on ethnicity to divide potentially threatening concentrations of power and to bind critical elements of the population to the state "by bonds stronger than simply fear or legalistic compliance."[29] Perhaps the most formal ethnic bargain was the one that shaped Lebanese politics after 1943. Recognizing the abiding strength of religious identities as opposed to national ones, Lebanese leaders, under French tutelage, entered into a gentlemen's agreement; it allotted posts from the presidency to seats in parliament to positions in the bureaucracy on a confessional basis in this nonmeritocracy.

[27] Waterbury, *The Egypt of Nasser and Sadat*, p. 349.

[28] Quoted in Nathan L. Whitten, *Rural Mexico* (Chicago: University of Chicago Press, 1948), p. 549. The quotation is repeated by Hansen, *Politics of Mexican Development*, p. 126.

[29] Cynthia Enloe, *Police, Military and Ethnicity* (New Brunswick, N.J.: Transaction Books, 1980), p. 7.

Kenneth Kaunda, president of Zambia, juggled tribal, ethnic, and sectional divisions masterfully. While carefully selecting his cabinet on an ethnic basis, he repeatedly chided state officials and politicians about their calls to the public based on ethnic identification. Raising such issues, he exhorted, could only foment conflict. But note, in a footnote to an article by Robert Molteno, how Kaunda constructed a government:

> 1969 and 1970 saw the step-by-step reduction of Bemba predominance. In January 1969 the President's new Cabinet included two additional Easterners and one additional member from North-western. In August the central committee was dissolved. The interim replacement committee included major Eastern and North-western leaders again. In September Vice-president Kapwepwe was stripped of his major portfolios, and three additions to the Cabinet were made from the relatively under-represented Central, Luapula, and North-western Provinces. And in November 1970 the President chose a new, Tonga-speaking Vice-president, Mr Mainza Chona.[30]

Certainly appointments based on personal loyalty, cooptation, and ethnic bargaining have constituted only a portion of the gamut of nonmerit recruitment into state agencies. Indira Gandhi, for example, made a series of appointments of chief ministers and party chiefs in the Congress based largely on what the new appointees were *not*. She sought new faces in the early 1970s to replace the entrenched ministers and party bosses, who demonstrated far too many centrifugal independent tendencies for her liking. The new chief ministers and party heads had no independent bases of social control and no role in the complex caste and factional alignments operating on the district and state levels. The results, however, disappointed Mrs. Gandhi, crippling the party and state agencies as other sorts of nonmerit appointments have done elsewhere. Frankel wrote,

> The reconstituted party organizations were even more ineffective as instruments of social transformation than the undivided party had been. . . . The new aspirants to power inside the party usually had no more ideological commitment to socialism than their predecessors, and with only few exceptions in the states, they represented the same socio-economic groups. Younger and less experienced than the established leadership, they enjoyed an even more narrow

[30] Robert Molteno, "Cleavage and Conflict in Zambian Politics: A Study in Sectionalism," in William Tordoff, ed., *Politics in Zambia* (Manchester: Manchester University Press, 1974), p. 95n.

and tenuous base of popular support. . . . Weakened by an uncertain tenure and the absence of an autonomous organizational base, they lacked the capacity to mobilize local followings on behalf of national policies.[31]

Where loyalties to other organizations besides the state or nation have run high and where the state's rules have confronted heavy opposition, state leaders have taken great care in making appointments. Their goal has been neither simply to construct a representative bureaucracy or military, in which the proportion of various ethnic groups in the state agency reflects the proportion in society at large, nor has their aim been to expand state authority by following formal organizational principles in extending the reach of the state. Allocations of posts, rather, have reflected the loyalty of particular groups, the threat of other groups, and the importance of specific state agencies. State leaders have assigned the most loyal elements, often the tribe or ethnic group of the leaders themselves, to the agencies, such as the military, potentially most threatening to state leaders and exercising the most control in society. (A good rule of thumb for quickly ascertaining the group most loyal to state leaders is to note the background of the minister of the interior and the commander of the palace guard.) Likewise, those from the least trustworthy groups have often been coopted into more marginal, low-budget agencies.

Shaul Mishal recounted that Jordanian King Abdullah assigned Palestinian elites to senior positions in the ministries of agriculture, economics, education, development, and foreign affairs. These appointments came after Jordan's annexation of the West Bank and its Palestinian population in 1949. Abdullah considered the Palestinians, as a group, much less trustworthy than the Bedouin tribal groups of the East Bank. Even among the Palestinians, the king rewarded those who had facilitated annexation and "also tended to use the appointments policy to placate or co-opt his enemies."[32] The real centers of power, however, were not the agencies under Palestinian direction but the Office of the Prime Minister, the Ministry of the Interior, and the army (the Arab Legion); in these areas those from Bedouin tribal groups constituted the most important appointees. "While trying to give the army a national character by recruiting Palestinians," Mishal

---

[31] Francine R. Frankel, *India's Political Economy, 1947–1977: The Gradual Revolution* (Princeton, N.J.: Princeton University Press, 1978), pp. 474–75.

[32] Shaul Mishal, "Conflictual Pressures and Cooperative Interests: Observations on West Bank-Amman Political Relations, 1949–1967," in Joel S. Migdal, *Palestinian Society and Politics* (Princeton, N.J.: Princeton University Press, 1980), p. 176.

wrote, "the central authorities encouraged the concentration of *loyal* (Bedouin, East Bank) elements in key positions and in elite combat units."[33]

Appointments based on personal loyalty, cooptation, ethnic bargaining, and other nonmerit criteria have limited the ability of states to make the binding rules in the society. Waterbury made this point regarding the Egyptian shilla: "By its very nature the *shilla* vitiates ideological and programmatic politics and maximizes the wielding of group influence for personal gain."[34] Mishal echoed the point for Jordan: "The absence of uniform procedures in the public service in terms of broad discretion in hiring and firing also led to weakness in the staff units of the Jordanian administrative system."[35] In exchange for appointments that have weakened centrifugal tendencies in state agencies, leaders have undermined their own tools of social transformation and political mobilization. The state's prerogatives have come to be bound in much the same ways that historical patrimonial regimes were limited. Yet, these limitations have developed in the context of a remarkable growth in the size and complexity of state organizations, permeating all parts of society.

Dirty Tricks

Perhaps no aspect of the politics of survival has received as much notoriety as "dirty tricks." These actions, at times initiated by top-ranking state personnel, have included illegal imprisonment and deportation, strange disappearances, torture, and death squads. Here, the difference from other sorts of politics of survival has been that state leaders have transgressed the very laws that could serve as the basis for instituting state social control. Dirty tricks include illegal methods or quick changes of the law to remove key state figures, preempting the emergence of competing power centers, and weakening or destroying groups in agencies already powerful enough to threaten the rulers' prerogatives. They include what Filipinos in the Marcos era called "guns, goons, and gold." Similar methods, as I shall discuss, have been used against nonstate personnel. At times, it is difficult to distinguish between breaking nonstate and state power centers because both state officials and nonstate figures have either formed important alliances or have been perceived to be in alliance.

Although probably the most difficult to document, dirty tricks have

[33] Ibid., p. 177.
[34] Waterbury, *The Egypt of Nasser and Sadat*, p. 346.
[35] Mishal, "Conflictual Pressures and Cooperative Interests," p. 178.

been among the most popular means of the politics of survival; there have been efforts to record these incidents during the last decade by Amnesty International, the U.S. State Department, and a small number of other human rights organizations. In some ways, dirty tricks have been the most obvious manifestation of the paradox of leaders' undermining their very own tools. Dirty tricks mean attacks on the state's explicit or implicit rules of the games, its legal code and established modus operandi, by the leaders of the state themselves.

Indian Prime Minister Indira Gandhi's maneuvering immediately before and after the night of June 25, 1975, provides concrete insight into a leader's fear of a growing power center and her loose use of the law to eliminate it.[36] Agitation had mounted steadily in India for the year before that fateful night, punctuated by the first assassination of a cabinet minister in the nearly thirty years since independence. Opposition parties grew in strength and increasingly used direct mobilization of the population to express discontent instead of their usual parliamentary tactics. Alarming to Mrs. Gandhi was the increasing unity of the opposition around the figure of Jayaprakash Narayan, in the so-called "J.P." movement. Almost a mythical figure in India, Narayan was a nationalist hero, who had given up politics to work for the welfare of the poor. In many ways, he now carried the mantle of Mahatma Gandhi. As the J.P. movement coalesced, Narayan sought to channel the growing unrest in India into "permanent institutions of peoples power."

If all that were not enough to raise the prime minister's fears, her longtime political opponent, Morarji Desai, was engaged in a "fast unto death" directed against her rule. As Narayan and Desai joined forces, her situation became increasingly desperate. The coup de grâce was a court decision handed down on June 12, 1975, finding Mrs. Gandhi guilty of campaign abuses in the election of 1971. Her supporters rallied behind her with the telling slogan, "Indira is India and India is Indira." But there was no denying that a new power center was growing, even gaining an important base within the state apparatus. On the same day as the court decision, came election results from Gujarat, where Narayan's and Desai's forces ousted Gandhi's Congress party and gained a majority in the assembly. As the crisis edged toward its denouement, in the morning of June 25, Narayan called from the rostrum of a huge rally for state workers to refuse to obey any "illegal" orders.

Several days earlier, Mrs. Gandhi had already begun her maneuvers

---

[36] The following account is adapted from Frankel, *India's Political Economy*, ch. 12.

to deal with the menacing power of the opposition. She moved loyal officials into key positions in the home ministry and intelligence bureau.[37] She wanted no opposition or hesitation in her own ranks when she chose to move. On June 25, India's president announced a Proclamation of Emergency at the urging of Mrs. Gandhi. Even before the cabinet was convened, security forces arrested Narayan, Desai, and a host of political officials, including elected state figures. The emergency effectively abolished recourse for Mrs. Gandhi's opponents through the law. Citizens, for example, could not use the courts to challenge the actions undertaken by Gandhi and her followers. She issued numerous decrees through the president, including the right to arrest opponents without charges and hearings and to detain them for up to two years. Playing fast and loose with the law, the prime minister silenced her parliamentary opposition and those officials of her own party who she felt sympathized with the opposition.

Dirty tricks and the other sorts of politics of survival, including the big shuffle and nonmerit appointments, have all reflected a lack of confidence in the state institutions. Most obviously in the case of dirty tricks leaders have lost trust in the institution of law itself, at least as it stood before they used it as an ad hoc weapon against opponents. However, their mistrust of state institutions has gone even deeper than their disillusionment with the law; it has included the agencies that potentially could generate sufficient support through political mobilization to counteract centrifugal tendencies. The politics of survival has severely limited the prerogatives of these state agencies. State leaders' means have wandered far from rational forms of administration in terms of efficiency in implementing policies. The state has become a labyrinth of public agencies absorbing large percentages of all workers, but the political survival goals of state leaders have taken precedence over efficient administration. Ability to implement social policy has consequently suffered greatly. Eugene Bardach noted that to get something done—a policy of any sort—states must assemble machines.[38] With the politics of survival, state leaders have effectively thrown monkeywrenches into the workings of those machines.

When successfully practiced, the politics of survival can lead to longevity for both regimes and particular leaders. Political stability has resulted even in the absence of what Huntington felt was the prime

---

[37] *Times of India*, June 26, 1977, cited in ibid., p. 545.
[38] Eugene Bardach, *The Implementation Game: What Happens After a Bill Becomes a Law* (Cambridge, Mass.: M.I.T. Press, 1977), p. 36.

requisite for such stability, political institutionalization.[39] In fact, as we have seen, keeping state leaders afloat may paradoxically have involved the systemic weakening of the state's agencies, a kind of deinstitutionalization. The insecurity of personal tenure in agencies, the sanctions against developing strong intrabureaucratic ties, and the primacy of loyalty over functional relationships have all worked against the development of a bureaucratic class within the state itself. Although much has been written about the emergence of such a social class in Third World countries, I am skeptical about the degree to which functional relationships, shared interests, and common perspectives among bureaucrats have developed in environments marked by the politics of survival. The stability of regimes and longevity of particular rulers can be as much a result of the repression of such factors as an outgrowth of political institutionalization.

After reviewing the literature on this distasteful side of politics, it is tempting to conclude that leaders of Third World states who have successfully displaced strongmen and achieved predominance have been pure while those in states not achieving these goals have all risen to power as cynical connivers and manipulators of personnel. Engaging in the politics of survival, however, has not meant leaders have never had the slightest interest in using the state as a vehicle for progressive social change. Indeed, these leaders frequently have ascended to power with full social agendas. They have faced the structural dilemma in power—the danger of fostering the growth of powerful state agencies in the absence of adequate capabilities for political mobilization; this has caused a critical shift in priorities. No agenda is worth anything if its sponsor has not lasted through the hazards of politics. Political survival, the central issue occupying the attention of state leaders, is the prerequisite for achieving any significant long-term social change. Programs for social change may still have been the basis for public rhetoric and even for policy statements and legislation, but at the apex of the state the politics of survival have denuded state agencies of capabilities to see those programs through.

STATE LEADERS AND POWER CENTERS IN SOCIETY: THE STATE AND CAPITAL

Despite actions by state rulers through the politics of survival that have weakened state agencies, these leaders have faced important boundaries to this sort of political behavior. State agencies, after all, have col-

---

[39] Samuel P. Huntington, *Political Order in Changing Societies* (New Haven: Yale University Press, 1968).

lected taxes and policed the streets, among other essential services. In the security realm, in particular, the logic of lessening centrifugal forces, if taken to the absurd, would leave the ruler without any means of defense against international and domestic violence. State leaders have had to play a very delicate game of restraining agencies sufficiently so they pose no threat to the rulers while allowing sufficient organization so the agencies can perform the tasks necessary for state and leader survival.

Another set of delicate choices facing state rulers has involved the existence of power centers outside the state organization. Such centers, with their independent mobilizational capabilities and individual perspectives on what sorts of rules the society needs, have posed similar threats to those of state agencies. Where such centers have been organizations with limited reach and small constituencies, as many of those run by rural strongmen in poor urban neighborhoods or rural areas, then rulers have confronted little immediate threat to their own tenure. The sum of social control local strongmen have exercised has prevented state leaders from developing the state's own mobilizational capabilities. But the threat to the state ruler's tenure by any single strongman has been negligible. The very fragmentation of social control that has bedeviled state leaders seeking to mobilize the population has also worked in their favor in terms of stability by resisting the development of social frameworks, personal ties, and common identities broad enough to be the bases for strong social classes that could challenge the course of the state. A myriad of sets of rules in the society has not made for a strong sense of common cause in broad collectivities; and for these parts of society, at least, a class analysis would seem misplaced.

The situation may differ considerably, however, for social organizations with a longer reach than those of local strongmen. In cases of large social organizations or those threatening to become large, rulers of weak states have had the same sorts of fears about independent mobilizational capabilities that they have harbored about powerful state agencies. They have also needed the services of some of these groups—even ones, such as large holders of capital, which can become powerful social classes. We can identify three sorts of means to deal with threats posed by such societal power centers.

Extending the Politics of Survival beyond the State

State rulers have employed some of the methods they have used against state agencies through the politics of survival against nonstate personnel. Of course, leaders have lacked the power of appointment in these social organizations; the big shuffle and nonmerit appointments have not been options. But rulers have used dirty tricks against other social organizations in numerous cases. The use of death squads by state leaders against student political activists, businessmen, political party leaders, and others, has spread from South America to Central America to countries as distant as Indonesia and the Philippines.

Widespread reports of illegal means against, among others, journalists, students, labor chiefs, peasant leaders have surfaced in Mexico.[40] The Mexican state, noted Johnson, "prefers extra-legal to legal means of dealing with the conflict, for to allow itself to be challenged in court would be a sign of weakness on the part of the official image." In the case of one well-known journalist, who the police held without charges in prison, the state simply "did not want him in court defending himself."[41] One of Mexico's leading scholars, Pablo González Casanova, pointed to the no-win situation that societal out-groups have faced in Mexico. "Supplication and silence are of little use, whereas protest and organization are the traditional roads to imprisonment, exile, and even death."[42]

The myth of Mexico as a strong state stems, in part, from a misunderstanding of the state's relationship to society. There is no doubt that the Mexican state has overshadowed organized social interests much more than in, say, the United States. Such dominance, however, has risen less from the state's monopoly of rule-making functions than its pulverization of large concentrations of rule-making ability outside the state organization. The result has been a fragmentation of social control among numerous small social organizations (dominated by caciques and other strongmen) and a state with limited social control itself. As I shall discuss in Chapter 7, the Mexican state has had difficulty in getting even high priority policies implemented in local areas along the designs formulated in Mexico City.

In Sierra Leone, too, dirty tricks have been used against large, threatening social organizations. For example, President Siaka Stevens moved against the Sierra Leone Labour Congress when it called two brief national strikes in 1981. He invoked emergency power, a favorite mechanism to open the door to various dirty tricks, and arrested 179 labor leaders and journalists. Security forces held them without charges for periods of up to a month.[43]

---

[40] Evelyn P. Stevens, "Legality and Extra-Legality in Mexico," *Journal of Inter-American Studies and World Affairs* 12 (January 1970): 62–75.

[41] Johnson, *Mexican Democracy*, p. 112 n.

[42] Pablo González Casanova, *Democracy in Mexico* (New York: Oxford University Press, 1970), p. 133.

[43] U.S. Department of State, *Country Reports on Human Rights Practices for 1981*, p. 221.

As in the case of state agencies, however, leaders have faced limits to the degree to which they can level society. Large businesses have produced goods that have earned much needed revenues in the world economy. Other social organizations have provided communication systems, trained personnel, and other important social goods. The demands by international and transnational actors alone, for debt repayment and for critical products of the country, have made it impossible for state leaders to weaken all power centers in the society heedlessly.

Constraints have been as great on the domestic side. Engaging in the politics of survival within the state organization has meant that state leaders have limited the ability of state institutions to provide the population with important elements for its strategies of survival. If social stability is to be maintained, then, other social organizations must provide those strategies. For the most part, state leaders have opted to accommodate smaller social organizations, run by local strongmen, to provide such strategies, since they have been the least threatening to political stability. The problem of capital, however, has caused state leaders special concern. Production is critical in creating viable strategies of survival, and economies of scale in production often demand large, powerful organizations, especially in manufacturing. Dirty tricks, then, clearly have their limits as leaders of weak states seek antidotes to their chronic lack of mobilizational capabilities.

Transforming Social Organizations into State Institutions

How have leaders of weak states dealt with the threat of large social organizations where dirty tricks or outright bans on their existence dare not be risked or have severe limits? How have rulers with limited mobilizational capabilities of their own tried to keep reins on other social organizations important in providing revenues for the state or components for the survival strategies of the population? One method has been to incorporate these organizations or their functions into the state organization itself or into state-allied institutions. The attractiveness of state socialism—or state capitalism, as it is sometimes called—has stemmed partly from the desire of state leaders to eliminate major power centers outside the state organization. Many leaders with socialist beliefs felt they could undermine both the tremendous social control engendered by capital and its pernicious rules of the game through nationalization of industries. They could in one fell swoop eliminate a threatening social class or preempt the creation of an embryonic social class.

In Egypt, Nasser and the Free Officers moved to change Egyptian manufacturing from a sector in which almost all key production and investment decisions were made by members of the urban bourgeoisie to one in which decision makers came from the state. After a final wave of nationalizations from 1961 through 1963, the state owned and operated all large-scale industries. Its nationalizations outside agriculture were worth about a half-billion Egyptian pounds.[44]

Nasser's fears of the power of private capital in the absence of his own mobilizational capabilities were quite tangible. An army-business alliance undertook a coup in Syria in 1961, which led to the demise of Nasser's cherished union with Syria. Reports also surfaced of approaches by Egyptian businessmen to the head of the military, Amir, to undertake action against Nasser himself.[45] Waterbury wrote of the motivations behind the nationalizations:

> Nasser was a leader acutely conscious of potential threats to his regime and his control. Whenever possible he anticipated these threats (real or imaginary) and tried to preempt them. He manifestly endorsed the notion that the best defense, in politics at any rate, is offense. Perhaps also he had a zero-sum image of power struggles and saw each incremental diminution of the resource and power base of likely adversaries as a proportionate enhancement of his own strength. Dismantling the upper reaches of the private sector therefore contributed directly and commensurately to regime strength by placing the levers of economic control in its hands.[46]

Almost as quickly as the private industries changed into state-owned enterprises, Nasser realized that some of the old problems appeared in new guise. Would the new state agencies not demonstrate centrifugal tendencies, as had other state agencies? Nasser had to deal with twin problems confronting his regime: (1) to assure efficient and growing production, at least to keep existing strategies of survival in society working and hold international creditors at arm's length, and (2) to prevent development of threatening power centers within the state itself. He responded by dipping into his trusted bag of tricks, affording himself some measure of control, although his mobilizational capabilities still remained limited. Once again, he relied heavily on his power of appointment, attempting to balance through his placements his need for industrial production and his fear of concentrated power in nationalized industries.

In appointing the new industrial managers, he had to face "the classic problems of securing the loyalty of the managers while guarantee-

---

[44] Waterbury, *The Egypt of Nasser and Sadat*, p. 75.
[45] Ibid., p. 74.
[46] Ibid., p. 78.

ing their efficiency."[47] Engineers topped the list of new managers, but "loyalty has been as significant as efficiency in appointing Egypt's managers."[48] Because he could never satisfy both his values of high production and prevention of threatening centers of power, Nasser vascillated toward his appointees. At one moment, he would tend toward intimidating the managers to prevent their development of power centers. Note the attack of Ali Sabri of the ASU in 1967: "However, it appears that in fact many of those who hold the levers of command in the nationalized enterprises and corporations of the public sector have carried out devious procedures for exploiting that sector while striving to maintain their positions for the longest possible time."[49] But, when the managers' fear led to downturns in industrial production, the next moment Nasser would leap to their side and move toward more decentralized operation of the state-owned industrial sector.

These drops in production posed other sorts of threats and constraints on the regime, many stemming from outside the country. With a stagnating industrial sector, Egypt's economic situation grew from bad to worse during the 1960s. A series of international debt crises resulted—the most serious in 1965—with heavy pressure applied by outside forces, especially the International Monetary Fund and the USSR, for internal changes. Domestically, per capita income plummeted in absolute terms, threatening existing strategies of survival. Little wonder that Nasser at times put aside his fears of power centers in order to promote more efficient management of the state-owned corporations.

In the end, Nasser's fear of the managers' establishing an independent base overrode his desire for efficient and growing production.[50] Again, his fears were not unfounded; he took a series of actions that cumulatively hampered industrial growth in Egypt. "The managers of the public sector could use their control of the means of production to consolidate that control, build empires, and otherwise enhance their power."[51] Nasser cut into their authority first by establishing a veritable layer cake of agencies over them—the Higher Supervision Com-

---

[47] Baker, *Egypt's Uncertain Revolution*, p. 178.

[48] Ibid., p. 180.

[49] Quoted in ibid., p. 184

[50] The opposite seems to have occurred in Brazil, where Peter Evans has written, "The most important resource that local partners may possess is political power, and the local partners with the most direct political leverage are state-owned firms." *Dependent Development: The Alliance of Multinational, State, and Local Capital in Brazil* (Princeton, N.J.: Princeton University Press, 1979), p. 212.

[51] Waterbury, *The Egypt of Nasser and Sadat*, p. 122.

mittee, the Central Agency for Audit, the Central Agency for Administration and Organization, the Legal Department, the Ministry of Planning, the Supreme Control Committee.

Next he moved to limit the managers by adding layers within each enterprise. Watchdog committees of the ASU engaged in direct and indirect surveillance of the managers. And, when in 1967 Nasser began to fear the growing control of the ASU and the centrifugal tendencies it clearly exhibited, he added watchdogs to watch the watchdogs. In the end each factory had a labor union, a joint labor-management consultative committee, and worker members of the board of directors, all in addition to the ASU Committee. "All four groups acted as 'popular' restraints on the managers," wrote Baker, "while their mutual rivalry prevented any one of them from assuming a too powerful position in the institutional framework. . . . The economic costs to Egypt of Nasser's political success were high."[52] For Nasser, the policy of incorporating threatening power centers into the organization of the state allowed him not only much closer surveillance but also the ability to restrain the growth of independent power bases in Egypt. The price he paid came in Egypt's disappointing economic performance from the time of the nationalizations until his death.

In Mexico, the effort to control threatening social organizations has taken some unusual twists and turns. Leaders have not so much incorporated such potential power centers into state agencies as they have into the dominant political party, the PRI. Exceptions to this rule have occurred, of course, as in the nationalization of the oil industry and its transformation into the state-owned Pemex Company. Some of the most interesting cases of Mexican leaders' attempts to prevent autonomous social power bases from developing, however, came during their incorporation into the PRI.

In 1937, President Lázaro Cardénas initiated the sector system within the party; this organized four broad social groups—peasants, laborers, the military, and what has been called the popular sector. Several years later, the party dropped the military sector, but broad organizations within the party have continued to represent the interests of the other three groupings.

The experience of the peasantry within this system has been telling. Although peasants in some regions had played a vital role in the Mexican revolution, even to the leaders of the revolution their independent-minded goals had been troubling. Also, the weakening of old

[52] Baker, *Egypt's Uncertain Revolution*, pp. 189, 192.

forms of social control before and during the revolution led, in areas such as Morelos, to more broadly based social organization than previously available to the peasantry. This solidarity directly threatened the urban leadership of the revolution, which was just beginning to consolidate its new role in the state.

The solution to the threat of a broad, independent base of peasants was twofold. First, it involved encouraging fragmentation of social control among the peasantry through accommodations with local caciques who had only limited spheres of influence (see Chapter 7). Second, the leaders' solution lay in party-dominated organizations. Incorporation into the PRI through the National Campesino Confederation (CNC), in effect, has helped eliminate peasants for the last half-century as a potentially united organization with significant social control, although economically they have suffered considerably relative to other major groups in society. "Since the time of Lázaro Cardénas in the 1930s," wrote Grindle, "peasants in Mexico have not been in a position to make sustained independent demands on the political system for attention to their problems."[53] This type of tight control prompted Carlos Chavira to write in his novel, *La Otra Cara de México*, "Why is it that we have an official party, which is no more than the Government disguised as a Party, whose single presence in the electoral field not only corrupts and nullifies every popular effort at self determination, but is in itself a negation of democracy?"[54] One Mexican bureaucrat assured peasants he was not trying to organize them. "We don't want to talk anything about 'organization.' That's what this government will not allow—organization. You can say what you wish and write what you wish and criticize as much as you like now and get away with it. But the moment you try to organize, they'll be right on top of you. This government will stand anything except organization."[55]

The Mexican answer to the problem of the growth of independent power centers in the society, however, has not been without its own set of problems. Foremost, once again, has been the issue of how to handle those who control capital. In the wake of the world depression of the 1930s, which severely curtailed Mexico's raw material exports and seriously shook its economy, Mexican political leaders opted for a policy of rapid industrialization. Willing to assume the risks of the creation of some power centers outside the state organization, they promoted industrialization through an import-substitution policy of high

[53] Grindle, *Bureaucrats, Politicians, and Peasants in Mexico*, p. 129. Also, see Dale Story, *The Mexican Ruling Party: Stability and Authority* (New York: Praeger, 1986), pp. 90–94.

[54] Quoted in Johnson, *Mexican Democracy*, p. 111.

[55] Quoted in Grindle, *Bureaucrats, Politicians, and Peasants in Mexico*, p. 161.

protective tariffs. By the time this policy began to have clear payoffs with heightened world demand during World War II, the PRI's sectoral system was already in place. Many members of the powerful new industrial class that had emerged by the mid-1940s never even became members of the party, let alone subsumed within sectoral confederations.[56]

In short, Mexican state leaders used the method of incorporation into the PRI as a means to restrain the growth of independent bases for peasants, labor, and a variety of other groups. Where such a policy of incorporation threatened major economic growth and efficiency, however, the presidents from Cárdenas on opted to allow a new industrial and agroindustrial class and its large-scale economic organizations to develop outside the state or party organizations. The problem has been that in the face of their own mobilizational weakness state leaders have allowed, even promoted, the growth of large power centers in Mexican society with significant concentrations of social control. The Egyptians of the 1960s effectively gave up rapid economic growth by subjecting manufacturing to the same politics of survival used with other agencies. The Mexicans gained rapid economic growth through industrialization for four decades, but they, in turn, gave up the kind of surveillance and control Nasser had over Egyptian industry. What means remain in such cases as Mexico for state rulers to prevent these large-scale organizations and their extensive social control from threatening the political leaders' prerogatives and tenure?

Accommodating Capital

The uncomfortable position in which state leaders have found themselves in dealing with major concentrations of capital helps explain the frequent, almost desperate, oscillations in political orientation toward it: between receptivity and coolness to foreign capital; between openness to private local capital and reliance on state-owned enterprises; between advocacy of tight control of state managers and allowing them a relatively free hand. Changes in state policy from import-substitution to export-led growth or from state socialism to incentives for private investment have stemmed not only from the search for optimal economic strategies. They have come, as well, from attempts to minimize the political difficulties of leaders in weak states: on one side of the ledger, fear of allowing large concentrations of social control to grow inside or outside the state organization when their own mobili-

---

[56] Hansen, *The Politics of Mexican Development*, p. 101.

zational capabilities are so low; on the other side, anxiety about increasing international pressure and growing domestic dissatisfaction with existing strategies of survival if the leaders themselves undermine economic efficiency and vitality.

State leaders who have chosen to emphasize economic efficiency over political control, as in Mexico, have had to find means to accommodate the new power centers in their society without permitting those power centers from becoming threats to them. At the most obvious level, such state leaders have dealt with powerful capital through cooptation, adopting a set of discriminatory policies that favor its large-scale powerful social organizations over smaller fragmented ones.[57] Rulers have used various means—including special prerogatives, discriminatory tax policies, appointments to state agencies, tariffs, income transfer policies, licensing, state expenditures—to convince leaders of such power centers that their interests lie in the longevity of the regime and its rulers.

In Mexico, many of the new industrial entrepreneurs of the 1930s and 1940s joined forces in the National Chamber of Manufacturing Industries (CNIT). Within a decade, it became a virtual partner to the Mexican state, influencing policy and winning special concessions for its members. Other chambers of businessmen and industrialists also joined the partnership. According to Hansen,

> Interaction between the various business chambers and the government is by now institutionalized and continuous. The chambers frequently phrase their demands in the form of proposed legislation; on other occasions they submit amendments to pending legislation at the invitation of the government. Their representatives now sit on numerous public-sector regulatory and advisory commissions and a host of other governmental bodies.[58]

The varying manifestations of the ties between states and capital demand a study of their own; this is not the place to develop a full typology of the wide range of state-capital relationships. Besides the links between state rulers and private local capital, those involving foreign capital and fairly autonomous state-owned enterprises must be considered. More important, the limited range of options open to state leaders has derived from the political weakness a society of fragmented social control has imposed upon them. Accommodations to

---

[57] For more on this line of analysis see Michael Lipton, *Why Poor People Stay Poor: Urban Bias in World Development* (Cambridge, Mass.: Harvard University Press, 1977).

[58] Hansen, *The Politics of Mexican Development*, p. 108.

capital have demonstrated how state rulers have sought simultaneously to promote high economic performance while keeping leaders of large social organizations from threatening political stability.

The art of balancing both goals—political stability and economic growth—may be less demanding for leaders of states whose societies produce wealth through the relatively easy process of extraction (such as mining and oil drilling). In such cases, state leaders can raise a large portion of the revenues needed to keep their series of accommodations viable and important state agencies well fed through rent (for example, petroleum sales or royalties). In nonrentier states, such as Egypt, India, and even Mexico and Sierra Leone (for all that oil and diamonds have lightened the load), leaders must promote complex organization; this effectively enhances production and state revenues, on the one hand, and political dangers to rulers with limited mobilizational capabilities, on the other.

STATE LEADERS REDUCED TO RUSES AND STRATAGEMS

In this chapter, I addressed two major questions: Why have some states continued to be weak, given all the resources and agencies at the disposal of their leaders? And, what have been the effects of such weakness on political life? The answers centered around the dilemma of state leaders. Their basic weakness in the face of continued fragmentation of social control has led them to a political style and policies—the politics of survival—that have prevented the state from enhancing its capabilities by not allowing the development of complex organization in state institutions. Rulers have used similar styles and policies to preempt the development of large concentrations of social control outside the state organization. Where complex organization is needed for the survival of the regime, as with the military and capital, state leaders have varied between tight reins, cutting into the efficiency of the organizations, and loose reins through accommodating, discriminatory state policies. They have also tried balancing powerful institutions against one another.

Many state leaders have carved out for themselves some area for maneuver in balancing and accommodating state-owned enterprises, local capital, and multinational firms. Effective use of budgets and other prerogatives have brought those who control capital to rely on existing regimes and present state leaders to assure their ascendancy. In some cases, such as Sadat's Egypt, state and local entrepreneurs, many serving foreign capital, were so close at times as to blur the distinction between the two.[59] It would be mistaken, however, to confuse such maneuvering of state leaders with either the ability to dominate rule making for society or even effective state autonomy. As long as the fragmentation of social control has continued, denying state leaders effective mass political mobilization, rulers have been reduced to ruses and strategems; they must build and rebuild coalitions and balances of power centers while using state resources to reinforce existing distribution of power and wealth in society. Such mechanisms may at times encourage economic growth, but they do not create a more capable, autonomous state.

[59] See Nazih N. M. Ayubi, "Implementation Capability and Political Feasibility of the Open Door Policy in Egypt," in Malcolm H. Kerr and El Sayed Yassin, eds., *Rich and Poor States in the Middle East: Egypt and the New Arab Order* (Boulder, Colo.: Westview Press, 1982), pp. 352–55.

CHAPTER SEVEN

The Triangle of Accommodation:
Implementors, Politicians, and Strongmen

IMPLEMENTORS

The political style at the top has had an important effect on those at a much lower level of the state hierarchy—bureaucrats entrusted with implementing policy. Implementors are usually far from the sight of state leaders, often even far from the sight of the top personnel in their agencies, and they pose little danger of creating power centers that could threaten the position of state leaders. Nonetheless, they have been crucial in determining whose authority and rules will take hold in region after region, the state's or the strongmen's. Scholarly literature on political and social change has unfortunately paid these implementors little heed.[1] The indirect impact of the politics of survival upon them, their centrality to the implementation of politics, and the calculus of social and political pressures they face have placed them in a critical role to influence whether states can actually accomplish what their leaders purport.

Who are these implementors? Grindle described them:

A corps of middle-level officials who have responsibility for implementing programs in a specific, relatively constricted area—a state, a district, a province, or an urban zone—and who are held responsible for program results by their superiors. This corps of individuals—the first and second ranks of the field administration—maintains frequent contact with national or regional superiors, but also has occasion to interact with the clients of government agencies and with opponents of the programs at local levels. These middle-level officials may have considerable discretion in pursuing their tasks and, even when it is not defined as part of their formal duties, they may have a decided impact on individual allocation decisions.[2]

---

[1] Often the causes for failure are sought far from these players. "Many observers," write Van Meter and Van Horn in their discussion of state policy failures, wrongly point "to insufficient planning or the inadequacy of the program itself." Donald S. Van Meter and Carl E. Van Horn, "The Policy Implementation Process: A Conceptual Framework," *Administration and Society* 6 (February 1975): 449.

[2] Merilee S. Grindle, "The Implementor: Political Constraints on Rural Development

In short, implementors have been strategically placed between the top policy-making elements of the state and most of the country's population. They have been the key switchmen in moving state resources originating in the main stations, the capital city, along the tracks to the villages, towns, and cities all over the country. Their job has been to imbue the purposes of top political leaders into the plethora of state institutions that has suffused society. Without implementors, state leaders do not have a chance at enforcing their rules. In Mexico, for example, the representatives of more than 750 state agencies, public enterprises, state commissions, and development trusts now bring the state's presence to the far corners of the society. State leaders have charged these middle-level public administrators with activating the programs and instruments designed to achieve the goals of policy and, more generally, to establish the state's rules of the game. In brief, implementors take the programs, legislation, and policy statements of leaders and, acting responsibly on those guidelines, make them the rules of daily behavior. This state personnel must make policy work at the ground level.

CAREERISM, RISKS, AND IMPLEMENTING POLICIES

Like state leaders above them, implementors may be analyzed using a simple model of risk analysis. Their leading role in changing the rules of the game has subjected them to pressure and risk from four groups. First, and most obviously, they have needed to consider their supervisors. After all, these supervisors have had to produce results while overseeing those below them in the bureaucratic hierarchy. Second, the intended clients of the program—those designated to benefit from, or be regulated by, the rule changes involved in the policy— pressure the implementors. Third, regional actors from other state agencies and from the state-sponsored party, if existing—that is, peer politicians and bureaucrats—have taken a keen interest in allocating resources and changing state rules within their jurisdictions. Finally, nonstate local leaders, strongmen such as landlords, moneylenders, local businessmen, have fashioned for the local population the existing strategies of survival, the rules of behavior; implementors jeopardize their social control through the state rules and strategies conveyed by the new policy.

In negotiating the maze of pressures and cross-pressures generated by all these groups, a leading motivating factor for implementors has

in Mexico," in Grindle, ed., *Politics and Policy Implementation in the Third World* (Princeton, N.J.: Princeton University Press, 1980), p. 197.

been careerism, a concern with their own security and possible mobility. Careerism provides a set of standards with which implementors can weigh pressures and evaluate any factor's possible impact on their professional standing. Where the accountability and control within agencies have been high, and especially where supervisors have been willing to protect their officials from other groups' pressures, agencies have tended to have high morale and follow in their official actions the purposes laid down in law and policy statements. Morton Halperin described highly motivated personnel as believing "that what they are doing makes a difference and promotes the national interest," at least as they understand it.[3] Even here, however, careerism stands out. "Above all," Halperin continued, "the career official must believe that there is room for advancement in the organization and that the organization is seeking to protect his opportunities for advancement."[4] One could add a flip side of the coin: the career official must believe the organization can protect him from ouster or demotion due to attacks by the opposition.

The politics of survival at the apex of weak states has tremendously diminished the coherence of the state, its accountability and control. First, nonmerit appointment of agency leaders—for example, recruitment on the basis of loyalty to the ruler or ethnic affiliation—has cut into efficient bureau operations and supervisory ability. It has also undermined the agency personnel's unity of purpose and the motivation that comes from the belief that toeing the line furthers national interest.

Second, and probably more important, the frequent shuttling in and out of new agency heads has had a devastating impact on policy implementation. New agency chiefs enter with their own policy agendas; by the very nature of policy and its assault upon existing rules, it challenges the interests of strongmen who receive disproportionate benefits from their own existing rules. The implementor must do battle with these strongmen, while risking an assault by them on the policy itself *and* on his or her career. The implementor must also pay considerable political capital in gaining the cooperation of peer bureaucrats, politicians, and party leaders in pushing policy forward. Where the big shuffle has resulted in chiefs moving in and out of the implementor's agency in a matter of months, and along with them their agenda of programs, implementors have become very reluctant

[3] Morton H. Halperin, *Bureaucratic Politics and Foreign Policy* (Washington, D.C.: Brookings Institution, 1974), p. 54.
[4] Ibid.

to confront the intense pressures strongmen can exert. They have been unwilling to pay the high costs of gaining the cooperation of peer officials in order to promote a policy that, more likely than not, disappears with its originator; with the new agency chiefs, no doubt, new burning priorities and innovative policies will come.

There is too much at stake, especially one's career, for implementors to become closely identified with any one policy of an agency chief whose tenure will most likely be counted in months rather than years. No career-minded bureaucrat wants to be identified as a zealot for a state policy, despite its popularity or unpopularity, if there is a strong chance that he or she will be left out on the limb of that policy long after its creators and the agency chiefs have turned to other endeavors.

In brief, I argue that the structure of society has an important indirect effect on policy implementation. We have seen how a society with fragmented social control leads to the politics of survival. In turn, I hypothesize, the politics of survival lessens backing and threats of sanctions from supervisors, thus making the implementor more attentive to possible career costs involving strongmen and peer officials. The result is a further weakening of the state's ability to make the rules governing people's behavior. In cases of extreme fragmentation of social control and a state with minimal mobilizational capacity, as in Sierra Leone, state coherence as evidenced in its control and supervision of implementors has been extremely low. These are the weakest states, where the declarations of intent by state leaders coincide the least with the actual rules by which people abide. In cases of states with middle-level capabilities, such as Egypt, India, and Mexico, the state has had more supervision within its agencies than in Sierra Leone. In every state, there is bound to be, as Anthony Downs has noted, a "leakage of authority" as a policy moves through an agency.[5] Where accountability and control have been crippled and where the big shuffle or similar means have consumed leaders at the top, as in Sierra Leone, that leakage can turn into a massive hemorrhage.

In Egypt, India, and Mexico, there has been more than a leak of authority, but the state's impact at the local level is still substantial. Careerism on the part of implementors in these cases has led to their resistance to the policies handed down from above. Their resistance most often has taken the form of what Bardach calls tokenism, which "involves an attempt to appear to be contributing a program element

---

[5] Anthony Downs, *Inside Bureaucracy*, (Boston: Little Brown, 1967), p. 134.

publicly while privately conceding only a small ('token') contribution."[6] However, their tokenism has not simply resulted in a disengagement of local society from the state, as Azarya and Chazan have argued occurred in Ghana and Guinea.[7] It has led, as we shall see, to the injection of state resources and institutions into the everyday lives of people and their strategies of survival throughout the country based on rules quite different from those official laws and policy statements.

Scholars and aid officials alike have singled out bureaucrats in the Third World for their slothfulness, lack of will, and absence of commitment to reform. These scholars have paid scant attention to the calculus of pressures these bureaucrats have faced that have made them so "lazy" or "uncommitted." Success for public policies neither waits around the corner in a "new breed" of implementor, nor will it be found in an exclusive focus on new management techniques. In fact, the politics of administration in weak states lies at the heart of problems with policy implementation.[8]

A consuming obsession for careerist implementors has been to prevent the upward flow of information to their supervisors and agency chiefs that indicates the implementors have not been "handling" the situation. As Bardach notes in the U.S. context, "A great deal of energy goes into maneuvering to avoid responsibility, scrutiny, and blame."[9] This generalization is even stronger for those Third World cases where constant concern among those at the top with the politics of survival has made officials in the upper reaches of the bureau even less patient with implementors who cannot keep local situations local. The implementor must hunker down while somehow assessing who may pass undesirable information upward and what can be done to stop it.

In one Egyptian village, the bureaucratic head of the village cooperative, Samir, found how risky it can be to press the state's rules at the local level. Facing pressure from the village headman (strongman), Anwar, to give him extra supplies of fertilizer and pesticide, Samir refused and distributed the state resources according to official regulations. The head of the cooperative board, a poor peasant who served

[6] Eugene Bardach, *The Implementation Game: What Happens After a Bill Becomes Law* (Cambridge, Mass.: M.I.T. Press, 1977), p. 98.

[7] Victor Azarya and Naomi Chazan, "Disengagement from the State in Africa: Reflections on the Experience of Ghana and Guinea," *Comparative Studies in Society and History* 29 (January 1987): 106–31.

[8] Among the first to point to the effect of the character of politics on administration in Third World states was Fred W. Riggs, *Administration in Developing Countries: The Theory of Prismatic Society* (Boston: Houghton Mifflin, 1964), see esp. pp. 55–56.

[9] Bardach, *The Implementation Game*, p. 37.

as Anwar's henchman, then filed an official complaint against Samir and had the other barely literate poor peasants on the board sign the letter of complaint. So far Samir has withstood the challenge to him.[10] Like other bureaucrats everywhere, however, he must be sensitive to giving an appearance of not managing his environment. In cases such as Egypt where support from superiors in the bureaucracy has been weak, largely due to the debilitating effects of the politics of survival, it may be small consolation to the implementor to know that the brouhaha arose from properly carrying out orders.[11]

Intended clients of social programs have not posed the most serious risks to the implementor. As in the case of the poor peasants in Anwar's village, they have often lacked the contacts and means to publicize failures in implementation or to reach and influence highly placed state leaders with damaging information about the poor implementation of policy. Even more crucial in neutralizing the intended clients has been their dependency in the local arena.[12] The social control of strongmen has stemmed from the strategies of survival they could provide, including the concrete services and goods, even if meager, they have supplied. As one poor fellahin in the Egyptian village put it, "Sure, Anwar is tight [with his money]. But what choice do I have? I can't go hungry."[13]

One price the poor peasants have paid for their pittance has been to grant the strongman the role as sole spokesman to state officials. In one Mexican village in the 1950s, Paul Friedrich found that Pedro Caso, a relatively wealthy cacique, had so established his role as middleman between the peasants and outsiders that his social control was at the highest level, that of legitimacy. Caso enviously guarded the village's "external relations with the priests, the outside creditors, and 'other exploiters.' "[14]

> First and foremost . . . the performances that legitimize his status
> are those that demonstrate his aptitudes or personal superiority—as
> a relatively lucid speaker with a certain dexterity in handling the

---

[10] This account is from Richard H. Adams, Jr., *Development and Social Change in Rural Egypt* (Syracuse: Syracuse University Press, 1986), p. 85.

[11] An indication of the lack of supervision in the Egyptian bureaucracy came in a newspaper article, "Cairo Journal: Bureaucrats Toil (27 Minutes a Day)," *New York Times*, July 20, 1987.

[12] Milton J. Esman and Norman T. Uphoff, *Local Organizations: Intermediaries in Rural Development* (Ithaca: Cornell University Press, 1984), pp. 182–84.

[13] Adams, *Development and Social Change in Rural Egypt*, p. 83.

[14] Paul Friedrich, "The Legitimacy of a Cacique," in Steffen W. Schmidt et al., eds., *Friends, Followers, and Factions: A Reader in Political Clientelism* (Berkeley: University of California Press, 1977), p. 277.

Agrarian Code, as a sophisticated arbiter of personal conflicts, as a tough and resolute competitor but also relatively tempered in the use of assassination. . . . Pedro's performance is not legitimizing because of moral goodness or even benefits to his public; rather, it satisfies a set of "hardnosed" and essentially amoral questions about his ability to lead and his effectiveness in knowing how to give orders and control the community.[15]

Rural and urban clients of strongmen, such as Pedro Caso, depend on these strongmen who have found the state's social policy threatening their own control. States undertaking reform have not targeted social policy at a free floating clientele but at people susceptible to the sanctions of the local, threatened leaders. Potential clients might face the inability to secure a tenancy, the denial of credit, the loss of a job, or even assassination. Their current working strategies of survival have tempered any inclinations they might have had to clamor for their rightful benefits from state policies and to finger the implementor as the villain in the implementation process. Moreover, their fear of undermining their strategies of survival, in which the strongmen play such an important part, have discouraged vulnerable peasants and workers from confronting government officials for not giving them their due.

With clients frozen by fear and superiors absorbed in the politics of survival, those groups most potentially damaging for the implementor have been peer officials and the local strongmen themselves. The implementor has often confronted a set of complex accommodations between these two groups. Local strongmen, through the social control they exercise, have performed critical functions for state and party personnel. They have turned out the vote (where there are elections), they have maintained stability, and they have provided access to constituencies. In turn, strongmen have received special benefits from the officials.

Like strongmen elsewhere, cacique Pedro Caso played an important middleman role as he developed relations with local state and party officials, using those relations as additional resources to strengthen his social control among the village peasants. "Pedro tries to legitimize his role by describing his friendship with politically powerful persons: compadres in nearby county seats, and 'very good friends' such as the former state senator, A. Madariaga Rios."[16] Caciques, such as Pedro Caso, have repaid the debt for the resources they have gained from

[15] Ibid., pp. 274–75.
[16] Ibid., p. 275.

officials' public acknowledgment of their role by getting out the vote for the PRI, insuring high membership in the CNC (the official peasant confederation), silencing dissenters, and more.

THE CASE OF CONASUPO

Bureaucrats charged with imposing a new set of rules have faced not only the local strongman but also strong local alliances between strongmen and other state and party officials that pose great threats to their careers. The experience of implementors of a new rural policy in Mexico during the 1970s reflects the sources of pressure on such bureaucrats.[17] CONASUPO, the state agency empowered to protect the consumer and regulate the staple products market, became the spearhead of the new rural policy. This policy was designed to counteract the poor productivity of peasant farmers by nudging them into the modern commercial agricultural sector. The agency's study group in 1972 pinpointed the problems of Mexico's peasant farmer: "It is necessary for him to produce a surplus, to retain the use of the surplus, and finally to invest it productively in the improvement of his production. The problem is that any surplus produced by the Mexican peasant is extracted by individuals and groups who make their livings by exploiting him."[18]

The CONASUPO solution to the problem was straightforward: to break the hold of the strongmen on the peasant economy. As CONASUPO officials put it, their goal was to "make the agency as agile as the *cacique* and the *coyote.*"[19] They sought an outright confrontation over social control between those in the environment of conflict, the state and the strongmen. Concretely, the agency heads planned for CONASUPO to supply the goods and services currently offered by the strongman, including consumer goods, farm inputs, health care, marketing services, credit, harvest-related services (e.g., storage and transport), and investment advice.

In 1973, CONASUPO established offices in each of the thirty-one federal states in Mexico to oversee the array of programs designed to deliver these goods and services. One clear message came through to the implementors from the outset: there could be no public scandal. CONASUPO had already surfaced in the newspapers of the late 1960s as

[17] The following case is adapted largely from Merilee S. Grindle's outstanding book, *Bureaucrats, Politicians, and Peasants in Mexico: A Case Study in Public Policy* (Berkeley: University of California Press, 1977).

[18] Ibid., p. 86.

[19] Quoted in ibid., p. 161.

a source of mismanagement and scandal.[20] Agency chiefs were now unwilling to brook more reasons for sensationalist newspaper accounts. Just as the British colonial civil servant in Sierra Leone had done a century before, the Mexican bureaucrat had to control the local environment sufficiently to prevent unfavorable information from flowing up to his superiors.

Where did the risks for the implementor lie? The pressures were not from the potential clients of the new rural policy but from peer state and party figures and private sector strongmen, including merchants and caciques. Both the governor of the federal state and merchants had the contacts necessary to allow damaging information to flow upward, through articles in the local press, for example; the caciques had also developed important strong ties. Grindle described the implementor's risk calculus. "The most important local demands upon him," she wrote, "come from the private sector, the governor, and other locally important political forces. In addition, he is the focus of performance demands from the central offices of CONASUPO. These demands are of two types: (1) to implement centrally determined policies, and (2) to solve local level problems without public scandal."[21]

The governors' base of support depended on their accommodations with the local strongmen who pressured the governors to help modify CONASUPO's plans; without threatening their own social control, governors focused their efforts on the implementor. Where the governor had had a hand in suggesting the implementor for his important post in CONASUPO, the governor's influence on the implementor was only enhanced. Certainly, if implementors would have become the champions of the subsistence farmers, the result could have been just the sort of scandal they had to prevent. Moreover, such a stance could have been downright dangerous. One community worker said, "CONASUPO wants to break the power of the *cacique* or the sons and grandsons of *caciques* who are often allied with the PRI and the CNC. There is some danger in this—pistols are still worn in many rural areas to deal with this kind of threat."[22]

In the end, the risks to the implementor posed by governors, caciques, and regional merchants outweighed those found in disregarding the charge from above "to implement centrally determined policies." As the inevitable big shuffle at the end of sexenio scheduled for 1976 loomed ahead, CONASUPO chiefs, as those in almost all of Mexi-

[20] Kenneth F. Johnson, *Mexican Democracy: A Critical View* (Boston: Allyn and Bacon, 1971), pp. 105–7.

[21] Grindle, *Bureaucrats, Politicians, and Peasants in Mexico*, p. 129.

[22] Quoted in ibid., p. 160.

co's agencies, became exceedingly cautious, focusing on how to position themselves for an entirely new assignment in the next administration. Their emphasis shifted from implementing the policy to keeping on the lid on at the local level. For the implementor, this only heightened the risks posed by local forces. In the end, CONASUPO's grand policy for replacing the cacique failed at the level of implementation.

Where the politics of survival are working at the apex of the state, those in the middle levels of administration learn that the calculus of pressures changes for them as well. No state can achieve predominance without local representatives pressing forward the state's social control, rules of the game, and strategies of survival. But the quality of implementation reflects the degree to which state leaders can mobilize support and encourage the emergence of differentiated, complex agencies. Where state leaders undercut those agencies at the top, implementation becomes crippled at the bottom.

ACCOMMODATION AND CAPTURING THE STATE AT THE LOCAL LEVEL

The state has become the grand arena of accommodation on at least two levels. The first has involved the top state leadership itself. As noted in Chapters 5 and 6, rulers have accommodated two sorts of social control not under their direct influence. In the case of local strongmen, as with Egypt's middle and rich peasants, rulers have traded a hands-off policy that allowed the strongman to build enclaves of social control for the social stability such strongmen could guarantee. These leaders have also dealt with much larger concentrations of social control, the so-called power centers, especially those organizing capital and security. Their accommodations with these organizations have come largely through a series of discriminatory and/or preferential policies.

The second set of accommodations has occurred at the local and regional level, where implementors, their peer officials (especially regional politicians and party functionaries), and strongmen have accommodated one another in a web of political, economic, and social exchanges. Their bargaining has determined the final allocation of state resources that have made their way to the region; it has shaped the nature of the insinuation of state agencies into village and town.

For those interested in discerning how Third World societies have been ruled and the influence of politics on social change, the local level often holds rich and instructive hints. Here the state, through its implementors, has become involved in bargaining relationships with strongmen. At the same time, intrastate or party-state bargaining occurs between implementors and other state and party officials. These two sets of related bargaining can be called the Triangle of Accommodation. The results have been unexpected state-society relations—unexpected, at least, for those who have observed only the politics of the capital city. The impact of state policies devised in the capital city may be quite different from that anticipated by a scholar looking only at the scope of public policies undertaken and the vast apparatus the state organization has available to effect those policies. Observers have all too often assumed that "once a policy has been 'made' by a government, the policy will be implemented and the desired results of the policy will be near those expected by the policymakers."[23]

Grindle summarized the web of local politics in Mexico as a "system of accommodation and payoff." Her CONASUPO case reflected how the system ultimately determined the disposition of vast resources in a manner substantially different from the state plan of 1972–1973; CONASUPO consumed more than 5 percent of the state's budget. "At the local level, as the example of CONASUPO's state representatives indicates, governors, deputies, senators, municipal presidents, and village leaders serve the party by mobilizing and delivering the support of their followers and are rewarded for their efforts with a variety of government controlled goods and services, which are frequently channeled through the bureaucracy."[24]

Explicit or covert bargaining among organized social interests, bureaucrats, and politicians is a hallmark of nearly every contemporary state. Even strong states, such as in France, find it a rarity to implement a policy so faithfully that the minister of education could confidently say, as the aphorism goes, what page of what text any child in the country is studying at any hour. More often local interests and local state officials can bend regulations through their bargaining. Their distortion of the intent of policy makers is limited, however, because of the scrutiny from superiors and the potential clamoring of clients who would stand to lose by any changes in adopted policy. In weak states, such constraints are far more feeble, and the bargaining can lead to major distortions in the use of state resources. Anemic supervision due to the politics of survival and the powerlessness of potential clients of reformist policies leave the bargaining among implementors, peer politicians, and strongmen much less encumbered by

---

[23] Thomas B. Smith, "The Policy Implementation Process," *Policy Sciences* 4 (June 1973): 198.

[24] Grindle, *Bureaucrats, Politicians, and Peasants in Mexico*, p. 179.

the power of state officials from above or by the demands of the mass of the population from below. The Triangle of Accommodation can become a set of institutionalized relationships with only occasional infringement from other forces.

World norms of what a state should do have undoubtedly influenced state officials at all levels about the purposes of the state. Top state leaders, with the strongest ties to outside institutions, have been especially prone to the impact of external norms about what their states should be able to accomplish. Their plans, as with CONASUPO's new rural policy for the 1970s, and their rhetoric have portrayed a continuing environment of conflict between the state and reactionary strongmen. Mexico's PRI chairman, for example, delivered a much-publicized speech in 1972 in which he said, "No ruler can base his support on *cacicazgos*. . . . *Caciquismo* should disappear in our time."[25] This rhetoric should not be dismissed lightly. Even as top political leaders, such as Nasser in Egypt and Rajiv Gandhi in India, accommodated the strongmen at the local level, they simultaneously used a populist strategy to insist on the illegitimacy of these same strongmen. They reasserted in their direct communications with the population what was belied in the action of their agents, the implementors: a commitment to the reformist role of the state and to the demise of strongmen.

The state leaders' direct access to the masses and the masses' access to the state through populist networks espousing state symbols have come to coexist with fairly unencumbered Triangles of Accommodation determining the actual disbursement of state resources and disposition of state policies. In some important ways, the state symbols espoused through the mass media and other means, such as election campaigns, have become part of people's strategies of survival. They are modified and reinterpreted in these eclectic strategies, however, in ways that promote the strongman's rules of the game. An Egyptian fellahin may have thus revered Nasser, demonstrated for Egyptian nationalism, and still signed the letter of complaint against Samir when he tried to apply the state's rules faithfully.

In Chapter 1 the conception I offered of a continuing environment of conflict with unremitting hostility between state and strongmen's organizations must be modified to reflect a more complex situation. The conflict between state and strongmen is most obvious at the level of the grand plans and rhetoric of the state leadership. That leader-

[25] Reyes Heroles quoted in Wayne A. Cornelius, "Leaders, Followers, and Official Patrons in Urban Mexico," in Schmidt et al., eds., *Friends, Followers, and Factions*, p. 349.

ship itself may be involved in an implicit accommodation with those it regularly attacks in speeches and slogans. Also, the state is not composed only of top leaders. But the accommodations between arms of the state, implementors and regional politicians, and strongmen can also mean the simultaneous existence of a rhetorical environment of conflict and arrangements in which arms of the state tolerate, even support, rules in conflict with those written in state laws and regulations. As Wayne Cornelius noted, lower-level state officials, implementors, and party personnel in Mexico have maintained a view of the cacique quite different from that posed in the rhetoric. These state and party functionaries

> are expected by their superiors to maintain social and political control of those segments of the population falling within their jurisdictions, as well as to secure high turnouts of PRI voters and participants in other forms of regime-supportive political activity. *Caciques* have found it so easy to gain and hold power in small communities, both rural and urban, because they make it so much easier for the ambitious, lower-echelon official to do his job.[26]

India's experience with policy implementation has revealed similar accommodations at the local and regional levels. "The system," wrote Myron Weiner, "gave a great deal of power to individuals at the local level who were often able to impede the carrying out of national policies."[27] Even as the Congress party sought to develop as a parallel state in the colonial period, it lacked direct access to the mass of India's population, the peasants. After independence, the party relied heavily on strongmen of one sort or another to deliver the vote. Of particular importance have been the rich peasants, who have not only asserted their social control locally but also as a group have become effective lobbies at the federal level and key players in party politics. The nexus of relationships among state, party, and strongmen, the Triangle of Accommodation, ultimately defined the character of India's state agencies' activities at the local and regional level. Even when Indira Gandhi sought in the 1970s to free herself of her dependence on strongmen, particularly the rich peasants, and to appeal directly to the

[26] Ibid., p. 350. Also, see Antonio Ugalde, *Power and Conflict in a Mexican Community: A Study of Political Integration* (Albuquerque: University of New Mexico Press, 1970), p. 122; and Friedrich, "The Legitimacy of a Cacique."

[27] Myron Weiner, "Motilal, Jawaharlal, Indira, and Sanjay in India's Political Transformation," in Richard J. Samuels, ed., *Political Generations and Political Development* (Lexington, Mass.: Lexington Books, 1977), p. 72.

electorate, the accommodations proved impossible to overcome without suffering unacceptable costs in terms of political stability.

The gap between Congress rhetoric and state practices became a subject of debate as far back as the 1950s, especially concerning India's vast rural sector. Nehru initiated agrarian reform policies to bring state benefits directly to the peasants. India's National Development Council followed Nehru's lead and approved a new and expanded program of cooperative development. Nehru and his planners hoped cooperative farming along with peasant-dominated panchayat institutions would link peasants directly to the state without the influence of intermediaries on the disposition of state goods and services. Frankel summarized the new plan:

> Institutional change, especially the organization of village cooperatives and panchayats, was . . . assigned the central role of rural resource mobilization. The planners envisaged that each panchayat would prepare a village production plan to ensure all cultivators a supply of credit for improved agricultural inputs; and to involve the entire community in the construction of capital assets through the digging of field channels, digging and maintenance of tanks, and contour bunding.[28]

Nehru, for his part, spoke in an imagery of direct unmediated relations with those who could benefit from the cooperative agricultural policy. "I shall go from field to field and peasant to peasant begging them to agree to it, knowing that if they do not agree, I cannot put it into operation."[29]

Rich peasants, who had developed bases of social control in the countryside and influence within the Congress, greatly feared the looming reforms. They used their position in the Congress first to water down considerably legislation regarding the plan. And when the program was finally implemented their role resulted in a monumental gap between plans and actual institutional effects of the reforms. At the main point of diversion, the state (provincial) level, stood the imposing Triangle of Accommodation forged by rich peasants, the state's regional politicians and implementors, and Congress party personnel. Their accommodations resulted not only in hefty voter turnouts for Nehru's Congress but also in rules of the game at the local level that mocked the intent of the state's cooperative agricultural policy and reinforced the strongmen inimical to Nehru's purposes.

[28] Francine R. Frankel, *India's Political Economy, 1947–1977: The Gradual Revolution* (Princeton, N.J.: Princeton University Press, 1978), p. 182.

[29] Quoted in ibid., p. 167.

As the only cultivators with access to sufficient resources either from savings or low-interest loans to experiment with and risk adoption of improved methods of cultivation, the more substantial landowners early acquired the additional prestige of being identified by the Block Development staff as "progressive" farmers in the villages. From this vantage point, it was a short step to assuming the role of intermediary between the Community Development administration and the more "backward" farmers to control access to "community" funds and services.[30]

In India and Mexico, as in Egypt, state leaders and agency chiefs constructed complex rural policies aimed at eliminating intermediaries and establishing direct state social control. Ironically, in each instance state institutions deeply penetrated rural life, but those institutions and the resources they brought reinforced control of existing strongmen. State resources did reach the village in each case, but strongmen distributed them according to their own criteria, not those set by state legislation, and used their distribution to reinforce their own social control. But the strongmen were limited, too; they did not have unlimited ability to apply their rules. The local accommodation restricted them to the bargain just as it did the other parties.

The Triangle of Accommodation at the local level has meant that no single group—not implementors, local politicos, or strongmen—monopolizes power. Local politics has reflected the bargaining strength of each of the actors. Implementors, as noted, have guarded against any damaging flow of information and have avoided scrutiny from above, but that is not all they have gained. Since they allocate so many resources that come through the state pipeline, they have often been in a strong bargaining position at the local level. In cases where accountability and control still have some meaning in their agencies, they have used their bargaining power to protect their careers by narrowing the parameters of what can be done with the resources they allocate. Where, on the other hand, effective supervision and support from above have all but disappeared, many have used their leverage for personal gain with little regard for the overall purpose of any given policy.

In India, the deterioration of supervision over implementors led to a situation in which "officers of the police, the judiciary, the state and local revenue and development services, and even the vaunted Indian Administrative Service, were all engaged in selling influence (often at

[30] Ibid., p. 197–98.

fixed prices and graded fees)."[31] In Tanzania, supervision was so lax that one observer found an alarming number of cases in which he could find no record of project implementation at all.

> One cannot know how many other achievements on the records in the capital of Dar es Salaam or the district headquarters throughout the countryside do not exist. Political systems under pressure from the center to produce solid development results were likely to exercise their own form of accommodation. The most common form of accommodation to date had been simply to pass false or inflated accounts of development results to superiors who were out of touch with local conditions.[32]

Whether supervision has deteriorated to almost nothing or not, bureaucrats at the regional and local level have remained key actors in determining who gets what and what others can do with it. The state bureaucracy, then, cannot avoid but being a major factor in local allocation of resources. The limitation on state power, of course, has been that the allocation may deviate tremendously from the prescriptions of law and policy statements in the capital city.

District leaders, state governors, local party chiefs—the local and regional politicos—have faced similar constraints and opportunities to those of the implementors. The closer the scrutiny from above, the more they have had to narrow the parameters of acceptable behavior. Where supervision has been lax, they could use their budgetary discretion, their contacts with top-level state leaders, and the force at their disposal for personal gain. Like the implementors, however, local politicos have been vulnerable to damaging publicity and dependent on those with effective social control, the strongmen, for any sort of popular mobilization they need to carry out.

Perhaps the most interesting figures of all in the Triangle of Accommodation have been the strongmen. They have come to rely on state resources, from contracts to handouts, in order to maintain the dependency of their segment of the population. Although the social control they have exercised enables these strongmen to make demands upon the state, the fragmentation of their petty baronies, their rules and organizations, has hurt them as well; in a few countries, although certainly not all, they have become a powerful influence even in capital city politics. Frequently, their inability to develop a significant organi-

[31] Ibid., p. 203.
[32] Clyde R. Ingle, *From Village to State in Tanzania: The Politics of Rural Development* (Ithaca: Cornell University Press, 1972), p. 254.

zational basis among themselves has meant that the actual volume of resources filtering through state agencies to them has been relatively small. In most countries, they have not been able to compete with the major power centers in society—capital, large labor unions, professional associations—in gaining disproportionate shares of state outlays. Their fragmented social control has not posed the same threat to a weak state with limited mobilizational capabilities that more unified centers, such as industrial capital, with fairly high mobilizational capabilities have. As a result, strongmen have witnessed a net outflow of wealth from their areas, but they have garnered a disproportionate share of that wealth coming back to the local area through the pipeline of state agencies.

In short, because effective maintenance of strongmen's social control, obviously in their own interests, in any case creates the stability enjoyed by a regime, there is little incentive for state leaders to invest a large proportion of state funds in areas of strongmen's control. Thus, while the state resources they garner may seem bountiful in the context of poor rural areas or urban slums, in countries such as Egypt and Mexico they have been a disproportionately small share of total state revenues. The larger sums are reserved for the bigger centers of power, such as private industry and state-owned enterprises, which can threaten top state leaders directly. Only in a case such as India, where rich peasants have managed to forge an effective national lobby, have these strongmen kept a fairly proportionate share of total state resources.

India, however, is the exceptional case in this regard. In other countries, such as Mexico and Egypt, the state has effected a major net outflow of wealth from areas controlled by petty strongmen. Hansen has noted the relative lack of power of the caciques at the macrolevel, compared to that of capital in Mexico:

> By making only insignificant expenditures on programs of agricultural extension, *ejidal* credit, rural and urban education, housing, and other welfare programs, the government has been able to channel a larger proportion of its limited resources into major development projects. . . . Likewise, most of the government policies designed to encourage the expansion of private investment have sacrificed the short-term interests of the Mexican laborer and *campesino*, and have concentrated the fruits of growth in the hands of a new industrial-agricultural elite.[33]

[33] Roger D. Hansen, *The Politics of Mexican Development*, (Baltimore: Johns Hopkins University Press, 1971), p. 221.

The larger power centers have squeaked the loudest, and consequently they have received most of the grease.

In proferring their strategies of survival, the strongmen have used a share of the state resources at their disposal to bind the population to them. Added to their land, credit, and jobs—the other elements upon which they have based the strategies of survival they offer their clients—are the bountiful, at least in local terms, resources of the state. Local leaders have become brokers for the contracts, jobs, goods, services, force, and authority that filter through the bureaucratic tentacles of the state. As one writer on Brazil put it, there has emerged a new "state-based political clientelism" in which clients have "looked to the public economy and the elites who controlled the distributional arm of the state to deliver the state benefits upon which they came to depend."[34] State resources, then, have become integral to the everyday lives of great portions of the population, but their disposition has been deeply influenced by local strongmen.

The latitude these strongmen have had in how they use the resources has depended in great part on the bargaining power of the implementors and political officials. It is difficult to judge overall whether strongmen have been hurt or helped in terms of social control as a result of their relations with the state. Adams has argued for Egypt that "the leverage that rich peasants enjoy over cooperative resources has been reduced" as a result of their interaction with bureaucrats.[35] The same may be true elsewhere.

In short, the strongmen have been wedded to state resources and personnel to maintain their local control and to gain new resources to enhance that control. Yet, their most basic purposes have been antithetical to modern norms of what a state should do. These norms have depicted the state as a mechanism to create a single jurisdiction—a rule of law in which the rules are the same from border to border; this is the desideratum of the modern state.

These strongmen—whether village chiefs, urban caciques, or rich peasants—have worked for precisely the opposite effect. They have sought to maintain their own rules and their own criteria for who gets what within much more limited bounds; their rules have been parochial and discriminatory rather than universal. In some respects they would like to enhance the state, or at least the resources it can make available to them, but they must also thwart the state from achieving

[34] Frances Hagopian, "The Politics of Oligarchy: The Persistence of Traditional Elites in Contemporary Brazil" (Ph.D. diss., M.I.T., 1986), p. 38.

[35] Adams, *Development and Social Change in Rural Egypt*, p. 86.

its leaders' most fundamental purposes and from being in a position to offer viable strategies of survival to the population directly.

Such contradictory impulses and the delicacy of the equilibrium strongmen seek in simultaneously embracing and foiling the state have led them to try to maximize control over as much of their environment as possible. As a result, they have found the parameters set by implementors and other state officials in the Triangle of Accommodation irksome. Commonly, to minimize such tension, strongmen themselves become the implementors, or politicos or party officials, or they place a kinsman or client in such a position. Sierra Leone, Egypt, Mexico, and India, each has exhibited varieties of such practices. Thus, many strongmen have captured parts of states. They have succeeded in having themselves or their family members placed in critical state posts to ensure allocation of resources according to their own rules, rather than the rules propounded in the official rhetoric, policy statements, and legislation generated in the capital city or those put forth by a strong implementor.

The Triangle of Accommodation, with all its bargaining and trade-offs, has had as debilitating an effect on state strength as the politics of survival. Accommodation at the local and regional level has stemmed indirectly from the fragmentation of society and the dilemma such fragmentation imposed on state leaders. Its impact has been to bring the political process full cycle, for the Triangle of Accommodation results in an allocation of state resources that reinforces societal fragmentation.

THE EFFECTS OF SOCIETY ON STATE AND STATE ON SOCIETY

Tokenism on the part of bureaucrats, frequent reshuffling of cabinets, and human rights abuses by state officials have neither been random or idiosyncratic happenings in the Third World, nor are they simply explained as the products of depraved, mendacious, or inept leaders and bureaucrats. Society's structure, I have argued in Chapter 6 and 7, has affected politics at the highest levels of the state and the administration of state policy at much lower levels. If we want to understand the capabilities and character of states—their ability to make the rules for their population and the degree to which the politics of survival predominate over other agenda items—we must start with social structure. Where social structure has not been marked by deeply entrenched strongmen or where such strongmen have been weakened, state leaders have had greater opportunities to apply a single set of rules, the state's rules, and build channels for widespread, sustained political support. In such instances, leaders have been in a position to pursue broad social and political agendas. The struggle for survival need not become so consuming as to negate the state's abilities to carry out other public policies.

These chapters have examined another set of circumstances, the case of states with low- and middle-level capabilities. Here social control has been vested in numerous local-level social organizations and perhaps several major power centers. These power centers have received the most direct attention of state leaders through public policies in their favor, state transfers of wealth to their benefit, cooptation of their leaders, or through state attempts to demolish their independent mobilizational capabilities.

Critically placed strongmen—for example, landlords, caciques, local businessmen, moneylenders—have usually not received the kind of attention leaders of power centers have, but they have played critical, if often overlooked, roles in the recent history of many countries. They have dictated rules of behavior for much of the population. Their ability to impose themselves between segments of the population and critical resources, such as land, credit, and jobs, has enabled them to offer many elements for their clients' strategies of survival. This structure of society, with its fragmentation of social control, has denied the state the ability to mobilize these clients politically. And, with few sources of support, state leaders have faced the dilemma of creating powerful agencies that could eventually generate such support but in the meanwhile could be very threatening. Many patterns have derived from the fragmented structure of society: the altered priorities of state leaders (survival over social change), the style of state politics (big shuffle, dirty tricks, and so on), the structure of the state organization (redundant agencies), the difficulties in implementing policy, the showering of capital with special prerogatives, the calculus of pressures on the implementor, and the capture of tentacles of the state.

Part III started with the fragmented social control exercised by local leaders and the effects of such fragmentation on politics—the impact of society on the state. In the end, we came full circle to the effect of the state—its resources, policies, and personnel—on society. That effect has been the strengthening of fragmented social control of local leaders and their particular rules. In short, a society fragmented in social control affects the character of the state, which, in turn, reinforces the fragmentation of society. Even the very weakest states have changed the institutional landscape of their societies to some extent and injected new resources into communities. In states somewhat higher on the scale of capabilities—Egypt, India, Mexico—the trans-formation has introduced state resources into the everyday minutiae of people's lives and strategies of survival. Overall, however, in many societies the distribution of social control has not changed radically from a weblike to a pyramidal configuration.

CHAPTER EIGHT

Conclusion

IN BOTH academic literature on the Third World and daily newspaper accounts, writers have portrayed states that represent, speak for, their societies. Third World state leaders have valiantly attempted to reinforce this image of the state as the natural spokesman for the people of society. Note the ironic comments of the hero in Nigerian Chinua Achebe's novel, *A Man of the People.*

> A man who has just come in from the rain and dried his body and put on dry clothes is more reluctant to go out again than another who has been indoors all the time. The trouble with our new nation—as I saw it then lying on that bed—was that none of us had been indoors long enough to be able to say "To hell with it." We had all been in the rain together until yesterday. Then a handful of us— the smart and the lucky and hardly ever the best—had scrambled for the one shelter our former rulers left, and had taken it over and barricaded themselves in. And from within they sought to persuade the rest through numerous loudspeakers, that the first phase of the struggle had been won and that the next phase—the extension of our house—was even more important and called for new and original tactics; it required that all argument should cease and the whole people speak with one voice and that any more dissent and argument outside the door of the shelter would subvert and bring down the whole house.[1]

A first look at the institutional landscape of practically all Third World societies today confirms the impression rulers have sought to impart. The state seems omnipresent, speaking for all the people with a single voice. Even in the far corners of societies, its institutions have penetrated local life. In many Asian, African, and Latin American countries, these institutions have had a continuing, resounding impact on people's daily habits.[2] States have grown in sheer size and resources

---

[1] Chinua Achebe, *A Man of the People* (Garden City, N.Y.: Doubleday, 1967), pp. 34–35.

[2] I, therefore, am not satisfied with the literature that describes most of the world's societies as "stateless societies." Although it is certainly true that the "idea of the state" is weaker in many societies, lacking a long historical and intellectual tradition as an institu-

almost everywhere since World War II. Their agencies and resources have become a major presence in societies, collecting taxes, setting prices, building clinics and schools, and more. Images presented by researchers in the literature on Latin America, for example, of strong corporate or bureaucratic-authoritarian states have reflected the impingement of state agencies on nearly every aspect of daily life.

One must go, however, beyond that first glance. Abner Cohen, quite rightly I think, criticized political scientists for limiting their inquiry far too severely to the formal aspects of organization.[3] Goode made a related point for economists, noting their preoccupation with the formulation of policy rather than its effectiveness and efficiency.[4] In the preceding chapters I have sought to show how one goes beyond first looks and formal institutions, studying and understanding such societies and their states. In these chapters I have sketched an approach or model of state-society relations as well as a broad theory of the interactive relations between state and society.

In many cases, the operative rules for people's behavior in these societies have not been established in state legislation or bureaucratic decrees. True, state agencies have insinuated themselves into the towns and villages of the society, and, in the case of states somewhat higher on the scale of capabilities, this penetration has resulted in monumental effects on social life. However, the distribution of revenues and services, as well as other consequences, has frequently run counter to those anticipated in official policy. This disparity between declarations of intent by state leaders in the capital city and the actual disposition of state resources has been most evident in microlevel social policies,

---

tion that embodies public power, the state as an apparatus *and* a developing idea has had considerable impact on almost all contemporary societies. Instead of "state societies" and "stateless societies," I prefer a continuum in which states as organizations vary in their ability to enforce the rules of the game—weak and strong states. On "state societies" and "stateless societies," see, for example, Kenneth H. F. Dyson, *The State Tradition in Western Europe: A Study of an Idea and Institution* (Oxford: Martin Robertson, 1980). More useful than Dyson's categories is a formulation, echoing Nettl, which states that "in different polities, or in the same polity in different historical periods, there will exist a greater or lesser degree of 'stateness,' depending upon the extent to which the major goals for society are designated and safeguarded by the state, independent of civil society." Metin Heper, "The State and Public Bureaucracies: A Comparative and Historical Perspective," *Comparative Studies in Society and History* 27 (January 1985): 86.

[3] Abner Cohen, *Two-Dimensional Man* (Berkeley: University of California Press, 1974), p. 7. For an important commentary on the formal-legal study of the state, see Harry Eckstein, "On the 'Science' of the State," in Stephen R. Graubard, ed., *The State* (New York: W. W. Norton, 1979), pp. 1–20.

[4] Richard Goode, *Government Finance in Developing Countries* (Washington, D.C.: Brookings Institution, 1984), p. 300.

although even in macrolevel fiscal questions, scholars still often have not looked very closely at the actual impact of policy.[5] This disjuncture between the state's rules of the game, as its leaders sought to establish the whole society as a single juridical whole, and the actual operative dictates of behavior in society stimulated the general questions that have guided this book: Why have so many Third World state rulers, with all the resources at their disposal, had such difficulty in having their state organizations implement social policies and in getting their populations to do what they want them to do? And why have a handful of other states succeeded much more in this realm? What sorts of effects on the state itself have derived from the resistance of organizations in the society to the state's efforts to direct people's daily behavior?

The approach, outlined in Chapter 1, begins with the struggle for social control, the actual ability to make the operative rules of the game for people in the society. Social control for the state entails more than insinuation, or penetration, of its agencies into society, more even than just successful extraction of resources. It includes the ability to appropriate resources for particular purposes and to regulate people's daily behavior. With controlled and selective disbursement of state resources, officials have the possibility of offering the main components, especially the major myths and symbols, for people's strategies of survival. Only then does the state have the prerequisites for effective regulation and the possibility of extensively mobilizing the population. The approach in this book, then, does not take state capabilities or autonomy as a given. It focuses our attention on how social control is actually distributed in society. The starting point for analysis is the environment of conflict; there is a struggle between state leaders, who seek to mobilize people and resources and impose a single set of rules, and other social organizations applying different rules in parts of the society.

In the remaining chapters, I presented a broad theory to explain why so many Third World states have fallen on the lower end of the spectrum in their abilities to achieve social control and effective appropriation of resources. Why have many Third World states remained weak or achieved only middle-level capabilities, and why have a few others been able to avoid such weakness? The initial part of the answer to those questions was developed in Part II. As with European society

---

[5] Goode makes this point in ibid., and his book is a corrective. For the impact of exchange rate, price, and credit policies of a weak state, see Victoria Anne Lawson, "National Economic Policies, Local Variations in Structure of Production, and Uneven Regional Development: The Case of Ecuador" (Ph.D. diss., Ohio State University, 1986).

prior to its great burst of state building in the sixteenth and seventeenth centuries, societies in Africa, Asia, and Latin America experienced rapid, deep, and universal debilitation of existing strategies of
survival—the very bases of existing social control. The blitzkrieg-like
extension of the world market from the late 1850s through World War
I made many of the existing rules in these societies irrelevant. Legal
changes in land tenure and revenue collection and new modes of
transportation paved the way for a much more fundamental penetration of the world economy to all parts of society, undermining existing
bases of social control. It was as if a great wind had swept through the
non-Western world, knocking Humpty Dumpty off the wall.

The theory here posits that the emergence of a strong, capable state
can occur only with a tremendous concentration of social control. And
such a redistribution of social control cannot occur without exogenous
factors first creating catastrophic conditions that rapidly and deeply
undermine existing strategies of survival, the bases of social control.
With the disruptions caused by the spreading European world system,
such conditions existed. Yet, only a minority of the new and renewed
states could today be classified as strong, even in an historical epoch
supporting strong states as the accepted international norm. Why?

Our answer suggests that the destruction of old forms of social control does not hold within it the blueprint for how Humpty Dumpty
will be put together again. The new concentration of social control was
by no means assured. In Asia, Africa, and Latin America, in fact, the
conditions in the half-century preceding World War I resulted in a
strong state in only one country in the world, Japan. Several factors
worked against the creation of conditions for the eventual emergence
of strong states. In Latin America and in societies that escaped formal
colonial rule altogether, for example, the alliance of European merchants and indigenous strongmen limited the ability of state leaders to
concentrate social control. Key players in the expanding world economy funneled resources into societies quite selectively, allowing for the
strengthening of caciques, effendis, caudillos, landlords, kulak-type
rich peasants, moneylenders, and others. Through credit, access to
land and water, protection, bullying, and numerous other means,
these strongmen fashioned the wherewithal for viable strategies of
survival for numerous peasants and workers.

Our attention was mainly on another major factor determining the
new distribution of social control: Western (especially British) policies
in colonial territories. Here, too, for many societies the effect favored
the emergence of new or renewed strongmen. Colonial policies, in
most cases, led to the reestablishment of fragmented social control in

societies in Africa and Asia, although as the case of Palestine indicated fragmentation was not a necessary outcome of colonialism.

Despite the overwhelming organizational resources found in today's states, compared to those in the hands of strongmen, state rulers have discovered that the legacy of such fragmented social control has continued to constrain them severely. Once established, a fragmented distribution of social control has been difficult to transform. State leaders could not easily dismiss conflicting sets of rules in society. Their central problem has been in political mobilization of the population.

To understand the continuing problem of political mobilization for state leaders demands a more differentiated view of the state. The state does not merely reflect the will and skill of its leaders. I have identified three important levels of the state organization and how they affect one another to determine overall state-society relations. First is the level of the central executive leadership. Besides its own particular policy agenda, its concerns include mobilization of support, creating effective arms or agencies to carry out its will, resolving the conflicting notions of the state's priorities among its agencies, and insuring its own political survival. Second is the level of the leadership in the central agencies of the state organization. These figures have their own personal and policy agendas; within their agencies they can use the power of appointment and patronage to forge a broad organizational view of the state's priorities. Finally, there are the state officials at the regional and local levels. We looked mainly at the implementors, those entrusted with inducing the population in particular regions to accept the state's rules of the game in the domain of their agency. As they seek to advance their careers, they are subject to multiple pressures, including those from supervisors, clients, peer officials, and strongmen.

Top executive leaders, as we saw in Part III, have been well aware that the sole means toward sustained political mobilization is through building state agencies and related political parties that can provide the primary elements for viable strategies of survival to the people in all spheres of their lives. Yet, there are big risks in creating effective agencies of this sort; each tends to become a centrifugal force—a power center, as Nasser called it—at a moment when the leader's counterweights, or centripetal forces, are limited. Building such state institutions can create powerful suborganizations within the state itself with an oligopoly of mobilizational capability, in which high bureaucratic and party officials can influence the overall channeling of support to the state that comes through political mobilization. Top state leaders in societies with fragmented social control have had, then, an intense dilemma. They have had to weigh their need to create effective agencies for political mobilization and security against the risks to political stability and their own survival, which come in creating potential power centers they cannot control.

The effects of society on the state—that is, the impact of fragmented social control and the consequent ruler's dilemma on political style and state preferences in distributing resources—have been monumental, as I outlined in Chapter 6. Fragmentation of social control and the difficulties in political mobilization have led to a pathological style at the apex of the state, the politics of survival. State leaders in weak states have taken to pulverizing the very arms of the state that could achieve their goal of mobilization. Their purpose has been to prevent leading officials in important agencies from using their own mobilizational capabilities against the central state leadership.

The top state leaders have also used a variety of techniques to deal with major power centers in society, such as industrial capital and organized labor. These methods have included cooptation, steering disproportionate amounts of state resources to them, absorption into the state organization, intimidation, and more. Here, too, state leaders have acted paradoxically, damaging the capabilities of these other social organizations to deliver even those benefits to society from which the top leaders indirectly receive major advantages. Again, they aim to thwart the emergence of organizations with independent-minded chiefs having more mobilizational capability than the state leaders themselves. At times state leaders have allowed power centers to grow, inside or outside the state organization, because they have felt they could not do without the services the centers have provided (for example, security and wealth from industrial production). The risks to the leaders have not subsided, however, simply because such centers supply more highly valued services than others. The dilemma of the state leaders still remains, resulting in vacillations and unpredictability in state policy toward the most powerful agencies and organizations inside and outside the state.

In circumstances of fragmented social control, the state has become an arena of accommodations. Not only have state leaders accommodated power centers, but they have also developed trade-offs with much less powerful strongmen. In exchange for resources and minimal interference in strongmen's exercising their own rules in the organizations they control, these strongmen have ensured a modicum of social stability in the cities and countryside, if not the same system of justice state leaders would have preferred.

At the regional and local level, bureaucrats have engaged in their own accommodations.[6] The politics of survival in the state capital have hurt the coherence of the state, lessening the pressures of supervision and control from above. At the same time, the local social control of strongmen has neutralized independent pressure on these bureaucrats from the potential clients at the local level, leaving pressure on implementors from these strongmen and from peer state and party officials. In many areas, these pressures have led to a Triangle of Accommodation; this formation has ironically allowed state resources to strengthen those strongmen and their organizations whose rules of the game conflict with the declared intentions of state leaders and the formal language of laws and regulations. Populist state leaders maintain the environment of conflict by pitting their rhetoric, legislation, and formal policies against the continuing social control of strongmen. On another level, however, these strongmen depend on state resources to maintain their control; they have learned to accommodate populist leaders and even, at times, capture lower levels of the state organization.

It is true that many states in the Third World are still infants in world historical terms. Some critics have argued that a principal reason for the weakness of so many is simply that not enough time has elapsed for them to become strong. My explanation has implicitly rejected such an argument. The structural circumstances to which I have pointed indicate conditions likely to perpetuate fragmented social control. Strongmen are not mere anachronisms; they have carved out protective niches for themselves, invigorated, as it were, by the dilemma of state leaders.

The image of the strong state found in the social science literature has stemmed in large part from the rapid expansion of the state organization in Latin America, Asia, and Africa during the last generation, as state leaders have set out to offer the elements for viable strategies to the populace and win people over to the state's rules. Also, when tested, state leaders have been able to depose most individual strongmen with little difficulty. But one must be extremely cautious before equating a growing state apparatus and ability to get rid of a strongman with state predominance. Individual strongmen may go, but the overall distribution of social control may remain remarkably constant. The bureaus of the state may become little more than the arenas for accommodations with other organizations. Their tentacles may

[6] On the notion of bureaucrats seeking their interests as another group in society, see Richard Kraus and Reeve D. Vanneman, "Bureaucrats versus the State in Capitalist and Socialist Regimes," *Comparative Studies in Society and History* 27 (January 1985): 111–22.

be captured by those with very different rules and principles from those expressed in the state's legal code, and state resources may be used to strengthen the very forces they aimed to eliminate. As Victor Azarya and Naomi Chazan have argued, one must discard the notion that all societies are state-centered (what they call the engagement paradigm). This is a world in which conditions have led, in some cases, to the "enfeeblement of the state."[7]

Azarya and Chazan's notion of enfeeblement of the state was drawn from the sub-Saharan African experience, where states have been weakest. Of course, a spectrum of state capabilities indicates variation in state strength. Among the cases here, the state in Sierra Leone has been lowest in capabilities. Even in the realm of regulating diamond mining, the state has found it cannot do much more than "make legal an activity which would have continued regardless."[8] The attention of its leaders has been on securing and maintaining power and thwarting the growth of serious power centers. Note Cartwright's discussion of the considerations going into the state's mining policy.

> Both from the viewpoint of the national leaders and of the chiefs, an enclave system in which the foreign mining companies paid revenue directly to the central government but otherwise did not create much disturbance was preferable to the uncertainties and challenges posed by the growth of an indigenous entrepreneurial class with autonomous financial resources and bases of operation beyond the chief's [and the state's] control.[9]

In many parts of Asia, the Middle East, and Latin America, the state has been higher on the spectrum of capabilities than that in Sierra Leone. Natural and historical factors have mitigated against the extreme sort of fragmentation of social control found in cases on the farthest "weak" end of the continuum of state capabilities. In Egypt, for instance, the topography of the country and the demographic distribution, which concentrated population in a relatively small number of settlements (about 4,000) along the Nile River, have tremendously eased problems of state access to all parts of society. Colonialism in India, while fragmenting in important ways, had at least two contrary effects. First, it created what one scholar called a "technical frame" for uniting India through improved communication and especially a com-

---

[7] Victor Azarya and Naomi Chazan, "Disengagement from the State in Africa: Reflections on the Experience of Ghana and Guinea," *Comparative Studies in Society and History* 29 (January 1987): 106–31.

[8] John R. Cartwright, *Political Leadership in Sierra Leone* (Toronto: University of Toronto Press, 1978), p. 252.

[9] Ibid., pp. 252–53.

prehensive set of administrative linkages, the famed Indian Civil Service.[10] Second, Gandhi's notion of the Congress as a parallel state gave that organization both comprehensiveness and experience in governing that counteracted India's extreme heterogeneity and fragmentation. The destruction of old bases of social control also occurred in the bloody Mexican Revolution and its aftermath, including the Great Depression and the activities of President Cardénas in the 1930s.

These factors helped make the current states in Egypt, India, and Mexico formidable contenders for social control throughout their societies. They have managed somewhat better supervision and control of their bureaucrats. In certain areas of policy making, they have shown far more capabilities than have "enfeebled" states. One could cite, for example, the Egyptian state's abilities in extraction of revenues, particularly from the rural sector, and the Indian state's abilities in organizing successful large-scale industrial enterprises. Nonetheless, the Egyptian, Indian, and Mexican states have continued to rely heavily on strongmen, although in each country state actions at some point led to the substitution of one set of strongmen for another. In these countries, the new and old strongmen have played by rules quite different from the state's laws. The politics of survival have been readily apparent in each case at the highest reaches of the state.

Supervision and control for implementors in these states, while certainly a reality to be dealt with, have tended to be uncertain, even capricious. As one study in Tamil Nadu in India indicated, field administrators felt they never know precisely what superiors will demand of them or how they will evaluate them. These implementors also believed their actions should not threaten their superiors and that they need handle sensitive situations themselves.[11] These administrators admitted only to sticking to the formal rules handed to them, but observations by researchers at the regional and local level in India, as well as in Egypt and Mexico, have indicated Triangles of Accommodation that have seriously modified the rules set out in state laws and policies. In these countries a major transformation has resulted by injecting state resources and institutions into villages and cities alike but on the basis of the continuing sway of the rules and social control of strongmen. Although these states certainly could not be classified as weak as Sierra Leone, it is also impossible to place them on the "strong" end of the scale of capabilities.

Israel has been one of the small number of Third World countries

[10] Satish Saberwal, "Modeling the Crisis: Megasociety, Multiple Codes, and Social Blanks," *Economic Political Weekly* 20 (February 2, 1985): 203.

[11] The study is cited in David C. Potter, *India's Political Administrators, 1919–1983* (Oxford: Clarendon Press, 1986), p. 237.

on the "strong" end of the scale, countries in which strongmen have not maintained a firm foothold. This absence of difficult-to-dislodge fragmented social control in society has by no means meant that Israel has been free of difficulties in establishing a professional bureaucracy to carry out laws and policies.[12] Nevertheless, the overwhelming majority of Israelis perceive the bureaucracy, along with the Knesset (parliament), cabinet, and local governments as each affecting their daily lives.[13] The weakness has not been lacking control of implementors by supervisors so much as overly centralized control, which has impeded contact with and participation of the public in policy implementation and coordination among different agencies of the state.[14] Israel, the state, suffers from a host of problems ranging from stalemates within the central executive leadership to leaking authority in the bureaucracy. Still, the consolidation of social control and the ability to mobilize the public have been relatively high compared to other countries in Asia, Africa, and Latin America.

A summary of my argument for societies with fragmented social control is presented in the interactive, self-reinforcing model depicted in Figure 8.1. The implications of this model are that slim prospects now exist for qualitative leaps in the consolidation of social control on

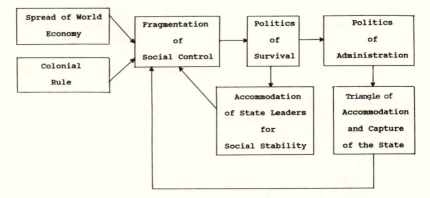

FIGURE 8.1. *An Interactive Model of Relations between Weak Third World States and Their Societies*

[12] David Nachmias and David H. Rosenbloom, *Bureaucratic Culture: Citizens and Administrators in Israel* (New York: St. Martin's Press, 1978).

[13] Ibid., p. 67.

[14] Ira Sharkansky, *What Makes Israel Tick: How Domestic Policy-Makers Cope with Constraints* (Chicago: Nelson-Hall, 1985). See, for example, his discussion of a policy called Project Renewal, pp. 125 ff.

the part of states in societies that now have fragmented social control. The strong bargaining position and the capture of tentacles of the state by urban and rural caciques, or any other such strongmen, have made the outlook for widespread political mobilization by state leaders in these societies even more remote. The dilemma of state leaders has intensified in many countries. Without mobilization, state leaders' ability to pursue innovative programs or to coordinate state agencies that can exercise significant autonomy in the face of other power centers remains limited.

DISLOCATING SOCIETIES: NECESSARY CONDITIONS FOR CREATING STRONG STATES

Strong states have been a rarity. In fact, Pierre Birnbaum, the prolific French political sociologist, once delivered a paper in which his two categories were "state societies," strong states, and "stateless societies," weak states.[15] By the end of his talk, the audience was not quite sure whether the first category included one state among all those in the world, France, or none at all. I would not be quite so extreme, but it is true that only a handful of Asian, African, and Latin American states fall high on the continuum of "stateness," or state capabilities. Israel, Cuba, China, Japan, Vietnam, Taiwan, North Korea, and South Korea have been among the highest in state capabilities from those continents.

Have some common historical conditions led to the emergence of strong states? Again, the importance of massive societal dislocation, which severely weakens social control, stands out as a necessary condition in all these cases. Societies must be weakened before a new distribution of social control is possible. All these cases of relatively strong states have occurred in societies in which major social disturbances rocked existing structures within the last half-century. The rapid, deep, and universal social dislocations associated with the spread of the world economy in the half-century leading up to World War I, and resulting nearly always in fragmented social control, were not necessarily the last such dislocations to take place.[16] New disruptive forces

---

[15] Pierre Birnbaum, "End of the State?" (Paper presented at the Hebrew University Political Science Departmental Seminar, Jerusalem, December 25, 1985).

[16] Japan is the only country in Asia, Africa, and Latin America not settled and dominated by Europeans (for example, South Africa and Australia) that emerged directly from the disruptions of the late nineteenth century with concentrated social control. Although Japan certainly had a new trauma in World War II, it was the earlier disruption that first led to a strong state. The fears caused by the Opium War in China and the

have undermined the bases of social control in some societies in this century as well (certainly not nearly as many as were dislocated previously by the spreading world economy), changing land-man ratios, undermining the resource bases of strongmen, and making old strategies of survival irrelevant in the conditions of disruption. As these dislocations weakened other social organizations considerably, the risks diminished for leaders of states and parastatal organizations to confront the old bases of social control.

The most common sort of twentieth-century dislocation leading to the emergence of strong Third World states has been a devastating combination of war and/or revolution, sometimes associated with massive migration. For China, Korea, and Vietnam, the succession of brutal war and revolution after the 1930s led to catastrophic organizational changes in everyday life. Landlords fled, and labor became scarce in all cases, thus changing the most fundamental bases of social control in society.[17] In both Korea and Vietnam, the military and economic effects of World War II and the subsequent revolutions were followed by yet more devastating wars. Russia had undergone precisely the same combination of forces in World War I and its revolution, followed by the onslaughts of the state against those seeking to refashion or maintain their social control in the new circumstances— first the White gangs in the civil war and then the Kulaks.[18] Yugoslavia experienced a similar succession of such dislocations during World War II and its aftermath.[19]

A second basis for major twentieth-century dislocations, weakening old social control and allowing new, has been mass migration. In Tai-

---

tremendous changes after Perry's landing in 1853 deeply shook an already weakening feudalistic structure. Tokugawa Japan fell as plans were bandied back and forth on how to strengthen the Japanese political organizations to deal with the outside threats. A number of the factors listed below leading to other strong states apply to Japan, but a key additional factor may have been its unique geopolitical situation of being just porous enough to allow military and economic world forces to weaken existing social control in the two decades before the Meiji Restoration but sufficiently nonporous to counteract outside forces acting to fragment social control anew.

[17] On China, see Chalmers Johnson, *Peasant Nationalism and Communist Power: The Emergence of Revolutionary China, 1937–1945* (Stanford: Stanford University Press, 1962); on Korea, see Bruce Cumings, *The Origins of the Korean War: Liberation and the Emergence of Separate Regimes 1945–1947* (Princeton, N.J.: Princeton University Press, 1981); on Vietnam, see Samuel L. Popkin, *The Rational Peasant: The Political Economy of Rural Society in Vietnam* (Berkeley: University of California Press, 1979); and John T. McAlister, Jr., *Vietnam: The Origins of Revolution* (Garden City, N.Y.: Doubleday Books, 1971).

[18] Reinhard Bendix, *Kings and People: Power and the Mandate to Rule* (Berkeley: University of California Press, 1978), pp. 567 ff.

[19] Johnson, *Peasant Nationalism*, pp. 121–22.

wan and Israel, massive migrations into the countries affected both
the old bases of social control of the immigrants and of the indigenous
populations. In Israel, the unsettling effects of in-migration of Jews
on their own social organizations was more than matched in importance by the flight and expulsion of Arabs, destroying most existing
bases of control among Arabs. Both Israel and Taiwan also suffered
from war. Israel's 1948 War of Independence, for example, which accelerated the influx of Jews and out-migration of Palestinian Arabs,
was also its most costly in human terms of all its wars, killing nearly 1
percent of the Jewish population. In Cuba, the revolution itself probably was not sufficiently widespread or brutal to undermine existing
social control; however, out-migration made the difference. The emi-
gration of approximately one million Cubans—especially the first fifth
or so who controlled key resources in Cuban society—out of a total
population of less than eight million gave important opportunities to
those who had seized the state apparatus to concentrate social control.
One Chilean official of the deposed Allende regime acknowledged the
importance of such migration for Cuba when he suggested that Chile's
socialist experiment failed because Chile did not have a Florida only
ninety miles away.

In brief, those states that have concentrated social control in Asia
and Latin America since World War II have succeeded only after a
series of wrenching social dislocations, many of which stemmed from
exogenous shocks beyond the control of state officials. Whereas the
last great world shock was the nineteenth-century spread of the world
market, some individual countries in the twentieth century underwent
equally devastating changes that weakened social control throughout
their societies. These twentieth-century catastrophic shocks have come
mostly in the form of war, revolution, and mass migration, often in
some combination. The only other twentieth-century phenomena that
have come close to these forces in weakening some societies have been
the Great Depression in the 1930s and famine. Major catastrophic
forces have been a necessary, but not sufficient, condition for the
emergence of strong states. We can suggest four sufficient conditions
once the existing patterns of social control have been broken.

SUFFICIENT CONDITIONS FOR CREATING STRONG STATES

World Historical Timing

The dislocation is more likely to lead to creating a strong state if it
occurs at a world historical moment in which exogenous political

forces favor concentrated social control. This was not the case outside Europe in the fifty years before World War I, making the Japanese experience all the more remarkable and exceptional. The weakening of old forms of social control in Africa and Asia then took place as Western states scrambled wildly for colonies and sought cheap and quick methods of rule in the vast and heterogeneous lands they had seized. Those methods often involved collaboration with dispersed strongmen coupled with divide-and-rule policies designed to prevent coordination among these strongmen.[20] Likewise, the intense, competitive scramble for new markets in the course of the Industrial Revolution led in noncolonies to numerous quick deals by Western entrepreneurs with strongmen, often bypassing formal political institutions altogether. The notorious experiences of several U.S. robber barons in Mexico in this regard are now legendary in parts of North America. In short, in the important world historical moment during the latter part of the nineteenth century, both colonial policies and the alliance of Western capital with indigenous forces fragmented social control.

In Chapter 4 I demonstrated how exogenous political conditions could act in the opposite direction, favoring the concentration of social control. In the world historical moment immediately following World War I, European states adopted a different approach. Many leaders now recognized that they had entered the sunset of empire. British strategists sought some stable form of rule in the Middle East to keep open routes to India and to stem Bolshevik expansion southward; they did not seek permanent British rule of the area. In the case of the Jewish community in Palestine, British rulers offered the idea for a Jewish agency that could concentrate social control in the society because they believed such an agency could be a vehicle to perpetuate British influence in that part of the world. For the Jews much more conducive conditions resulted, encouraging the creation of institutions that could later form the basis of a strong state than for indigenous leaders in earlier colonial situations.

Similarly, in the generation between the end of World War II and the beginnings of detente around 1970, a world historical moment favorable to the concentration of social control existed. For one, the new then vibrant United Nations system, on both a rhetorical and institutional level, trumpeted the cause of the state as the sole voice of the people. Probably even more important was the consolidation of the

---

[20] The Japanese, once they too became colonialists, may have been the most extreme of the colonial powers in both weakening existing social control and in resisting the cheap and quick divide-and-rule method. Japan's hard rule in Korea and Taiwan may, therefore, be an additional factor explaining the emergence there of stronger states.

Socialist World System under the Soviet umbrella, which gave important political support and shelter to state leaders concentrating social control through Socialist principles.

Military Threat

Related to the issue of world historical timing is a second "sufficient" condition for the emergence of strong states—the existence of a serious military threat from outside or from other communal groups in the country. Such a threat changes the risk calculus of state leaders. Concentrating social control necessarily entails its own risks, for it involves challenging directly the prerogatives of other powers in the society. Political leaders are most often risk-averse when it comes to questions of their own political survival, and, if possible, they would avoid dangerous confrontations with the parties now holding those prerogatives. But the combination of a weakening of strongmen generally and the threat from outside can induce leaders to take those risks. The possibility of political demise from external sources rises if leaders fail to mobilize the resources now garnered by strongmen. Also, the accommodation in which leaders buy social stability in exchange for a hands-off policy towards strongmen seems much less tenable when stability in any case is threatened from the outside.

Possibly the structure of post–World War II politics has sufficiently minimized external risks so that few state rulers have felt the need to confront strongmen in order to vastly increase their mobilization of resources. The bipolar configuration of power between the superpowers has created an extraordinary international stability. Not one state has disappeared in this generation due to war. Only one has split because of war; Pakistan has become Pakistan and Bangladesh. Military hostilities have produced only minimal border changes; the 1967 Arab-Israeli War is an exception, but even there none of the parties has claimed most changes to be permanent. Invasions, such as those in the Iran-Iraq War and the Ethiopia-Somalia War, have often failed to achieve their intended effects. In short, even where the necessary condition of rapidly weakened social control exists and where outside political forces, such as colonialism, favored concentration of social control as society reconstituted itself, the current international security of even weak states may act against leaders' concentrating control. Such a situation contrasts with the much greater threats faced by seventeenth-century European princes, who could expect dire consequences for failing to increase resources substantially by confronting the prerogatives of feudal lords. Michael Howard wrote that at least until 1945, states "came into existence and defined their boundaries by the use, or the threatened use, of force."[21] Only in the postwar era has this changed.

It is striking how in the relative security of the bipolar world those countries in Asia and Latin America with strong states have stood out as stark exceptions. Those countries mentioned as strong states, including Israel, Cuba, Vietnam, and the Koreas, have been exceptional because they have actually been invaded at least once since World War II. Japan, China, and Taiwan have been the only exceptions. In the case of Japan, its leaders' fear of invasion, of course, came on the eve of its state consolidation, starting with the Opium War and the Perry expedition of 1853. In the instances of China and Taiwan, although there have been no actual full-scale attacks, rulers certainly have had enough cause to believe an invasion could occur. In brief, war itself and the threat of war induce state leaders to take unusual risks to consolidate social control, creating a strong state.

The Basis for an Independent Bureaucracy

A third condition important for creating strong states is the existence of a social grouping with people sufficiently independent of existing bases of social control and skillful enough to execute the grand designs of state leaders. Bureaucrats of the state, both those at the tops of agencies and the implementors in the field, must identify their own ultimate interests with those of the state as an autonomous organization. Where social processes—social mobilization or social differentiation—have produced individuals whose primary interests and loyalties do not lie with existing civil social organizations, the possibility exists for forging the interests of both state rulers and officials. The medieval European town played an important role in the creation of such an autonomous class, the burghers, outside the framework of feudal society. The burghers developed important experience in law, administration, and concepts of citizen rights in the free cities of Europe. At a critical juncture, many city burghers felt their own interests could be furthered through the expansion of the state, and they joined forces with the prince. In Palestine, Jewish Russian emigrés, who gained important practical and ideological experience in the aftermath of the Bolshevik Revolution, played a key role in establishing effective central political institutions. After a series of hard-nosed clashes with Ben-Gurion, they joined forces with him to execute his grand conception for Palestine and the Jewish people.[22]

---

[21] Michael Howard, "War and the Nation-state," in Graubard, ed., *The State*, p. 101.

[22] Yonathan Shapiro, *The Formative Years of the Israeli Labour Party: The Organization of Power 1919–1930* (Beverly Hills: Sage, 1976).

Although there will always be important differences among actors in the state concerning the state's real interests, strong states can emerge only when the shared notion that there should be an autonomous set of state interests exists and when bureaucrats believe those interests coincide with their own. A society, such as that in Lebanon, where primary loyalties are still with religious sects, ethnic groups, regional organizations, and the like, has difficulty in producing independent cadres for the state.

The social groupings from which state bureaucrats can be drawn must not only be sufficiently independent of prevailing forms of social control. They must also have people with the requisite skills to concentrate social control over a wide territory. Creating effective strategies of survival on a society-wide scale demands technically competent personnel. It also needs those who can evoke and manipulate the all-important symbols that "package" the more material side of these strategies. One constant criticism of Nasser's efforts to offer elements for viable strategies, for example, was the lack of ideologically sophisticated personnel who could give content to his broad concepts, such as socialism and Arab nationalism. In Cuba, Fidel Castro's cooptation of the Communist party personnel immediately after his takeover in 1959 provided him with a group experienced in organizational works *and* educated in a comprehensive ideology.

Skillful Leadership

Finally, skillful top leadership must be present to take advantage of the conditions to build a strong state. Rulers must be competent at a number of levels. They must carefully select bureaucrats who can and will proffer strategies of survival to the population based on the principles of the leaders. Also, they must have a keen eye toward the changing risk calculus. Leaders must know when to move and against whom; changing conditions demand pragmatism in their approach.

Because it is easier to recognize skillful leadership with hindsight than to delineate its characteristics, it becomes a residual category; but it is impossible to escape as an important condition for creating strong states. So many founding leaders—among them David Ben-Gurion, Fidel Castro, Ho Chi Minh, Kim Il Sung, and Mao Zedong—of the handful of strong Asian and Latin American states stand out in history, in part precisely because of their skills in taking advantage of conditions to concentrate social control.

In summary, whether states end up on the strong or weak end of the scale depends on the distribution of social control in society. For that distribution to change dramatically, highly disruptive forces must first weaken existing strategies of survival, the bases for social control. Such forces caused massive dislocation throughout the non-Western world a century ago. Other forces at that time, however, led to the reestablishment of highly fragmented social control in almost all of Asia, Africa, and Latin America. That pattern later affected independent states in the postwar period of the twentieth century, keeping them relatively weak. And the politics of survival at the top and the Triangles of Accommodation at the bottom of such weak states, in turn, reinforced social fragmentation.

The relatively rare instances in which strong states did emerge in the Third World came only after another onslaught of highly disruptive forces, once again undermining existing bases of social control. But even such dislocation was not in itself sufficient. For example, Mexico's brutal revolution followed by the added dislocation of the Great Depression in the 1930s severely weakened old strategies in that society. Under the leadership of Cardénas, these factors did result in some concentration of social control; however, other conditions were insufficient to lead the Mexican state beyond the midpoint on the scale of state capabilities. The threat of a U.S. invasion had declined substantially by the late 1920s and 1930s. Also, a series of lackluster state leaders preceded and followed Cardénas. Finally, Mexico's major effort at concentrating social control came at least a decade before other serious efforts to build strong states in the Third World. The 1930s did not offer the same sort of supportive world political conditions for the emergence of strong states that the late 1940s and 1950s did, when the new UN celebrated the norm of states as the predominant rule makers in their societies and when a second world system existed to give shelter and support to consolidating state leaders. In the end, the Mexican state could not and did not take advantage of weakening old bases of social control to impose a single, effective set of rules on Mexican society.

Can policy performance be substantially improved in weak states? Scattered materials indicate that in certain cases the answer is yes. Kohli showed that even within the constraints posed by the implicit accommodations between state leaders and strongmen in India, there were important regional differences in the success of implementation of reformist policies.[23] He singled out at the regional level regime

---

[23] Atul Kohli, *The State and Poverty in India: The Politics of Reform* (Cambridge: Cambridge University Press, 1987).

characteristics—leadership, ideology, and organization—and the class basis of the regime in power.

Sharpe pointed in the Dominican Republic to the ability to change the calculus of pressures on the implementor, in effect breaking up the Triangle of Accommodation.[24] In the absence of supervision and control from above, there must be some countervailing pressures on implementors to counteract the influence of strongmen and peer politicians, if policy is to be implemented fairly faithfully. Only forces permanently ensconced in the region can play that role, thus neutralizing the ability of strongmen to wait them out as often occurs when the countervailing forces are temporary foreign-aid officials. Effective countervailing forces must also have sanctions they can apply affecting the implementor's careerist goals as, for example, independent communications lines to the capital city that could bring damaging information about the activities of the implementor. Finally, these forces must be rather impervious to the sanctions against them that those in the Triangle of Accommodation could apply. In the 1970s in parts of Latin America, bishops and parish priests of the Catholic Church played such a countervailing role. In Sharpe's Dominican case, their presence was critical in the creation of a new village cooperative that threatened the strongmen's social control.

The existence of Kohli's conditions or Sharpe's countervailing forces, however, remains a rarity, and the overall constraints against vast improvements in policy performance continue to be overwhelming in societies with weak states. Without severe social dislocations and additional conducive conditions, it is unlikely that new strong states will emerge in the foreseeable future. New policies, management techniques, administrative tinkerings, more committed bureaucrats are all inadequate to change the structural relations between weak states and strong societies: the effect of society's fragmented social control in weakening the state and the effect of a weak state's politics and administration in reinforcing fragmented social control in society.

[24] Kenneth Evan Sharpe, *Peasant Politics: Struggle in a Dominican Village* (Baltimore: Johns Hopkins University Press, 1977).

Assessing Social Control

UNFORTUNATELY, ascertaining the differences among states in their capabilities or the degree of social control they have exercised in their societies has been about as difficult for social scientists as actually establishing social control has been for state leaders. None of the indicators designed by social scientists has been terribly successful in revealing variations in state capabilities. Nevertheless, all existing measures do point to important differences between Third World states and others taken in aggregate and among Third World states themselves.

Two sorts of problems have plagued indicators. First, for the most part they usually rely on aggregate figures that tell more about the general assignment of resources than about their actual use. In other words, indicators of capabilities tend to measure "extraction" much more than "regulation of social relationships," "penetration," or actual "use of resources" in ways determined in designated state offices or agencies. For example, it will do us little good in assessing state social control simply to know that a state has a huge number of police or military personnel on its payroll. The level of coherence of the state may be so low that most security forces effectively take their orders from outside the state, from those with rules quite different from the ones espoused by state leaders.

Second, a number of indicators do not distinguish effectively between social and material resources (for example, population size, GDP) and state abilities to extract or employ those resources. This lack of differentiation has been the problem for the most common indicators, those devised to measure military potential, such as that by Ray Cline.[1] Cline's numerical ranking of power ranged up to 523 points for any single country (USSR), and Third World countries varied from 128 for Iran all the way down to 1 for Singapore; Egypt scored 72; India, 58; and Israel, 37. The disparities in rankings of military potential, however, tell us little about *state* capabilities, the ability to

[1] Ray S. Cline, *World Power Assessment 1977* (Boulder, Colo.: Westview Press, 1977). Also see, Wilhelm Fucks, *Formeln sur Macht* (Stuttgart: Deutsche Verlags-Anstalt, 1965); and Klaus P. Heiss, Klaus Knorr, and Oskar Morgenstern, *Long Term Projections of Power* (Cambridge, Mass.: Ballinger, 1973).

employ societal resources, relying instead on differences in energy sources, territory, population, and so on, somewhat adjusted according to national will and national strategy. One fairly straightforward method exists to partially overcome that problem of lacking differentiation between societal resources and state capability but not the problem of how resources appropriated by the state are actually used; one can compare countries on the basis of the percentage of GDP in the state sector or a related statistic such as "general government consumption" as a percentage of GDP. Although such indicators may be quite misleading without knowledge of state coherence, they do point to a significant degree of variation among states. According to World Bank figures, for example, general government consumption as a percentage of GDP averaged 12 percent for so-called "developing economies" in 1985 (precisely the same as in 1965) while industrial market economies averaged 17 percent (up from 15 percent in 1965), almost 50 percent higher than the rate in developing countries. Among my cases, there was considerable variation: Mexico, 10; Sierra Leone and India, 12; Egypt, 23; and Israel, 31.[2] One problem here is the low reliability of many of these statistics and the different meanings of the figures for various countries.

Other problems of comparability also abound. Rentier states may rank high in the percentage of GDP in the state sector but may have achieved such ranking with very little ability to affect behavior in their societies. Saudi Arabia, for example, has been able to achieve the number two-ranking among all the states listed in its state consumption expenditure as a percentage of GDP. Its high place on the list derives from the relative ease in garnering state revenues from the sale of the country's main, and practically only, resource—oil. Similarly, Mexico's ranking could be expected to rise if oil revenues rise significantly as a share of the total income, but moving up in the percentage of GDP in the state sector may not coincide with increased capabilities as defined here.

An attempt to go beyond looking at state consumption as a percentage of GDP in assessing state social control has been to put such figures (or related ones) in some sort of context. W. Arthur Lewis, for example, attempted a rough computation of the minimal expenditures necessary by Third World states in order to aim for widely accepted targets these states demand of themselves.[3] Appendix Table 1 breaks down his results.

[2] *World Development Report 1987* (New York: Oxford University Press, 1987), pp. 210–11.

[3] W. Arthur Lewis, *Development Planning: The Essentials of Economic Policy* (New York: Harper and Row, 1966), pp. 115–16.

APPENDIX TABLE 1. *Minimal State Expenditures to Achieve Development Targets*

Purpose	Percentage of GDP
General & economic administration	6
Education	3
Health	2
Welfare Services	2
Captial expenditure on public works	3
Captial expenditure by State enterprises or state lending corporations	4
	20

Source: Adapted from W. Arthur Lewis, *Development Planning: The Essentials of Economic Policy* (New York: Harper and Row, 1966), pp. 115–16.

In other words, a state will need to spend at least 20 percent of GDP to build the means necessary to gain access to the population and to offer the components for people to construct viable strategies of survival. It should be added that Lewis's figures do not include two expenses quite substantial for many states, armed forces and debt repayment. For Third World states from 1980 to 1984, military expenditures as a percentage of GNP averaged more than 6 percent. The lowest figure for any continent in 1984 was a shade under 2 percent for Africa.[4] Also, debt repayments plus interest have skyrocketed as a share of, GDP for many Third World states. Not including unguaranteed private debts, quite large for some countries, and debt related to military purchases, debt service averaged over 6 percent of GNP for non-oil producing Third World states in 1985 (up over 200 percent from 1970).[5] If we add in minimal figures for defense and debt servicing, then, we come to a total considerably more than Lewis's 20 percent, probably a number in the area of 30 percent.

One way of assessing social control of states is to compare this 30 percent goal with actual figures. Radian, for example, pitted Lewis's figure against the tax ratio of various countries, the ratio of all taxes

[4] U.S. Arms Control and Disarmament Agency, *World Military Expenditures and Arms Transfers, 1986* (Washington, D.C.: Defense Program and Analysis Division, 1987), pp. 59–62.

[5] *World Development Report 1982* (Oxford: Oxford University Press, 1982), pp. 134–35.

to GDP.[6] This ratio shows "the proportion of national income that is 'compulsorily' transferred from private hands into the government sector for public purposes."[7] The tax ratio in 1969–1971 for forty-seven Third World states came to only 15.1 percent, and, even with additional sources of income such as foreign aid and loans, the figure falls far short of the 30-percent goal.

Only two states exceeded the Lewis minimum, ten states came close to the figure, and thirty-five fell considerably short; eight of those short-falls collected revenues amounting to less than 10 percent of the gross product. Even the two states above the Lewis figure, Zaire and Zambia, should be regarded with some skepticism because they are rentier states and their mines make revenue collection relatively easy. In fact, one survey showed that a number of states increased their taxes considerably by taxing large companies involved in mineral export.[8] There is little indication that either Zaire or Zambia has leap-frogged ahead in the ability to use tax monies to insure state social control. World Bank statistics lead one to the conclusion that the situation had not changed radically by 1985.[9]

In short, most states fall short of gaining compulsory transfer of resources from private hands in order to pursue even their leaders' minimal goals. In a frequency distribution, the biggest group of countries by far in the late 1960s was of a tax ratio in the 11 to 15 percent range, about half of needed revenues to pursue accepted goals.[10] It should be added, though, that most Third World states improved their tax ratios from the early 1950s to the 1970s, some from increased tariff revenues but also from more internal taxes.[11]

Other similar attempts have been made to place revenue collection, or state consumption, in a broader framework. Organski and Kugler,

[6] Alex Radian, *Resource Mobilization in Poor Countries: Implementing Tax Policies* (New Brunswick, N.J.: Transaction Books, 1980), p. 11.

[7] Raja J. Chellia, "Trends in Taxation in Developing Countries," *International Monetary Fund Staff Papers* 18 (July 1971): 258.

[8] Ibid., p. 269.

[9] *World Development Report 1987*, pp. 210–11. The World Bank and other suppliers of such data, such as the United Nations in its *United Nations Statistical Yearbook* report only general government consumption, excluding public domestic investment. If we add an additional 5 percent for such investment, the so-called developing economies still fall short on average of even 20 percent of GDP in the state sector.

[10] Chellia, "Trends in Taxation," p. 262.

[11] Chellia's study was updated several years later with results remaining fairly consistent. Raja J. Chellia, Hessel J. Baas, and Margaret R. Kelly, "Tax Ratios and Tax Effort in Developing Countries, 1969–71," *International Monetary Fund Staff Papers* 22 (March 1975): 187–205.

for example, devised a measure that related the actual tax collecting done by a state (the real tax ratio), not to a global figure, but to the taxable capacity of each country in question.[12]

$$\text{Tax Effort} = \frac{\text{Real Tax Ratio}}{\text{Tax Capacity}}$$

Again, the measure reveals significant variation in state capabilities. The "normal" line in Appendix Figure 1 indicates states with tax efforts in which actual collected taxes match the country's estimated tax capacity (i.e., a ratio of one). States such as Israel and Egypt, falling above the "normal" line, have ratios considerably higher than one, indicating that the states' performances are above the norm. On the other hand, states such as Lebanon and Mexico, falling below the "normal" line, have tax efforts of less than one; they perform less well than what would be expected given their economic resources.[13] One of the most interesting and innovative attempts to build on this method has been by Lewis Snider.[14] He finds Israel's capacities very high; Egypt's high; India's about average; and Mexico's very low. Kugler and Domke elaborated the model first set out by Organski and Kugler in a subsequent article, attempting to operationalize the notion of political capacity of industrialized states.[15] Here they used this equation:

$$\text{Relative Political Capacity (\textsc{rpc})} = \frac{\text{Actual Extraction}}{\text{Expected Extraction}}$$

Of course, all these sorts of measures do not tell very much about social control beyond the state's ability to mobilize or extract revenues. Questions of establishing rules of the game in other realms are not touched. One attempt in the early 1970s to operationalize political performance generally and "decisional efficacy" as part of overall performance proved extremely unwieldy with little impact on subsequent work.[16]

[12] A.F.K. Organski and Jacek Kugler, "Davids and Goliaths: Predicting the Outcomes of International Wars," *Comparative Political Studies* 11 (July 1978): 141–80.

[13] Ibid., p. 151.

[14] Lewis W. Snider, "Political Capacity and the Credit Worthiness of Governments: The Development and Validation of a Measure" (Paper, Program in International Relations, Claremont Graduate School, Claremont, Calif.).

[15] Jacek Kugler and William Domke, "Comparing the Strength of Nations," *Comparative Politics* 19 (April 1986): 39–69.

[16] Tedd Robert Gurr and Muriel McClelland, "Political Performance: A Twelve-Nation

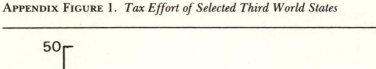

APPENDIX FIGURE 1. *Tax Effort of Selected Third World States*

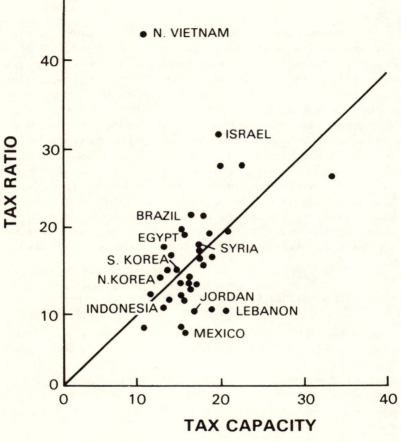

Ratio of Real Tax to GNP versus Tax Capacity Cross Section: 1970

Source: A.F.K. Organski and Jacek Kugler, "Davids and Goliaths: Predicting the Outcomes of International Wars," *Comparative Political Studies* 11 (July 1978): 152.

Another school, that interested in international political economy, has begun to assess differences in states' capabilities in a way that comes closest to the conceptions developed in this book—through an evaluation of the strength of states vis-à-vis their own societies. Peter Katzenstein, for example, has sought to differentiate strong and weak states by looking at "the number and range of policy instruments [that] emerge from the differentiation of state from society and the centralization within each."[17] According to Katzenstein, a state with a large number and wide range of such instruments, such as Japan, has a better developed "policy network"; it is therefore stronger than one without such a number and range of instruments, such as the United States. Stephen Krasner has added a useful classification system to help gauge the strength of states.[18] Appendix Table 2 is an adaptation of his system.

Unfortunately, the works of this school help only minimally in distinguishing Third World states from one another empirically in their capabilities. To date, most authors in this field have been interested in advanced industrial, democratic states and have assessed "policy networks" only for those states. The policy networks in even the weak European states far outstrip those of most Third World states. Also, the concept of policy network must be applied qualitatively, case by

APPENDIX TABLE 2. *Strength of the State vis-à-vis Society*

	Resist Private Pressure		Change Private Behavior in Intended Ways		Change Social Structure in Intended Ways	
	Yes	No	Yes	No	Yes	No
Weak		X[a]		X		X
Middle	X		X			X
Strong	X		X		X[b]	

Source: Adapted from Stephen D. Krasner, *Defending the National Interest* (Princeton, N.J.: Princeton University Press, 1978), p. 57.

[a] Or sometimes.

[b] Or often only slowly.

Study," Sage Professional Paper, Comparative Politics Series, vol. 2 (Beverly Hills: Sage, 1971).

[17] Peter J. Katzenstein, "Conclusion: Domestic Structures and Strategies of Foreign Economic Policy," *International Organization* 31 (Autumn 1977): 892.

[18] Stephen D. Krasner, *Defending the National Interest* (Princeton, N.J.: Princeton University Press, 1978), p. 57.

case, without giving an easy measure for comparing numerous states. Nonetheless, a qualitative analysis of the policy networks of the states used as illustrations in this book showed that Sierra Leone has had an exceedingly small number and range of policy instruments and falls in the weak category of Table III; Mexico, Egypt, and India (in that order from stronger to weaker) have had greater policy instruments and may be ranked as middle; and Israel has had an extensive policy network and can be ranked as strong.

As noted above, most quantitative measures of state power or social control fail to sort out state-society relations sufficiently. Beyond tax ratios, few statistics serve as good summary statements of state capabilities in achieving even the population's compliance, let alone other elements of social control including "participation" and "legitimation." One set of figures that does reflect the variability of states in using control to mobilize the population into state institutions and rules is school enrollment data.[19] These data for the late 1970s corroborated the rank ordering for my five cases that came from the qualitative analysis of policy networks, although Mexico ranked somewhat higher on this single measure than it did in the qualitative analysis. School enrollment figures at the primary and secondary levels as a percentage of the school-age population for Israel were 88; Mexico, 81; Egypt, 59; India, 53; and Sierra Leone, 26. The average percentage for Third World countries is about 58, compared to 61 percent for my five cases; for non-Third World countries the figure is close to 90 percent. The school enrollment rates confirm a modest gain in the capabilities of Third World states from 1950 through 1975; in that period school enrollments grew by an average of slightly more than 4 percent, or less than a fifth of 1 percent each year.

[19] The data are adapted from Charles Lewis Taylor and David A. Jodice, *World Handbook of Political and Social Indicators*, vol. 2, 3d ed. (New Haven: Yale University Press, 1983), pp. 163–65, 251–53.

A Controversy over How Disruptive the Nineteenth Century Really Was

A RAGING DEBATE has taken place among scholars over just how destructive were the state policies discussed in Chapter 2 and the capitalist penetration these policies facilitated. Morris D. Morris has led a revisionist school against prevailing opinion concerning nineteenth-century India: "On the whole, then, I would argue that there is a stong likelihood that the traditional sector, generally speaking, did not decline absolutely in economic significance and therefore did not constitute a depressing element in the performance of the nineteenth century economy. It is even possible that absolute growth occurred."[1] Similarly, McAlpin has challenged the notion that Indian increases in cotton production came as a result of a switch in land use away from food crops; the increase, she argued, came from an extension of land under cultivation, a process far less disruptive.[2] Kumar demonstrated that landlessness and debt existed even before British rule in India and did not simply result from colonial rule.[3]

Such works raise important questions about the notion of a mythical idyllic past in the precapitalist era and the deleterious effects of capitalism in the late nineteenth century. No doubt, some could insulate themselves better than others from changes in life situations. Many peasants, McAlpin's findings indicate, simply did not become very price responsive for much of the nineteenth century and were thus less subject to the vagaries of the market. Despite these arguments, however, one cannot conclude but that there was immense pressure on existing social arrangements during this period. Even the very evidence of these authors intimates that the expansion of the world economy forced enormous changes in people's life conditions.

[1] Morris D. Morris, "Towards a Reinterpretation of Nineteenth-Century Indian Economic History," *The Indian Economic and Social Review* 5 (March 1968): 9. Those who are not specialists on India have been influenced by Morris's work. See, for example, Tony Smith, "The Underdevelopment Literature: The Case of Dependency Theory," *World Politics* 31 (January 1979): 256.

[2] Michelle Burge McAlpin, "Railroads, Prices, and Peasant Rationality: India 1860–1900," *Journal of Economic History* 34 (September 1974): 665.

[3] Dharma Kumar, *Land and Caste in South India* (Cambridge: Cambridge University Press, 1965), pp. 34, 45, 190.

Kumar found, for example, that for seven districts surveyed in Tanjore all but one had falling wages in the last quarter of the century; the decline was substantial, between 13 and 42 percent. Other statistics confirm that while India's exports grew in value by 280 percent during this period, its real industrial wages at constant prices fell about 30 percent per capita.[4] Kumar noted that "the beginning of a trend towards the payment of money wages can be discerned, particularly for casual labourers and cash crops, but the pace of monetization was both slow and uneven."[5] Yet, the numbers of landless agricultural laborers rose substantially, indicating also, Kumar asserts, a decline in handicraft industry. Peasant debt, too, grew quickly. Morris also pointed to the sorts of changes producing transformation in life situations: the growth of factories for the production of cotton and jute, the expansion of coal mining, and the like.[6]

Rao takes McAlpin to task for minimizing the effects of railways but not looking in a disaggregated manner at statistics on the increase in area of cultivation and the persistent proportion of food grains grown. Rao argues that increases in cultivated areas came as the penetration of capitalism, which the railroads precipitated, threw people back into agriculture, reabsorbed as poor agricultural workers in the mammoth agricultural expansion. The area under cash crops increased significantly in the second half of the nineteenth century, while the area under food grains increased as well, especially where railways *had not* penetrated.[7] The effect was much more disruptive on the lives of peasants than McAlpin's undisaggregated figures might indicate.

Even in many of the sanguine interpretations of the spread of capitalism to peasant societies, then, an image of substantial and rapid demographic, occupational, and production changes filters through. The evidence does not support those interpretations that attempt to build a rather stable picture of the late nineteenth century. With all the changes in life situations—place of residence, type of job, items produced, relations to land, and ties to other classes—people's needs changed drastically. Market forces greatly weakened the existing organization of people's lives.

[4] K. Mukerji, "Levels of Living of Industrial Workers," in V. B. Singh, ed., *Economic History of India 1858–1956* (Bombay: Allied, 1965), pp. 658–59.

[5] Kumar, *Land and Caste in South India*, p. 146.

[6] Morris, "Towards a Reinterpretation," p. 10.

[7] G. N. Rao, "Political Economy of Railways in British India, 1850–1900," *Artha Vijāna* 20 (December 1978).